Simon Napier-Bell has been a composer, songwriter, record producer and author, but he is best known for having managed such artists as the Yardbirds, Marc Bolan, Japan and Wham!. Under his management, Wham! became the first Western pop group ever to play in communist China. He is the author of three other acclaimed books about the music industry – *You Don't Have to Say You Love Me*, *Black Vinyl White Powder* and *I'm Coming to Take You to Lunch* – as well as a memoir, *Sour Mouth, Sweet Bottom*. He is CEO of the Pierbel Entertainment Group and continues to consult, write and broadcast, most recently directing documentary films on subjects ranging from Frank Sinatra to the decriminalisation of homosexuality in Britain. Simon lives in Thailand.

SIMON NAPIER–BELL

THE
BUSINESS

A History of Popular Music from Sheet Music to Streaming

unbound

First published by Unbound as *Ta-ra-ra-boom-de-ay* in 2014
This paperback edition first published in 2022

Unbound,
Level 1, Devonshire House, One Mayfair Place, London, W1J 8AJ
www.unbound.com

Grateful acknowledgement is made to the following for permission to reprint lyrics:
'Tutti Frutti' Words and Music by Dorothy Labostrie, Joe Lubin and Richard Penniman
© 1955, Reproduced by permission of Sony/ATV Songs, London W1F 9LD; 'Revolution'
Words and Music by John Lennon and Paul McCartney © 1968, Reproduced by
permission of Sony/ATV Tunes, London W1F 9LD; 'Rip It Up' Words and Music by John
Blackwell and John Marascalco © 1956, Reproduced by permission of Peter Maurice
Music Co Ltd/Sony/ATV Songs, W1F 9LD; 'Fuck tha Police' Words and Music by Andre
Romell Young, Lorenzo Jerald Patterson & O'Shea Jackson © 1988, Reproduced by
permission of the Universal Music Publishing Group (UK), London SW6 1AH

Typeset by Bubblegum

A CIP record for this book is available from the British Library

ISBN 978-1-78352-937-7

Printed and bound in Great Britain by Clays Ltd, Elcograf S.p.A

1 3 5 7 9 8 6 4 2

CONTENTS

FOREWORD

The man in front of me was a jelly gorilla. His short-sleeved white shirt revealed flabby runnels of spare fat flowing down the underside of his arms like melting liver sausage. Sitting at his desk, the top of his stomach reached right up to his neck. He was three hundred and fifty pounds of collapsing flesh. How he could manage to pull all this weight upwards and get it balanced on two legs was amazing. But he did. And we shook hands.

This was Mike Stewart, president of United Artists Music, New York. Standing next to him was his sidekick, the company's vice-president, Murray Deutch, polished and petite, like a life-sized porcelain figurine.

Just five foot seven, Murray was packaged in an exquisitely cut charcoal suit with a perfectly knotted tie and a stiffly pressed collar. At the bottom of his suit, his shoes shone like black onyx. At the top, his rose-apple face stuck out like a dollop of pink mayonnaise on a prawn cocktail. This was Mike Stewart's pet sycophant – a plaything for the boss. In the middle of our meeting a shoeshine boy knocked at the office door. Mike flipped him a quarter and told Murray to have a shoeshine.

"I don't need one," Murray told him.

Nor did he. His shoes were like mirrors. But Mike snapped back, "Murray, if I tell you you're gonna have a shoeshine, you're gonna have one." So Murray concurred.

This was 1966. Through a stroke of luck I'd written the lyrics to a hit song, 'You Don't Have To Say You Love Me'. Writing songs wasn't what I really did, I was a manager, though that was also due to a stroke of luck. One day out of the blue the Yardbirds had phoned me and asked if I'd like to manage them. 'Well – yes please!'

The lyrics for 'You Don't Have To Say You Love Me' had been co-written with Vicki Wickham who was a producer at *Ready Steady Go!*, Britain's top pop show. She was also a friend of Dusty Springfield, who'd found the song in Italy and asked us where she could get English lyrics for it. We knew nothing about writing songs but had a go at it. Next thing we knew the song was number one.

And because management was turning out to be hard work, I thought, "Maybe this is what I should be doing."

United Artists misguidedly thought the same. They approached me and Vicki and asked if we'd like to sign an exclusive songwriting agreement. Apart from a nice advance they also offered a flight to New York to meet the head of the company, Mike Stewart, which is why we were there.

Mike had an idea. "Murray – why don't you take Simon and Vicki over to the Brill building."

He turned to us, "You know about the Brill, don't you? It's where all the top songwriters work. Murray will show you round."

Mike's dapper little servant led us off to see something we knew about but had never seen.

It was a building heaving with activity – cramped small offices, people running in and out of the passageways, everyone seemingly knowing everyone else, badly lit, hugely atmospheric but equally claustrophobic. This was the American music industry in microcosm. In this building were publishers, pluggers, music printers, demo studios, but most important of all – songwriters.

Murray took us to a floor on which every door had a six-inch square window to see in through, like prison cells. Inside each room was a pianist at an upright piano and someone else sitting on a stool beside them. Pianos were banged, melodies hummed, chorus lines sang, and phrases tossed around between piano-players and stool-sitters. There was no air-conditioning. The temperature in the street was in the eighties. In here it was more like the nineties.

"They all work 10 to 6, five days a week," Murray told us. "They write America's hits. We want you to join them."

"But who are they?" we asked. "Who on earth agrees to sit in a little sweatbox and slog away at writing songs in such an atmosphere?"

Murray opened a door. "Neil," he said. "I want you to meet a couple of guys from England. They've just written one of the greatest songs ever."

Turning from the piano we saw Neil Sedaka. Three years earlier his song 'Breaking Up Is Hard to Do' had been number one. So why was he slaving away in here?

Vicki knew him; she'd booked him on *Ready Steady Go!* a few months previously. "Neil," she asked, "why on earth do you spend your day working in a tiny room like this?"

He grinned. "Well – the truth is – I'm under contract. But that's not really the reason. It's just that… This is how we do it. And we love it. We're all here. All songwriters together."

Vicki shook her head in disbelief.

Murray opened the next door. "Carole. Meet two friends from England."

The face at the piano turned towards us. It was Carole King. Carole had written one of the most memorable hits of the early sixties, 'Will You Still Love Me Tomorrow'. It was unbelievable that the reward for having done so was to be imprisoned eight hours a day. Vicki knew Carole too, and asked her, "Why do you work in a place like this?"

"It *can* be a bit of a nightmare sometimes," Carole admitted.

It was incredible – like a car factory – a conveyor belt of songwriters.

Murray shut the door. "Burt Bacharach worked here until last year too," he told us. "All the great songwriters do. We want you to join them."

When we got back to the office Mike Stewart was tucking into his lunch – a bucket of Kentucky fried chicken and a half-gallon milkshake. "Whad'ya think?" he asked, spilling crispy bits into his lap. "You wanna stay here for a few weeks and work with the best? We'll pay your accommodation."

We both shook our heads.

"Do you want to know what these guys earn?"

We didn't. It was irrelevant. Our lives were about London. I tried to explain that back home I had the Yardbirds to manage and Vicki had a job producing *Ready Steady Go!*.

Mike got tetchy and banged his desk. "You just don't get it, do you? In this business, the song is the one and only commodity. Don't let anyone tell you otherwise. The history of music publishing is the history of the music industry. Forget records, forget TV shows, forget rock groups – they're a mere triviality. Songs are forever. When you've finished your time in this business, all you'll have left is the songs. You guys should stay here and get rich."

We both knew if we were serious about wanting to be top songwriters we should stay and work in that dreadful building. Even worse, we ought to try and make friends of these two men – a slag heap of falling flesh and his perfectly tailored pet frog.

Without even looking at Vicki I knew what she was thinking – it wasn't us who didn't "get it", it was these guys. They were completely ignorant about the cool world we inhabited on the other side of the Atlantic. They knew nothing about pop groups and pirate radio, Kings Road and trendy nightlife, lazy dinners and easy sex. As far as we were concerned the music business was a British thing; America was just a backwater. Why would anyone want to exchange the pleasures of swinging London for a songwriters' Alcatraz?

"I'm sorry," I told Mike. "We really need to get back to London." Vicki nodded in agreement, and he gave a helpless shrug.

But back in London managing the Yardbirds, I soon found I needed to know more about music publishing. In fact, bearing in mind I was managing one of the world's top rock groups, I thought it was about time I learnt more about the music industry in general – how it worked, how it had come into existence, how it had managed to get by without me for a hundred years. So I started reading.

Twelve months later I felt better informed. But I've been surprised ever since by how few other people in the business know anything about it, so I decided the time had come to write it all down in one book.

Mainly I wanted to show the business-side of things, and although I call it a complete history, of course it's nothing of the sort, in fact it's as incomplete as you can possibly imagine. I've simply chosen a meandering path through the lives of assorted hustlers, entrepreneurs, songwriters, artists and executives who helped bring the music industry from its beginnings three hundred years ago to what it is today.

Mostly it's a story of how the desire to make money (and then make more money), created an industry. Which now looks like it's in decline.

(Though perhaps it's not!)

We'll have to wait and see.

1

Ta-ra-ra-boom-de-ay
THE BEGINNING OF THE MUSIC BUSINESS

This is how Britain got started in the music business.

In 1710, the British parliament passed a law protecting an author's rights in his written work – the Statute of Anne. A piece of writing, once it had been published, or made public, would remain the author's exclusive property for fourteen years. This could then be extended for another fourteen years. And because music could be written, it too was given the same legal status.

There was also a proviso that an author had the right to assign his rights in a work providing there was a signed and witnessed contract. So if a music publisher could persuade a songwriter to sign a piece of paper assigning him a song, the publisher would become the owner of the song.

Previously, the only business in music had been the simple one of paying musicians to play and charging people to come and see them. But now music could be owned, just like property. And anyone who owned a piece of music could print copies of it and sell them for whatever price he chose.

The court had created the music industry.

This is how America got started in the music business. It was a British colony. And when it won the War of Independence it kept the copyright law Britain had given it.

What pushed the industry forward was not so much the public's love of music, or the musicians' love of playing and writing it, but the music publishers' desire to make money from it. Eventually it was America that kicked the music business into high gear and turned it into a multi-million dollar industry, but it was Britain that started things off.

The first big step was in December 1810 when Samuel Chappell, who had a piano store in Bond Street, signed an agreement with Johann Baptist Cramer, England's best-known concert pianist and composer. Chappell and Cramer would set up a joint publishing company that would print and sell all of Cramer's music, including his best-seller, the definitive work on piano technique, '84 Studies for the Pianoforte'.

Cramer then wrote to all his musician friends telling them about the new company and asking them to publish their work with it. One of them was

Beethoven, who, because he considered Cramer to be the world's best pianist, let the company publish his new piano concerto, which Cramer named the 'Emperor'.

Cramer's contacts brought in top classical composers from all over Europe and Chappell was soon considered to be amongst the top music publishing companies in Britain. But after seven years Cramer decided he was doing more for Chappell than Chappell was doing for him, so he left and set up on his own. In 1834 Samuel Chappell died and in due course the business passed to his son Thomas.

Tom was a moderniser. He wasn't as stuffy as his father. He wanted to publish popular music as well classical. Classical music sold only on the reputation of the composer. For a new work to sell better than the last took a very long time – concerts had to be arranged and played and the time needed to turn a classical work into a hit was often several years. Popular music was totally different. Popular songs could be engineered into hits in a matter of months. But it was a tough business.

The other top publishers were Novello and Boosey. Novello published only classical music, but Boosey had moved into popular ballads for the middle classes – genteel love songs and broken-hearted laments. Tom Chappell decided to do the same.

Promoting new ballads wasn't at all genteel. Publishers fought to get the best songs from the best writers, and then they had to be made popular. Nobody wanted to hear songs they didn't know so new songs had to be force-fed to the public. The best way was to persuade top ballad singers to feature them in their concerts. To persuade them they were bribed – from the very beginning, that was the nature of the music business. No song was played till someone was paid.

It could be expensive but sales of songs could be huge. The money made from the sheet music of 'The Last Rose of Summer' or 'Darby and Joan' justified almost any expenditure on promotion. The most famous singer at the time was contralto Dame Clara Butt. After Queen Victoria told her, "I have never liked the English language before but in your mouth it is beautiful," Boosey gave her a royalty on the sheet music sales of every song she helped promote.

(Dame Clara, not the Queen.)

Tom Chappell wanted to find an alternative to the cut-throat nature of the ballad business, and eventually he found one – musical theatre. His next big signing was Britain's most successful songwriting team, Gilbert and Sullivan.

Gilbert and Sullivan wrote light-hearted operettas that made them the darlings of the middle-class. Sullivan wrote the music and Gilbert the words, and their shows were in the classic style of British comedy, absurdity with a straight face. The music was jolly and the characters were familiar types from the Victorian era – shopkeepers, thieves, policemen, judges. The trick was to tell an outrageous story in a deadpan way.

This was the second half of the nineteenth century – a taxi to the theatre was a carriage pulled by a horse. Streets were lit by gaslight, as were most of the theatres. Onstage light came from footlights shining on the performers unattractively from underneath. A poor show couldn't be saved by making it look spectacular, the lighting to do that didn't exist; a comedy had to be truly funny, a musical show had to have stunning songs. And Gilbert and Sullivan's did.

Every show was packed with catchy tunes, easy to remember and not too hard to play on the piano. More than 60 per cent of middle-class families in Britain had a piano and nearly all of them bought sheet music of Gilbert and Sullivan's songs.

By the 1890s their songs had made Chappell the number one music publisher in Britain.

In America, by the 1880s, a hundred years after the end of the War of Independence, there had been an influx of immigrants from Europe. Over 250,000 of these were Jews, the majority of them having fled persecution. Although most of these immigrants were well educated, there was little chance of them finding good positions in businesses that already had management in place, but the entertainment industry had vacancy signs all over it. It was new, and there was no one at the top to object to newcomers moving in. It revolved around actors, singers, dancers, writers, and choreographers – all of them quirky, forceful and idiosyncratic. There was no room in entertainment for people who made judgments based on race or class or sexuality; the only thing that mattered was profitability.

Jews came from a non-proselytising culture. They didn't try to convert people to their way of thinking, nor did they object to other people being themselves – the entertainment business provided them with an ideal opening. And the quickest way in was through songwriting or music publishing.

As in Britain, publishers bought songs as cheaply as they could, then tried to popularise them and sell sheet music, and it was this popularising of the song that was key to the business. If the song became a hit it might sell thirty or forty thousand copies at 50 cents each, and with three or four hits a year a publisher could make a comfortable living. No one considered music publishing to be a profession from which one could get truly rich, but in 1894 something happened that raised the possible rewards to another level.

Aged eighteen, Charles K. Harris lived in Milwaukee and wrote songs that he sold to travelling minstrel shows for a few dollars each. He managed to publish one of his songs with a New York publisher, Witmark & Son, who agreed to pay him one cent for each copy sold. From friends in New York, Harris heard the song was doing well, but when his first royalty cheque arrived it was for just 85 cents.

He was furious. He decided he would never give another publisher one of his songs and he set up his own publishing company in a rented room. On the wall, he hung the 85 cents cheque he'd received.

Isidore Witmark, the publisher who had sent it to him, retaliated by hanging the sheet music of the song on his own office wall, telling friends he was "framing the song as a prize failure".

But the last laugh was with Harris. The next song he wrote was 'After the Ball', the best-selling song ever.

It was a deliberate tearjerker, about a man who dumped his girlfriend when he saw her kiss another man. He leaves in a huff and refuses to speak to her again, then hears she's killed herself with grief. And it turns out the man he saw her kiss was her brother. Again it was the plugging that made the song a hit, and preceding the plugging was the bribing.

To start with Harris was a bit stingy. A young tenor, Evan Williams, was due to sing a concert at the Los Angeles Theatre and Harris asked him to sing 'After the Ball' four times. He wrote a letter to the theatre's treasurer. "I am enclosing my cheque for $10. If Mr Williams sings it all four times you are to give him the $10. If he sings it only three times you are to deduct $2.50. In fact, deduct $2.50 for each omission and return the money to me."

When this failed to get the song going, Harris splashed out lavishly. He paid five hundred dollars to James Aldrich Libbey, a well-known baritone for the right to put his photograph on the cover of the sheet music and to sing it at a concert that bandleader John Philip Sousa would be attending. Sousa liked the song so much he made an arrangement of it and for the next six months played it once an hour at the 1893 Chicago World Fair where he and his band were in residence. Over twenty-seven million people attended the fair, equivalent to half the population of the USA, and by the end of the year the sheet-music had sold over two million copies, an unheard of amount.

As the song's publisher, as well as its writer, Charles K. Harris made all the money for himself. He then became a music business bore and lectured the industry on how things should be done. "A new song must be played, hummed, and drummed into the ears of the public, not in one city, but in every city, town, and village, before it ever becomes popular."

Harris's success with 'After the Ball' prompted other amateur songwriters to follow him into publishing. And as soon as they became publishers they started sending out their own 85 cent cheques.

Many of them had a background in sales – buttons, neckties, socks, corsets. They looked at songs as just another product to be sold. Popular songs weren't art, just a commodity.

Edward B. Marks had been a button salesman. In his spare time he wrote rhymes. Joseph Stern, a necktie salesman, played piano and wrote tunes. Stern and Marks combined their talents to write songs and start a publishing business from a basement on East 14th Street with "a 30-cent sign and a $1 letter box". They too decided on the tearjerker route. Their first hit was 'The Little Lost Child', about a policeman who came across a waif in the street only to find, when he got back to the police station, it was his own long lost daughter. With some cash in the bank, Stern and Marks hired other writers to write songs for them. One was Leo Feist, a corset salesman who had been writing songs in his spare time. Stern and Marks gave Feist a lowly job in the firm but when one of his songs became a hit Feist demanded to be made a partner. Instead, he was shown the door.

So Feist started his own company and became the first publisher to come up with a slogan: 'You Can't Go Wrong With A Feist Song'. He also stole all the staff from Stern and Marks – pluggers, writers, arrangers, and even the extremely inventive accountant, Mr Anderson, whose creativity with royalty statements worked wonders for the profits. Whenever a songwriter received one, he would say, "Another one of Anderson's fairy tales."

Aaron Gumbinsky was the son of a sock salesman. Aged fourteen, he'd run away to join a circus and renamed himself Harry von Tilzer. He wrote songs for his own song-and-dance act and eventually managed to sell one to publishers Shapiro Bernstein for fifteen dollars, 'My Old New Hampshire Home'.

When it sold a million copies Shapiro Bernstein offered von Tilzer a partnership. It would cost them less than the royalties they owed him and it meant they could publish his future songs. Von Tilzer was a fancy dresser and liked to wear a formal suit with a high stiff collar, which made visitors presume he was the man in charge. After a while he decided that's what he'd like to be. So he left Shapiro Bernstein and started his own company – Von Tilzer Music.

By the beginning of the 1890s, the old generation of New York publishers (Bond, Kennedy, Fisher, Smith, Howley, Haviland) had completely faded away, outclassed by the energy and innovation of these newcomers (Marks, Stern, Feist, Harris, Witmark, Shapiro, Bernstein, von Tilzer) nearly all of them Jewish immigrants, or children of immigrants.

They all understood that the essential link between a newly written song and the sale of its sheet music was the plugger. "He it is," wrote music sociologist Isaac Goldberg, "who by all the arts of persuasion, intrigue, bribery, mayhem, malfeasance, cajolery, entreaty, threat, insinuation, persistence and whatever else he has, sees to it that his employer's music shall be heard."

Leo Feist hired pluggers to sing in public places – on the platform of a train station, in Times Square, a saloon bar, a theatre balcony, a pool hall – anywhere a crowd gathered.

Edward B. Marks told people the best songs came from the gutter. "There was no surer way of starting a song off to popularity than to get it sung as loudly as possible in the city's lowest dives." He went out himself each night, buying drinks for the performers and distributing chorus-sheets to the customers. "Sixty joints a week", he claimed. "The Alhambra Music Hall was expensive because you had to buy drinks for the boys in the band and there were twenty-six of them; the Haymarket was dangerous – bullets flew frequently – and you could only get in by joining a club called the Welsh Rabbits, at the cost of drinks for all."

Other pluggers would go to the music counters of department stores with hundreds of copies of the song printed on the cheapest paper, then stand and sing it while selling them for ten cents each. Every department store had a grand piano allotted by the hour to publishers for their pluggers to play and sing new songs.

At Witmark & Son, the preferred method of plugging was 'booming'. It meant buying a dozen or so tickets for a vaudeville show and placing pluggers in the audience. When the performer sang, they joined in, and applauded wildly afterwards. Sometimes a singer would pretend to forget the words and a boomer would stand up in his seat and prompt him by singing along.

At Shapiro Bernstein, Louis Bernstein took his plugging crew to the bicycle races at Madison Square Gardens and the audience got it full in the face. "They had 20,000 people there. We'd have a pianist and singer with a large horn. We'd sing a song to them thirty or forty times a night – it was forced down their throat. They'd cheer, and they'd yell, and they'd boo, but we kept pounding away at them. When the people walked out of there they'd be singing the song. They couldn't help it."

The most elegant way of promoting songs was with a series of photo slides showing the story in pictures. Publishers sent them to all the top vaudeville singers to project as they sung the song. These became the pop videos of their day. Some were put together cheaply with library pictures, others were hugely extravagant, with photographers travelling to Florida or California. Most expensive of all was a slide show made for the song 'Red Wing', about an Indian girl who loses her lover in battle. The publisher of the song, F. A. Mills, wanted to use real Red Indians for the photographs and by chance there were a couple of dozen in town appearing in a burlesque show on Broadway. Sparing no expense, he took the lot at $5 a day each. But there was a misunderstanding. Mills hadn't been aware that Red Indians believed each time a person was photographed they lost a day of their life. Fifty pictures meant fifty days' pay for each Red Indian.

When songs became popular, the masses bought them to sing round the piano at home for their Saturday night entertainment. In turn of the century New York nearly every home had a piano, rich and poor. Poor parents bought them to give their children a backstop way of earning a living if they failed to complete their education.

When Harry Ruby was a child he lived with his family on the lower East Side. In the 1920s he became a top songwriter. "All the families around us were poor. But they had pianos… you could buy one for a hundred dollars and pay it off on time payments. They'd hoist it up to the apartment on a rope."

Because music publishers depended on sheet music sales, it was important that even the most amateurish pianist could play their songs easily. They were forever looking for a foolproof formula. Songs were made simple, chords uncomplicated, rhythms obvious. Melodies had a range of no more than one octave, often less. Publishers told their songwriters to compose to a common format – 32 bars divided into four sections – an 8-bar theme, a repeat of it, a different 8-bar theme, a final repeat of the first one – AABA.

This became the standard for all pop songs. The familiarity became addictive. The listener waited with pleasure for the places in the song where he knew the changes would come, and with equal pleasure for the return to the original tune. Melodies had predictable intervals and familiar harmonies. There was no point writing something cunningly clever if it couldn't easily be played and sung round the family piano. The new breed of music publisher pushed aside tricky ideas and stuck to one simple formula – the money-making formula.

Occasionally hits came from thinking quietly alone, but not often. Songwriting was not seen as an art. Each company employed full-time songwriters, up to a dozen of them, working from nine to five in cramped rooms, mixing old bits with new, searching for musical phrases and clever words, banging on tinny pianos.

Harry von Tilzer was interviewed by a newspaper reporter writing about the area at 28th Street and 5th Avenue where music publishers had their offices. To make its sound cut above the noise of the traffic coming in through the windows von Tilzer had doctored his rather expensive Kindler & Collins piano with strips of paper on the strings to give it a more percussive sound. When he sat down to play, the journalist told him, "Your Kindler & Collins sounds exactly like a tin pan. I'll call the article, 'Tin Pan Alley'."

Britain had a Tin Pan Alley too.

Besides popular music for the theatre and ballads for the middle-classes, the third arm of the popular music business was music hall, which operated much like America's vaudeville. The competition was daunting; there were dozens of small publishers, many of them housed in a short back alley off Charing Cross Road called Denmark Street.

Most of them paid their songwriters no royalty and bought songs for as little as £5 flat payment. 'Any Old Iron' and 'My Old Man Said Follow the Van' wouldn't sell to the middle-classes but sheet music of these songs could be sold to every pub pianist in the country.

The leading publisher in the field was Francis, Day & Hunter. Brothers William and Harry Francis had sung in a minstrel group with Harry Hunter. To get their songs published they'd teamed up with David Day who had experience in publishing. Francis, Day & Hunter was now the most successful publisher in the field of music hall songs, with a huge catalogue and an office filled every day with artists looking for new material. One of the company's most successful writers was the music hall star Joseph Tabrar. He arrived one day when there was an unknown singer in the office looking for a song with which to launch herself. While she was being played a few, Tabrar sat in the corner and wrote 'Daddy Wouldn't Buy Me a Bow Wow', then offered it to her. She turned it down. It couldn't possibly be any good, she said, if he'd written it so quickly. So he gave it to Vesta Victoria who made it the biggest hit of the season, and the unknown singer stayed unknown.

Like the ballad business, the secret of success in music hall was to pay top artists to publicise your songs. Sometimes the singers were also given exclusive rights to the song so no other singer could perform it. Other times the singer received a penny a copy on the sale of sheet music even when the writer was getting nothing.

It wasn't just music publishers who short-changed songwriters, writers did it to each other. Singer Charles Coburn was an occasional songwriter but got his name on far more songs than he actually wrote. 'The Man Who Broke the Bank at Monte Carlo' was written by Fred Gilbert but Coburn managed to buy it from him for £10. He took it to Francis, Day & Hunter and asked for thirty. They gave him £5 plus a royalty and he ended up making six hundred.

There was plenty of interaction between America and Britain. Hit songs moved easily across the Atlantic in both directions. But usually as stolen property.

The USA didn't recognise British copyright. As a result, British music hall songs were often copied verbatim by American publishers, credited to a new author and printed as sheet music with nothing paid to the British publisher.

A British publishing company's only hope of getting money for its music in the USA was to assign its songs to an American publishing company to register on its behalf. Francis, Day & Hunter did this with T. B. Harms, one of New York's old-time publishers. But these arrangements sometimes turned out to be less gentlemanly than expected.

In 1891, Harry Dacre, one of Francis, Day & Hunter's British songwriters, went for a holiday in the USA and took his bicycle. When he arrived he had to pay duty on it. The friend who met him at the pier jokingly remarked, if he'd come over with a bicycle built for two he would have had to pay double. The phrase stuck in Dacre's mind and he used it to write his first song on American soil, 'Daisy, Daisy, Give Me Your Answer Do'.

Because his work was published by Francis, Day & Hunter, the American rights for the song would eventually pass to T. B. Harms in accordance with their agreement. But with the songwriter right there in New York, Tom Harms, the owner of the company, couldn't resist cajoling him into signing his song directly to T. B. Harms. So Francis, Day & Hunter ended up losing it.

This lack of respect for each other's copyright laws led to endless disputes between British and American publishers and courts on both sides of the Atlantic tended towards a national bias.

'Ta-ra-ra-boom-de-ay' was a song copyrighted by Henry J. Sayers in Massachusetts. He gave a copy to British singer Lottie Collins while she was visiting. When she got back home she changed it around a bit and gave it to a London publisher as her own. Then she worked up a dance routine. In a wide-brimmed Gainsborough hat she delivered the verse like a virgin and the chorus like a whore – neckline plunging, legs kicking, white petticoat flying. And on the word 'boom', she gave her petticoat an extra hoist to reveal diamante garters.

In due course, the London publisher received a writ from the American publisher claiming the song was Henry J. Sayer's. The British publisher's defence was that the song was more than twenty-eight years old and was therefore out of copyright. They claimed it had been around since before the American Civil War and was an old negro song with exceedingly vulgar lyrics. The judge asked to have them read out in court.

Counsel for the defence stood and delivered. His deadpan recital of the verse's bawdy words caused sniggers around the courtroom. But it was when he arrived at the chorus that things got out of hand. As the first 'Ta-ra-ra-boom-de-ay' left his lips the entire public gallery burst into song and continued for four complete choruses before the judge managed to regain control.

The song, he decided, was in the public domain. It was anyone's to do with as they pleased.

2

Around and Around
THE BEGINNING OF RECORDS

In 1877 Thomas Edison invented the phonograph, well… sort of!

Edison produced a machine with a horn, a stylus, and a cylinder covered with tinfoil that recorded sound. Other people had already got close.

Frenchman Édouard-Léon Scott de Martinville had produced a machine with a horn, a stylus, and a cylinder covered in lamp-blacked paper. When someone sang into the horn the stylus traced the sound waves onto the paper; clever stuff, but of little use – you could see them, but you couldn't hear them.

Another Frenchman, Charles Cros, left a sealed document at the Académie des Sciences in Paris describing a process for recording and reproducing sound virtually as Edison finally did it. But writing about it and doing it weren't the same thing. His paper remained sealed until after Edison had built his machine. So Edison got the patent.

Edison was born in Ohio in 1847. At age fifteen he began to study telegraphy, four years later he got a job with Western Union where he invented a device to electrocute the cockroaches in the office. He then devised a telegraphic printer that he sold to the Atlantic and Pacific Telegraph Company, Western Union's biggest rival, for $30,000.

In 1867 that was an enormous amount, like a million dollars today, and with the money Edison set up a factory and started inventing more things. In due course he came up with what he called a phonogram. When someone sang into the horn, instead of the stylus tracing sound waves onto paper it indented them into tin foil. For playback, when the cylinder was revolved the stylus followed the indentations and sent the same sound back up the horn that had previously come down it.

Edison took his new machine to the office of the *Scientific American*, and in its next issue it made a report. "Mr. Thomas A. Edison recently came into this office, placed a little machine on our desk, turned a crank and the machine inquired as to our health, asked how we liked the phonograph, informed us that it was very well, and bid us a cordial good night. These remarks were not only perfectly audible to ourselves, but to a dozen or more persons gathered around."

The recordings were of poor quality and couldn't be copied, but Edison, who was a master of publicity, glossed over the weaknesses and lavishly described the possibilities. "You can have a phonograph in your parlour with an album of selected phonographic matter lying beside it. You can take a sheet from the album, place it on the phonograph, start the clockwork and have a symphony performed; then, by changing the sheet, you can listen to a chapter or two of a favourite novel; this may be followed by a song, a duet, or a quartet..."

In fact, you could do no such thing, but Edison was working on it.

When some investors turned up and offered to pay him $10,000 for the rights to market the phonograph, with a 20 per cent royalty on sales, he agreed. Several machines were made and rented out to people who earned money by demonstrating their recording abilities to crowds, at department stores, or fairs, or wherever they might gather – getting them to speak into the machine, or sing, or cough, or most popular of all, to laugh; then letting them hear it back.

In 1878, a reporter from the *Philadelphia Press* attended a demonstration. "Laughter and whistling and singing and sighing and groans – in fact, every utterance of which the human voice is capable – was stored in that wondrous wheel and emitted when it was turned."

At the height of this craze, some of these demonstration machines were earning $1,800 a week in rentals, yet only one man, Dr William Channing writing in the *London Illustrated News*, accurately forecast what these machines would really be used for. "Certainly, within a dozen years, some of the greatest singers will be induced to sing into the ear of the phonograph."

For the moment though, people became bored with these novelty machines and Edison himself got on with inventing other more important things – movie cameras, light bulbs, and the thing he prided above all others – the electric pen wiper.

Meanwhile an American scientist, Professor Charles Tainter, and his partner in invention, a Scot named Chichester Bell, were trying to come up with a phonograph which had a better recording surface than Edison's. Professor Tainter had a passion for tea and employed an assistant, Fred Gaisberg, who was coached in the art of tea-making and tasked with providing a dozen perfect cups a day.

In due course, Tainter and Bell came up with a phonograph almost identical to Edison's except that it used a cardboard cylinder coated with wax into which a groove could be cut. The two inventors called it a graphograph, and despite its close similarity to Edison's phonograph they were granted a patent.

It immediately attracted attention from investors who wanted to market it as a dictation machine. Edison objected, saying it was a virtual copy of his machine. Tainter and Bell, feeling protected by having received a patent, admitted it was, and offered Edison a share of their company.

Miffed, Edison refused. But rather than suing them for infringement of his patent, he infringed theirs, changing the cylinder on his own machine for one coated with wax. So Tainter and Bell sued *him* instead.

Just as patent lawyers on both sides were gearing up for their day in court, a glass tycoon called Jesse H. Lippincott stepped in. With Tainter and Bell he formed a company to produce and sell their machine, the American Graphophone Company. He then bought the rights to market Edison's machine too. Now the two warring factions were part of the same organisation, each producing a slightly different product.

Instead of selling the machines, Lippincott decided to hire them out. In due course the two manufacturers – Edison on one side, Tainter and Bell on the other – came together and formed a single company called Edison Bell, but things went too slowly. And when Lippincott's strange marketing scheme finally collapsed, Edison bought the whole thing back and started again.

While this was going on a company in Washington DC had been set up called the Columbia Graphophone Company. It was the idea of a group of Congressional stenographers who were planning to persuade their colleagues in Congress to abandon shorthand in favour of dictation. They had obtained rights to manufacture the Bell-Tainter version of the recording machine before the company had merged with Edison, and although they saw the machine as a secretarial device, they also saw its potential as entertainment and began to build a repertoire of recordings. This was the beginning of America's most famous record company – Columbia – later known as CBS, and now owned by Sony.

To find and record talent, this company of Congressional stenographers employed Professor Tainter's tea-maker, Fred Gaisberg. It was a shrewd move for his talent at tea-making turned out to be nothing compared with his talent for recording. The music he recorded for the new company was a mixture of marches played by the US Marine Band, and negro songs sung by Billy Golden, a white man pretending to be black.

This was the Columbia Graphophone Company's earliest repertoire, and because there was still no satisfactory process for duplicating cylinders, four machines were used to record four separate cylinders. Normally, to get enough volume, the singer would put his head right into the top of the horn. But when he was recording with four horns at once he had to use a midway position between the four, which meant singing extra loudly.

It was a strain. And if a song sold well the singer might have to come back and sing like that all day long for a week.

Then another inventor appeared, Emile Berliner.

Berliner was born in Hanover and came to the USA when he was nineteen.

He'd invented a microphone for the telephone and sold it to Bell Telephone for $25,000 plus $5,000 a year. With sufficient funds to start working on something new he chose recorded sound and came up with a machine that played a flat disc.

In 1887 he received a patent on his disc machine whose stylus traced sound waves from side to side rather than up and down. He called it the 'gramophone' and gave the instrument a public debut at Philadelphia's Franklin Institute.

Berliner's gramophone consisted of a hand-cranked turntable on a baseboard with a soundbox and horn. Billy Golden, the black-sounding white singer, took Fred Gaisberg to meet Berliner. During the meeting, Berliner recorded Golden's voice using a muzzle and a rubber hose to carry the sound to the flat disc. Gaisberg later said he was "spell-bound by the beautiful round tone of the flat gramophone disc".

Master recordings were made on zinc discs covered in a thin layer of beeswax and cold gasoline through which the recording stylus cut a groove. After they'd been immersed in acid, there was a groove strong enough to carry the sound box and needle across the record. The sound it produced was not only clearer than the cylinder recorder, it was louder. Gaisberg asked Berliner if there was any way he could help.

For the moment there wasn't. Berliner first wanted to work out how to make a 'mother' from the master disc, which he could use to press duplicates. It took two years; then he called Gaisberg back. He now wanted artists to record.

Gaisberg bought him all the singers he'd worked with at Columbia. Since it was now possible to make duplicates, songs only had to be sung once. Because performers would no longer get extra money for singing all day, it was agreed they would receive $25 a title. And because there were no contracts involved, after they'd sung for Berliner, they could make extra money by going back to Columbia and singing the same songs over again.

Berliner offered his first list of discs for sale in April 1895 but the quality wasn't good enough. He was coating the zinc discs with vulcanite, a hardened form of rubber that had a tendency to develop heat spots. Gaisberg noticed a company in New Jersey selling buttons made from a material called shellac, a resin from India produced from the secretions of the lac bug. Berliner tried it and it worked perfectly.

To set things properly in motion Berliner now needed money. He rustled up a bunch of people who agreed to join together in an investment consortium – some steel jobbers, a clothing manufacturer and a building contractor. Between them they came up with $25,000.

In 1896 Edison returned to the fray. He launched a new 'Spring Motor Phonograph' selling at $40. At Columbia, where they'd been pressing ahead with their Bell-Tainter version of the cylinder machine, they were taken by surprise. They'd thought Edison was out of the picture for good. To compete with his new machine they rushed out a spring-wound graphophone at $25.

Edison lost ground, and Columbia riled him further by moving into plush new offices, Edison mortgaged his factory to come up with cash for yet another new machine, 'The Home Phonograph', then focused his efforts on Europe. Which turned out to be exactly what Emile Berliner was doing.

Berliner had sent William Owen, one of his sales staff, to scout for opportunities in London. Owen had taken rooms at the Hotel Cecil in the Strand and with a few samples of merchandise set about building a new company from scratch. The name he'd chosen was The Gramophone Company.

Owen intended The Gramophone Company to be nothing more than a sales company for Berliner's American-made flat disc player. From the American factory, he purchased parts that could be assembled into finished machines in London. Before long he'd sold 3,000 of them, together with 150,000 records he'd also imported. He then moved to offices in Maiden Lane, off the Strand.

He had plenty of competition. Edison had set up in London too with very persuasive advertisements. "What will you do in the long, cold, dark, shivery evenings, when your health and convenience compel you to stay indoors?" The answer of course was to buy an Edison phonograph for two pounds two shillings, "the Finest Entertainer in the World".

Owen fought back by selling the Berliner gramophone with "two kinds of gramophone needles". One that "reproduces the voice with almost the same volume of sound as is given by the artist when singing". And an alternative 'pianissimo' needle that "subdues the tones and gives a very soft sweet effect as of a voice heard in the distance".

Owen decided the only way to win this battle was to begin recording and pressing discs locally. In 1898, Berliner sent over his nephew, Joseph Sanders, to sort out the pressing, and Fred Gaisberg to find artists to record. When the ship docked Sanders went to Hanover, where Berliner's brother owned a telephone factory, to set up a German record company – Deutsche Grammophon. In London, Gaisberg went to the company's offices at Maiden Lane and set up his recording gear.

On the ship he'd made friends with an American vaudeville artist, Burt Shepard, who turned up at Maiden Lane with some of his friends, all top music hall stars. Not understanding what the word recording meant, they'd turned up in full stage gear and make-up.

Just a week after disembarking, Gaisberg started recording, and one of the first songs was Burt Shepard's 'The Laughing Record'.

In the next few years William Owen and Joseph Sanders started to build The Gramophone Company into a Europe-wide operation, forming partnerships in each country and taking majority shareholdings. By 1900 they had companies in Spain, Italy, France Portugal, Switzerland and Belgium. Everywhere they went Gaisberg made recordings that demonstrated the machines' capabilities. Because of its close links with Britain, even India became a good market for them and they opened an office in Calcutta. They weren't aiming at colonial settlers but at Indians themselves.

By then 'The Laughing Record' had sold over half a million in India alone. Fred Gaisberg wrote, "In the bazaars of India I have seen dozens of natives seated on their haunches round a gramophone, rocking with laughter, whilst playing Shepard's laughing record."

For the local market, Gaisberg recorded one of Calcutta's most famous divas, Goura Jan, "a Mohammedan, rather fat and covered with masses of gold... her teeth were quite red from betel-nut chewing".

When she came to the studio, Goura Jan arrived with "four musicians... a bearer for her pipe and to prepare her betel nut, an ayah, or black girl attendant, one coolie to fan her, another girl to carry her cuspidor, and a coolie to carry the traps".

Back in London, William Owen bought a painting from an artist fallen on hard times, Francis Barraud. It was of Barraud's late brother's fox terrier, Nipper, listening at the horn of a talking-machine to his deceased owner's voice. Barraud had named the picture 'His Master's Voice' and Owen paid him £100 for it.

The picture was painted with an Edison cylinder machine, which could record, and was often used for dictation. Owen asked Barraud to over-paint it with a Berliner flat disc machine, which could not record. It made the likelihood of the dog listening to his master's voice an unlikely scenario, but Owen wasn't worried by the discrepancy.

The American end of the Berliner company was also building a large catalogue, most of them quite second rate, the chief criteria for recording artists being a loud voice and a low fee. The company also made classical recordings, but the quality was rarely as good as the recordings they received from Fred Gaisberg in London.

Columbia's popular catalogue was little different from Berliner's and still included the singers Fred Gaisberg introduced them to years earlier, like Billy Golden. For classical, they used singers from the Metropolitan Opera House, but they cost a lot. Bass singer Edward de Reszke charged $1,000 a record, and the Met's star soprano, Marcella Sembrich, asked for $3,000. To cover these costs, Columbia sold its classical records at $2 each. Sales were small but at least it gave the company a touch of class.

Edison, the third company, covered the same range of material as the other two and also had a high class label called Blue Amberol. It wasn't really that classy. They used just one singer, Arthur Collins, who adjusted his accent from operatic areas to negro songs as needed. And because there were still no exclusive contracts for singers, as soon as he'd finished he went round to Berliner and recorded them all again.

It was in Europe that the Berliner company was doing best, but it wasn't unopposed. In France they met stiff competition from two brothers, Charles and Émile Pathé.

The brothers started out with a bar in Pigalle where they installed an Edison phonograph to entertain the customers. The reaction was so overwhelming that they contacted Edison and asked to be his French licensee.

They started producing an Edison-based machine with 200 workers in a barn near the village of Chatou just west of Paris. When they renamed their machine 'Le Coq' it was so successful they had to increase the workforce to 3,500, expanding the factory to twenty acres. They specialised in recording Parisian opera companies and supplying them to Edison in America, who used them to compete with Columbia's recordings of stars from the Metropolitan Opera.

Even so, Columbia was no competition for the Berliner company, which was way out in front simply because it had a flat disc machine, and it wasn't long before Columbia started looking at Emile Berliner's patents to see if they could be broken. They picked the toughest copyright lawyer in the business, a devout Christian, but only on Sundays. From Monday to Friday, the lawyer co-habited with the devil, devising any scheme possible to break his opponents' copyrights. He saw an opportunity with the arm that held the stylus. It moved freely, guided only by the groove on the disc. The arm of the Bell-Tainter cylinder machine also moved freely in the groove. So did trains on their tracks and tramcars on their rails, but the lawyer pounced on it and sued for infringement of patent.

Before the court could make up their minds about it, Berliner began to have problems within his own organisation. In America, marketing of the flat disc machine had been given to a separate company. The man in charge was Frank Seaman, who felt his cut of the profits was insufficient. Someone must have told Columbia's patent attorney about his dissatisfaction because he suddenly re-directed his infringement action at Frank Seaman hoping it would pressure him into siding with Columbia against Berliner. It did. Seaman stated in court that he considered Berliner's patent to be an infringement of Columbia's.

Columbia and Seaman then settled out of court, announcing an agreement "for legal protection and commercial advantage". They would set up a new factory to manufacture a flat disc talking-machine called the Zonophone.

Out-smarted, Berliner got hugely depressed. Feeling pushed out of the business he'd created, he gave up the fight and got rid of his staff.

His principal engineer, Eldridge Johnson, was not so defeatist. He'd worked for years making continuous improvements to the Berliner flat disc machine including a way of fixing paper labels on the discs. He wanted to fight on, so Berliner gave him the company and turned his attention to inventing the helicopter.

Johnson, now able to say the company had no connection with Berliner, counter-sued, claiming the Zonophone infringed the company's rights. And he won.

In celebration, Johnson re-named his company Victor. With William Owen's permission from London, he started selling a new machine in the USA with a logo of Nipper listening to the gramophone – The Victor Talking Machine. In Britain, Owen too decided he would use the logo for the British company and changed the name under which the company sold its records to HMV – His Master's Voice.

Without ever having discussed how they might divide the old Berliner company, William Owen and Eldridge Johnson suddenly found themselves controlling two separate entities – Victor in America and HMV in Britain. They drew up a formal agreement, splitting the world between the two companies and agreeing on ways to co-operate. It meant there were now four major record companies in the world. In America; Victor, Columbia and Edison. In Britain; HMV.

3
The Song Is You
MAX DREYFUS

In 1888 the SS *Aller* steamed into New York harbour packed with immigrants from Germany and Britain. Amongst the passengers on deck was yet another of the thousands of Jewish immigrants fleeing from prejudice and persecution in Europe – Max Dreyfus, a fourteen-year-old boy in shorts.

Young Max had boarded the ship in Bremen, taken there by his father from the family home in Baden in Southern Germany. Now, as the ship prepared for disembarkation, Max was taking a first apprehensive look at his new country.

The Civil War had been over for twenty years and New York was booming. The Brooklyn Bridge had just been finished and with it came New York's first cable car. Great landmarks were being built – the Statue of Liberty, the Metropolitan Museum of Art, Madison Square Gardens, and the Metropolitan Opera House.

Bicycle lanes had been opened right across the city and cycling had been declared 'safe' for women. The popular song of the moment was 'The New York and Coney Island Cycle-March Two-Step'.

Your yacht and fishing may be fine,
but they can't compare,
with pleasure rare,
that wheeling gives to all mankind.

Max would be staying with his Aunt Lena in a nice part of Brooklyn. Just across the water was Lower Manhattan, which was the bottom rung for Jewish immigrants fleeing from persecution in Russia and Eastern Europe. They lived in the Bowery, crammed into decaying tenement buildings or foul doss houses converted from broken-down warehouses.

Further uptown, between 20th and 50th Street, was where middle-class immigrants tended to settle. And above that was uptown, where wealthy merchants and upper middle-class New Yorkers lived in fine houses, dining in elegant restaurants and visiting the opera and concerts of classical music by the world's finest musicians, which is what Max dreamt of being. His ambition was to become a world-famous concert pianist.

The chances were small. On the other hand there was a thriving new industry in popular music. New York's obsession with nightlife meant there were theatres and vaudeville shows, saloon bars and cafés, scattered all over town, nearly every one of them with some sort of live music.

For the last twenty years, the most popular music had been 'minstrelsy' – white entertainers with blacked-up faces and white lips, singing songs with a rhythmic lilt and a banjo accompaniment, parodying black southerners. Now vaudeville was taking over. Blacked-up singers were still popular, but they appeared as a single act on a bill featuring many other acts. Some of these blacked-up singers were black themselves, parodying their own race, but most were white. Until recently the majority had been Irish immigrants, now Jewish immigrants were taking over. A Jewish face wasn't well received on a vaudeville stage, but blacked-up it was acceptable. It was part of a ritual that Jewish entertainers went through to establish themselves – by becoming black a Jew announced his allegiance to America – by singing black music he showed his modernity.

For a while, Max lived with his aunt in Brooklyn and got a job selling fabrics in a furnishing store. Every free moment he went to the area round 28th Street and 5th Avenue where most of the music publishers had their offices, talking his way into their offices, showing off his prowess on piano. Eventually, at Howley & Haviland, a long established firm, he got a job providing piano accompaniment for singers demonstrating songs.

There was a new partner in the company, Paul Dresser, the son of a Catholic German immigrant. He was an ex-vaudeville entertainer, now in his thirties who composed tunes but couldn't write music. Max wrote down Dresser's hummed musical phrases giving them chords and structure, turning them into songs and writing a piano part.

He quickly became indispensable and Dresser thanked him, not by offering him a share in the songs, or by raising his salary, but by helping him with his English, explaining that it wasn't 'Srow zee bal', but 'TH-row TH-e ball'.

He made Max practise them over and over until he sounded properly American.

Eventually Dresser had a monster hit, a maudlin tearjerker called 'On The Banks of the Wabash', and it sold millions. Dresser and his company were now rolling in money, and Max, who'd done his bit in turning Dresser's hummed melody into a hit song, felt he should get an increase on his $6 a week. When it was refused, he went looking for work elsewhere.

The person who agreed to pay him an extra dollar a week was Isidore Witmark, whose company had started the whole new upsurge in publishing by sending Charles K. Harris that cheque for 85 cents.

At Witmark and Sons, Max Dreyfus found himself working for a publisher who specialised in coon songs – syncopated ditties with derogatory lyrics about the oddities of the negro character – watermelon-chicken-loving country buffoons, good for a smile and a dance but not much else.

In the days before amplification, these performers had to bellow the songs to be heard at the back of the hall. As a result they were called 'coon shouters', and the titles of the songs they shouted were appalling. 'If the Man in the Moon Was a Coon', 'Every Race Has a Flag but the Coon', or the hugely popular, 'All Coons Look Alike to Me'.

This last one was written by a vaudeville singer who himself was black and called himself 'The Unbleached American', Ernest Hogan. Black people found the song so offensive that a white man could intimidate them just by whistling the first two bars as they passed on the street.

Hogan justified having written it by saying, "with the publication of that song, a new musical rhythm was given to the people". He was talking about the hint of ragtime that flowed through the song, and perhaps what he said was true; the rhythm used in these coon songs opened the public's ear to a new musical style. And in 1899 it became a craze.

Scott Joplin's 'Maple Leaf Rag' introduced America to something new. At its best ragtime expressed the intensity and energy of urban life in modern America; it was thrilling, even rather sexual. Listeners felt as if social restraint was being removed, allowing them to flow with the music.

But like every fad that came along, it was swallowed up by an industry intent on quick profiteering. Most people never got to hear ragtime as a piano performance, just as an endless flow of second-rate popular songs.

As ragtime became popular, Max Dreyfus moved on. This time he went to T. B. Harms, Witmark's chief rival, the company who'd stolen 'Daisy' from Francis, Day & Hunter while their songwriter was holidaying in New York.

For the first time Max was given freedom to spend his time composing songs. Determined to finally make his mark, he churned them out, many of them ragtime melodies with lyrics by one of the company's staff writers – 'Hello, ma Baby!', 'A Carolina Cake Walk', 'Bound with a Golden Chain', 'A Bow of Blue'. There were dozens of them, sometimes one a day, but very few achieved any sort of success.

At T. B. Harms, Max Dreyfus, like all the other writers of popular songs, was writing in the same formularised fashion. It was a long way from being the classical composer and world-class concert pianist he'd dreamt of becoming, and he was just about to give up trying to be a songwriter when he finally got a hit.

It was a piano instrumental called 'Cupid's Garden'. But when he heard his hit being played by pianists all over town – in bars and saloons and restaurants –

instead of inspiring him, it depressed him. It sounded so ordinary, so uninspiring, that Max realised he simply didn't have the knack to be a great songwriter. And if songwriting was ruled out, the only way left to make his fortune from music was as a publisher.

Harms was a speciality publisher. The company spent less time than the other publishers on plugging songs to vaudeville and focused instead on getting songs into shows on Broadway, mostly revues or burlesque featuring a mish-mash of different music. This was what Tom Harms was best at. He'd been doing it for fifteen years, not only paying producers to use his songs but also loaning them rehearsal money in return for the publishing rights to any new songs they used. But Tom Harms was getting old.

Sometime previously, Max's younger brother Louis had arrived in America and gone to the southern states to sell picture frames. By letter, Max had been educating him in the ways of the music business and he now suggested they borrow money from their family in Germany and take over T. B. Harms. Once Louis had agreed, Max went to Tom Harms and persuaded him to sell the brothers a 25 per cent share and let them run the company.

Max decided they should concentrate on the company's greatest asset, its contacts with Broadway. But when he started going round theatre producers trying to persuade them to use the company's songs he realised the quality of its material was no longer good enough. He needed to find new writers who could compose specifically for the stage.

Another publisher, Edward B. Marks, supplied him with just the right person.

Marks had a weekend house on Long Island. One day someone knocked on the door and asked if he could audition for a job. He was Jerome Kern, aged eighteen.

Kern came from a well-respected middle-class family. Like the Witmarks and the Dreyfus brothers, they were Jewish immigrants from Germany. At school he started writing songs and contributed one to the end-of-term minstrel show. People said it was the best song of the evening and the local yacht club asked him to write a revue for them. When the show went well, Kern walked out of school and told his parents he was going to make a career out of songwriting. Surprisingly his father was supportive. He was a piano salesman and viewed a career in music as perfectly normal.

Young Kern had a niece whose family knew Edward B. Marks and Kern persuaded her to take him to meet the publisher at his holiday house on Long Island. Marks made Kern sit down and play the piano. Although he didn't look enthusiastic at the time Marks later admitted he'd been impressed by "the little fellow with tight green pants".

Because he had no vacancies for a pianist Marks suggested Kern work in his 'jobbing' department, "dealing with bills and invoice". Kern accepted, and for nine months he learnt about the finances of music publishing. Then his grandfather died and left him a substantial sum of money.

Kern went to see Marks and told him he'd like to buy a share of the company. Marks told him he was being cheeky, so Kern went down the road to T. B. Harms and asked to see the manager, Max Dreyfus.

Dreyfus was sitting in his office in a morning suit with a beautifully cut Prince Albert coat draped over the piano next to a silk scarf and top hat. And young Kern, a bit of a snob about clothes, was impressed.

When Kern played the piano, Dreyfus was equally impressed. He offered him a job as a staff writer and asked how much he was currently earning. Kern told him seven dollars a week but Dreyfus misheard eleven. And offered him twelve.

"He said he wanted to imbibe the atmosphere of music," Dreyfus recalled later. "I decided to take him on and to start him off by giving him the toughest job I had – selling music." So Kern became a plugger.

Kern thought it best to leave the suggestion about buying shares till later, but within weeks of starting he'd begun to notice a visible lack of money around the place. The offices were scruffy and Max never again dressed as smartly as he had the morning they met. When Kern asked him about it Max admitted he'd hired the hat and coat to attend a funeral. So Kern decided to make his proposal.

Lately, Max and Louis had upped their share in T. B. Harms to a majority. To do so they'd borrowed too much and promised to pay it back too quickly; they were over-stretched and needed funding. If this teenager wanted to help them out they could hardly refuse. But the teenager was no fool and by the end of the day he was a 25 per cent shareholder in T. B. Harms.

Max, though, was delighted. He not only had the perfect new writer to work with, he now had the money to run the company as he wanted to.

4

Give My Regards to Broadway
THE AMERICAN MUSICAL

In the music business, 'The British Invasion' usually refers to the period in the 1960s when the Beatles burst into America followed by a stream of British pop groups. In fact, the first British invasion was much earlier. It was at the start of the twentieth century, when Broadway was invaded by a new style of British stage show from which the classic American musical would evolve.

In Britain in the nineteenth century, the Gaiety Theatre in London became the first theatre to install electric lighting to light the stage from the front. The result was that shows could rely more on spectacular staging and less on music and dialogue. With this in mind, George Edwardes, who for ten years had been the production manager for all of Gilbert and Sullivan's operas, resigned and moved to the Gaiety Theatre.

Edwardes wanted to try something new – an alternative to Gilbert & Sullivan's clever satire for the upper middle-class. He envisaged musical plays with modern dress, cheerful songs and sharp dialogue, something a bit more mass market. Most important of all was to make the shows spectacular, so he decided on a chorus of fashionable young ladies, reminiscent of music hall but actually quite respectable, the Gaiety Girls.

Putting on a show of this type was expensive. Music hall had no sets – a show could run for as little as one night and still make a profit – a musical play took rehearsals, scenery, a cast, an orchestra and the rental of a theatre for a fixed period. If it didn't run for at least three months the promoter would lose money.

Early in the nineteenth century London didn't have enough people within range of its theatres for big musical productions to be financially viable. But in 1863 London's first underground train came into service, the Metropolitan Line. People could come into London for a show in the evening and be back home by midnight – from Swiss Cottage or South Kensington or Moorgate. This helped tremendously with the success of Gilbert & Sullivan's operas.

In the early 1890s, just as George Edwardes was ready with his new shows, the Underground expanded again – to Chesham on the Metropolitan Line and to Hounslow, Wimbledon and Whitechapel on the District Line. This meant five times more people could get to a West End show. For George Edwardes it was a present from heaven – an audience from the suburbs.

From his very first production, Edwardes was onto a winner. Light plays and sharp dialogue with songs weaving in and out of the story.

Edwardes had no ear for music and not much understanding of dramatic writing, but he knew exactly what the public liked. His masterstroke was his chorus of fashionable young ladies. In 1896, *The Sketch* described their costumes as "in accordance with the very latest and most extreme modes of the moment". Gaiety Girls were polite and well behaved, giving the impression of ideal womanhood.

In fact, they were just shop assistants, picked up by Edwardes according to his fancy and sent off to tutors to be taught song and dance, good diction, and social skills. The Gaiety Girls were his obsession; he reveled in his control over them, and there was always at least one with whom he was having an affair. The whole structure of his business was designed to give him an endlessly evolving harem of pretty girls – too fat or too thin, they were fired – not smiling enough onstage, or smiling too much at one person, they were fired.

Edwardes needed to keep his girls single but encouraged them to dine out with male friends at fashionable restaurants. Then he spied on them, paying headwaiters to report back. He was a puppet-master, a snooper, a control freak, and a dirty old man.

And the most successful theatre producer in Britain.

The composers and lyric-writers Edwardes used were not from the world of operetta, nor from music hall, they were well-educated gentlemen. The two who contributed most were Ivan Caryll and Lionel Monckton.

Caryll was a bourgeois Belgian turned bourgeois Briton. He'd studied at the Liege Conservatory before coming to England and marrying Maud Hill, Gilbert & Sullivan's favourite leading lady. George Edwardes hired him as musical director for his shows, but amongst London high society Caryll was more famous for his extravagant dinner parties than his music.

Lionel Monckton was the eldest son of Sir John Braddick Monckton, the Town Clerk of London. He was educated at Charterhouse and Oxford and became drama critic for the *Daily Telegraph*. For a hobby he wrote songs but he was twenty-nine before he managed to place one, 'What Will You Have To Drink', in the revue *Cinder Ellen Up Too Late*.

It wasn't much, but it gave him the confidence to approach George Edwardes and propose himself as a songwriter, and Edwardes paired him with Caryll.

Once Monckton and Caryll had made a name for themselves, the composing of popular songs became an acceptable profession for gentleman to pursue. Other than Monckton and Caryll, the nucleus of George Edwardes' group of writers were all upper middle-class; Paul Rubens, educated at Oxford University; Howard Talbot, born in America but educated at London University; Sidney Jones, Trinity College Dublin; Adam Ross, King's College Cambridge; Owen Hall, an Irish-born theatre critic and solicitor; and Percy Greenbank, another qualified lawyer.

Because he'd walked out on Gilbert and Sullivan, who were published by Chappell, Edwardes had thought Tom Chappell would feel awkward dealing with him. So he took the songs for his first show to a rival publisher, Hopwood & Crew.

A year later Tom Chappell retired and bought in a new managing director, William Boosey, the adopted son of John Boosey, Chappell's biggest rival.

William Boosey had been a school-friend of Lionel Monckton at Charterhouse. They'd "shared the distinction of sitting at the bottom of the classical form". So Boosey contacted Monckton and asked him to introduce Edwardes.

At the meeting that followed their differing views dovetailed nicely. Edwardes saw songs as something that would make people come to the show. Boosey saw shows as something that would make people buy sheet music. A deal was struck whereby Chappell would join Edwardes as co-producer in all his future shows and would publish the music from them. And the big new market for these shows would be America.

For years British popular music had been openly stolen in America; sometimes songs were given new words, sometimes simply credited to new writers. When Gilbert and Sullivan's shows toured America, the writers received nothing. But in 1886, at a convention at Berne in Switzerland, an international copyright agreement in due course was signed by most European countries.

In America the leading publishers reorganised themselves into the MPA – the Music Publishers Association. Although the USA was not a signatory to the Berne Convention, the MPA decided foreign copyrights would be honoured from then on.

Almost at once a British musical show stormed Broadway. It was *Florodora*, with a sextet of petite girls, each five foot four and 130 pounds, singing flirtily at six young toffs with Mayfair accents.

> *MEN: Oh tell me, pretty maiden, are there any more at home like you?*
> *GIRLS: There are a few, kind sir, but simple girls and proper too.*

George Edwardes was furious. Although the show was by Owen Hall, one of his regular writers, for this show Hall had defected to a different producer, Tom Davis. As usual though, William Boosey had managed to get hold of the publishing for Chappell.

In America, Chappell normally allowed its copyrights to be administered by T. B. Harms, but seeing the show's enormous success on Broadway, William Boosey decided Chappell should now open its own office there. So he went to New York and hired George Maxwell, the Englishman he'd previously hired to run the American office of Boosey.

His foresight was masterful. As he'd anticipated, the rivalry created by *Florodora*'s success triggered George Edwardes into rushing his own latest hit onto Broadway. It was *A Chinese Honeymoon*, his biggest success to date, which had run for more than 1000 performances in London.

About an English couple who inadvertently break China's kissing laws, the show's final number had the irresistible title, 'Martha Spanks the Grand Pianner'. In New York it ran for almost as long as *Florodora*.

Following its success, Edwardes persuaded Owen Hall to return to the fold, then wiped the floor with Tom Davis by sending a succession of successful shows to Broadway – *The Girl from Kays*, *The Orchid*, *The Spring Chicken*, *The Girls from Gottenberg*, *Our Miss Gibbs*, *The Sunshine Girl*.

The flow was endless. During the first fifteen years of the 1900s over thirty British musicals opened on Broadway.

If a show was produced by George Edwardes, the publisher would be Chappell. Its New York office became one of the three publishing companies most linked to Broadway musicals, but with its shows arriving ready-made from London there was little work to be done. For the other two publishers, Witmark & Sons, and T. B. Harms, each song placed in a Broadway show was the result of hard work and persuasion. The people being persuaded were the three American producers who dominated Broadway, Florenz Ziegfeld, George M. Cohan, and the Shuberts.

Ziegfeld was the son of a Chicago music teacher. His first venture into show business was with 'dancing ducks'. This was achieved by placing normal ducks on a heated metal floor and drowning their squawks by banging on a drum. Shortly afterwards, his father was appointed music director for the 1890 World Fair and sent his son to Europe to seek out musical talent for the event. He came back with nothing more than an oversized muscleman but recovered his costs by exhibiting him at the World Fair in flesh colored tights, charging people to feel his biceps.

The experience gave Ziegfeld Jr. a taste for theatrical promotion, though not for musclemen. He took to promoting young women in similarly skin-tight costumes and soon developed a taste for theatrical excess. In 1906 he put on his first Ziegfeld Follies, an American equivalent of the *Folies Bergères* with non-stop music, billed as 'fifty of the most beautiful women ever gathered in one theater'. The high spot of the first follies were *The Taxicab Girls*, almost naked, with red flags saying 'for hire' and headlights stuck in their crotch.

The Follies were a wild success. Each show had to top the previous one, with more girls, fewer clothes, grander sets and increasingly outrageous finales. It soon became clear that performing a song in the Ziegfeld Follies would make it successful regardless of its true value. The Follies became the best short cut to a hit, and although Ziegfeld never published songs himself, he was ready to cut a deal with any publisher in town providing the price was right.

George M. Cohan was an Irish-American whose family were travelling vaudeville performers. As a baby, George joined them on stage as a prop. As a boy, he sang and danced. As a teenager, he was paid by a New York publisher to Americanise music-hall songs from Britain.

This was before the two countries had started honouring each other's copyrights and what Cohan did was nothing more than 'song laundering'. He would take an English popular song and make it into something the American company could register as its own. He could do as little or as much to it as he liked. The publisher would get a hit and sell fifty thousand copies; Cohan would get just ten dollars cash. But he benefitted from learning about the construction of songs and what made them into hits. And he was building his name as a songwriter.

In 1904, when he was twenty-six, Cohan put on his first Broadway show, *Little Johnny Jones*. It included two of his own original songs, 'Give My Regards to Broadway' and 'The Yankee Doodle Dandy Boy'. He'd wanted to publish the songs with Witmark & Sons but ended up putting them with a small publisher because he'd been afraid to knock on the door of such an important company. "They were the big song publishers in those days…. I figured it would be useless to try…"

On several occasions he passed the Witmark offices cursing them as he went. "Just goes to show how smart those babes in there are… here I am, the best songwriter in America, walking right by their door with four or five great big sure-fire hits under my arm."

But after the success of *Little Johnny Jones* he got up the courage to go and see them. His apprehension had been unwarranted and they remained his publishers for the next twenty-five years.

Cohan wrote, directed, choreographed, produced, and performed in all his shows. He became the biggest star on Broadway. He knew every trick there was about rousing an audience and improving the box-office takings. He regularly used 'boomers' in the audience who cheered at certain songs and sang along with others to encourage an encore. And he knew the value of patriotism. Somewhere in every show he would make sure the Stars & Stripes was on display. "Many a bum show has been saved by the flag," he explained.

The last of the three great American theatre producers were the Shubert brothers – Sam, Lee and Jacob. Children of an alcoholic father, they were forced to find work from the age of ten. While Lee Shubert sold newspapers outside a local theatre, Sam found a way inside and persuaded the director to give him a small part. Over five years Sam rose from bit-part actor to assistant treasurer of the Grand Opera House, and he pulled his brothers up behind him.

On the East Coast, the Shuberts eventually owned thirteen theatres. Sam produced New York shows, Jacob out-of-town ones. But when they went outside their regular territory to present a farewell tour for actress Sarah Bernhardt they came up against the Syndicate. The Syndicate was a national association of shady theatre owners who monopolised ticket sales. In every city where the Shuberts tried to do their Sarah Bernhardt show they found themselves unable to book a theatre. So they started doing the Bernhardt show in a tent. The public loved them for it, and so did the press. The Shuberts were happy too. The tent held more people than a theatre so they made more money.

The main thing was – the Shuberts loved musicals and they owned Broadway theatres. So music publishers loved the Shuberts. And in the case of Witmark, the love was mutual. Although the Shuberts had theatres, Witmark had Broadway's favourite composer, Victor Herbert.

Herbert was born in Ireland and bought up in Austria. To most people that made him a German with the gift of the gab. By all accounts, he was a charmer. The philanthropist Andrew Carnegie said he liked Herbert's music more than anyone else's.

Herbert started as a flute player in Stuttgart, moved on to cello and was selected by Johannes Brahms to play in a chamber orchestra for Franz Liszt's 72nd birthday. Having married one of the stars of the Stuttgart Opera he emigrated to America and found work by socialising at New York's best German café, Luchow's, handing out cards saying "solo cellist from the Royal Orchestra of his Majesty, the King of Wurtemberg".

He became assistant conductor of the New York Philharmonic and took advantage of his position to provide it with orchestrations. He then did the same for symphony orchestras in Detroit, Philadephia and Boston. But it was when he fell in with some writers of popular songs that Herbert truly blossomed.

Herbert found he had a great talent for popular tunes, and coupled with his gift for orchestration he was soon writing shows for Broadway – light opera, not unlike Gilbert & Sullivan's, but without the verbal bite – *Babes in Toyland, The Red Mill*, and *Mademoiselle Modiste*.

Straddling the two worlds of popular and classical music, he became the best-known and best-connected composer in America. Probably the most loved too.

And Witmark published it all.

Isidore Witmark paid Herbert more for his works than any other writer the company published. He also tried to stem Herbert's wild spending, but complained it was hopeless. "His motto might have been 'Easy come, easier go'."

The other specialist Broadway music publisher was T. B. Harms, run by the guileful Dreyfus brothers. Although they hadn't been happy about Chappell setting up a New York office, the brothers went out of their way to maintain good relations with William Boosey.

They were prepared to play the long game and wait for Chappell to come back to them. They also found themselves playing the long game with Jerome Kern. Nearly a year after they'd benefitted from his investment they'd still had no success with his songs so Max persuaded him to work as a rehearsal pianist for shows. If an extra number were needed Kern could step in and dash one off on the spot.

Kern didn't make himself easy to work with. When Max finally managed to place one of his songs in a show, Kern went to the theatre where it was being rehearsed and looked through the arrangement. It didn't please him; so he walked round the stage picking up the orchestra parts and left the theatre with them.

Max suggested he take some time off and visit England to savour the British theatrical scene. But when Kern arrived the first thing he saw was American – a giant poster of Bert Williams.

Williams was America's best-known black vaudeville singer and on a billboard outside the Shaftesbury Theatre he was standing on top of an iced cake. The show being advertised was *In Dahomey*, the first-ever musical with an all-black cast and an all-black creative team. The producers, though, were white.

One of them had discovered a female impersonator and was planning to launch him in New York through a not very good British musical called *Mr Wix of Wickham*. He asked Kern if he could provide some songs to improve it.

When it opened on Broadway the critics focused mainly on the transvestite. "He contrives to let his masculinity shine through", said one. But another found something nice to say about Kern. His music, said Alan Dale of *The American* "towers in such an Eiffel way" that "criticism is disarmed".

Kern took confidence from these comments and started taking over the publisher's role, pushing his new songs directly to theatre producers. Lyricist Edward Laska turned up at the Harms office one day when Kern was doodling on the piano. "I got to the Harms building and there was my young friend as usual, with a straw hat on, of which the top was knocked out, and a long black cigar in his mouth, being cold-smoked – I don't think I ever saw him really smoke one."

Laska had been asked to write a song lampooning the trendy phrase 'to spoon', would Kern like to collaborate? They knocked up a song and went round to see the theatre producer who'd asked for it. Not only were they kept waiting but several people who arrived after them were shown into the producer's office ahead of them. Kern got angry and dragged Laska off to see another producer, Charles Frohman.

Frohman's assistant listened to the song, liked it, but criticised the lyric. Laska started to say they would alter it but Kern grabbed him and dragged him off to the Shuberts' office where he demanded to see Lee Shubert himself.

The Shuberts had just opened a new show by composer Reginald De Koven. Kern lied and said it was De Koven who'd sent them, so Lee Shubert agreed to put their song into a new show from London, *The Earl and the Girl*, replacing a song by Percy Greenbank and Ivan Caryll.

'How Would You Like to Spoon With Me?' would be sung to gentlemen in the front stalls by chorus girls sailing over their heads on swings.

Afterwards, out in the street, Laska slapped Kern on the back. "We kids, nineteen and twenty respectively, gleefully went into an apothecary's to have a couple of ice-cream sodas."

Still only twenty, Kern was becoming a bit pushy, but getting in with the Shuberts was quite a coup. A few years later it would lead to a song that triggered the creation of Broadway's biggest star ever.

The show was *La Belle Paree*, a revue produced by the Shuberts in which they were trying out a new performer. He was Al Jolson, a young Jewish man who blacked-up his face. And the extraordinary song Kern and his lyricist came up with was entitled 'Paris is a Paradise for Coons'.

London town is mighty strong for colored brown or even yellow octoroons,
But lordy me, to have a jubilee just save all rag-a-time tunes for Paris, that's
the Paradise for coons...
Here the Frenchmen cheer for black monsieur de Jig,
and all the ladies want to see Mamzelle de Nig.

When Jolson came on and sang it, the first night audience failed to applaud. They were bored. From the first note the show had been sluggish, and by the halfway point they were restless. The sight of a blackface singer was the last straw, and they barracked him.

The next evening, when it came time for Jolson's song, he walked to the front of the stage and read out the critics' reviews of the previous night – all of them bad. He then asked the audience, would they prefer the show to continue or hear him sing some Stephen Foster songs. They chose the singing.

The next day the Shuberts promoted him to a major role in the show, and by the end of the week he was the principal attraction.

La Belle Paree ran for 104 performances and Al Jolson went on to become America's biggest star of musical theatre. Without Jerome Kern's dreadful coon song it would never have happened.

5

Alexander's Ragtime Band
IRVING BERLIN

In 1906, the trendy dance in London was 'Sausages for Tea'.

Two lines of dancers faced each other, men on one side, women opposite, and advanced, keeping their heads down until nearly touching, then throwing them back as they retreated.

This was how London's new generation danced. Children of the upper middle-classes, dressed in dinner jackets and evening dress. The music was the cakewalk, the latest piano music from America, but the words the dancers sang to them were decidedly British. And like military music, the emphasis in their movements fell solidly on the 1st and 3rd beat of each bar.

> *When we are married we'll have*
> *Sausages for tea*
> *Sausages for tea*
> *When we are married we'll have*
> *Sausages for tea*
> *Sausages for you, and*
> *Me*

It may have been profoundly English, but young toffs dancing to the cakewalk and singing silly words was the first indication that American black music had the ability to influence popular culture across the world.

The second was 'Alexander's Ragtime Band'.

Henry Waterson made a great deal of money dealing in diamonds, and lost a great deal of it gambling on horses. He was almost completely deaf. When music publisher Harry von Tilzer boasted he'd made a fortune from music without being able to read a note of it, Waterson went further; he told friends he planned to do the same without being able to *hear* a note of it.

He formed a music publishing company with Ted Snyder a young songwriter who'd just had a hit with 'Wild Cherries Rag'. Like so many other songwriters, Snyder was now eager to climb up the ladder and find other songwriters to publish.

The first one he found in his new partnership with Waterson was a singing waiter, twenty years old, working in a cheap restaurant in Union Square.

Issy Baline was yet another Jewish immigrant, but on a different level from Kern or Dreyfus. Issy's family had been chased from Russia by a pogrom against Jews. His first memory was as a three-year-old, lying in the road on a blanket, watching the family house go up in flames, torched by bigots.

The family arrived in New York without a penny and when Issy was eight, his father died. He was too young to help support his family, but rather than burden them with another mouth to feed, he left and existed as a street-boy – selling newspapers, picking up dropped coins, sleeping in a filthy rat-infested warehouse for which he had to pay 15 cents a night. "You got a cubbyhole to sleep in, open at the top, and you were always scared that somebody would reach over and steal your pants."

During all that time his sole ambition was to become a singing waiter. When he finally became one he got a new ambition – to become a songwriter. He was always scribbling words on paper and got an idea for a song from reading about the 1908 Olympic Games in London. The Italian marathon runner entered the stadium in the lead but crumbling at the knees. The crowd surged forward and pushed him toward the finish line, which caused him to be disqualified. Issy's song would be about an Italian-American barber who bet his entire shop on the marathon runner, only to see him lose.

In due course, trying to sell his idea, Issy arrived at the offices of Waterson & Snyder with the lyrics. Waterson, despite being deaf, could at least read, and after he'd scanned through the words he agreed to pay twenty-five dollars for them, including the melody. Issy was planning to write the melody later with the help of the pianist at his restaurant. But he didn't admit it – he needed the twenty-five dollars too badly. Waterson told him, "Just you trot into the next room to the arranger and he'll take down your tune for you."

Issy had never written a tune before; he only did lyrics. But with twenty-five dollars at stake he stood there and improvised. A few months later the song became something of a hit.

His next idea was for a comic song sung in a New York Jewish accent – 'Sadie Salome Go Home'. Sadie Cohen, a local girl, gets a job as a stripper and woos her customers with *The Dance of the Seven Veils*. But Moses, her boyfriend, grumbles.

This time one of his employers, Ted Snyder, wrote the music. It was a bigger hit than the first, enough to persuade Waterson & Snyder they should offer Issy a position as staff lyricist – twenty-five dollars a week plus royalties.

It seemed a good deal; most songwriters were still not getting royalties and even when they did they were paltry (which these would probably be too). But that didn't bother young Issy. He had a new job.

And he had a new name too. The one he'd persuaded them to print on the sheet music.

Irving Berlin.

"What is it that makes a song a hit?"

In the first decade of the twentieth century it was a question everyone was asking.

"Popular music has become a fad from Maine to California" announced *Music Trades* in 1907.

Newspapers were full of features on how hits were written. Nobody wrote for fun, they wrote for money; they all understood exactly what the popular song business was about.

Fred Weatherly, who would later write 'Danny Boy' by appropriating the tune of 'Londonderry Air', believed hits came from the simplest melodies. "Why should a musician despise a simple melody and think himself great for constructing discords and dull phrases?"

"Write according to the market," said Edward B. Marks.

Black vaudevillean Bert Williams was totally practical about it. He said his songs were not so much written as assembled. "The tunes to popular songs are mostly made up of standard parts, like a motor car."

No one puzzled over this question of what made hit songs more than young Irving Berlin. He'd had his first small hit, but the big one had so far eluded him. One evening he was having his hair cut when he met a friend and suggested they go to a show.

"Sure," his friend said. "My wife's gone to the country."

In Berlin's brain a bell sounded.

"Bing! There I had a commonplace familiar title line."

He persuaded his friend to forget about going to the show and work on a song instead. But the lyrics they came up with were too ordinary, and for Berlin, too wordy.

"All night I sweated to find what I knew was there and finally I speared the lone word – just a single word, that made the song – and a fortune… 'My wife's gone to the country! Hooray!' That word gave the whole idea of the song in one quick wallop…"

In the course of six verses and choruses Berlin managed to repeat the wallop 48 times, and six months later it became his first number one.

Hooray! Hooray! Hooray!

Because Henry Waterson was afraid Irving Berlin's success would make him look for a better publishing deal elsewhere, he suggested that Berlin should become an equal shareholder with him and Ted Snyder. In fact he went even further;

he made Irving Berlin president of the company, which now became Waterson, Berlin & Snyder. Berlin was now his own publisher.

Berlin had begun to write his own melodies and found it made songwriting much easier. "Writing both words and music I can compose them together and make them fit. I sacrifice one for the other. If I have a melody I want to use, I plug away at the lyrics until I make them fit the best parts of my music, and vice versa."

For a while he'd been trying to figure out how to incorporate black rhythms to a popular song. His answer was 'Alexander's Ragtime Band'. The song wasn't a real rag, it was just a clever pop song, a *very* clever one. A mix of black and white styles with military overtones, not classic ragtime but with a syncopated feel similar to the rhythm of American speech, and touches of black American dialect.

Having finished the song, Berlin didn't have much confidence in it, and both Waterson and Snyder were as cool about it as Berlin himself. But another member of the staff, Max Winslow, was certain it was a hit and refused to let them give up on it. Winslow pushed the song everywhere. He instructed all of the company's seventy-five pluggers to work on it non-stop, and he sent copies to singers and bandleaders all over America.

After a few months it began to sell, but only in dribbles, becoming popular in what Berlin described as "a mild pale-pink way". When it finally it took off it was by an unusual route, via a well-known vaudeville singer performing in Chicago. She was Emma Carus, a German immigrant who claimed she'd learnt the negro dialect from a man called Frog Eyes. She hooked onto the lines of black dialect in Berlin's lyrics and shouted them like she was singing a coon song.

Normally, to become a national hit, New York had to come first but from Chicago the song spread to vaudeville performers all over the country and by mid-summer it had sold 500,000 copies. By the end of the year it was up to a million, and then it shot around the world.

'Alexander's Ragtime Band' started a global dance craze. Amongst other things, it began to popularise the gramophone. Reading the sheet music and banging away on a piano wouldn't suffice. To dance to it you needed a record, and something to play it on. So all over the world the sales of gramophones increased, even as far away as Russia and China.

The song's international success was the first indication that American black music had the ability to influence popular culture across the world. Even though the song's black influences came second-hand through the writing and performance of white musicians, it was from that moment on that popular music all over the world began to incorporate the beat and singing nuances of American black music, however subtly.

But that was to evolve gradually. There was one other change that came at once.

Irving Berlin's song bought a new kind of rhythm to the dance floor, ending the tradition of using military bands for dancing. Old-fashioned dance music had emphasised the 1st and 3rd beats of each bar, the 'on-beat', which was also the rhythm of genuine ragtime. But for this song Berlin had used a rhythm that could be heard in the music of southern blacks in New Orleans, the rhythm of Africa, with the emphasis on the 'off-beat'. By copying it Irving Berlin changed popular music forever.

Clapping your hands on 2 and 4 became the new beat of popular song.

6

Stardust
MAKING IT, 1910 STYLE

Personality, personality, that's the thing that always makes a hit.
Your nationality or your rationality, doesn't help or hinder you one bit.

This wasn't an Irving Berlin song, nor was it by a Tin Pan Alley rhyme-merchant, it was the philosophy that would one day be embraced by rock stars, 'the singer not the song'. In 1910 it was an unheard of concept, except from Eva Tanguay.

Tanguay was the artist who didn't fit, and she was the biggest. The public were bored with old-fashioned music they wanted ragtime and excitement.

From the beginning, the music industry was led by business, not art. When artists sometimes showed the way, it was because they were essentially business-minded themselves, like Eva Tanguay. She took the raw material of her own performing ability and turned it into something saleable. Making a lot from very little, many people would say.

Before the mid-twenties, there were no microphones, only megaphones. The most popular singers were the ones with the biggest, loudest voices. With men, that meant booming baritones; with women, big black blues voices. Or shrill crazy ones like Eva Tanguay. Her voice was sheer madness!

On stage Tanguay simulated sexual satisfaction; slurring, screeching, punctuating her songs with cackles; bouncing her voice from its highest to its lowest and back again. She poured bottles of champagne over her head, danced like a demon, flailed her arms, flung back her head, and shimmied her breasts. Her bra was just an encumbrance. The law said she had to wear one onstage, but she didn't much care if her breasts stayed inside of it or flopped out. Her voice was just average but it raised the roof. And her songs were outrageous, 'It's All Been Done Before But Not The Way I Do It', or 'Go As Far As You Like'.

Aleister Crowley, the English occultist, was besotted by her. "She cannot sing, as others sing; or dance, as others dance. She simply keeps on vibrating, both limbs and vocal chords... I could kill myself at this moment for the wild love of her."

Eva Tanguay was born in Quebec, the daughter of a doctor, but moved to Massachusetts with her family when she was six. Her father died soon after and from then on Tanguay sought constant attention. Left with a penniless mother, she started working in the theatre at the age of eight. As a chorus girl she upset the others with too much shimmying. When another girl criticised her, Tanguay choked her till she turned blue and lost consciousness. When it got into the papers she fell in love with notoriety. Her story was a template for creative artists before and since; the need to be in the public eye, and feel the love of an audience, triggered by childhood misfortune and wretchedness – from Irving Berlin to Ethel Waters to Madonna.

Eva Tanguay was a provocateur. Her songs were outrageous and she was a plotter of new looks. Her costumes were manic – bells, leaves, feathers, seashells, and coins. After the Lincoln penny was issued, Tanguay appeared in a coat made from 4,000 of them. Her most outrageous dress was just a whisp. "I can fit the entire costume in my closed fist," she boasted.

At her peak, she earned the highest salary of her day, $3,500 a week. Wads of $1,000 bills were her stock in trade. When someone accidentally walked in front of her as she hurried to her dressing room she grabbed a hatpin and stabbed them in the belly. When the police came to arrest her she threw a roll of bills at the nearest cop and shouted, "Take it all and let me go, for it is now my dinner time."

If these things got into the papers, it was usually because Tanguay put them there. Anything that happened to her, she used for publicity. When her jewels were stolen she kept it on the front pages for days.

Whirling madly onstage she got terrible cramps. After shows, to unknot her leg muscles stagehands beat them with wooden staves. Her aim was to spin so fast "no one will be able to see my bare legs".

Tanguay was a rock star before they existed. She arranged her own coast-to-coast tours and broke box office records everywhere. She was a poor singer, an indelicate dancer, and her hair was piled up in a tangled mess. But it worked.

The only British artist who came close to her in outrageousness was Marie Lloyd. She worked in music hall and was every bit as provocative. When Lloyd came to America she got a reputation for being even bluer than Tanguay. It was all winks and leers, all to do with the manner in which she delivered the songs. After she had a hit with 'She'd Never Had Her Ticket Punched Before' she became the target of an English 'Vigilance' committee opposing music-hall licences. When she was summoned before the committees she sang two of her bawdiest songs, 'Oh! Mr Porter' and 'A Little of What you Fancy'; but she sang them in such innocence that the committee could find nothing wrong. Not content to leave it at that, Lloyd then launched into the classic drawing-room ballad 'Come Into the Garden Maud' and sang it in such an obscene way that the committee was shocked into silence.

The third in a trio of outrageous women was from France. She was Mistinguett, and her ability to outrage was the equal of the other two women. Jean Cocteau said of her, "She was of the animal race that owes nothing to intellectualism. She incarnated herself." It could equally well have been said about Eva Tanguay.

Her real name was Jeanne Bourgeois and she began by singing popular ballads as she sold flowers in a restaurant. A friend nicknamed her 'Miss Tinguette', and she kept it.

In the world of popular music she was France's first major export and played in both London and New York. She sold herself as a Parisian fantasy; the queen of *le spectacle risqué*, the highest paid female in the world with legs insured for half a million francs.

Like Eva Tanguay, she used sexuality and outrageousness to hold an audience that couldn't be reached any other way. Without amplification, musical finesse would barely reach the tenth row. To grab the barracking balcony, sexual imagery was needed, and a hearty bawl. Jean Cocteau called Mistinguett's voice, "that of the Parisian street hawkers".

She not only started the trend for female entertainers to wear enormous headdresses, she helped initiate the Apache dance "in which the male dancer tries to demolish the female dancer, as spectacularly as possible, and usually succeeds".

There wasn't much she didn't know about selling herself sexually, whether from the stage or in more personal circumstances. "A kiss can be a comma, a question mark, or an exclamation point," she said. "That's basic spelling that every woman ought to know."

Someone else using outrage to overcome lack of amplification was Julian Eltinge (rhymed with '*melting*').

Eltinge was the American female impersonator who spiced up Jerome Kern's first Broadway show, *Mr Wix of Wickham*. He didn't sing much but was still chased by music publishers; to have a song played behind his act was as good as having him sing it. In Britain he played a show for King Edward VII who presented him with a white bulldog. *Variety* called him "as great a performer as there is today".

Offstage, to counter any suggestion he might be homosexual, Eltinge smoked cigars, went to ball games, was seen with pretty women and regularly got into bar room brawls.

In London, music hall star Vesta Tilley was doing exactly the opposite. She was a woman impersonating a man – Burlington Bertie, a wacky good-for-nothing, who sang songs about the indignities of coming from a good family but not having a penny to his name.

What price Burlington Bertie,
The boy with the Hyde Park drawl,
What price Burlington Bertie,
The boy with the Bond Street crawl?

Offstage, like Julian Eltinge, Vesta Tilley found it necessary to emphasise her real sexuality, wearing copious amounts of jewellery to compensate. People thought of her as a symbol of female independence but it was always the men in her life who controlled her. First she was managed by her father, then by her husband, Walter de Frece, a music hall owner. When he was knighted for charitable work, he made his wife give up singing. When she disappeared from the London stage, songwriter William Hargreaves wrote a new song on the same theme as Tilley's for his wife, music hall star Ella Shields. She, too, dressed in a dinner jacket and wing collar, but presented herself as a sham toff, not from the upper classes at all – 'Burlington Bertie from Bow'.

Meanwhile, Vesta Tilley's husband became a Conservative Member of Parliament and the original Burlington Bertie became Lady de Frece.

Although all these artists were hugely popular, none of them made recordings until later in their career. To the music industry, their principal value was to publicise songs for which sheet music could be sold in abundance. But there were four other artists who already, at this early stage of the recording industry, were helping push the new technology into the public ear.

The biggest problem for an artist was how to adapt their stage voice to the limitations of recording acoustically through a horn, but one popular singer had a voice that proved ideal, big and understated.

Bert Williams was the first black singer to reach the mainstream of popular entertainment. When Ziegfeld hired him to perform in 'The 1910 Follies' it was considered totally shocking; a black performer had never before performed with a cast of white dancers. Some of the dancers delivered Ziegfeld an ultimatum saying Williams should be fired.

Ziegfeld held firm. "I can replace every one of you except the one you want me to fire."

When a bartender at the Astor Hotel tried to put Williams off drinking there by telling him drinks for coloureds were $50 each, he pulled out a wad of fifties and ordered him to pour a round for everyone at the bar.

After his Broadway successes, Columbia Records signed Williams to an exclusive recording contract and he became the first black artist the company had ever promoted without reference to his race. Columbia described his recordings simply as "inimitable art".

Equally inimitable was the occasional, strangely intense chord that could be produced by four unaccompanied performers singing continuous four-part harmony in the style known as 'barbershop', "a tingling of the spine, the raising of the hairs on the back of the neck, the spontaneous arrival of goose flesh on the forearm".

The American Quartet were the ultimate specialists in this and for their two record companies, Victor and Edison, it was a godsend – something that sheet music could never capture.

The American Quartet included two renowned lead singers – John Bieling and Billy Murray. They were signed to Victor for discs and Edison for cylinders. On stage they used no theatrics or strange outfits, just stood still and sang. But on record more was sometimes needed. When they recorded 'A Cowboy Romance', background effects were called for "the clatter of hoofs, the whinnying of horses, and the 'yipping' of the cowboys". It took hours to get it right and needed a great deal of yipping, causing John Bieling's voice to suffer a strain from which it never recovered.

Billy Murray, who'd encouraged him, wasn't too displeased. Left on his own he became one of America's top solo recording stars, one of the few able to make records that outsold sheet music of the same songs.

As did the Castles.

Vernon Castle was an actor whose speciality was playing an inebriated gentleman elegantly falling about the stage, trying to hide his condition. At a rowing club he met Irene Foote, the daughter of an eminent doctor, whom he married over her father's objections. They went to Paris with a revue that failed and to earn their fare back home they got a job dancing at the Café de Paris. Within weeks they'd become the rage of Parisian society, doing the latest American dances. At home their success was so widely reported that they returned as superstars. Victor Records signed them as the 'front' for a series of dance records.

The Castles opened a nightclub, a restaurant, and a dance school. They re-invented the foxtrot and popularised their new version in *Watch Your Step*, a Broadway revue written especially for them by Irving Berlin. They were trendsetters in every way; they had a lesbian manager and an all-black orchestra. But although their fame came from "teaching America to dance from the waist down", their real contribution to the music industry was to help popularise records.

But one other artist did even more.

Standing head and shoulders above all others as the first truly great recording star was Enrico Caruso.

Classical voices had built-in amplification and opera houses were designed to further amplify the sound created onstage. As a result, when it came to live performances, opera singers had an edge on everyone else. But there was something else too about opera that served the emerging recording industry particularly well.

A classically trained male tenor had exactly the frequency range best suited to acoustical horn recording. Not much was lost, whereas sopranos lost a lot, as did baritones. Victor Records and Caruso helped each other; Victor helped popularise Caruso, and Caruso helped make records a permanent part of American life. He made more than 260 recordings for the Victor Talking Machine Company and earned millions of dollars from royalties.

For a few thousand dollars Caruso could be persuaded to record almost anything, but mostly he recorded grand opera. The sheer quality of his voice convinced the non opera-loving public to buy his records and almost everyone had at least one. It should never be forgotten that it was opera rather than popular song that gave the record industry its first superstar.

Caruso's first recordings were made for The Gramophone Company. Early in his career, he was appearing at La Scala in Milan when Fred Gaisberg, on his way to Rome to try and get permission to record the Pope, stopped by. Hearing about the great new tenor at La Scala, Gaisberg asked if he could record him. The terms Caruso sent back were scandalous – he would sing ten pieces for £100. When Gaisberg requested permission from William Owen in London, he received the answer, "Fee exorbitant, absolutely forbid you to record".

Gaisberg went ahead anyway, deciding to cover the amount from his own pocket if he had to, and hiring a hotel room in which to record them. "Dressed like a dandy, twiddling a cane", Caruso sauntered down Via Manzoni and entered the Grand Hotel. He wanted "to get the job over quickly as he was anxious to earn that £100 and to have his lunch".

The arias included 'Celeste Aida' and 'Studenti! Udite!', and were instant bestsellers. It was these that resulted in Caruso being booked at Covent Garden and the New York Met. More importantly, they led to Victor Records making him America's first superstar recording artist.

Caruso always dressed immaculately, took two baths a day and smoked Egyptian cigarettes, but in 1906 he was arrested, charged with committing an indecent act in the monkey house at Central Park Zoo. The New York court found him guilty of pinching a married woman's bottom and he was fined $90.

Caruso said the monkey did it.

7

The Winner Takes It All
PIRATING AND OTHER PROBLEMS

In 1905 a bankrupt fishmonger almost killed off the British music industry. Music publishers called him 'The Pirate King' because all over London he sold cheaply made copies of sheet music on the street. People liked them. His sheet music sold for just pennies, less then a tenth of the normal price.

The music business was the biggest popular entertainment business in Britain and sheet music was its principal product. Records hadn't yet caught on and even people who couldn't play the piano bought sheet music. They liked to have a song's words in front of them, with a picture of the singer who popularised it on the front page.

But the sale of pirated music on the street was destroying the publishers' profits, which meant they had less money to invest in new songwriters and the plugging and advertising of their songs. Things were in a downward spiral.

William Boosey of Chappell explained later in his memoirs, "Popular songs only required two or three pages of paper and they could be photographed or litho'ed in any old shed or barn which happened to be handy. They could then be retailed to an army of street hawkers for distribution."

Popular songs were being sold on the street for as little as two pence, compared with up to three shillings and sixpence for the real thing, twenty times more. William Boosey persuaded the other publishers to take affirmative action and join Chappell in a Musical Defence League. They employed strong-arm men to raid the premises of the printers and tackle hawkers in the street. But the seized copies were replaced as fast as they were taken. "At 7 o clock one evening, one of our agents had 38 copies seized at a street stall. The agent went to the stall at 8.30pm and seized 30 copies; at 9.45pm 25 copies; at 10.15pm 16 copies."

At first the publishers found it difficult to get public opinion on their side; people thought it served them right for selling sheet music at such an exorbitant price to start with. So the publishers announced they would spend nothing more on new publishing. They would issue no new contracts, print no more sheet music, place no more advertisements in newspapers. Popular music was such a large part of public entertainment it was like shutting down TV today. Printers were put out of work and newspapers shriveled in size as advertising disappeared.

Simultaneously, Chappell spent £10,000 prosecuting the bankrupt fishmonger. Chappell won the case on the basis of 'conspiracy'. The hawkers, they claimed, conspired with others to reprint and sell the music, which made it an imprisonable offence.

Chappell's success prompted composer Sir Edward Elgar to join the publishers in petitioning parliament for a bill with real teeth – the Copyright Act of 1906. Afterwards, hawkers selling pirated music found themselves going off to jail for twelve months and the illicit trade stopped dead.

In America there was a reverse situation in progress. This time with recordings – not records, but piano rolls. The top music publishers had formed a cartel to keep the prices artificially high, sharing the profits between them.

When President Theodore Roosevelt learnt of this "giant music monopoly" controlling the majority of new works, he demanded Congress deal with it at once.

During the first ten years of the century, people gradually became aware of the gramophone. In 1906 Victor had launched the Victrola – the first machine to have an internal horn. It sold so many that the word Victrola became the word Americans used for a gramophone. But what the public were even more familiar with was another mechanical method of creating music – the pianola.

The pianola was an upright piano with an opening above the keyboard into which a roll of punched cardboard was put. You wound up the spring, turned the switch, and the piano automatically played the song exactly as the pianist had recorded it. If a top pianist had made the piano roll, playing it on a pianola gave you a perfect reproduction of his performance right in your living room. Most people considered it far superior to a scratchy gramophone record.

In America, the principal manufacturers of this instrument, and the principal suppliers of piano rolls to use with it, were the Aeolian Company. James F. Bowers, president of the Music Publishers Association, had discreetly set up an arrangement with the Aeolian Company. It would pay a 10 per cent royalty for exclusive rights to all the popular songs of the MPA's members, which meant all the currently popular music in America. No one else on the market could get a look in – neither instrument manufacturers nor publishers outside the MPA.

In 1909, when the scheme came to Roosevelt's attention, he immediately proposed legislation. Composers welcomed it, and amongst those who testified before Congress in its support was Victor Herbert. But the major publishers – Witmark, Leo Feist, T. B. Harms – fought it. They were happy with their 10 per cent royalty. Congress wasn't.

A new copyright law was passed which gave the publishers many benefits. But one it did *not* give was an exclusive right to license their music to the Aeolian Company at 10 per cent. Instead it was decided that once a song had first been published it would then become available for anyone to copy by any mechanical means, providing they paid the correct royalty. And Congress decided the royalty should be two cents – two thirds of which would go to the publisher and one third to the writer.

For the publishers it was a big reduction in income, for the Aeolian Company it was a big reduction in outgoings. For songwriters it was a bonus. Most of them hadn't been paid anything by the publishers from the previous deal with Aeolian, now they would at least get something, as would all the smaller publishers who hadn't been able to join the elitist Music Publishers Association.

There was one more benefit. Although the law had been introduced with piano rolls in mind, there was another mechanical method of reproducing music to which it would also apply – the gramophone.

In Britain, legislators followed the American Congress and produced their own law. William Boosey, who had been happy to have the government intervene on the publishers' behalf over pirated sheet music, was this time incensed.

In essence, British law followed American law, but instead of the publishers being paid a compulsory two cents per recording, the British parliament decided on a remuneration of 5 per cent of the marked price of the record. If the composition occupied only one side of the record and another composition occupied the other side, the amount paid for each song would be just 2.5 per cent, and as in America this fee had to be divided between composer and publisher. But the publisher who licensed the song to the first record company would have no control over the price that any subsequent record company might sell it for.

William Boosey was furious. "Imagine such a condition of copyright prevailing in the book world! An author publishes a work, say, at 10 shillings; a publisher round the corner publishes the same work at sixpence. On a compulsory remuneration of 5% what becomes of the author's property?"

Whatever the pros and cons of the new laws governing recordings, most music publishers considered records to be little more than a gimmick. The principal commerce of the music industry was the sale of sheet music. And it was booming as never before.

In America, the original boom in sheet music sales had been partly due to Woolworths. Frank Woolworth loved music and played the piano. In the early 1890s he'd told his local store managers they had to start selling sheet music. At first they objected, but he forced them to, telling them to discount it heavily. The success that followed caused Macy's to follow suit.

By 1912, twenty years after the boom first started, Macy's counters were the most important in America, selling hundreds of millions of copies each year. But for the music publishers, there was no point in coming up with all these hit songs if the sheet music couldn't be sold at a profit. And Macy's were forever demanding bigger discounts from the publishers, eventually offering them just six cents a copy.

For a songwriter, six cents a copy would be a dream. For a music publisher, with the costs of popularising and advertising the song, six cents simply wasn't practical. But Macy's wouldn't budge.

So the publishers hatched a plan.

Macy's had a slogan, a sign they hung in all their stores, 'Never Undersold'. If you could find anything sold at Macy's selling for a cheaper price elsewhere in town they would refund you the difference.

Led by Witmark and Leo Feist, several big New York publishers agreed to pool all their titles for six months absolutely free. They would then sell them at Rothenberg & Co (the only store in town that had a music counter to rival Macy's), for just one cent per copy. The sale would be advertised with a full-page advertisement in the *New York Evening Journal*. The plan was not so much to sell sheet music at Rothenberg, but to disrupt Macy's, and on the first day of the Rothenberg sale each of the publishers sent all their staff to Macy's to buy sheet music.

Isidore Witmark, the perpetrator of the plan, was thrilled with its execution. "Max Meyer was staging his little act at Macy's. After buying some tinware in the household department, he went to the music department and ordered a long list of numbers which the salesgirl wrapped up. Then he offered to pay a penny a copy for them."

The salesgirl consulted with the manager who was in a complete quandary about what to do about these people coming in and showing him the Rothenberg advertisement. The lowest price he could let them go for was the price he'd paid – the wholesale price of six cents. Isidore Witmark's friend Max "started to walk away, keeping up a long harangue, at intervals of which he dropped pieces of tinware sounding like cannon reports".

With dozens of other publishing company employees re-enacting the same show throughout the day, Macy's relented. Within a week they sorted out new terms with all the major music publishers.

Throughout these disputes, there was one publisher who kept himself aloof from them, yet was happy to benefit from any advantages that flowed from them.

Max Dreyfus was getting a reputation for the deftest player in the pack. In 1906 Tom Harms had died. His remaining shares in T. B. Harms had been distributed between the current shareholders, which gave both Jerome Kern and the Dreyfus brothers an increased interest in the company. Max Dreyfus then produced another benefit from his death.

Before he and his brother Louis had taken over T. B. Harms, Tom Harms had been less than straightforward in acquiring the song 'Daisy' from the British publisher Francis, Day & Hunter. As a result the British publisher had stopped dealing with T. B. Harms and had set up an American company of its own. Increasingly, they were finding the going tough, and now, with Tom Harms removed from the picture, Max tempted them back.

For the Dreyfus brothers it was an extraordinary deal to pull off – Francis, Day & Hunter (America) would be owned one third by Max Dreyfus, one third by Louis Dreyfus, and one third by Fred Day.

With the addition of Francis, Day & Hunter's copyrights, T. B. Harms became the biggest publishing house in America. And in case a little more luck were needed, five years later, in 1911, Harry Lauder, a Scottish music-hall singer who in Britain was Francis, Day & Hunter's most important writer, broke the American market.

Lauder toured America twenty-two times, usually on his own train. He became the highest-paid performer in the world, performed at both the White House and Buckingham Palace, and was knighted.

And Max Dreyfus got the publishing.

8

Pennies from Heaven
ASCAP AND PRS

Just as stars came and went, so too did the earning power of their songs. The songs were still remembered, still sung, still loved, but by now everyone had the sheet music and the songs no longer earned the publisher any money. Often, the cost of popularising the song had equalled the profits from the sale of sheet music. The song was known and sung and whistled all over the world but no one earned anything.

Music publishers got together to work out how they could make money from songs that were no longer hits but still in people's minds. The answer was to ask for payment every time the songs were played. Restaurants, cafés, theatres, parks, pubs, hotel lobbies and bars – if a song was being played, someone had to pay. For people who'd never paid before, it sounded outrageous.

It wasn't a totally new idea. A few years earlier Puccini had come to New York for the premiere of *The Girl of the Golden West*. When he heard his melodies being played by orchestras in restaurants he asked his American publisher how much this brought him. He was shocked when he was told 'nothing'.

Puccini explained that in Italy there was a copyright organisation, SIAE, that required payments for all public performances, but American publishers weren't sure about it. They worried it might make it more difficult to promote new songs. Normally the publisher paid the musicians to get the song played; now they'd be asking the musicians to pay the publisher.

In Britain the same discussion was going on. William Boosey said Chappell would have nothing to do it. He dismissed the French and Italian habit of collecting fees whenever music was performed as "vexatious rights of performance that never have and never will be understood here".

Nevertheless, on both sides of the Atlantic, many publishers and writers were coming round to the idea, and America got there first.

Victor Herbert, a composer rather than a publisher, was the principal driving force behind it. And George Cohan, also a writer and not a publisher, was keen to make the new society, if it could be formed, an organisation that would include both publishers *and* writers.

In his work in the theatre Cohan was both artist and producer. He was used to seeing conflict between the artistic temperament of performers and the business-minded viewpoint of producers and theatre managers. Since he saw things from both sides he was aware of the rising conflicts.

Backstage conditions on Broadway were dreadful; contracts contained a 'satisfaction' clause, which meant the performer could be fired on the spot for anything a producer might think of. There was no limit to what was called 'free rehearsal' – a straight play might need ten weeks, a musical eighteen, and nobody got paid till opening night.

Artistes also had to provide costumes, sometimes even period ones. Often a player would invest money in costumes only to be dismissed as 'not satisfactory', or be left holding the can when the show folded before opening. And they also had to pay their own transportation, which meant out-of-town strandings were frequent.

For some time Cohan had been proposing some sort of joint association made up of both actors and producers which could look for mutual solutions to problems. And since all the problems in the world of theatre had equivalent ones in the world of songwriting, a society that would include both publishers and writers appealed greatly to Cohan so he became an immediate supporter.

The first meeting was held in a private banqueting room at Luchow's restaurant, the best German food in town. Whether it was at the request of the North German Witmarks, the South German Dreyfus brothers or the Austrian Irishman Victor Herbert nobody knew, but to the disappointment of those who came, only nine of the thirty-six people invited showed up.

Missing were Irving Berlin and Jerome Kern who were worried that the new organisation might impinge on their independence. But despite the sparse crowd the meeting went ahead and an attorney outlined the society's objectives. To confuse those who thought there might be an undue German influence on the society, the man appointed to be chairman was an Englishman. He was the person who had at different times had run the New York offices of both Boosey and Chappell, George Maxwell, stately and dignified, rapping with his signet ring to concentrate his listeners' attention.

Although the new society included two top songwriters, Vincent Herbert and George M. Cohan, it was clear from the outset that publishers, not writers, would wield the most influence.

A month later there was a second meeting, this time held at the Hotel Claridge. One hundred people turned up to it and by the time it was over a new society existed: ASCAP, the American Society of Composers, Authors and Publishers.

Two months later, Britain got the same thing. On 1st April, 1914, the first meeting of the Performing Rights Society took place just off Piccadilly Circus.

The concept was identical. Top publishers and writers came together to try and collect licence fees from hotels and other places where orchestras played music. William Boosey overcame his earlier objections and agreed to become the PRS's first chairman.

It was soon obvious these societies were simply an extension of music publishing. By becoming members, songwriters effectively became part of the music publishing industry; writing and publishing were no longer seen as different occupations, they were simply different aspects of the same business, known by the media as 'the song racket'.

As in America, the PRS was an exclusive club in which top writers sided with top publishers, not with young aspiring writers. Similarly, top publishers found their interests best served by siding with top writers, not with new publishers trying to break into the business. Composer or publisher, once you were a member of one of these societies you were part of the same elite. Second graders were excluded, whether publisher or writer.

The payment plan for members was similar in both societies, complicated, and favouring those with most influence. Both PRS and ASCAP planned to collect a flat fee from every venue that played music – restaurants, hotels, amusement parks, pubs, fairs, or department stores. To begin with, most refused to pay up. During the first couple of years the societies only managed to collect from concert halls and other seated performance venues; even so, considerable new earnings came into the societies and had to be dispersed. At the end of its first year, after covering its operating costs, ASCAP announced it would pay out what was left equally between composers and publishers according to their class, AA to D.

Because the biggest publishers were likely to have the largest number of currently successful songs, it was also likely that their music would be the most played. So they were designated AA and got the largest share. At ASCAP, unsurprisingly, Witmark and T. B. Harms were the top two publishers, with Victor Herbert and George M. Cohan as the top two writers. Everyone else came next. And next again. And so on, with voting rights designated in the same manner.

At PRS there were no surprises either; Lionel Monckton was the top-rated writer, Chappell the top-rated publisher. Between them they took the largest share of the income.

9

Pack Up Your Troubles
FIRST WORLD WAR

The first big hit of the First World War was sold for £5.

Jack Judge, a British music hall artist, made a five-shilling bet with a friend that he could write a song in an afternoon good enough to sing in his act that night. He wrote it, sang it, and collected his five shillings.

When music publisher Bert Feldman offered him a flat fee of £5 to buy it outright, Jack Judge took the money and ran. "Not bad for an afternoon's work", he thought.

Well it certainly wasn't bad for Bert Feldman; the song was 'It's a Long Way to Tipperary'. It sold over a million copies of sheet music and became the biggest-selling British song of World War I. And Feldman wasn't even paying a royalty.

Britain's second wartime super-hit was set in motion by Clara Davies.

Fifteen years earlier Mrs Davies had been one of George Edwardes' tutors, helping to turn shop assistants into Gaiety Girls. A pushy woman, she founded the Welsh Ladies Choir and had a son called Ivor, who went by the surname of Novello rather than Davies.

There was a touch of the aesthete about Ivor Novello, cigarette holders and azalea-coloured trousers, and he dabbled in writing songs. When posters went up calling for people to enlist in the army, Clara taunted her son, "What a pity," she said, "that you aren't capable of writing a wartime song as good as 'Tipperary'."

Ivor refused to rise to the bait and said he had no intention of even trying.

"Alright, dear," she sighed, "but one of us two is going to... and if you won't I will." And she quickly dashed off something called 'Keep the Flag A-Flying'.

It was awful, and he told her so. But it set him thinking.

A few days later a tune popped into his head so he called Lena Ford, an American friend who lived in London and dabbled in lyric writing. When she arrived at his flat Ivor sat down and played it on the piano. "I want words that conjure up images of the homes the young soldiers have left and the families waiting for them to come back again."

Just as he was saying this, the maid came in and put more wood on the fire.

'Keep The Home Fires Burning' was heard everywhere – in music halls, palm courts, tea-lounges, family parlours and bandstands. The British Army took it up and spread the tune around France. French soldiers began to sing it in their own language and in some countries people even thought it was the British National Anthem. When America entered the war the song gained a new life and became popular in the States.

To publish his song, Ivor Novello took it to Boosey (not William Boosey of Chappell, but Boosey Music, the publishing company run by William's cousin Thomas). Because his song was popular music, not classical, Novello was sent to see Harold Booth, who ran a subsidiary company, Ascherberg, Hopwood & Crew (the publisher of George Edwardes' early shows).

Harold Booth was a fancy dresser with a fruity voice that he used to seduce people into the sharpest of deals. He also ran a company that relayed West End plays on the telephone and had the concession for supplying opera glasses in London theatres. He suggested a royalty of three pence per copy and twenty-five pounds advance. Generous enough, until Novello got home and realised he'd signed for three years and would have to give the company all the songs he wrote during that time.

But Novello did all right. Lena Ford, the friend who wrote the lyrics, was offered no share in the royalties and before she could complain a German airship dropped a bomb on her flat in St John's Wood and killed her. The sheet music sold two million copies.

Novello, keen to do his bit for the war effort, then joined the navy. He trained as a pilot, crashed his plane and wound up grounded. Bored with his naval office job he wrote twelve songs for a new musical, *Theodore & Co.*, which ran at the Gaiety Theatre for the rest of the war.

In America, the big song of the war was 'Over There' by George Cohan. When he heard that President Wilson had signed a document declaring war he wrote it in thirty minutes – a warning to the Germans that the Yanks were coming.

Vaudeville singer Nora Bayes recorded it and put her picture on the sheet music which sold one and a half million copies. Caruso's version made even more impact. With his Italian 'r's rolling longer than a Scotsman's, it was laughable, yet he sang it with such passion that your hair stood on end when you listened, and half a million people bought it.

The music industry has consistently found ways to make the best of bad times. In an economic recession, sheet music or a record gives longer lasting entertainment for the money than a theatre ticket. And during a war, songs can help people forget or remember as necessary, or stir up passions, or calm them down. Whatever's needed, the music business can provide it, and always at a moderate price. No one understood that better than Leo Feist.

For the past twelve years all George Cohan's songs had been published by Witmark, but 'Over There' would be an exception. Leo Feist had set his mind on getting it for a special project he was planning, and to make sure he did he was prepared to pay Cohan the biggest song advance ever known – $25,000.

There was no doubt about it, Feist was a terrific salesman and a brilliant schemer. Having got hold of Cohan's song he commissioned all his contracted songwriters to write war songs – as many as they could. He selected the best, added 'Over There', and put them into a folio entitled *A Nation's Songs: The Popular Songs of America at War*.

Feist then paid more to advertise it than any publisher had ever spent before. One single advertisement in the *New York Times* cost him $5,000 – perhaps the equivalent today of spending a quarter of a million. Under the heading, 'Music Will Help Win The War' he wrote, "A Nation that sings can never be beaten… Songs are to a nation's spirit what ammunition is to a nation's army."

He went on to call them 'Stimulants of the National Spirit'.

The song titles were meant to be a model of patriotism but in reality they sounded like jokey music-hall songs. 'We're All Going Calling on the Kaiser', 'We'll Knock the Heligo Out of Heligoland', 'I'd Like to See the Kaiser with a Lily In His Hand' and 'Keep your Head Down Fritzie Boy'.

There were thirty of them and Feist marketed them at 15 cents each or seven for one dollar. He told the public it would be an act of patriotism for the songs to be sung at every vaudeville show in the nation.

He finished the advertisement with an endorsement from a top member of the military, Major-General Wood. "It is just as essential that the soldiers know how to sing as it is that they carry rifles and know how to shoot them."

Feist also printed the songs in a *Pocket-sized Songbook for Soldiers and Sailors* and sold it to half the American fighting force – two million copies. Call it hype or masterful song-plugging, one way or another he proved that utterly average songs could make a great pile of money.

Finding himself on a roll, Feist then encouraged publishers to pay attention to the wartime paper shortage. He lectured them on reducing the size of sheet music and suggested they discard the usual single-page insert. No one objected. It saved thousands of dollars in paper costs, reduced shipping charges and increased profits. Even rival publisher Edward B. Marks approved. "A great many other parts of the War Machine fell down lamentably – the service of supply, the shipyards, the airplane manufacturers – but Tin Pan Alley did a swell job."

Florenz Ziegfeld also did his bit. In his *Follies of 1915* he dressed his chorus girls in military uniform and had one of them appear bare-breasted to personify 'liberty'. And because of the patriotic context no one complained.

Also doing their bit by turning a crisis into an opportunity were the heads of Britain's two biggest record companies – HMV, and the British arm of Columbia.

At the beginning of the war, afraid it might be considered an unsuitable thing to do, retailers refused to stock records. Columbia's British subsidiary faced bankruptcy but they had a new general manager from New York, Louis Sterling. He called his staff together and told them to find every recording they could that might be termed "patriotic, stirring, or inspiring", then rush them out as 'war records'. Within ten days the situation had turned around and dealers started buying again.

At HMV, William Owen had faced the same problem, but Louis Sterling had now solved it for him. Owen took advantage of the improved situation by issuing the records a country at war really wanted to hear – not marches and hymns but sentimental heart-breakers, songs which reminded them of good times at home. HMV sold more copies of 'Keep the Home Fires Burning' than any record previously. And then it sold even more of 'Roses of Picardy', a melody by Haydn Wood given lyrics by Fred Weatherly that were even more sugary than those he did for 'Danny Boy'.

The game bounced back to Louis Sterling. He stole a march on HMV by signing exclusive contracts with all the musical shows running on the London stage. One by one he took their casts into Columbia's studios and recorded them. Then shipped the records to Europe and marketed them to the troops.

The British record business was now totally in the hands of these two highly competitive Jewish New Yorkers. And they did it nothing but good.

William Owen's next idea was for HMV to issue a series of records featuring the sounds of war – heavy artillery, planes swooping overhead, officers shouting orders, tanks revving helplessly in the mud. The man who volunteered to go and record these sounds was William Gaisberg, brother of the company's recording chief, Fred. He particularly wanted the sound of a gas attack.

He got it, but gassed himself in the process.

In wartime America record sales were going well. Of the big three companies – Victor, Columbia and Edison – Victor was in the lead. They sold their most special acts on what they called their 'Red Seal' records – one-sided and of especially high quality. But it was nothing but bluff. The quality was identical to their regular records, the only difference being they gave you just one side to listen to and were sold for $2 as against 'Black Seal' for 75 cents, which gave you two.

Record sales were helped for all three companies by the government insisting on a wartime 'black' night in theatres and vaudeville. It meant a night when entertainment had to be found at home and family parlours rang to voices around the piano. Or gramophone records.

Britain didn't have black nights, just boom nights. The war had given a huge boost to musical theatre and shows were packed everyday of the week. Soldiers on leave from the trenches didn't want to watch Ibsen or Shakespeare, they went in their thousands to musicals like *The Maid Of The Mountains* or *Chu Chin Chow*. A third musical in London, *The Bing Boys Are Here*, featured an early song by Ivor Novello that hadn't been successful. When 'Keep the Home Fires Burning' became a hit, the theatre management changed the name of the earlier song and added it to the billboard outside. Originally it was called, 'The Garden of England', now it was called, 'Keep the Home Flowers Blooming'.

Jerome Kern, too, was cashing in on the British wartime boom in musical theatre, travelling backwards and forwards from the States to Britain, writing songs for shows on both sides of the Atlantic.

During a trip to London, Kern's American producer, Charles Frohman, introduced him to an English songwriter, P. G. Wodehouse. They got on brilliantly and Kern went back to New York promising to return the following month. But the night before he was due to leave for England he stayed up all night playing poker and missed the boat. It was the RMS *Lusitania*, the first passenger ship of the war to be sunk and Charles Frohman went down with it.

Kern, undaunted, took the next boat to London and told Wodehouse he was no longer tied to Charles Frohman and they could go into partnership. They agreed to bring in another British writer, Guy Bolton, and the trio clicked like crazy. Within months the first Bolton & Wodehouse & Kern show was running on Broadway. The trio found a niche at New York's Princess Theatre where their shows ran throughout the rest of the war, all with smart dialogue and snappy names – *Have a Heart, Oh Boy, Leave it to Jane, See You Later, Kissing Time, Oh My Dear*.

In *Vanity Fair*, Dorothy Parker said seeing their shows was her favourite indoor sport. And in the New York Times a letter appeared in their praise, later rumoured to have been written by a young Lorenz Hart, still at university.

This is the trio of musical fame,
Bolton and Wodehouse and Kern.
Better than anyone else you can name
Bolton and Wodehouse and Kern.

For most publishers, competition to get to the top of the chart was intense. To plug their new songs publishers were paying performers like Eddie Cantor and Al Jolson ever-increasing amounts of money to sing them. Sometimes the cost of promoting a hit could rise as high as $75,000 and many publishers paid out more to plug a song than could be recouped by its subsequent sales. But to stay in the race they had to do it.

In 1916 American publishers, realising that to survive they had to stop making these payments, formed the Music Publishers Protective Association, the MPPA. Just one publisher refused to join the new society, T. B. Harms.

The Dreyfus brothers said there was no need for their company to join because all its songs were written for Broadway shows and printed with a notice saying they could only be performed live in the show for which they were written. Max Dreyfus told Mills that T. B. Harms had "never been involved in the evil practices that MPPA sought to curb". (In other words, paying famous artists to perform their songs.)

But it wasn't quite true. Jerome Kern's wartime success with P. G. Wodehouse and Guy Bolton, had helped spotlight T. B. Harms as the place that new writers would most like to be. But the Dreyfus brothers, concerned that every new writer who joined the company would also be earning money for Kern, decided to form a new company simply called Harms. Kern kept his shares in T. B. Harms, and therefore in his own work, but the new company was for the Dreyfus brothers' future expansion.

It enraged the other music publishers because Max straight way started plugging the new company's songs by paying vaudeville singers to sing them. And since he'd never joined the Music Publisher's Protective Association, the other publishers were powerless to punish him.

In 1917, incensed by the society's lack of bite, they signed up to a new code of practice; they would immediately stop paying singers to plug their songs. They thought, if everyone stopped simultaneously there would be no disadvantage to anyone in doing so, they would simply save money, lots of it. And if anyone cheated they would be fined $5,000.

The first was Leo Feist.

Feist's latest offering was 'I Didn't Raise My Boy To Be A Soldier'. An inspector on behalf of the publishers alerted the MPPA to a vaudeville theatre where he'd heard the song played a dozen times during the course of one show. The opening act sang it, dancers danced to it, a conjurer produced rabbits out of a hat to it, performing dogs barked to it, the pit orchestra played it in the interval, and the last four performers each sang it again.

The MPPA copied the strong-arm tactics that British publishers had used ten years earlier to stop street hawkers. They paid ex-policemen to disguise themselves as federal officers and sent them to Woolworth in Chicago to seize Feist songs from the counter. It wasn't the loss of sheet music that hurt him, it was the loss of face; Feist liked being respected. But his cheating had worked; the song became the year's bestseller and once it reached the top of the chart he paid his fine and fell into line with everyone else.

Strangely, although these publishers would fight furiously with each other at meetings of the Music Publishers Association, they managed to sit amicably together when they attended meetings of ASCAP. But it was all a charade. None of them wanted to stop paying vaudeville singers to plug their songs, they just wanted everyone else to stop. They would sign their name to new rules, only to rush back to their offices and discuss with their staff ways they might bypass them. Someone, they thought, would always be stealing a march on the others.

And of course, they were right.

When the war finished, it was clear to everyone it had been a boom time for the business of popular music on both sides of the Atlantic. In America sentimental songs had sold best and sheet music sales were huge; 'Till We Meet Again' 3.5 million, 'I'm Forever Blowing Bubbles' 2.6 million, 'Joan of Arc, They're Calling You' two million.

In Britain, the biggest sellers had been 'It's a Long Way to Tipperary', 'Keep the Home Fires Burning', 'Pack Up Your Troubles', and something that wasn't pop at all, Sir Hubert Parry's 'Jerusalem'.

But the most striking development was the way the war had popularised the gramophone. There wasn't a single army barracks in Europe that didn't have one. Most soldiers went to war having never seen one and got back home intending to buy one. On both sides of the Atlantic, six months after the war finished, nearly every home with a returning soldier also had a gramophone.

People no longer gathered round the piano to sing songs; they listened to their favourite artists singing them instead.

10
Cheek to Cheek
JAZZ AND JEWS

After the war America found its music industry being run almost entirely by Jews.

When there were openings for new employees, whether administrative or creative, other Jews were usually given preference. But although Jewish bosses helped their own kind first, they had no list of preference for who came second. Mostly they still believed they'd come to a land of equal opportunity and felt badly when they saw any section of society being prejudiced against. Irish immigrants were regarded equally with Italian, black Americans equally with white; the best person got the job and black Americans tended to find work with Jewish-run companies more easily than with non-Jewish ones.

On the other hand, musically, the Jews running these publishing companies avoided their own likes and dislikes and provided the public with whatever it wanted, even when it meant selling them coon songs, whose hurtful nature they must have been aware of. They had no time for emotion; music was just a business.

After the First World War, people in the music business in New York began to hear jazz, a new style of music played by black musicians arriving from New Orleans and Chicago. The popular music business had already benefitted from the success of ragtime, which white songwriters and composers had assimilated into their own music, but jazz was something altogether different. It appeared to engage the Jewish psyche in a way that previous styles of American music hadn't.

Unsurprisingly, jazz was born in a city with a unique social outlook. New Orleans was the only city council in the South that showed a tolerant attitude towards African music, even prior to the Civil War allowing it to be played at Sunday slave parties in Congo Square while other cities banned it completely. New Orleans also had the first Opera House in America, where rich plantation bosses imported top operatic stars from Italy and slaves were allowed to listen outside the window.

In 1898 the Spanish–American war ended. Troops coming back from fighting in the Caribbean landed in New Orleans with European brass instruments and sold them cheaply. Within a few years the number of brass bands in town doubled.

The terrible climate, the foul sanitation, and the preponderance of mosquitos, kept them all in work. The city was damp and hot with no sewage system; it had the highest infant mortality rate in North America, and the shortest life span. Funerals were non-stop, and they always used a band. The prevalence of death was a major role in the birth of New Orleans music, as was the tendency to dance and party, even when someone was being buried.

The city's mix of cultures, from the poorest black plantation workers to middle-class Creole half-casts, meant the partying was done to hugely differing styles of music. At posh parties, conservatory trained Creoles performed with classical correctness; at more raucous events untrained black musicians preferred improvised music, using the loose intonation of African chant rather than the precise tuning of European tradition.

The city had some thirty different dance halls, each one frequented by a different social class based on colour, family, money and religion. Guitarist Danny Barker played with Chris Kelly's band.

> *Each one of those caste systems had its own trumpet player, and Chris Kelly played for those blues, cotton-picking negroes, what they called in those days "yard and field" negroes. They were real primitive people who worked in the fields… They would give a ball at the New Hall, which was the young men's charity hall… the undertakers would be glad because there were three or four bodies…*

To try and control prostitution the town council created Storyville, a special area for places of entertainment. Jammed with clubs, bars, restaurants, dives and brothels, it was there that the city's various musical styles began to coalesce into a common New Orleans style. But the US Navy, less tolerant of prostitution than the town council, moved in to shut it down. Musician John Provenzano watched it happen.

> *The scene was pitiful… a veritable shambles of Negro and white prostitutes moving out. With all they had in the world reposing in two wheel carts or on wheelbarrows, pushed by Negro boys or old men, the once Red Light queens were making their way out of Storyville to the strains of 'Nearer My God To Thee' played by a massed combination of all the Negro jazzmen of the Red Light dance halls.*

Arnold Loyacano, a bass player, was one of many people who decided it was time to move north, which for most musicians meant Chicago. "No one knew we were leaving because if we didn't make it good and had to come back, that'd look pretty bad. They paid us twenty-five dollars a week in Chicago – the salary was the big thing. We'd been making a dollar a night in New Orleans."

Most of them arrived there with next to nothing. Singer Alberta Hunter ran away from home "when I was eleven years old with a nickel and a dime – just fifteen cents – in my pocket".

The first wave of musicians from New Orleans had been the ones who hadn't been doing so well at home, but bit by bit the best musicians arrived too – pianist Jelly Roll Morton, cornettists King Oliver and Louis Armstrong, drummer Zutty Singleton, pianist Tony Jackson – everyone wanted to come north and cash in. And by the time they got there, they found the music they'd been playing for years in New Orleans had become known as 'jazz'.

The place they most wanted to play was Dreamland, Chicago's top jazz nightspot. By 15, little Alberta Hunter had developed her voice and got herself a gig there. "It was big and always packed, and you had to be some singer... there were no microphones... singers then would go from table to table singing to each table, hustling dollars in tips, but nobody at the other tables would get mad when they couldn't hear you."

One young arrival in Chicago was Lil Hardin who arrived from Memphis with her family when she was 20. Passing a music store she was mesmerised by all the sheet music in the window and decided to go in and buy a song she'd heard people whistling on the street.

I hummed it over to the salesman, and he sat down and played it over to me. Well, he didn't play it very well so I asked him if I might try it over. He readily consented and was very surprised that I played it on sight as well as adding something to it. When I finished he had me try out other numbers and then asked if I'd like the job demonstrating music... Oh! But mother was indignant. "The very idea, work! And above all things, for only three dollars a week! I should say not young, lady," she said. Well, in no time at all I sold her on the idea... I got busy playing all the music on the counter, and by 2pm the place was packed with people listening to the 'Jazz Wonder Child'.

Within weeks Lil had been hired by a jazz band to play with them at the De Luxe Café for $27.50 a week plus $20 a night tips. And a short while later she was working at Dreamland. One night Louis Armstrong came in and Lil Hardin was set to become Lil Armstrong.

For Chicago's black musicians, Dreamland became a social club; for white musicians it was a fun place to go slumming. One of them was songwriter Gus Kahn who one night heard pianist Tony Jackson sing 'Pretty Baby'. A few dollars changed hands and soon afterwards the song was published by Jerome H. Remick. Added to Jackson's name on the sheet music was not only Gus Kahn's but another songwriter's too, Egbert van Alstyne, both sharing Jackson's credit.

And his royalties.

For publishers in New York this new music from Chicago remained undiscovered. Even Chicago publishers were slow to see what was in front of them, except the black ones like pianist Clarence Williams. Previously he'd run New Orleans' first black publishing company with trumpeter A. J. Piron and they'd signed a song from Louis Armstrong when he was just fifteen. "I was young and very green. I wrote the tune 'Sister Kate' and someone said that's fine, let me publish it for you, I'll give you fifty dollars. I didn't know nothing about papers and business and I sold it outright."

When New Orleans musicians started their exodus to Chicago, Williams and Piron followed them and were surprised to find there were no other black publishers in Chicago. Clarence Williams visited a regional music convention and took singer Lizzie Miles. "He took me on account of my powerful voice. It was the largest crowd I ever sang to and we were the only two coloured out there."

Roger Graham, a locally based white publisher, grabbed an opportunity everyone else missed. One of the bands from New Orleans was white, the Original Dixieland Jazz Band. Graham approached the band and explained how much money they might make if they gave him their songs to publish. So the Original Dixieland Jazz Band gave him every New Orleans song they'd ever heard of and put their names on all of them.

The band then moved on to New York where they got an engagement at Reisenweber's restaurant, joined by Sophie Tucker, a Russian Jewish immigrant. Previously she'd worked as a black-faced 'coon shouter' but with the Original Dixieland Jazzband she was appearing plain faced as 'The Last of the Red Hot Mammas.' The band's stint at the restaurant attracted wildly enthusiastic audiences and Columbia sent someone down to record them. Afterwards they decided the tracks couldn't be released because of their "ostensibly vulgar nature", so Victor jumped in, recording the band and releasing 'Livery Stable Blues', with a whinnying cornet and a mooing trombone.

The band was much liked by New York musicians, including Vincent Lopez, a pianist in the band playing at the Pekin Restaurant. "The event of Dixieland on Broadway changed the entire fabric of the entertainment world. After listening to them, we made the switch from schmaltzy music to the drive of Dixieland…"

When their booking at Reisenweber's ended, the Original Dixieland Jazz Band toured Europe and in London even played for King George. Despite the rave reviews they received wherever they went there were other people who disliked the new sound with a passionate hatred. When a jazz band from New Orleans was booked for a boxing contest in LA, the journalist from the *Los Angeles Times* called them "a vile imitation of music".

Strangely, someone else who disliked this new music was W. C. Handy, New York's most respected black publisher. Originally from St Louis, Handy was an educated musician and a thinker. As a boy he'd fallen in love with a guitar in a shop window and picked berries to buy it without his parents' permission. His father was furious. "What possessed you to bring a sinful thing like that into our Christian home?" Handy went back to the shop and swapped it for organ lessons, then switched to cornet.

Later he left home and moved to Memphis where he formed a military band that played ragtime. He wrote 'Memphis Blues' which his band recorded for Victor. It was at the height of a tango craze so the next song he wrote was 'St. Louis Blues'. "I tricked the dancers by arranging a tango introduction, breaking abruptly into a low-down blues." But Handy's music wasn't jazz, and wasn't improvised; it was played in the traditional manner of a European marching band.

Since 1918, Handy had been in New York, publishing blues and ragtime, working from an office in the Gaiety Theatre building owned by George M. Cohan. He didn't at all like the new music coming from Chicago and complained to his aunt about the number of mistakes the musicians made. She told him, "Honey, white folks like to hear colored folks make some mistakes."

But while the best-known black publisher in town took a dislike to the new music, most of the Jewish ones seemed to love it. Perhaps it was jazz's emotional directness, or something in its improvised phrases that reminded them of Klezmer dance music where instruments often mimicked the human voice. Either way, jazz hit a nerve with the Jewish people who ran the music business and the songwriters they employed.

For hard-nosed Jewish businessmen, simply liking jazz wouldn't have been enough to affect their commercial judgment had they felt there was no market for it. But it quickly became obvious there was, especially when its essential essence was watered down a little and made to sound more familiar.

By the end of the First World War, and during the thirty years that followed, nearly all the top popular songwriters in America were Jewish and nearly all of them used elements of jazz in their compositions. Popular music as America came to know it during the next three decades grew almost entirely from this relationship between black and Jewish cultures.

For both black and Jewish Americans the music industry was a shortcut from their individual backgrounds to a higher level of society, and although profit was its principal motive the American music industry was mostly a force for good. For black Americans it was a doorway into mainstream American culture, and the door was left open for them by the Jewish-run music industry.

11

Prohibition Blues
DON'T DRINK, DANCE

Victor Herbert was having dinner at Shanley's restaurant on Broadway one evening when one of his songs was played by the orchestra. It was nothing new – this happened in almost every restaurant in America, especially with Victor Herbert songs. But on this occasion Herbert got angry. Why should people all over America play his songs without paying him? And the next morning he went to see his lawyer.

It was the test case ASCAP had been waiting for, and the PRS too, for they knew that what happened in America would eventually happen in Britain. ASCAP had been unwilling to risk the society's money fighting a dispute of this type; it had taken a rich songwriter to do it for them.

Three months later Victor Herbert won. The court's judgement was something most composers and publishers, and even ASCAP, had given up hope of ever obtaining. The judge's summing up changed the business of music publishing forever.

"It is true that the music is not the sole object, but neither is the food... The object is... a luxurious pleasure not to be had from eating a silent meal. If music did not pay, it would be given up... the purpose of employing it is profit, and that is enough."

ASCAP had already been collecting money from concert halls, but now every venue in America that featured live music would have to pay a licence fee – restaurants, bars, dancehalls, bandstands, seaside boardwalks, county fairs, even city parades used by stores like Macy's to advertise sales.

But for some music publishers, whatever their profit it never seemed enough.

By the early 1920s, a growing number of them had already begun to see their product as paper rather than music. Half a cent's worth of paper printed with a song and lyrics would fetch 60 cents – a 10,000 per cent profit on raw material. But to run a publishing company from that standpoint was a big undertaking.

In the mid-twenties Leo Feist had an America-wide set-up: a printing press in every city ready to roll out copies of any song with which he could tickle the public's fancy. Along with the printing presses there were pluggers in each city, ready to visit entertainers playing in local vaudeville shows and cafés, and there were sales people who pushed the songs at music counters in departments stores.

Back in New York there was another team of pluggers, the ones tasked with giving each song its first whiff of success so that its popularity could start to be spread across the country. The total operation involved hundreds of people.

To feed them with sufficient product Feist had to run his New York songwriting operation like a conveyor-belt. Dozens of songwriters sat daily at pianos banging out tunes or phrases or lyrics that could be combined together into a final song. The daily outflow of songs was like the daily outflow of cars in Detroit, a necessity to satisfy local dealers across the country. The pressure was enormous, and songwriters ended up being nothing more than a cog in a wheel of a machine designed to turn bits of paper into a saleable commodity.

One of the first tasks each morning was searching the newspapers for topical stories the writers might be able to use as a basis for the day's songs, and nothing was more topical than Prohibition, it was discussed in the press constantly.

The principal push for making alcohol illegal came from two organisations: the Anti-Saloon League, a federated church in the state of Illinois; and the Women's Christian Temperance Union who, seemingly unaware of the definition of temperance, were calling for complete abolition.

During the First World War these two societies had deemed it unpatriotic to use much-needed grain to produce alcohol. They manipulated the public towards their point of view by pointing out that most of the largest brewers were of German origin. By the time the war ended they'd managed to persuade a majority of politicians that alcohol was the cause of most of the woes in American society. Congress was being pressured to do something about it and the music industry watched and worried. Music and alcohol had always been close companions. It was difficult to think of them being separated.

In 1919 it happened. Well, almost! Congress passed the 18th Amendment forbidding the manufacture or distribution of alcoholic beverages, but for the moment it had no effect because there was no firm definition of what an alcoholic beverage was. Later in the year, though, the Volstead Act was passed and defined it as any drink with more than .5 per cent alcohol by volume, which meant anything but water, coffee, tea, or soda pop. Prohibition would come into effect on 6th January 1920, but songs about it were already streaming out.

Leo Feist was one of many publishers who sought to benefit from the publicity it could give a song. Although most publishers hoped abolition would never happen, their own viewpoint didn't matter, business was business, and they were just as happy to publish songs for the abolitionists' cause – 'The Lips that Touch Liquor Shall Never Touch Mine', 'The Drunkard's Child', 'Take the Sparkling Wine Away'.

But the best songs on the subject were not on the abolitionist side; songwriters liked their drink. The first big hit was 'Alcoholic Blues', by Edward Laska and

Albert von Tilzer. Then Irving Berlin chipped in with 'How Dry I Am', a lament to the lack of alcohol in his highball.

And then there was 'Prohibition Blues' by Ring Lardner, a famous sports columnist. Lardner had dabbled in songs before but without much success. This time he did better. He got Nora Bayes to publicise it and grabbed a $250 advance for the song from publishers Jerome H. Remick.

Nora Bayes was dull but a big star. An advertisement by Victor for her records summed it up nicely. "Nora Bayes, with her inimitable foolery and clean fun, her admirable imitations and clever and witty songs..."

Witty maybe, but hardly hilarious, and never with any innuendo. As an artist Nora Bayes was clean and proper, but when it came to money she was sharp and not too straight dealing. She married several times making sure she bettered herself each time.

The second marriage was to songwriter, Jack Norworth, who wrote 'Take Me Out to the Ball Game'. Thereafter his wife received a co-credit on all his songs, including 'Shine on Harvest Moon' which they performed together in Ziegfeld's Follies. In fact, neither Norworth nor Bayes was the real writer of the song, it was by their accompanist, Dave Stamper.

For twenty-one years, Stamper worked as an accompanist at Ziegfeld Follies. He couldn't read and write music, so whenever he composed a song he got someone else to write it out for him and register the copyright. Often, they registered it for themselves. Bayes and Norworth made Stamper wear make-up on stage to look as if he was Japanese, making it less likely he would be interviewed by journalists.

Not surprisingly, for agreeing to record 'Prohibition Blues', Nora Bayes demanded a 'cut-in' from Ring Lardner. Although Lardner had written both the words and music, Bayes got a one-cent royalty on sheet music and had her name on the cover as co-writer.

It was strange how easily songwriters acquiesced with these arrangements. Usually, in the creative arts – theatre, literature, painting – artists were extremely possessive of their creativity and objected strongly if someone else suggested they had some input into the work. But in the world of popular music, songwriters mostly shrugged and accepted it; writing songs was a musical sleight-of-hand rather than art.

These cut-ins were the publishers' new trick for getting songs performed by famous artists. As with Nora Bayes and 'Prohibition Blues', the singer would be credited as a co-composer and get a royalty. Once started, this tradition never went away again, and for the publishers it cost nothing; it came out of the songwriter's share.

Of all the 'cut-in' singers, Al Jolson was the best known. Each year between five and ten songs he sang would enter *Variety*'s Top 10. Since he was usually listed as co-writer it put him amongst the country's most successful songwriters.

Yet he never wrote a note.

On one occasion he overruled the Shuberts, for whom he was doing a show and who had a contract in place with Max Dreyfus requiring them to give T. B. Harms all the songs from their show. Jolson insisted that the principal song from the show would go instead to Witmark "as a mark of respect" of their long friendship.

The real story was a bit different. Jolson had asked Buddy De Sylva and Joe Meyer to write him a song for the show. He'd then taken it to Jerome H. Remick and asked for $5,000 cash and a cut of royalties. The office manager told him he didn't have enough cash on hand, would he accept $1,000 in cash and two promissory notes for $2,000 each?

"Fuck you," Jolson said. Then went down the road to Witmarks who handed over the full $5,000 in cash. The song was, 'California Here I Come'.

Cut-ins were soon go to in a new direction. The music industry was about to enter a decade where places to dance became the principal places of musical entertainment.

In Britain, abolishing alcohol was not under consideration, which was just as well because there was huge new investment going into dance halls. The first of these was about to open in Hammersmith, in West London, and was known as a Palais de Danse.

The Palais de Danse was something new. Aimed at working and lower middle-class customers, it would offer elegant dancing to the best bands in the country. No matter how well they dressed up, ordinary people were not going to get into the Savoy to dance to the New Orleans, or into the Cecil to dance to Jack Payne. But now they could go to the Hammersmith Palais or similar dance palaces.

The American court's decision over the collection of performance royalties from public places had considerably bolstered the PRS's confidence in collecting money from places of entertainment. The society had already made inroads into collecting money from upmarket venues like the Savoy Hotel; now, bolstered by the US court's decision, they could tackle these new dance halls too. If these Palais de Danse opened all across Britain the PRS could find itself collecting royalties far in excess of its original predictions.

Hammersmith would be the first. It had once been a tram depot in down-at-heel Shepherds Bush. As the area turned middle-class the tram shed became an ice-rink with "the only Palm Court in the district where teas and light refreshments will be most daintily served". But with the war over and incomes increasing it was being given another revamp, this time as an exotic palace for elegant dancing.

The internal design had a Chinese theme, featuring "lacquered columns, decorative fretwork and a pagoda roof with Chinese lanterns". The dance floor was made of Canadian maple and there would be two sessions per day at which instructors and dancing partners could be hired. For investors it looked like big business. And with performance royalties to collect, it looked like big business for the music industry too. But there was a snag.

To make a good return on investment, these new Palais de Danse needed to work with a crowded dance floor. By far the majority of the songs played for dancing were classic four-to-the-bar rhythms. Before the war these had been danced to with the two-step, but in 1914 at the Jardin de Danse in New York, a vaudeville star called Harry Fox invented something new.

Fox combined two slow steps with a sort of trotting movement that caught on as no dance had ever done before. Publicised by the Castles and the Dolly Sisters, it was nicknamed the 'Foxtrot' and quickly became the standard way to dance four-to-the-bar rhythm. The problem was, Harry Fox's way of dancing used up a lot of dance floor. If more than half a dozen couples did it everyone bashed into everyone else. The numbers at these big new Palais de Danse would be substantial, with as many as six hundred couples on the floor at the same time. Doing the foxtrot would be impossible.

But just before the opening of the Hammersmith Palais, a dancer called G. K. Anderson arrived from America and teamed up with British ballroom champion Josephine Bradley. Together they developed a less-invasive foxtrot. It required only a small space from which the couple never strayed. Each couple could now come to the dance floor, establish their own small territory, and perform the full range of required steps without going to war with the rest of the clientele. This 'on the spot' dance would provide a totally new way for the masses to enjoy music.

Soon the Hammersmith Palais became just one of hundreds of similar dance halls all over Britain – Sherry's in Brighton, the Locarno in Liverpool, the Lido in Croydon – they were endless. Tony's, in Birmingham, was decorated in an 'Eastern' theme, the hall representing a mosque with prayer mats hanging from the walls and a ceiling painted with stars. The Ritz, in Manchester, advertised itself as 'The Dance Hall of 1,000 Delights'.

A customer visiting one in Bolton wrote down this impression.

Orchestra, nine men in dinner jackets, start a tune. Large groups of each sex, segregated and concentrated round door, break up and mingle into couples. Common mode of approach is simply to touch girl on elbow. At the end, men walk straight away from their partners not escorting them off the floor. Sexes accumulate in their original separate groups round door.

It was nothing like dancing at the Savoy or the Cecil, but for British music publishers these were gifts from heaven – the new dance palaces, the American court's pronouncement on performance royalties, and now the new dance – between them these three things changed the direction of popular music. In Britain, the place to promote new songs was no longer the music hall, it was the dance hall.

12
I Got Rhythm
BLACK MUSIC GOES MAINSTREAM

In America, the best place to make hits was still where it always had been, on Broadway.

Musical shows were booming as never before, and with them the Dreyfus brothers. They'd made a deal with all the theatre producers – every writer had to be contractually free to give their songs to Harms. If a producer chose a writer who couldn't or wouldn't do so, he had to be replaced. For agreeing to this, producers were paid a royalty on each piece of sheet music, an arrangement known in the Dreyfus office as 'graft contracts'.

Besides Jerome Kern, Max Dreyfus had now picked up two of the hottest new young theatre writers, George Gershwin and Vincent Youmans. But Max had a good relationship with all the best writers whether they were signed to Harms or not. Victor Herbert, Buddy De Sylva, Bert Kalmar, Harry Ruby; they all socialised with him. And whenever they did Max let them know how much better off they would be if they published with him too.

By now, the normal royalty for a top writer was two cents for sheet music and one third of the statutory two cents mechanical royalty paid for records or piano rolls. Max made sure that Harms's writers received more – three cents for sheet music and half the two cents mechanical royalty. And he sent them royalty statements every quarter rather than the customary twice a year.

Jerome Kern did even better. Through his investment in T. B. Harms he now earned eight cents a copy for sheet music. And his income from stage royalties was running at $3,000 a week.

For Max, an extra bonus from publishing Kern was the close relationship T. B. Harms had developed with Chappell in London, publisher of Kern's wartime co-writers Wodehouse and Bolton. At the end of 1919 this relationship blossomed into something more.

Chappell's William Boosey was holidaying on Long Island at the home of Ivan Caryll, the Belgian who'd written George Edwardes' early musicals. For the last five years Caryll had been living in New York, writing and conducting musicals, publishing them with Max Dreyfus at Harms.

William Boosey admitted to being "considerably worried as to the future of our American house". Sitting in Caryll's Italian garden, Boosey asked what changes he should make to the way he was running things.

Caryll suggested, "Close Chappell's office in New York and make a deal with Max Dreyfus to run Chappell's business in America."

"Very well," Boosey said, "let's follow your suggestion. Will you ring up Harms on the telephone."

Caryll called Max Dreyfus and five minutes later the deal was settled. Harms would represent Chappell in America; Chappell would represent Harms in Britain.

While Chappell and Harms were getting married, music and alcohol were getting divorced.

President Herbert Hoover called it 'The Noble Experiment'; everyone else called it 'Prohibition'. On 16th January 1920 it became illegal in the USA to manufacture, sell, or drink alcoholic beverages. Unable to operate at a profit, big restaurants with musical entertainment closed down.

Edward B. Marks feared the worst for the song business. "We were told that with Prohibition people would spend more time at home around the piano... but depressed hypocritical people do not sing."

Even so, Marks adapted to the situation more quickly mostly due to his nose for trends. "The public of the nineties," he said, "asked for tunes to sing... But the public from 1910 onwards demanded tunes to dance to."

He'd done well in picking up material from black artists – dance songs with a black tinge. And he got it right, because Prohibition promoted speakeasies, and speakeasies were for dancing.

In the big cities new places sprang up as quickly as the old ones closed. New York lost fifteen thousand licensed saloons but by the end of the year it had 30,000 speakeasies. Moreover half-a-dozen states, including New York, passed laws banning local police from investigating violations of Prohibition. Hoagy Carmichael described the Roaring Twenties as "a bang of bad booze, flappers with bare legs, jangled morals and wild weekends".

As speakeasies became the new place for Americans to dance, front parlours became the new place for them to listen to famous entertainers. The gramophone was taking over from the piano.

In America the two principal record companies were Victor and Columbia. Coming third was Edison, but because of its continued use of cylinders rather than flat discs it was losing ground to the fourth placed company, Brunswick. In Britain, the market was dominated by two companies HMV and Columbia UK.

When records were successful the profits could be huge. In 1921 Enrico Caruso died and Victor made two million dollars by issuing a folio of his best records under the title *They Needed a Songbird in Heaven So They Took Away Caruso*. Buoyed by the profits, the company paid nine million for a half-share in Britain's HMV. It was a good deal; it was the same half-share they'd sold for fifty million a few years earlier. With it, Victor became the leading record company in the world, both in terms of size and cash in hand.

But Caruso's memorial folio marked the end of opera as a major force in record sales. The big new winner was jazz. Firstly, because it delivered a unique performance each time it was played; secondly, because jazz was a cheap buy for the record companies and everybody loved it.

Chicago was in the middle of a jazz boom. On the South Side, the jazz was black, with Johnny Dodds, 'King' Oliver and Louis Armstrong. On the North Side it was white, with Muggsy Spanier, Wingy Manone and Eddie Condon. The two styles were easily discernable. Condon observed, "some people play so differently from others that it becomes an entirely new set of sounds". The blacks preferred a more laid-back tempo with a continuously improvised ensemble; the white players pushed the tempo, played more frantically and gave solos to each instrument in turn.

White jazz musicians tended to play popular tunes of the day; black musicians played tunes of their own – rags, blues and bar songs. It wasn't long before speakeasies on the South Side featuring black jazz musicians became the haunt of music publishers looking for songs they could pick up cheaply. If they were lucky and got there before a record company, they could buy a song for thirty dollars. The record company would then turn up and give the musicians fifty dollars to record it. From royalties for record sales alone the publisher would get his thirty dollars back. On top of that the record would be an advertisement for the sheet music.

Some publishers were out to take advantage of the black musicians' unsophisticated ways in business, but not all of them. Edward B. Marks found himself frequently seduced into buying songs he didn't really want by the delightful people who came to his office. "When they gathered around a piano and harmonized, they could make anything sound good... We got a lot of slaps in our wholesale buying of ragtime numbers, but we also got a lot of pleasure... They played it right out of their heads and an arranger took down the notes as they played.... Not many of those first coloured composers read music."

But Marks was being fooled. Most of the black musicians who went to his office were accomplished musicians fully able to read and write music. In front of a white publisher they chose not to; they preferred to play the fool and speak in dialect. One of them was arranger and composer Eubie Blake. "They didn't want to think that Negroes read music... But all of us could read – you have to write parts out, don't you, you're a musician. But you didn't let the white people know that."

There were also one or two black publishers. One was Perry Bradford, who as far back as 1901 had co-founded one of the first black publishing companies, Gotham-Attucks Music. Later it fizzled out because too many people refused to deal with a company owned and run by blacks. But Perry Bradford was now back in business, looking to change the way white people perceived black artists.

The nature of northern cities was changing. In 1910, three out of every four black Americans lived on farms, and nine out of ten lived in the South. By 1920, one and a half million blacks had moved north looking for work. Chicago's black population grew by 150 per cent, Cleveland's by 300 per cent, Detroit's by 600 per cent.

In New York, Harlem had become the capital of black America. It attracted black intellectuals and artists from across the country. "The world's most glamorous atmosphere," said young Duke Ellington when he first visited.

James Weldon Johnson called it "the recognized Negro capital... the Mecca for the sightseer, the pleasure seeker, the curious, the adventurous, the enterprising, the ambitious, and the talented of the world".

Even so, the best place for a black music publisher to set up business was where the whites did it – on Broadway. Perry Bradford had his office in the Gaiety Theatre building in Times Square, which made George M. Cohan his landlord.

Having "walked out two pairs of shoes" trying to persuade record companies to record black artists, Perry Bradford ended up at Okeh Records, a label that specialised in imported recordings from Europe, mostly marching bands and light classics. There he met the boss, Fred Hager and gave him a lecture on the growing black population in Northern cities and how it was producing new consumers for recorded music. Bradford persuaded Hager to record 'Crazy Blues', something he'd written for Mamie Smith, a singer he had under contract. He promised it would be bought by twelve million black people.

Fred Hager had already received threatening letters saying Okeh would be boycotted if the company had "any truck with coloured girls in the recording field". But after consulting with his marketing manager, Ralph Peer, he decided to go along with Perry Bradford's idea and aim Mamie Smith at the black market, something never tried before. Okeh's advertisement for her record included the words, "those who desire to help in any advance of the Race should be sure to buy this record as encouragement to the manufacturers for their liberal policy".

In the event, Perry Bradford's estimate of twelve million sales was optimistic; it only sold a million. But that made it the largest selling record ever by a black artist.

At Okeh the credit for pulling this off went to Ralph Peer, who'd been given the job of marketing it. Up to then Peer's job had been buying recordings of light classics by overseas artists. "We had records by all foreign groups. German records, Swedish records, Polish records, but we were afraid to advertise Negro records."

He decided to list Mamie Smith and all future black artists under the title 'race' records. It was the name by which records by black artists of all types would be known for the next forty years.

By now pianist and publisher Clarence Williams had moved from Chicago to New York and taken an office in the same building as Perry Bradford. Williams decided to copy Bradford and went to Columbia where he told them they too could sell a million records with a black singer. Due to Columbia's shares being traded speculatively on Wall Street, the company had recently gone into liquidation and was being run by its creditors. The man in charge was looking for cheap investments that might reap rich rewards, so Williams found him receptive. The singer he had in mind for Columbia was Bessie Smith, who'd failed her previous audition for a record company by stopping in the middle of a song, and saying, "Hold on, let me spit."

Williams coached her through the niceties of record company etiquette and at Columbia she got through her recording without incident. The result was another black hit, 'Cemetery Blues', this time written and published by Clarence Williams.

When this sold more than Mamie Smith's record had for Okeh, Columbia decided to focus almost entirely on jazz and blues. The people at Okeh were concerned this might eclipse the company's sudden rise to prominence so Ralph Peer hatched a plan to put it back on top as the number one jazz label. He would travel America with portable recording equipment.

During the course of 1923 he visited Chicago, Atlanta, and St. Louis, and recorded dozens of acts. Some were unknown, while others, like Louis Armstrong, King Oliver, and Bennie Moten, were already on the way to fame.

Peer was twenty-nine. He had a babyish pink face and liked to dress in a white linen jacket, dark shirt and light-coloured tie. Working in the southern states where it was too hot for such things, he usually looked liked a disheveled all-night party-goer.

Before his arrival in each city, Peer would advertise in local newspapers. Each artist was paid a $25 fee for the recording from Okeh Records, but Peer was also doing some business on the side for himself. He insisted the artists record only original songs and presented the writers of each song with a publishing contract agreeing to pay them five cents for each 100 records sold.

As he toured America building Okeh's catalogue of recordings, Peer was also turning himself into America's number one publisher of black music. A year or so later Okeh Records found themselves paying Peer, their employee, two cents per record as the publisher of all the records he'd recorded during the time they'd been paying him a salary. At just five cents per 100 to the writers, it meant Peer kept 99 per cent of all the money he received.

Although Peer was doing well he was waiting for something even better – the day when black music would outsell white and his publishing catalogue would rocket in value.

Now two more black publishers sprang into action. The first was Cecil Mack, who twenty years earlier had been another co-founder of Gotham Attucks Music, along with Perry Bradford. The second was pianist-composer, James P. Johnson.

Mack and Johnson got together and wrote a stage show called *Runnin' Wild*. It included a song that Johnson had written in 1913, 'The Charleston'. It had no lyrics so Mack provided some, becoming the co-writer of the biggest hit ever to which nobody knows the words.

As a dance, 'The Charleston' had originally been developed in black communities in the Southern states. After *Runnin' Wild* was a hit on Broadway it became an international obsession. In reality, by the time the whole world was doing it, there wasn't much left of the original dance. Originally, the sequence of steps was just a lazy twisting of the feet. But in Harlem clubs they started adding a kick, throwing the feet forward and backward and making an occasional tap on the floor. The producers of *Runnin' Wild* saw these changes and incorporated them into the routine in the show. And for the next five years that's how the world danced.

Despite the success of this and other all-black musicals on Broadway, once a black artist left New York and headed south things deteriorated fast. In 1920, the Theatre Owners Booking Association, was formed to cover vaudeville bookings in the South and Midwest. TOBA, as it became known, also stood for 'Tough On Black Asses', because with an admission price of only 25 cents it was none too comfortable

It was none too comfortable for the artists either. Production budgets were so tight that after the usual deductions the remaining weekly pay package was around $20 a person; even so, top black performers from big-time vaudeville were often on the bill. Ma Rainey, Bert Williams and Bessie Smith used to perform on this circuit for a fraction of their usual fee just to reach the southern audience. And without the restraints of a middle-class white audience, they had the freedom to sings songs and tell jokes of a type that could never be performed on a Broadway stage. Southern vaudeville on the TOBA circuit had a tradition of lewdness that went way beyond what was acceptable in any northern city. Favourite songs included, 'You Got the Right Key But the Wrong Keyhole', and 'Big Long Slidin' Thing'.

When the 'The Charleston' took off as a dance hit, it was the first time ever that record sales had outnumbered sheet music sales. But although 'The

Charleston' became the biggest selling record yet, an equally big surprise was the extraordinary demand for orchestral arrangements. Every musical combo of two or more instruments throughout the world needed a band arrangement of the song, and the publishers willingly supplied them.

And who were they?

Well of course – as with any song that came from a Broadway show – it was the Dreyfus brothers at Harms. Which was good for Cecil Mack and James P. Johnson because it meant they got their royalties. Though even with Harms as the publisher, not every black songwriter would get paid.

Cole Porter was just starting to make a name for himself. He hadn't yet written a Broadway show but he was writing songs for reviews. There was one song in particular that he enjoyed singing and which always got great applause, 'I'm in Love Again'. He wasn't sure where he'd found the tune but at least it was his own lyric and he'd put them together to make a song for a revue called *Greenwich Village Follies*. Many people said it was the best song in the show and in due course Porter received a telegram from the Harms office offering him "an excellent royalty to publish this song and do everything to make a big hit out of it".

Shortly afterwards Porter heard the same tune played in a high-class speakeasy so he went accross to the band and asked who'd written it.

"Oh, a Harlem nigger wrote it," the bandleader told him.

Cole Porter was unabashed. "I shall be surprised if I don't make a lot of money out of it."

13

On the Radio
WIRELESS KILLS AND RESCUES RECORDS

When it came to radio, President Hoover was more generous than he had been with alcohol. Immediately after the war he loosened government controls and since then radio stations had been opening at an ever-increasing rate. In 1922, the big four broadcasters set up shop – AT&T, General Electric, RCA and Westinghouse. These four companies quickly gained control of one fifth of the country's 600 radio stations, trying to make sure that in every region theirs was the strongest signal. From then on radio became an essential part of the song business.

In 1923 the top-of-the-range radio set in America was the Radiola Grand made by Westinghouse. It cost $325, came in a mahogany case, had four valves and a horn speaker. To raise or lower the volume you pulled out or pushed in one of its four valves.

On the other hand you could buy a $9 Harko crystal set for use with headphones. This involved jiggling a metal rod the size of a matchstick with a piece of crystal on the end against a larger piece of crystal in a small cup. If you hit lucky you found a radio station. If you wanted to change stations, it might take you ten minutes to find the next one. And you might never find your way back to the original one.

Somewhere between the Harko crystal set and the Radiola Grand, was the average price for a radio set. They were streaming out of the shops and manufacturers couldn't keep up with demand. It was the same story in Britain and all over Europe.

Virtually all the music on network radio was by live musicians, but many of the best bands refused to play on radio. In an interview with *Metronome*, bandleader Ben Selvin said, "Radio in its present stage is a menace to the artist who broadcasts; its publicity value dwindles into insignificance when compared to the harm that it does… The tonal balance perfected in the phonograph recording studios is utterly lacking in radio reproduction."

Actually that was rubbish. Recordings were still made through an acoustic horn whereas radio had an electronic microphone with more sensitivity and a larger frequency range. Anyway, radio stations didn't care what Ben Selvin thought, they preferred to employ local bands, which they usually didn't pay. The government granted radio licences on the basis that radio was a public service, so stations were not allowed to carry advertisements. As a result, station owners insisted it was impossible to pay for the use of music. They thought musicians who played on air were sufficiently rewarded by being made well-known and could use their new found fame to find work elsewhere.

As a result, local bandleaders trying to make a name for themselves often changed the way a hit was arranged to give it their own special touch. Jerome Kern was particularly upset by this and told Ira Gershwin he would try to stop his songs being played. But it was beyond his control.

In Britain, radio didn't get started until 1922. Six private companies, including Marconi and General Electric, got together to form the British Broadcasting Company. It was a private enterprise licensed by the Post Office, free to choose its own programming, a great deal of which was music, but with no advertising.

Prior to radio starting, sales of British sheet music had been booming, outselling those in America, pushed perhaps by the new craze for dancing by the lower classes. Lawrence Wright, a songwriting publisher, had astonishing success with 'Wyoming Lullaby', selling three million copies of the sheet music, which in relation to Britain's population would be like American sales of seven million, an impossible figure. But publishers soon found radio reducing their sales figures. To compensate, the PRS requested the government to consider radio stations paying performance royalties. As usual, before deciding anything the government looked first at what was happening on the other side of the Atlantic.

In America, because virtually all radio music was by live musicians who weren't paid, publishers benefitted. Unpaid radio bands were more than willing to accept the $25 bribe publishers doled out for having a song plugged. However, having plugged the radio stations to get their songs played, publishers then complained that because songs were heard so often nobody needed to buy them. There was no doubting the power of radio to sell music. A new Irving Berlin song, 'All Alone' was performed live on radio just once by the Irish tenor John McCormack and in three weeks sold 250,000 copies from that one and only radio play.

Publishers weren't sure whether this sort of thing was good or bad. On the one hand radio could create a hit more quickly – very useful for a music publisher with a cash-flow problem who needed to generate some urgent income. Not so good was that over-exposure shortened the life of a hit from a year to just a few months. Sheet music sales sank from 200,000 per hit to just 20,000, and when local radio stations started switching from live music to records and played nothing else for several hours a day, publishers realised their songs were effectively giving radio stations free programming.

Through ASCAP, music publishers set about demanding payment – not for each song played, but as an overall licence for music whose copyright belonged to its members, similar to their licensing of restaurants. To get it they would have to persuade the government that radio plays were 'performance for profit', as in the restaurant case. Radio stations would then have to pay performance royalties each time a song was played on air.

The test case arrived in 1922 when ASCAP brought an action against Bamberger Department Store in Newark, New Jersey. Music played on loudspeakers throughout the store came from WOR, a local radio station. No advertisements were heard except at the beginning of the broadcast when the store manager announced "L. Bamberger and Co., One of America's Great Stores, Newark, New Jersey." The court decided that by playing songs from the radio to entertain its customers the department store was using music for commercial gain. This made it a public performance for profit, which meant the copyright owners were due payment.

With this ruling ASCAP began collecting licensing fees from radio stations all across America. Initially they employed agents in each territory on a commission basis. They established a charge for each radio station according to its size, then gave the agent 30 per cent of what he managed to collect from each one in the city where he lived and 50 per cent from stations further afield.

The charge wasn't related to which songs were played, it was a blanket charge for playing music in general. Some radio stations tried to opt out and play music that came only from writers who were not ASCAP members. But that meant they couldn't play current hits, or old ones either, so one by one the stations gave in and paid up.

When the money reached ASCAP it wasn't paid to the individual copyright owners of the songs played; it was divided up as before with top publishers and songwriters receiving the most and lesser ones the least.

As the twenties progressed, radio gave millions of Americans free access to music. Record and sheet music sales plummeted and the music publishers, instead of looking for new ways to run their business profitably, reacted by telling ASCAP to demand increased fees for radio licences. Radio stations saw ASCAP as greedily grabbing money from a struggling new industry and because a large number of radio stations were owned by newspapers, ASCAP and the music publishers got a terrible drubbing.

It was made worse when the much-liked and trusted head of ASCAP, George Maxwell, was kicked out. He'd always kept his British nationality and the ASCAP board decided it was unsuitable for someone who had never become a naturalised citizen to head such an important American institution. Perhaps it was just that Maxwell was too even-handed in dealing with disputes between writers and publishers. Either way, not having him there certainly didn't improve things.

The new president of ASCAP was Gene Buck, pleasant but weak. And by now the Music Publishers Protective Association had a new person in charge, Claude Mills, a one-legged Texan who'd lost his limb in a railroad accident and had never been a music publisher or songwriter. He'd run vaudeville clubs and was known for his no-nonsense, forthright approach, but not for his charm. To control a bunch of New York publishers, he seemed perfect.

Claude Mills, as head of the MPPA was also on the board of ASCAP as the publishers' representative. Effectively this made him the most powerful person in the organisation and he immediately proposed that MPPA and ASCAP share a telephone switchboard. They could jointly buy the latest and best one and save money by sharing the salaries of the girls operating it. To ASCAP songwriters, it looked like the publishers were taking over. And that's how it looked to outsiders too.

With Mills as part of the new executive and George Maxwell no longer around to charm everyone, ASCAP found itself on the receiving end of so much bad publicty that it offered a free ASCAP licence to any radio station owned by a newspaper if the paper would give them good press. By the end of the year ASCAP had 250 newspapers under its belt. But it still got bad coverage. And it wasn't just MPPA and ASCAP that got abuse, it was the whole world of music publishing. Everybody loved popular music but music publishers were generally reviled.

Yet despite their bad press, without music publishers there would have been no music business in the first place; there would have been no Irving Berlin, no Jerome Kern, and no Broadway shows. True, it was their insatiable desire for profit rather than a love of music that had fuelled the creation of the popular song industry, but the great songwriters would never have been writing songs in the first place if music publishers hadn't invented a way to make money from the process.

Perhaps the public's dislike of music publishers was based in anti-Semitism. Jews were accepted as long as they were quiet and retiring and this particularly showed itself with performers. Al Jolson and Eddie Cantor, the country's two top singing stars, were actually Asa Yoelson and Isidore Iskowitz, yet they chose to hide their Jewishness by performing with black face make-up. Even Jewish bandleader Ted Lewis found it necessary, rather daftly conducting his orchestra with a blacked-up face and white lips.

In Britain, following news of ASCAP's legal triumph over the radio stations, the government again followed American precedent and ordered the BBC to make payment to PRS in the same way. The PRS then copied ASCAP's way of dividing its income, with the top publishers and writers receiving the most.

Despite this bonus in royalties, British music publishers were torn between radio being a benefit or a disaster. In America, radio had been blamed for a fall in sheet music sales though it was possible that Prohibition was also a factor. It was certainly a factor in the lack of royalties from American dance venues. British publishers were benefitting from the boom in glossy dance palaces from which the PRS received performance royalties. America was doing its dancing in mob-controlled speakeasies where ASCAP hadn't a hope of collecting anything.

Record sales were down in both countries too. But the reasons might have been more complex than just radio over-exposure. In comparison with the best radio sets, records sounded tinny. What was needed, and every record manufacturer knew it, was a system of electrical recording. Radio provided the basic technology for such a thing, but no one had yet managed to construct an electric recording system.

Recording acoustically was a nightmare for the musicians. Walls had to be bare, floors hard, felts on piano hammers filed down, the string bass replaced with a tuba. Worst of all, everything had to be played as loud as possible. Pianist Gerald Moore was commissioned by HMV to record a Brahms lullaby. "I protested that it was impossible to bang out the notes of a lullaby. I should wake the baby." So he played it as normal and afterward the piano couldn't be heard beneath the orchestra.

Singers stood right in front of the recording horn and bellowed into it, and when jazz bands recorded they jostled and shoved to get in front of the horn for their solos. As a result, the most famous jazz soloists were not always the best but the ones with the toughest elbows.

For years the major record companies had been working to develop a method of recording electrically but so far nothing had materialised. In 1924, an answer was found, but not by someone in the record business. It came from Western Electric's research laboratories in New Jersey, where there was a technical staff of 1,200 people. The system would increase the upper frequency range from 2,000 cycles to 6,000, and at the bottom end string basses and bass drums would be properly heard. More importantly, musicians wouldn't have to crowd around a single horn or play loudly; they could stand wherever they wished and play as normal. It was just what the industry needed. But Western Electric wasn't in the habit of selling its inventions cheaply. They wanted a royalty paid on each record sold.

Victor were the only people who knew about this. Eldridge Johnson, who was still head of the company, had been dealing in secret with Western Electric, but when the contract finally arrived he dithered. He was unwell, suffering from depression, so it sat on his desk in the office unsigned while he stayed at home. And during that time Columbia heard about it.

Pathé, the French record company, had a pressing plant in New York. It was to them that Western Electric had sent their test waxes to be pressed into records for evaluation purposes. Their insistence on secrecy was so absolute that curiosity got the better of Pathé's boss, Frank Capps, and he listened to one of the discs. What he heard stunned him. Instead of keeping quiet about it, he immediately sent one of the test pressings to his friend Louis Sterling at Columbia in London. Sterling was so astonished by what he heard he got on the next boat to New York.

Sterling managed to push Western Electric into a deal. They would offer Columbia a licence on the same terms as they were offering Victor – $50,000 plus a royalty – but then Sterling hit an obstacle. Western Electric stipulated that only American companies and their affiliates could acquire the system. Sterling's British rival, HMV, would be allowed to use the system because Victor had bought half of its shares the year before. But Columbia America hadn't a penny to spare and there was no way they could buy out Columbia UK. The only way Sterling could ensure that Columbia UK obtained the new technology was to buy out Columbia America. He took a bank loan from J. P. Morgan and bought 60 per cent of the US company's shares – 51,000 of them at $50 each. Then, knowing his company's access to electrical recording would put it in a strong position, he also bought the German company, Carl Lindstrom A. G., and Nipponophone, Japan's largest record corporation.

In 1925, *Talking-Machine News* noted, "England is now in fact 'top dog'… The tremendous developments of the Columbia Gramophone Company Ltd places that company in the position of the leading and most powerful gramophone company in the world…"

So radio, which to start with looked like it would wipe out the record business, had ended up saving it by giving it the electric microphone. And Columbia UK, with its new electronic recording technology, had overtaken Victor as the world's number one record company.

14

Don't Trust Nobody
PUSHY PUBLISHERS, DODGY PRODUCERS

Paul Whiteman was one of the world's great opportunists. He called himself the King of Jazz but he was no such thing, he was simply the King of Publicity. He started with a mediocre dance band in San Francisco, then moved to New York. Along the way he happened to meet Ferde Grofé.

Grofé was a pianist of French extraction who came from four generations of classical musicians. He was also a brilliant arranger and Victor Records hired him to arrange two tracks for them, 'Whispering' and 'Japanese Sandman', both containing hints of jazz. Because the company had no artist available to front the tracks, Grofé suggested they should be released with Whiteman's picture on the front. Victor agreed and released the two songs together; one on each side of what became the first two-million selling record.

Whiteman rose to the occasion. He hired press and publicty agents, declared himself the 'King of Jazz' and never looked back. All he'd done was put his photograph on the right record at the right time. At least he had the good sense to immediately hire Ferde Grofé who became the band's pianist and regular arranger, incorporating little hints of jazz into Whiteman's dance band arrangements. Whiteman then employed one top jazz soloist for each instrument in the band and played dance music that had jazz solos interspersed throughout. Musically he was totally dependent on Grofé.

Whiteman was not only the King of Publicity, he was the King of Moneymaking too. Leo Feist retained him for ten thousand dollars a year to look over songs and make adjustments, but it was Grofé who did the work. On *Variety*'s chart of hit records, Whiteman's recordings of Feist songs were a permanent fixture – 'Wang Wang Blues', 'Three O'Clock in the Morning', 'I Miss My Swiss'. Eventually there were eleven official Whiteman bands in New York alone, plus forty more around the country, all playing only arrangements Grofé had done, Whiteman had recorded, and Feist had published, all run and controlled from Whiteman's New York office.

Duke Ellington said, "Paul Whiteman was known as the King of Jazz, and no one as yet has come near to carrying that title with more certainty and dignity." But Ellington played the music business game almost as well as Whiteman and was just saying what was best for him.

To the average person jazz might mean 'Alexander's Ragtime Band' or 'The Charleston', but for most jazz musicians it was improvisation that was the core element. Ellington and Whiteman were similar in that their bands didn't really play jazz at all, they played interesting, modern, dance-based arrangements with jazz solos interspersed. Whiteman went the white way, Ellington the black.

He took a residency at the Cotton Club, a smart whites-only late-night cabaret in Harlem. The club's shows reproduced the racist imagery of the times depicting blacks as exotic savages in Southern plantations. Ellington was expected to write 'jungle music' for an audience of whites.

Whiteman, on the other hand, began integrating the classics into his work. He paid arrangers to make dance arrangements of great classical pieces, but the public didn't take to them. In a final attempt at self-grandeur he commissioned George Gershwin to write a modern 'classical' piece for his orchestra, 'Rhapsody in Blue'. Gershwin only wrote the melody and piano part; the meat of the piece, the orchestration, was provided by Ferde Grofé.

When Whiteman premiered it at the Aeolian Hall, Dr Isaac Goldberg wrote, "It was a birthday for American Music, even an emancipation proclamation, in which slavery to European formalism was singed away by the ascending opening glissando of the Rhapsody." But Dr Goldberg was actually a great friend of Gershwin and overlooked the fact that Gershwin hadn't scored the piece. Even the opening glissando hadn't been Gershwin's idea. He'd written it as a fast ascending scale played with the instrument's keys, but just for fun, while the orchestra was in rehearsal, the clarinettist did a gliss.

Some critics praised the work – Olin Downes of the *New York Times* liked its "caprice, humour and exotic outline".

Others weren't so sure – Deems Taylor of *The World* thought it suffered from, "want of self-criticism and structural uncertainty".

Many thought it was total rubbish. In *The Tribune* Lawrence Gilman wrote, "How trite and feeble and conventional the tunes are… Weep over the lifelessness of its melody and harmony – so derivative, so stale, so inexpressive."

Whatever they said of it, and whatever Gershwin and Whiteman claimed it to be, the real truth was, Gershwin's 'Rhapsody in Blue' was little more than a piece of film music. And it had nothing whatsoever to do with jazz.

Real jazz meant Chicago's Southside. Songwriter Hoagy Carmichael wrote about it in his memoirs. "The joint stank of body musk, bootleg booze, excited people, platform sweat. I couldn't see well but I was feeling all over, 'Why isn't everyone in the world here to hear this?'"

Jazz joints weren't always such paradise. The biggest downside of Prohibition was to make the majority of musicians who earned money playing live music work in illegal surroundings – speakeasies run by mobsters. And Chicago was the worst of the worse.

Cornet player Jimmy McPartland had a band that played at Tancil's, a speakeasy in the Cicero area of Chicago where Al Capone was taking over.

One night a bunch of tough guys came in and started turning tables over to introduce themselves. Then they picked up bottles and began hitting the bartenders with them, also with blackjacks and brass knuckles... The thugs tore the place apart... The mobsters would break a bottle over some guy's head, then jab it in his face, then maybe kick him. They made mincemeat of people. I never saw such a horrible thing in my life. But we kept playing – period.

Lincoln Gardens was safer. It was a huge venue, big enough for one thousand people to dance, and it had the best jazz band in Chicago – King Oliver's band, with Louis Armstrong on second trumpet.

Armstrong and Oliver had a trick that left everyone thrilled. Whenever a tune had a break in it one of the lead instruments would improvise a couple of phrases. If the break was for the cornet, Joe Oliver would stand up and take it, playing something different every time. Yet miraculously Armstrong would stand with him, playing exactly the same thing, but in harmony.

Armstrong explained.

King and I stumbled on something that no other two trumpeters ever thought of. While the band was just swinging, the King would lean over to me, moving his valves on his trumpet, make notes, the notes that he was going to make when the break in the tune came... When the break came I'd have my part to blend right along with his. The crowd would go mad over it... Pretty soon all the white musicians from downtown Chicago would come there after their work and stay until the place closed.

Armstrong may have been playing the underneath line in the breaks but people soon realised it was him rather than King Oliver who was the real star. He went to New York and played for a year with Fletcher Henderson's band, then back to Chicago to form his own group and play at Dreamland. Okeh Records got in on the act and asked him to form a special recording group – the Hot Five – the best five jazz musicians in Chicago. They would meet up at Okeh's Chicago studios round 5am after they'd finished their various jobs round town. There they made what came to be considered the greatest ever examples of Dixieland jazz, the template for all similar bands to follow – amongst them, 'West End Blues', 'Muskrat Ramble', 'Heebie Jeebies', and 'Twelfth Street Rag'.

Okeh started pushing Louis Armstrong as something more than just a jazz musician. With each record they gave away a picture of him; it was the first time a record company had done such a thing with a black artist. Armstrong left Dreamland and was booked into Chicago's Erskine Theatre, featured as 'The World's Greatest Trumpet Player'. To start with it was just hype, but within a year people right across America would be calling him just that.

The music industry was quickly absorbing jazz into the mainstream of American popular music. But although the 1920s would be remembered for artists like Paul Whiteman, Duke Ellington, Bessie Smith, and Fats Waller, neither they nor Gershwin's fake-jazz 'Rhapsody in Blue' gave a true representation of what the decade's real popular music was. It was the ordinary songs – the everyday gimmicky sentimental popular songs – churned out every week by professional songwriters to be whistled and hummed for a few months and then disappear.

Some of the artists who sang them disappeared as fast as the songs they sang, but songwriters seemed to have a longer life; most of them went on turning out hits for years. And while not all of them could be as famous as Irving Berlin or Jerome Kern, many of the lesser-known ones were actually in the top league too. Gus Kahn, for instance, earned almost as much as Berlin, and so did Walter Donaldson who was signed to Irving Berlin's publishing company. Behind them came a host of others – Harold Arlen, Buddy de Silva, Harry Warren, Al Dubin, Jimmy McHugh, Bert Kalmar, Harry Ruby, Billy Rose – most of them from Manhattan, most of them sons of families who bought a piano on tick and had it winched up to the apartment and delivered through the window.

These were the writers who wrote songs for Broadway. But while songs from Broadway shows filled 25 per cent of the *Variety* song chart each week, the other 75 per cent was filled with the same ever-changing mix of popular songs that had always been there – from novelty tunes, to dance fads, to sentimental slop. Each publishing company needed its fair share of this stuff in order to survive. To come up with it they depended on staff writers paid between $100 and $150 weekly, with their weekly money deducted from any royalties they might earn whenever they had a hit.

This second tier of songwriters faced an endless struggle. Nominally, they were paid the accepted standard rate of "two and thirty-three" – two cents per copy for sheet music and 33 per cent of the 2c royalty paid on the sale of each gramophone record. From this, an average Top 10 hit might earn them a total of around $5,000, but usually the writer, or co-writers, had to split that amount with two or three other people – the artist who promoted it, the bandleader who played it on the radio, or simply the publisher, demanding an extra share.

By now, these 'cut-ins' were considered an essential part of the business. It wasn't even something that was kept secret. *Variety* called it "the new racket" and claimed bandleaders and singing stars received "from $1,000 to $20,000 a year as salary charged against royalty" on the songs supposedly written by them.

Music publisher Jack Robbins formed a joint company with Paul Whiteman to publish books. The first one was, *Inside Story on How to Write a Popular Song*, written by *Variety*'s editor, Abel Green. In it he emphasised the importance of making an 'arrangement' with one of the recognised bandleaders who would "need to be compensated with royalty interests" and credited on the sheet music. "Most bandleaders," he said, "consider it a poor week if they are cut in on less than fifteen new songs."

Another of Robbins' publications was a book of music that orchestras could play in silent movie houses; hundreds of short musical pieces and phrases to suit every type of emotion or action. When the new film arrived at the beginning of the week, the orchestra leader would go through the book picking out suitable pieces for each key point in the film, then cobble them together to make a continuous musical accompaniment.

Robbins was an opportunist. One night he saw Duke Ellington perform and got a new idea. "I want you to write me the score for a musical show," he told Duke.

"By when?" Duke asked.

Robbins, not sure how long these things were meant to take, answered "Tomorrow?"

Ellington, also unsure, agreed. "That night I sat down and wrote music for a whole show. I didn't know composers were meant to take six months off in the mountains or by the sea in order to compose music for a show."

Robbins had offered Ellington $500 advance if he did it, so that night he went and pawned his wife's engagement ring. The next morning he swapped the cash for Ellington's score for a musical, complete with four totally new songs. Robbins added other songs and put together a show with an all-black cast called *Chocolate Kiddies*, then sold it to the Admiralspalast theatre in Berlin.

It was billed as a 'Neger-Revue' and featured twenty 'entertainers', eleven musicians and a conductor, all of them black. It was the first time anyone in Germany had seen black people do a show in a theatre. After the last number on the opening night the audience just sat there. Silent.

When Sam Wooding, the conductor, turned and bowed he was shocked. "They started hollering 'Bis, Bis'… we thought they were saying 'beasts'…"

The band fled the stage but when they reached the wings the stage-hands explained that 'bis' was German for encore. So they went back and took a bow.

The show ran for sixty-five performances and was the hottest ticket in town. It then played Hamburg and toured Scandinavia, Hungary, Austria and

Czechoslovakia. After two years Jack Robbins came home a rich man and settled down to build a publishing company.

Someone else benefitting from travel was Ralph Peer. He'd now moved on from recording black music for Okeh and was recording country music for Victor. He was doing it on exactly the same basis as he'd done with black music – all songs had to be original and they all had to be signed to his publishing company.

It wasn't the first time Peer had recorded country music; he'd started while he was still searching out black talent for Okeh. One time he'd arrived in Atlanta and been unable to find any black talent. Okeh's local distributor knew a fiddle player called John Carson whom he reckoned could sell a few records round town. Since Peer already had a hall booked he agreed to do it. He took the resulting recording back to New York and pressed a few records for the Atlanta distributor.

It was so bad that we didn't even put a serial number on the records, thinking that when the local dealer got his supply that would be the end of it. We sent him 1,000 records, which he received on a Thursday. That night he called New York on the phone and ordered 5,000 more sent by express and 10,000 by freight. When the national sale got to 500,000, we were so ashamed we had Fiddler John come up to New York and do a re-recording of the numbers.

Despite his success with the material he'd recorded, Peer freely admitted he didn't enjoy being in the studio with hillbillies and blacks, he preferred hobnobbing with high society at the opera or growing prize-winning gardenias in his garden. When a journalist asked to what he owed his success, he said it was due to "knowing where lightning is going to strike". Then added, "how in God's name you can detect that I don't know". But it seemed Peer could. Over and over again.

In 1927, Peer returned to the southern states with Victor's new 'Orthophonic' recording equipment. "If I can't get 'em in town," he said, "we'll go to the woods." In Bristol a singer called Jimmie Rodgers was meant to come in with his band but had a quarrel with them and turned up alone. Peer gave him $100 to sing.

If he'd thought Fiddlin' John Carson was bad, Peer considered Rodgers even worse. But like Fiddlin' John Carson, Rodgers proved a huge success, and when his song 'Blue Yodel' became a hit, Peer signed him to management.

Rodgers was the first country singer to be heard nationally on radio. And although he endlessly repeated his first success, making 'Blue Yodel 2', then 'Blue Yodel 3', and so on, he also recorded many of the best country songs of the period and performed them live across America. He became recognised as the first 'great' of country music. But 'Blue Yodel 13' brought him bad luck.

Shortly after he recorded it, he died of tuberculosis.

The recordings of all of these country artists were passed on to Victor, the company that paid Peer his salary. Victor had steadily expanded since the early twenties, and with American Columbia having been bought out by its British subsidiary, Victor had become far the most important record company in America. Its head of recording was Nathaniel Shilkret, who didn't much like Peer. "He was paid $80 a week and expenses. He took several trips and the next year asked for a raise."

Grudgingly Shilkret agreed to the raise but Peer had a better suggestion. Why not leave his salary at the original $80 per week but add a percentage of two cents for each track he recorded.

Shilkret was outraged. "No one on the musical staff had been offered a royalty for his arrangement or compositions, and here was a man collecting royalties with other men's compositions!"

Shilkret shouldn't have been so upset. He frequently used other people's compositions to his own benefit. In 1925 'The Prisoner's Song' became the biggest hit of the year selling over a million records and a similar amount of sheet music. The artist Vernon Dalhart had turned up at the studio with a song written by his cousin. Shilkret said the tune wasn't good enough and instantly composed a new one. After the session he searched the waste bin and found the crumpled piece of paper on which the lyrics had been scribbled. He added some more verses and claimed the song for his own. The result was a lengthy court case at the end of which the singer got the money for the lyrics (really his cousin's), and Shilkret was deemed composer of the music. But Shilkret ended up with neither credit nor royalty. Under the terms of his agreement with Victor the company took everything he composed during the period of his employment.

While record executives industry scrambled grubbily through waste bins, Broadway provided a more elegant path to success. It had found a new musical sophistication. Some people credited it to Jerome Kern, but Kern credited it to Prohibition. Of his current show, he said, "I wrote this music with a view of having it appreciated by people who come to the theatre without any alcoholic stimulation."

He believed that to hold a sober audience's attention, they had to be given more than "the jazzy types of entertainment" that previously could fill a Broadway theatre. And even if Kern was the only composer whom Prohibition had influenced to write better music, that was enough, because what Kern wrote influenced everyone else.

The new music that composers were creating for Broadway was subtler and more harmonically advanced, often with distinct jazz influences. The words were better too. Ira Gershwin and Lorenz Hart were replacing the previous generation's sentimentality with subtle nuance, and musical comedy had become the primary medium for promoting great songs.

There was only one major writer not doing musical comedy on Broadway. Irving Berlin.

In 1920, with producer Sam Harris, Berlin had bought his own theatre, The Music Box. He put on a new revue each year. It was the perfect way to promote his best new songs and it meant he was totally in charge of his own life – songwriter, publisher, theatre owner, producer. But because it was revue, some of the sophistication that was finding its way into songs for Broadway musicals tended to be missing.

Berlin claimed it was deliberate. "Ease, naturalness, everydayness… it is my first consideration when I start on lyrics… easy to say, easy to sing, and applicable to everyday events…"

Musicologist Isaac Goldberg put it more bluntly. "His words, however clever, yet maintain contact with *hoi polloi*."

Not exactly criticism, but to make sure no one thought otherwise Berlin gave himself an annual PR budget of $750,000. He was particularly concerned the public should think of him as a hard-worker and not a dilettante. Once, when a journalist asked about his way of writing songs, he replied, "I sweat blood between 3 and 6 many mornings, and when the drops fall off my forehead and hit the paper they're notes"

The publicity worked. To most Americans he was their greatest ever writer of popular song, but to the music industry he was also an exceptional music publisher. He'd long ago parted company with Henry Waterson and set himself up as Irving Berlin Inc.

He was a publisher of guile second only to Leo Feist or Max Dreyfus. He always kept business uppermost in his mind; never let the songwriter side of him dominate when a deal was being discussed, nor let the business side intrude when he was writing a song. When it came to running his company he was a traditionalist. He didn't change the old-fashioned way of doing things and was doubtful of those who did; success came from running things as they'd always been run. Several times a week he went round music stores to make sure his songs were in stock. With his finger he checked for dust on top of the piles of sheet music. If he found some, it meant they weren't selling, which called for an inquest when he got back to the office.

He had a general manager who was the day-to-day business face of his company, Saul Bornstein, an unlikeable person who delighted in the way he introduced himself to people. "My first name is Saul. My second is Oscar. My last is Bornstein. And you know what that spells!"

He wasn't joking. He was a bullying son-of-a-bitch and a petty crook. Perhaps Berlin thought that was the sort of general manager a successful publishing company needed. And he may have been right. Bornstein could always be relied on to take the tough approach.

Harry von Tilzer published a song called 'When My Baby Smiles at Me' and persuaded bandleader Ted Lewis to make it his theme tune. Then he learnt Irving Berlin had written a song called 'When My Baby Smiles'.

Von Tilzer proposed the two of them meet and compare songs. When they did everyone present agreed the songs were not at all alike, the problem was simply with the titles. It was suggested they toss a coin for it, but because Saul Bornstein was a close friend with Claude Mills, the MPPA chairman, Berlin felt on safe ground and refused. Sure enough the MPPA 'discovered' the Berlin song had been registered with them prior to the von Tilzer song, and the following week Saul Bornstein placed a large advertisement in *Variety* saying so.

Abel Green, the editor of *Variety*, took an intense dislike to the relationship between Saul Bornstein and Claude Mills. He disapproved of both men and had already written in the paper that Claude Mills, was "little better than a megalomaniac looking after only himself".

On behalf of MPPA's members Mills had taken over the collection of mechanical fees from record companies. He collected them into his own office before passing them on to individual publishers after taking 5 per cent commission for himself, on top of his salary from MPPA. When Abel Green spoke up out about this, Mills was forced to hand it over to MPPA's general manager Harry Fox who renamed the department the Harry Fox Agency and separated it from the rest of MPPA.

The truth was Mills' chicanery was only a symptom of everything that went on in the music publishing business. Publishers met in meetings at ASCAP or MPPA, decided on new rules to restrict their promotional activities, then immediately broke them, hoping every one else was being bound by them. A good example was when ASCAP decided to start enforcing payment of performance royalties by vaudeville theatres. For many publishers, vaudeville was still the principal method of popularising their new songs and they thought it should be exempt. Some of them cheated and formed subsidiary companies that were not ASCAP members, thus being able to give music to vaudeville at no charge.

Shapiro Bernstein formed a non-ASCAP subsidiary called Skidmore Music which openly looked for songs suitable for vaudeville shows. The boss, Louis Bernstein (who was boss of Shapiro Bernstein too, of course), had a visit from two writers with a new song just perfect for vaudeville, 'Yes, We Have No Bananas'.

To make a new chorus, the writers had taken two out-of-copyright musical phrases, one from Handel's 'Messiah', the other from 'My Bonnie Lies Over the Ocean'. It was an extraordinary hotch-potch – a Handel chorus, a banana insert, and the last line of a folk song, *'Hallelujah, bananas, oh bring back my Bonnie to me'*.

Bernstein liked the idea but wanted some of the lyrics re-written. The entire office joined in and contributed one line each, but when they'd finished there seemed to be a bit of Cole Porter in the verse. Louis Bernstein suggested the two writers go down the road and check it with Porter's publisher, Max Dreyfus. When they got there Max scanned through the melody and decided it definitely breached Cole Porter's copyright but kindly suggested some changes that would make it OK.

The song went out published by Skidmore Music, thus allowing vaudeville theatres to avoid paying ASCAP performance royalties. When it became an instant hit the only objections came from Saul Bornstein who had done exactly the same as Louis Bernstein – set up dummy corporations on behalf of Irving Berlin to avoid MPPA and ASCAP's rulings.

Berlin's use of Bornstein to make his sharper publishing deals was shrewd to say the least. Although everyone knew Bornstein was a cheap crook no one wanted to confront Berlin with it, he was too respected. In public he was endlessly modest. "We depend largely on tricks, we writers of song, our work is to connect old phrases in a new way, so that they will sound like a new tune." But behind the scenes he pushed his own songs ruthlessly.

One day he got a call from singing star Belle Baker. She was about to open in *Betsy*, a new Ziegfeld show with a score by Rodgers and Hart. But they were overworked. With another Broadway show opening the evening before they hadn't come up with the sort of show-stopping song she was used to. "There isn't a Belle Baker song in the score," she told Irving, "and I'm so miserable."

Irving agreed to go over to her apartment. He took half a song with him, something he'd written ages ago and thrown into his box of rejects. Belle loved the first two lines but there wasn't a bridge, so she made coffee while Berlin stayed late and found one.

Trouble was – Berlin couldn't just go shoving songs into someone else's show, he at least had to tell the producer. So he phoned Ziegfeld.

Ziegfeld said it was impossible. His contract with Rodgers and Hart forbade songs that weren't theirs.

So Belle Baker refused to go on.

Ziegfeld relented. "Berlin, you can do it, but for God's sake don't tell Rodgers and Hart."

The show wasn't much good. The first night audience was restless and as the show progressed Belle could feel them slipping away from her. Almost at the end came the Irving Berlin song, 'Blue Skies'.

The audience was rapturous. They cheered Belle crazily, pushing her to do one encore after another. Some reports said there were twenty-five, some said twenty-eight, but they all agreed on one thing – on the last encore Belle blew her words, like old-time vaudeville performers used to, so the plugger in the audience could stand up and sing them for her. A spotlight came on and a figure in the front row stood up and bellowed out the chorus. It was Irving Berlin, and the audience erupted yet again.

Rodgers and Hart were not amused.

15

Let's Do It
SPECIAL RELATIONSHIPS

In 1925 William Boosey sent a wire to Louis Dreyfus asking him to come to London and discuss some urgent business. When he arrived Boosey said he'd decided it was time to retire, would Louis be interested in the job of managing director for Chappell? If he accepted, the board would offer him some shares in the company and appoint him forthwith. Louis agreed, and from then on the Dreyfus brothers were running the most important publishing companies on both sides of the Atlantic.

As head of Chappell, Louis Dreyfus' first priority was to sell British music in Britain; the American catalogue that Chappell licensed from Harms had to come second.

One of Louis' principal aims was to ensure there were better arrangements in place for both countries to collect performance royalties from the other. He quickly got himself onto the board of PRS from where he was able to enter into direct negotiations with members of the board of ASCAP, including his brother. Before long, there was a new agreement between the two societies.

For Louis, life in England was sometimes puzzling, sometimes petty. He was surprised at the amount of backbiting and politics in Chappell's offices. One of the company's songwriters said he would prefer to work at home on Thursdays. Louis told him not to. "When you are at home writing on Thursday, the assassins in the office are undermining you. And then when you come to work on Friday, you've got to spend the day re-solidifying your position."

He was surprised too by the BBC's snobbery about popular music. The BBC was no longer a private corporation owned by a consortium of the biggest electrical manufacturers, it had been re-constituted under a royal charter and was now non-profit-making, funded by a licence bought by all radio users. Radio licences which in 1921 had numbered just 3,500, were now up to four million, and 46 per cent of everything on the air was music.

This new BBC had adopted the motto, "Nation Shall Speak Peace Unto Nation". For some reason this precluded it from playing currently popular music until late in the evening. Yet it insisted it *was* playing popular music; it's just that what it deemed popular was music from fifty years ago – Gilbert & Sullivan,

Franz Lehar, and even music from George Edwardes' shows. Louis Dreyfus shouldn't have minded, it was mostly published by Chappell, but he and Max would have preferred to hear their current music on the radio – shows from Broadway by Rodgers and Hart, Vincent Youmans and Gershwin.

The BBC felt it had a moral duty to educate the British people to better things than that. Popular music was treated like an alcoholic drink, something people could be allowed a little of at the end of the day. It was only broadcast late in the evening, usually by the band at the Savoy Hotel, or the Cecil.

Because the bands at these upmarket hotels played very few show tunes Louis Dreyfus decided Chappell should invest in putting on West End musicals by their American writers, as Harms did on Broadway. He started in 1925 with *No No Nanette*, which ran for 800 performances in London before moving to Broadway.

One of the results of the BBC's pompous attitude to popular music was an abundance of commercial stations broadcasting to London from Europe, mostly with American sponsors. These programmes came from such stations as Radio Hilversum, Radio Normandie, and Paris Radio. They included The Kraft Cheese Show, the Rinso Radio Show, Cadbury Calling, and Feenman's Laxative Show. British publishers found them more straightforward to deal with than the BBC. Instead of a cash bribe being paid to get a song on the air, three minutes airtime could be bought legitimately, paid for by cheque to the radio station.

In some ways the BBC's patronising attitude to popular music helped the sale of gramophones. If you wanted popular music at home, you had to have one. The recent introduction of new machines with electronic amplification had given a huge boost to the record industry and sales of the new machines were impressive, three million during the first year. Proportionately, more British people had gramophones than Americans since young people depended on them as their only source of current popular music. Particularly popular were portables, good for picnics or using in the garden, and selling for as little as £3 to £9.

There was no doubt about it, the advent of electrical recording had triggered a new interest in records which were now no longer seen as elitist. At the turn of the century they'd sold for £1 each; now, HMV had two discount labels, Twin and Cinch, and Columbia had Phoenix and Regal. In Woolworth's, cover versions could be bought on the Crown label for as little as sixpence.

The new electronic method of recording had started to give rise to new styles of singing. One of the most popular new artists was Whispering Jack Smith whose ultra-soft singing style was the result of being poisoned by gas in the

First World War. A letter he received from a British fan was much publicised in the press.

> *When I'm feeling blue and all alone I get one of your records out and play it softly until it seems you are sitting there right here with me understanding all the rotten things that make up my life… I lost both my sons in the war, and there's a big ache left where there used to be a feeling of gladness… you have done more towards soothing that ache than anyone else in the world.*

Not everyone was happy with the gramophone's newfound popularity. Classical composer Constant Lambert had a particular dislike for it. "At one time a cautious glance round the room ensured one, through the absence of a piano, that there would be no music after dinner. But today the chances are that one's host is a Gramophone Bore, intent on exhibiting his 57 Varieties of soundbox…"

Somerset Maugham was more enthusiastic. "We all congratulate ourselves that the radio and gramophone have driven from our drawing-rooms the amateur pianist and the amateur singer."

Sir Hugh Allen, the director of the Royal Philharmonic, hated pop records with a passion, yet he also saw value in them. "It may be readily admitted that the recording companies have published and sold as many of their repellent, devastating and sordid noises as they could, but it must be remembered that without the financial help of what is loosely called jazz we should never have had the symphonies of Beethoven or Bach's Mass in B minor."

It was interesting – the record business had initially blasted off on the input of Caruso and opera. In those days records sold for four times as much as they did in the mid-twenties by which time classical music had to be subsidised. But because of the industry's history, no one ever considered simply scrapping classical music as uneconomic. Instead, the principal record companies on both sides of the Atlantic felt it was their duty to use some of the profits from popular music to subsidise it, and no one ever suggested otherwise.

Louis Sterling, head of Columbia UK, summed it up succinctly. "Boiled Beef and Carrots paid for Beethoven."

To most Americans in the music industry, Britain in the twenties seemed something of a backwater, yet Britain now owned Columbia, the largest record company in the world. And in Britain, records and sheet music sold far more per capita than in the USA. Certain aspects of British life helped to develop its popular music industry more swiftly than the American industry. For one thing, there was no Prohibition, which meant a much lower rate of crime in places where music was popularised by dancing.

Britain also had a different attitude to jazz, treating it as a separate but serious form of music. It didn't need to justify itself by aspiring to be something better, like Gershwin's efforts with 'Rhapsody in Blue'. When Constant Lambert composed 'The Rio Grande Suite' it wasn't a popular songwriter searching for respect by turning jazzy tunes into something classical; it was a serious composer incorporating jazz influences to show off his populist sophistication. Perhaps it was just as pretentious, for although Constant Lambert liked jazz he had no time at all for modern American songwriting. He blamed 'New York Jewry' for the "tearful, lovelorn quality" of current songs like 'Dancing with Tears in my Eyes'. He preferred hits from the pre-1920s. "The singer's hat is at a jaunty angle, his gloves are in his hand, he suffers no inhibitions as he walks down the pier, receiving the glad eye from presumably attractive girls…"

The top British name in popular music in the 1920s was bandleader Jack Hylton, to whom the top publisher, Lawrence Wright, paid a retainer, just as Leo Feist did to Paul Whiteman in America. For one new song, 'Me and Jane In a Plane', Wright hired an aeroplane from Imperial Airways which flew low over Blackpool Tower on a summer bank holiday releasing hundreds of copies of the song's sheet music while on the bandstand below Jack Hylton's band played it, with young men in striped blazers crooning the words through megaphones.

Wright became the best-paid songwriter in Britain, mainly by looking after his own music publishing. Among his biggest hits was 'Among my Souvenirs', and he also founded the weekly music newspaper, *Melody Maker*. He was probably best known to the public for his exotic promotion of the song, 'Shepherd of the Hills'.

Wright went to America and composed it during a live broadcast of a transatlantic phone call to his London office where it was taken down by Jack Hylton, whose band performed it at the Alhambra at 8.40pm that same night. Wright called it 'the 3,000-miles-a-second-New York-London hit'.

Like Leo Feist in America, Lawrence Wright led the way in getting singers and bandleaders to plug his songs. The difference in Britain was that the BBC was the only radio station. They objected to graft and let it be known anyone caught receiving money for plugging songs would be dismissed. But the truth was, even after 10pm, the BBC still needed the top artists on its airwaves, so graft continued and stern warnings were usually all that was forthcoming.

When one singer, Talbot O'Farrell, was reported to be getting £1,000 per year from Lawrence Wright, the BBC decided to deal with it by banning song titles being announced on air, which incensed the publishers. PRS fought the battle on their behalf, refusing to renew its licence with the BBC, which meant the BBC would be unable to play 90 per cent of the music it was currently playing.

No sooner had the BBC given way and agreed to go back to announcing song titles than a new bill was proposed in Parliament that threatened to kill the British music publishing business stone dead. It would ban performance royalties altogether.

The bill proposed that in future the sale of sheet music would constitute the sale of a performance right in the music purchased. To cover this, two pence would be added to the cost of sheet music. PRS hired the author and barrister A. P. Herbert to attack the bill and he did so in no uncertain means. He told MPs they'd disgraced themselves by allowing such a bill to slip through and that it should be "killed stone dead as an insult to the craft of music".

While Louis Dreyfus accustomed himself to the parochial nature of all this, Max in New York was as focused as ever on getting the best from all his writers.

"The writers. The writers. Always take care of your writers. Without them you're nothing." It was Max's eternal refrain at Harms' four o'clock staff meetings.

There were always some publishers who paid their writers simply to churn out non-stop songs, but there were others who found time to work with them more closely. History proved how worthwhile it was. Max Dreyfus told his writers he considered each of them to be a son and each of their songs a nephew. Certainly, it was from giving them a parental type of attention that he built the biggest music publishing company in the world.

Max knew his job didn't end with signing the best songwriters; he also had to coax the best out of them. Songs were never written simply to fulfill his employees' need for something to plug. Max's policy was to turn songwriters into stars. He found the best songwriters and had them write shows for Broadway. Then he helped finance and put on the shows.

When he first signed Richard Rodgers and Lorenz Hart he asked them if they wanted an advance and explained to Rodgers how he did his accounting. Contracted writers were permitted to draw up to $200 a week to be deducted from royalties when they became due. Rodgers immediately said he and Hart wouldn't want an advance.

Dreyfus stared at me with a look of disbelief. "All right," he said, "if that's the way you want it, but I'll tell you one thing. In all my years in the publishing business, this is the first time anyone has ever turned down an advance." Then he put his arm around my shoulder, and I suddenly realized what it was to be one of Max Dreyfus' boys. "There's one thing I want you to promise me," he said. "If you ever need money, I don't want you to go to anyone else but me. From now on, don't ever forget that I'm your friend."

Max was an astute businessman and despite his generosity toward writers he was well known for being careful with money. He had two country houses but only used them for entertaining. Otherwise he lived at the Astor Hotel in the heart of theatreland, and when he wasn't entertaining he ate lunch there alone – tomato juice, an egg, and crackers.

Just a few steps away were Harms' offices. Max would potter round them in slippers and a grey cotton office coat, soft-spoken and not given to showing much emotion. But his morose exterior was deceiving. He loved mixing business with pleasure and made the office into a social club for writers. During the week all the important songwriters of the day would drop into his office for a chat – George Gershwin, Harry Ruby, Bert Kalmar, Joe Meyer, Buddy De Sylva, Vincent Youmans – to Max, all of them were 'his boys'. "To get into the orbit of Harms was every composer's dream," said lyricist Irving Caesar.

Through this approach, Max got from his 'boys' as many complete musicals for Broadway as other publishers got single hit songs.

On Friday afternoons, Irving Caesar would go to a ball game with Max, then on to one of his country houses where the guest list would include 'the most favoured boys'. The barn had been turned into a bowling alley; there was also fishing in a private stream and horse riding on a private half-mile track. In the evening there was wine, cigars, and German food. 'The boys' would try out their latest compositions at the piano and afterwards things could get rowdy. At a birthday party for Victor Herbert, America's finest songwriters ended up throwing raw steaks at each other.

But it wasn't the songwriters that captured Max's heart; entertaining them was just a matter of good business. Nor was it their songs, because his real musical passion was opera. It was the ownership of them.

Because he had no children of his own he treated his copyrights as if they were his offspring, protecting and nurturing them. When someone told him about a mutual friend whose son had died in a road accident, he added, "At least you'll never suffer that particular agony."

Max replied, "But I have songs that go into the public domain."

For all their charm and bonhomie, it was as well to remember the extraordinary power the two Dreyfus brothers had in the music business. They were not benefactors to the industry, they were solely in it for profit, and they were running the most important publishing companies in both Britain and America. Moreover, both of them had senior positions on the publisher's committees of the respective collection societies, ASCAP and PRS. Behind the closed doors of these societies there was no knowing what leverage they exerted for the benefit of the two companies they ran. More easily seen was the commercial result of their business acumen, with nearly all the top writers on both sides of the Atlantic signed to their companies. They held on to them by paying them well, treating them as family, and always backing them up, even when they made mistakes. Like Jerome Kern when he wrote 'Ka-lu-a'.

Back in 1920, the year's first issue of *Variety* had come out without its usual front page. Instead of headlines and news stories, there was a full-page advertisement that read more like some sort of police notice.

WARNING
THIEVES AND PIRATES!
and those who live on the efforts of other people's brains
DON'T IMITATE, COPY OR STEAL
any part of
DARDANELLA
The Biggest Musical Hit of the Past 20 Years

It was a brilliant ad – both in terms of selling a new song to the music industry and in protecting its copyright. What the publishers particularly wanted to do was protect the song's boogie style counter-riff played on bass and piano. It was the way the riff worked against the melody that gave the song its unique catchiness.

After several years had passed, Jerome Kern, deliberately or maybe inadvertently, took the counter-riff and used it in a song he was writing, 'Ka-lu-a', published of course by Max Dreyfus at T. B. Harms.

Inevitably, the publisher, Fred Fisher, who had bought the song from the original writer for $100 and put his own name on it as composer, took action – he sued for one million dollars damages.

Max, as always, stood behind his songwriter and rustled up some star witnesses to speak in Kern's defence, including conductor Leopold Stokowski, Metropolitan Opera music director Artur Bodanzsky, and operetta composer Victor Herbert.

Kern's defence was that the bass figure wasn't unique. It had been used in many classical pieces long ago and was therefore out of copyright, and the three expert witnesses argued that point most articulately.

Fred Fisher's argument was less erudite. To support his claim that the bass line and melody formed a joint copyright, he illustrated how it could completely change any tune by playing the hymn, 'Nearer My God to Thee' against the same wriggling bass line.

Judge Hand thought the whole thing was a waste of the court's time. He called it "trivial pother" and demanded that the two sides meet in his chambers where Fisher offered to settle the matter for a suit of clothes. Kern, tetchy and humourless as always, considered such a settlement an insult to his reputation and rejected it, whereupon Judge Hand ruled in Fisher's favour. The riff, he ruled, was an "essential and substantial" part of Fisher's copyright. Fisher was awarded $250 in damages and Max Dreyfus had to assign him half the royalties.

Another of Max's writers causing him trouble was Cole Porter.

Porter's melodies were superb and his lyrics as sharp as any to be heard on Broadway, but he simply refused to focus on his career. From a family with money, and married into even more of it, he was homosexual, flamboyant and a playboy. But he was so terrified of failure that he pretended to be a playboy who only wrote songs as a hobby.

In London, Louis Dreyfus was now publisher of Britain's most famous hedonist, Noël Coward.

Coward had made his name with his first West End play, *The Young Idea*, about "birth control and sexual liberation; drink, drugs and dance-crazy clubs; divorce and adultery". He'd followed that with *London Calling*, a smash review that ran for two years. Since then his fame had gone up and up.

He was a songwriter, actor, singer, playwright, novelist, and above all, a celebrity. He conveyed a light-hearted approach to everything he did, claiming to have written many of his plays in a single day and being bored with the fact that novels could take him as long as three weeks. Yet he was dedicated to work and his most famous quote was, "Work is even more fun than fun."

Importantly too, he was homosexual. So Max and Louis thought he might provide just the right influence for Cole Porter.

In 1925, Cole and his wife let it be known they would be in Venice for the summer. Two of Max's other writers would be there too, Richard Rodgers and his lyricist Lorenz Hart, who was also homosexual. And Louis, in London, heard that Noël Coward was also planning to be there.

In Venice, Cole Porter soon met up with Coward and socialised with him and his boyfriend Jack Wilson. Coward scolded Porter for his fear of plunging into work and offered himself as living proof that a successful songwriter could combine a decent career with a lavishly decadent lifestyle. When Rodgers and Hart turned up and joined in the scolding, Porter was really put under pressure.

The occasion was set in progress when Rodgers, walking along the seafront at the Lido, bumped into Noël who then introduced him to a "slight, delicately-featured man with saucer eyes and wide grin".

It was Cole Porter, whom Rodgers had never met before. Porter then invited Coward, Rodgers, and Lorenz Hart, to have dinner at the Palazzio Rezzonico, which he and his wife had rented for the summer.

Rodgers described being picked up from the hotel where he and Hart were staying. "Promptly at seven-thirty, Porter's private gondola pulled up outside our hotel. Larry and I got in and were wafted down the Grand Canal and deposited in front of an imposing three-story palace."

Inside, they were ushered up a vast staircase and at the top waiting for them were Cole Porter and his wife Linda, together with Noël Coward. After dinner, they went to the music room where Porter asked Rodgers to play some songs on the piano. Coward then played and sang some of his too; then it was Cole Porter's turn.

Richard Rodgers was hugely impressed. "As soon as he touched the keyboard to play 'a few of my little things' I became aware that he was not merely a talented dilettante, but a generously gifted theatre composer and lyricist."

Both Coward and Rodgers nagged Porter about his lack of commitment to composition and Coward reminded him, as he'd reminded so many people before, that work could be even more fun than fun.

Rodgers told Cole, with a talent like his he should be focusing on getting success for himself rather than wasting his time in Europe playing his songs for friends at dinner parties. Cole responded to Rodgers by telling him he'd discovered the secret for writing hits. "As I breathlessly awaited the magic formula, he leaned over and confided, 'I'll write Jewish tunes'."

This from one of the few non-Jewish songwriters in America.

The Venice meeting had the desired effect; Porter got back to New York a changed man. The dilettante had disappeared and in his place was someone dedicated to succeeding. He started working as he'd never worked before, apparently enjoying it even more than he'd previously enjoyed being a playboy. He wrote *La Revue des Ambassadeurs* for the launch of a new café of the same name and it received more critical acclaim than anything he'd ever done. It included 'Let's Do It', a song so close to Noël Coward's style that it was impossible not to see the master's touch in it, coming as it did directly after their meeting in Venice. Moreover, back in London, Coward commandeered the song for his own use and for the next forty years sang it at nearly all his live shows.

It seemed impossible that Max and Louis Dreyfus hadn't in some way plotted Cole Porter's 'chance' meeting with Noël Coward. Having a brother on each side of the Atlantic was quite a special relationship.

16

Brother, Can You Spare a Dime?
HOLLYWOOD TAKES OVER

"Who the hell wants to hear actors talk? The music, that's the big plus!"

Harry Warner just didn't get it, which was odd. Drama was one of the most popular things on radio – drama with speech but no pictures. Then people went to the movies and watched drama with pictures but no speech. And people like Harry Warner didn't think there'd be a market for combining the two.

From the mid-twenties on Warner had been developing their Vitaphone system, more or less a long-playing record, a method of playing music in sync with a silent film but not of letting characters speak. Hollywood became obsessed with synchronized theme tunes; if they gave the song the same name as the movie and the song was played on radio, it publicised the film. Who cared if the title was rubbish? Australian songwriter Ted Ward turned up at United Artists to find he had twenty-four hours to write a hit song with the title 'Woman Disputed, I Love You'.

Never mind, everything was possible in the movie business; the next morning he handed them one.

Warner Bros finally tried a singing-dancing movie, *The Jazz Singer* featuring Al Jolson. Apart from the musical numbers it was basically a silent movie yet everybody's favourite part wasn't the dancing or even the singing, it was the one tiny bit in the film where Al Jolson spoke, when he came charging onstage and told the audience, "You ain't heard nothing yet!"

We hadn't. A year later Hollywood was turning out screen versions of Broadway musicals as fast as it could – all-talking, all-singing, all-dancing movies. Hollywood went mad for musicals, and when all the old Broadway shows were used up, the songwriters were sent for to write more.

Everyone was seduced by Hollywood. You went there to make money and you gave your bosses what they asked for, no questions asked. In return you lived a golden life. It was the era of the swimming pool and the tennis court. You could leave the office and get home in time for a couple of sets before dinner.

In July 1929, *Variety* wrote: "Never before in the history of Tin Pan Alley has the average songwriter enjoyed such affluence and influence."

What they were talking about was the new Hollywood custom of taking a sequence in a film and asking ten different songwriters to propose a song for it.

Although they were all paid for their efforts, only one song would be chosen. The other nine writers would have a song they could sell elsewhere and enough dollars in their pocket not to have to.

In just one year the audience for talkies had grown to seventy million. Movies could make hit songs. *Variety* had often told its readers, if the song isn't there the picture can't help it, but this was no longer true. Many a second-rate song was selling like crazy. If a publisher had a song in a movie, all he had to do was print up orchestrations for radio bands to play, then sit back and wait for the hit.

Hollywood was eagerly pulling in all the top songwriters, guaranteeing them up to $35,000 a year, with Rodgers and Hart topping the tree at a whopping $1,000 a week.

When they accepted it, Rodgers and Hart were in New York. Larry Hart went ahead to Hollywood, with Richard Rodgers planning to follow three weeks later. Because he'd heard stories about uncouth louts rising to be top Hollywood moguls, he was apprehensive. His worst fears were confirmed when he arrived at the studio and was shown in to meet Jack Warner.

> *He was just like the producers in the funny stories. He sprawled over the table and said, "Vell, now you're here, you got to get to work. And I don't vant none of your highbrow song-making. Music vit guts ve got to have – songs vit real sentiment."*

Rodgers didn't know where to look. But he was being sent up. When he turned his eyes back to Jack Warner, Larry Hart was standing behind him, and they were both helpless with laughter.

Warner's music department was in the hands of Lou Warner, Jack Warner's son, and Buddy Morris, son of the overseas sales chief. They decided they should expand laterally and buy up companies that controlled anything used in the production of musical films. They started by buying Brunswick Records, not because they wanted to get into the record business but because the Brunswick factory pressed Vitaphone records, the discs used in movie houses to play sync music tracks with movies. They then decided Warner should control all the music copyrights in its talking pictures; if not, they worried they would be held to ransom by music publishers. So in July 1929 they started looking around to see which publishing companies they could buy.

Witmark was the obvious first target. For a longtime the company hadn't been doing well yet it had a vast catalogue of show songs going back thirty years. Warner offered $900,000 and the ageing Witmark family couldn't resist. Warner would use the company as a vehicle to publish all new musical compositions that came their way. They called together their songwriting teams and told them that in future everything they wrote would be assigned to the film company whether it was used or not.

Other studios were thinking along the same lines. Paramount grabbed Famous Music; Fox Studios went for Red Star Publishing; RKO's cash seduced Leo Feist; and MGM picked up a majority shareholding of Jack Robbins' company for nothing more than a $75,000 loan, and then bought Mills Music too. Hollywood was devouring the music publishing industry.

For a while, some of the biggest music publishers hung on and rejected offers from Hollywood. But on the morning of 24th October, 1929, the New York Stock Exchange suffered a panic sell-off of shares. The market bounced back a bit that afternoon but on the ensuing Monday it plummeted. America was in the midst of the Great Depression.

The crash hit the remaining publishers hard. At Harms, Max Dreyfus found most of his writers had lost everything. They came to him for help and he obliged. In the afternoon he called staff arranger Russell Bennett into his office. "This morning I cleaned out that desk," Max told him, "I'm no longer a millionaire."

Warner pounced. Harms was the biggest music publishing company in America. For four million dollars the Dreyfus brothers sold Harms, Chappell-Harms, De Sylva Brown & Henderson, Remick Music, T. B. Harms (Jerome Kern's publisher), and New World Music (George Gershwin's). Warner Studios was now the biggest music publishing company in the world.

With the sale of Harms, Max Dreyfus was rich again, but his sales contract with Warner prevented him from starting a new company for five years. He had to stay and work with them, overseeing their new publishing empire. The sign on his door called him 'Executive Head of Warner Publishing'. His contract called him an 'advisor'.

"All hooey," he said. "Picture people don't take advice. They give orders."

Of the other publishers who'd sold out to Hollywood, some were making better use of their new affiliation than others. MGM had picked up Robbins music for a song, offering Jack Robbins a $75,000 loan in exchange for 51 per cent of the company. Everyone thought he was crazy for accepting, but afterwards, operating with a minimum of expense and no professional staff except himself, Robbins took advantage of being part of the MGM group and hired uniformed pages to stand in the lobbies of MGM movie theatres selling sheet music and recordings of songs from their new musical, *Broadway Melody*, which featured music published by his now jointly owned company. Before long Robbins' remaining shares in the company were worth double the value of the whole company before he sold out to MGM.

Buddy De Sylva was doing well too. Immediately after he'd tied up with Warner, his company got a hit with 'Sonny Boy', written in just an hour by Lew Brown and Ray Henderson after a phone call from Al Jolson, (who as usual got a share). On the back of this success De Sylva had urged the same two writers to drum up some ideas for a stage musical and now they'd set a new record – four shows running on Broadway simultaneously.

Edward B. Marks and the few other publishers who'd refused to sell out to Hollywood were upset by the way the movie industry was changing popular songs. In movies, music served a different purpose to musical shows. Musical shows on Broadway were a way of popularising songs so sheet music could be sold. In films the purpose was simply to bring in movie-goers by the million. So the new music publishers – the studios – no longer demanded their songwriters write simple 32-bar songs in a standard format. Composers were free to compose songs in whatever way they wanted so long as they bought in the audience. This produced some great music, but for the publishers dependent on selling printed sheet music it meant another slump in profits – it added extra pages and extra printing costs and the final songs were not easily played by amateur pianists. So the publishers who hadn't sold out were now being squeezed out instead.

But just as some of these more traditional publishers were on the point of giving up, everything changed. The studios had overplayed their hand. Too many musicals had been made and there weren't enough good songs to go round; moreover, the Depression had changed moviegoers' tastes. They no longer wanted music and glamour; they wanted action. All of a sudden Hollywood lost its enthusiasm for music publishing and retreated as fast as it had attacked. Having spent nine million dollars buying major shareholdings in music publishing, Warner now turned the day-to-day running of its music holdings back to the former owners. Songwriters imported to Hollywood were sent back to New York at the expiration of their contracts. The music staff at big studios was cut down, sometimes to a single person. Overnight, Hollywood stopped using popular songs almost completely; if a musical sequence was needed here and there it would be written by the few trained composers still on salary – Alfred Newman at United Artists, Max Steiner at RKO, and Leo Forbstein at Warner. Those people were now responsible for all the music in all the films their studios produced. They wrote lyrics, made orchestrations and conducted the final recording sessions using as few musicians as possible.

Music mania had died. In 1931 just one musical was made – *The Smiling Lieutenant* starring Maurice Chevalier. Amongst all the movie companies there was a drop from 143 songwriters employed in 1929 to just twenty in 1931. De Sylva Brown & Henderson, flush from successes on Broadway, even managed to buy themselves back from Warner for three million dollars.

Warner's new stock in trade was cheap gangster movies made up of unscripted brawling and gunfire, with unknown actors and maximum violence. It was what Depression era audiences seemed to enjoy most. The studios also lost their interest in the record companies they'd bought. Like everything else during the Depression, records weren't doing well. In the years following the stock market crash, record sales dropped from 104 million to six million. All three of the major labels, Victor, Columbia and Brunswick dropped their most expensive artists. The best-selling recording in 1931 was 'Little White Lies' by Johnny Marvin, which sold 40,000 copies compared with 350,000 for a best-seller three years previously. Warner decided they'd made a mistake buying Brunswick Records, it had caused them nothing but problems, so they sold it to American Record, a wholesaler of three-for-a-dollar records to mail-order-catalogues. And Victor, having dropped to second place behind American Record, had to move into the discount record market. They cut down on location recording and dismissed Ralph Peer.

In the USA, at the end of 1932, business of all sorts was operating at less than half its 1929 volume. Cities had soup kitchens and people sold apples on the street corner. The total amount paid in wages across the country was 60 per cent less than previously. For every four cars produced in 1929, only one was produced now. Foreign trade slumped, blue chip stocks fell, coal prices plummeted, and there were over thirteen million unemployed – one in four of the national labour force.

Yet amongst all this gloom there was one growth industry. Two out of every five homes in the USA now had a wireless set. During a time of slump and low wages it was the best value there was in entertainment.

The Great Depression had created radio lift-off.

17

Same Old Song And Dance
BRITISH RECORD COMPANIES RE-ALIGN

In Britain record sales had dropped from ten million to 4.5 million and Columbia and HMV were forced into a merger. The new company would be EMI – Electric and Musical Industries, under the management of Louis Sterling.

Meanwhile, Max Dreyfus, rich again from having sold out to Warners, had used the money from the Warner deal to buy the remaining shares in Chappell. It meant that both the top record company and the top publishing company in Britain were controlled by New Yorkers – Louis Sterling at EMI, and Louis Dreyfus at Chappell.

Despite both being Jewish-American immigrants, Sterling from Russia, Dreyfus from Germany, the two Louis were hugely different. Louis Dreyfus was charming but scheming; he liked to compromise, but only if he ended up better off than the person with whom he was compromising. Sterling was impatient; he wanted an instant solution to everything and usually found one.

At Chappell, Dreyfus was happy to be quietly in charge behind-the-scenes. At EMI, Sterling liked to be upfront and visible. He immediately fell out with the company's new Chairman, Alfred Clark, who prior to the merger had been the top man at HMV. For the next eight years, despite sitting on the board together, they only corresponded by letter. Sterling thought the HMV team were dull and uninspired but called the team he'd bought with him from Columbia an "active, aggressive, intelligent organisation".

The new company was enormous. It included Pathé Frères in France, Carl Lindstrom and Electrola in Germany, Columbia Nipponophone in Japan, Pathé Orient and the China Record Co. in China, and GramCo in India. There were subsidiaries in Australia, Italy, Spain, Romania and South America, and fifty factories in nineteen countries. It was also linked to Victor through the American company's shareholdings in it.

EMI was by far the biggest record company in the world. To celebrate its birth Louis Sterling opened Britain's best recording studio in Abbey Road, North London. To stimulate record sales his engineers designed a new EMI gramophone to sell for one pound six shillings and four pence. And to better train his salesmen he told them they must always wear a hat and carry a packet of cigarettes, even if they were non-smokers. One of them was L.G.Wood who thirty years later became EMI's managing director. "You wore a hat in order to be able to take it off when you greeted the retailer, and you could also offer them a cigarette."

Before the Columbia–EMI merger, realising there was going to be a big future in gramophones, a young stockbroker called Edward Lewis had decided to invest in a company that manufactured them. He bought a small company called Decca, the manufacturing arm of a company called Duophone. But within weeks of acquiring it, he was telling friends, "A company manufacturing gramophones but not records is rather like one making razors but not the consumable blades." So when he heard that Duophone's other division, the Unbreakable Record Company was in trouble, he stepped in and bought that too.

When Decca's first records appeared, *Phono Record* told its readers, "Decca have carried out intensive research so as to attain the best acoustic results, and the methods adopted are based on the very latest practices."

Actually, it was a load of rubbish, something written by the Decca press office. There had been no intensive research; they'd simply covered the walls of the studio with thick curtains to deaden the sound. And unlike EMI, which was experimenting with using multiple microphones, at Decca they stuck to the old method of using a single microphone and letting the musicians and singers find the correct balance between them.

The first important artist released on the Decca label was Ambrose and his Orchestra, the new band at the Savoy Hotel. Shortly afterwards, Edward Lewis pulled the remarkable coup of tempting Jack Hylton's Band away from EMI. Hylton was the biggest artist in Britain. In an average year his band played two performances on every day of the year and travelled in excess of 60,000 miles. In ten years the band had recorded 1,700 sides and sold seven million records.

To get him, Lewis had offered 40,000 shares and a place on the Decca board. Hylton was not from the same upper middle-class background as the rest of the board; he had the wrong kind of accent. Sigismund Mendl, the chairman, was furious. "You don't have that sort of man as a director," he complained.

Lewis over-ruled the complaints and the Jack Hylton Band gave Decca its first big hit – 300,000 copies. It was an amazing figure for such depressed times and it greatly riled EMI. Lewis then riled them even further by having his private notepaper headed with the words, "Jack Hylton & his Orchestra now record exclusively for Decca". The biggest problem for him came from Ambrose, whose orchestra had been Decca's number one act before the arrival of Hylton. He solved it by having a chat with Louis Dreyfus at Chappell.

Dreyfus had been planning to take Chappell into the record business too and had bought the British rights to Brunswick, but he was now having second thoughts.

Lewis persuaded him to give up the idea and sell the rights on to Decca. Once he'd got them, he switched Ambrose to the Brunswick label where he was once again the biggest artist on the label, though only the biggest British artist, because amongst Brunswick's acts from America were Bing Crosby and Duke Ellington.

Decca's new connection with America's top artists helped Jack Hylton. When the Ellington band came to play a tour of Europe, Decca arranged to get Hylton onto the French leg of the tour making it a two-band show. A British journalist saw Hylton dining with Ellington at Bricktops, the top jazz venue in Paris. He confirmed what Sigismund Mendl had feared about him being of the wrong class.

Jack Hylton was there too. Flabby and pot-bellied like an English pork butcher; he was rocking grotesquely in his chair. Overwhelmed by heat and liquor, he had a red, congested face and was splattering food on his neighbors and wiping it off mechanically when it fell on his jacket. Alongside him, Duke gave the impression of a prince of the blood, on whom had been imposed the company of a stupid upstart.

Jack Hylton was one of many bandleaders who fell foul of the BBC for taking payment for playing songs. The London *Daily Express* came into possession of a letter that proved payments were being made to British bandleaders for plugging songs on radio broadcasts. The letter was from nine London music publishers sent to the top bandleaders telling them from now on there would be a set scale for plugs. Tired of bidding against each other, these nine publishers had united to try and limit their expenses by agreeing to pay no more than £1 a play to get songs plugged on air.

This sort of graft was made worse by the BBC paying no fees to bands that played on air, the prestige of playing for the BBC being considered sufficient compensation. After the revelations in the *Daily Express*, the BBC agreed to start paying the bands the Musicians Union minimum rate, but bandleaders would have to give up selecting the music they played. The BBC naively believed this would stop the problem but it simply led to the American system of 'special arrangements'. The bandleader was paid by the publisher to make a new arrangement of each song each time it was played. If he played the song ten times he'd get paid for ten different arrangements, though he certainly wouldn't make them.

It was a nicer term to use than bribe but straightforward bribing was happening too. And cut-ins. The Music Publishers Association set up a study group to look at the situation and their report said, "agreements among publishers are farcical and as soon as they decide on some unanimous action, some immediately break their pledges".

A letter was sent to every bandleader telling them the BBC would no longer allow "the acceptance of special orchestrations, gifts or direct or indirect money payments from publishers, in consideration of their performing the works of particular publishers..." It asked bandleaders to give a written undertaking not to accept payments from publishers to play specific songs during a broadcast.

The bandleaders unanimously refused. They jointly announced that none of them had ever done such a terrible thing, nor ever would. How dare the BBC make such a vile and demeaning insinuation.

The BBC was forced to apologise. And everything went on as before.

18

Set 'Em Up Joe
BOOZE MAKES A COMEBACK

The music business has always been full of opportunists. They see an opening and grab it. They may not be fully qualified; they may not have really earned the right; but they jump in and grab it and hang on, then build something out of it.

In the early part of the century Paul Whiteman was asked to provide his photo as the face for a recording by someone else. When it was a hit he grabbed the opportunity to turn himself into the biggest bandleader in America – *The King of Jazz*, no less.

Ralph Peer had his lucky break the day Perry Bradford came wandering into Okeh Records and asked them to record Mamie Smith. The resulting hit gave Peer the opportunity to become one of America's biggest music publishers.

Jack Robbins bumped into Duke Ellington and took advantage of the moment by asking him to write a musical. He pawned his wedding ring to pay for it and ended up making a fortune from a hit show that travelled all over Europe.

But the biggest opportunist of all was Jack Kapp.

Kapp's big opportunity came in 1925 when Brunswick Records asked him if he could travel round the southern states finding new artists for the company. When he found a few good ones, Brunswick put him in charge of signing their entire roster. He became known in the trade as a "man of no taste, so corny he's good". He built up the best stable of biggest-selling artists of any record label including Bing Crosby, Mae West, the Mills Brothers, Isham Jones, the Casa Loma Orchestra, Guy Lombardo, and the Dorsey brothers. But Kapp's opportunistic masterstroke was to take advantage of Brunswick's sloppy business procedures. At the company's expense, and without anyone knowing, he signed all the artists to himself personally.

In 1932, in the new mood of American optimism that followed the end of Prohibition, Kapp travelled to London and talked with Edward Lewis at Decca Records. Kapp told Lewis, if he agreed to invest in a new company, Kapp would bring with him almost the entire artist roster of Brunswick. Lewis promised $250,000 if Kapp could assemble a complete recording, merchandising, and distributing operation that could compete with Victor or Brunswick.

Unlike EMI, which was an amalgamation of Columbia and HMV, both founded by expatriate Americans living in London, Decca was the first truly British record company. For it to gatecrash America was truly audacious, but it did. The new company was American Decca, with Kapp as its president. The first recording sessions were scheduled and *Variety* reported that Decca's discs would be sold for 35 cents or three for a dollar. Kapp believed cheap records by top artists would outsell the seventy-five-cent ranges of Victor, Columbia and Brunswick. But Decca's first batch of records turned out faulty. The records were warped and improperly grooved and Edward Lewis had to save the day with an extra injection of $400,000 – more than his original investment.

Even with that, Decca's first year was nearly disastrous. Some of its most demanding creditors were its own artists. Hugh Mendl, the chairman's son, worked in the New York office. "Bing Crosby and his brother Everett were very understanding and wouldn't take the royalties when there weren't any to pay, whereas Guy Lombardo used to send his brother up, looking very Italian and Mafia-like, and sit in the outer office until they got the money."

What kept Decca going was the jukebox.

Until the thirties they'd been called 'nickel in the slot' phonographs. But when the Depression left people with no cash for a night out, dancing to a machine that played records was a good substitute. 'To jook' was southern black slang for 'to party', so places that had a 'nickel in the slot' phonograph became known as jook joints. And from there the word jukebox came into being.

The repeal of Prohibition and the re-opening of drinking establishments, coincided with several manufacturers developing new and better ones. For each speakeasy that closed, five new places opened in their place – bars, taverns, or saloons – and for a nickel, a drinker could escape the Depression for three minutes.

The jukebox put the overall choice of music programming in the bar-owner's hands. Local music styles could be given preference – hillbilly in South Eastern states, blues and jazz in black areas. And with no censorship, saloon bar jukeboxes always had plenty of bawdy songs or sexually suggestive blues.

Record sales in the USA had fallen so badly that an average hit only sold 25,000 records but with jukeboxes Decca found its niche. It alone operated 100,000 of them and with jukebox operators changing records every two or three weeks it was a great way to both plug records and sell them. Decca sold records to jukebox operators at 21 cents, and very soon jukebox sales were accounting for 40 per cent of the company's total output.

By the end of 1933 there were around 250,000 jukeboxes spread across America accounting for nearly half the total record sales in the country. It was a shot in the arm for record companies, but not for music publishers and writers. In

1909, when the copyright law was enacted, listening to mechanically reproduced music in public places had usually meant end-of-the-pier peep shows. Congress decided this was a method of advertising songs and therefore not subject to a royalty. The decision had never been repealed so from jukeboxes there were no performance royalties.

But if that was a downside for publishers, the upside was that jukeboxes were a plugger's dream. New songs could be put onto them and pluggers would go from bar to bar putting in a few nickels and checking the listeners' reactions. If they didn't catch anyone's ear, they were quickly replaced with other new songs.

Jukeboxes, though, were only a stopgap. What really put the music industry back on its feet was Hollywood.

In 1932, Warner Studios decided to try another musical. They chose two songwriters with Broadway experience, Al Dubin and Harry Warren, both signed to Warner through Remick, one of the publishing companies the studios had bought during their buying spree.

The film was *42nd Street*. Intended as a low-budget movie set amongst Manhattan show business, Warner's modest plans for the movie were spoilt by the unexpected brilliance of the dance director, Busby Berkeley, a Broadway choreographer doing his first movie. He had a sixth sense for what a film camera could see that a theatre audience couldn't and the production cost mounted with each new dance sequence.

But what a turn around! On 9th March 1933 the film premiered in New York and when Warner saw the crowds that turned up for it, they turned on the promotion. They filled a train with starlets and showbiz reporters and sent it steaming around the country. *42nd Street* became the biggest grossing film of the year taking in $2,300,000 – a profit of two million dollars. Musicals were back with a bang.

In 1934, eighty-four were produced, of which Warner made sixteen. In Hollywood there was a one hundred times increase in the creation of original music, not just for musicals but for expensive dramatic productions too. Classically trained screen composers were found, signed and publicised, and film posters included strange names the general public had never heard of – Ernst Toch, George Antheil, Leopold Stokowski, and Erich Wolfgang Korngold.

The studio's musical dogsbodies also came into their own. Max Steiner, Alfred Newman and Leo Forbstein were put in charge of expanded music departments and began to get their names on the end titles. Warner employed a full-time symphony orchestra and other studios had agreements for the exclusive services of the best remaining West Coast musicians. 20th Century Fox even used trained musicians to help edit their films.

In 1929, before the Depression, Irving Berlin had gone to Hollywood during the brief boom in music-making but hadn't had a good experience. He'd written songs for a United Artists movie called *Putting On The Ritz* but had been unable to control the process to his liking. He felt he'd had a sub-standard director and bad sound recording equipment.

For his next movie he came up with a story he'd written himself, *Reaching For The Moon*, and persuaded United Artists to back it. It started out all right but half way through United Artists got cold feet and Berlin lost all confidence in himself. "I developed the damndest feeling of inferiority. I got so I called in anybody to listen to my songs – stockroom boys, secretaries. One blink of an eye and I was stuck."

At the last minute United Artists held a press screening of the movie. When it wasn't well received they decided to change it from a musical to a comedy and cut out all the songs except the title theme. Berlin went back to New York vowing never to do movies again. But his return to the East Coast coincided with the Depression. Broadway was in a slump.

Producer Charles Dillingham had so little money he had to put on Jerome Kern's new show with nothing but drapes for a backdrop. And then he did a bunk with the takings. Shortly afterwards Ziegfeld went bankrupt. Then the Shuberts. The only person Irving Berlin could find to work with was Sam Harris, his partner in the Music Box Theatre he owned.

Berlin had a new show in mind but their theatre had a tenant they couldn't evict; George Gershwin's *Of Thee I Sing* was proving totally Depression-proof. So Sam Harris hired the New Amsterdam theatre, and with a budget that was half of what Berlin used a few years earlier, they mounted *Face The Music*. By Depression standards it was a smash, running for 165 shows, which encouraged them to do another one, *As Thousands Cheer*.

The new show included Berlin's big Depression-busting song, 'Easter Parade'. Inspired by the optimism of 'Pack Up Your Troubles In Your Old Kit Bag', he'd written it during the First World War and called it 'Smile and Show Your Dimple'. It had flopped miserably, but now, with the first line changed to 'In Your Easter Bonnet' it turned out to be just what people needed to lift them out of their depressed mood.

The female lead was Ethel Waters, the first black woman to star on Broadway, a perfect example of someone being lifted out of depression. She'd been born to a thirteen-year-old girl who had been raped. Her debut as an entertainer was for $10 a week at the Lincoln Theatre in Baltimore – not as grand as its name suggested, it was long overdue for demolition. She'd grown so tall she was billed as Sweet Mama Stringbean, and from there things got even worse. She ended up at Edmond Johnson's Cellar at 132nd and 5th, one of Harlem's seediest hangouts, frequented mostly by transvestite hookers.

"The last stop on the way down", she recalled. "After you worked there, there was no place to go except into domestic service."

As Thousands Cheer was Irving Berlin's biggest ever Broadway hit. The show rescued him completely. As co-producer he took 40 per cent of its profits and a further cut for being composer and lyricist. He also took six cents a copy on the sheet music, which was published by his own company. And to celebrate the show's success, NBC Radio ran a five-programme retrospective of Berlin's first twenty-five years as 'America's greatest songwriter', playing all his biggest hits starting from 1910 with 'My Wife's Gone To The Country'.

With the Depression leveling out and Prohibition about to end, Berlin decided it was time to have another try at breaking into Hollywood. And within months of going back there he'd shamed all the other music publishers at their own game.

In 1933, RKO Pictures had enjoyed a moderate success with *The Gay Divorcee*, a cheaply made movie starring Fred Astaire. Astaire, whose Broadway career had faded and whose film career hadn't yet taken off, had done it for next to nothing. He'd had no choice; the RKO executive who auditioned him wrote on his report sheet, "can't act, slightly bald, also dances".

The studio's temporary boss, Pandro Berman, was only there because the real boss had suffered a heart attack and was away recuperating. Wanting to make a name for himself quickly he'd paired Astaire with Ginger Rogers. Although the film was based on a Broadway show by Irving Berlin most of the songs were replaced by new ones written by an RKO staff writer. When the movie was a success Berman decided he wanted to top it.

Which was exactly the moment Berlin turned up. He didn't want to go back to United Artists with whom he'd had a bad experience and he felt there was more chance of keeping control of a movie at RKO than at Warner or Fox. So there he was on the doorstep just when Berman was planning to make another movie as much like *The Gay Divorcee* as possible, except better. And what could make it better than Irving Berlin himself writing the music?

In keeping with the position he was aspiring to as Hollywood's number one film composer, Berlin demanded a number one fee – a one-off payment of $100,000. It was an unheard of sum, three times more than any songwriter had ever asked for before. Berman offered him $75,000, and Berlin said OK, providing he got 10 per cent of the movie's gross takings.

The deal was settled at 10 per cent of the gross over $1,250,000. Berman reckoned if the movie topped $1,250,000 he would be a hero with the RKO board, so paying a percentage wouldn't matter.

The film was *Top Hat* and it took three million dollars in its first year, earning Irving Berlin $300,000. But he'd negotiated more than just that. The songs were his. They were signed to his publishing company. The studio had no hold on them and earned no money from them.

To other Hollywood studio bosses it was unspeakable idiocy – studios always took the rights to songs. And to other publishers it was astounding audacity – who would dare propose that to a film studio?

Only Irving Berlin!

19

Heard it All Before
MUSIC STAGNATES

"Sammy! What are you doing here?"

"Well, I have this song."

"*You* write songs?"

Sammy Cahn was a teenager trying to sell his first song. Lou Levy was a friend from high school. Since leaving he'd earned his living by winning the dance competition at the Roseland Ballroom every week then selling the silver cup back to them for $7. Next door was the Roseland Building, full of one-room offices housing hopeful new music publishers. There was a great atmosphere in the building – brash, hypey, and endlessly confident – a good place for bumping into someone and making a deal.

Sammy and Lou's chance meeting led to them forming a publishing company, Leeds Music. Lou got the job of running it; Sammy and another friend, Saul Kaplan, would write the songs. Youthfully optimistic, they sent one of their first efforts to bandleader Jimmy Lunceford and a few days later Sammy Cahn got a call. "What a thrill, what a kick, what happiness! Mr. Georgie Joy of the Santly-Joy Music Company…."

Mr. Joy said he wanted to publish their song, 'Rhythm Is Our Business'. Since this was a legitimate publisher, their friend Lou and the new publishing company they'd formed with him went completely out of Sammy and Saul's thoughts; they rushed to sign the song to Mr Joy. They shouldn't have done.

"We were later to learn that this very nice man was actually taking advantage of us, because what we didn't know was that Mr. Joy knew Lunceford had already recorded 'Rhythm Is Our Business' for the Decca label and it was the flip side of 'Stardust'."

The easiest way for any publisher to make money for nothing was to get a 'B' side. The 'A' side was what sold the record but the mechanical royalty for the 'B' side paid exactly the same amount. A 'B' side by Jimmy Lunceford meant automatic sales. But by signing with Santly-Joy, Sammy and Saul had given up the share of royalties that would otherwise have gone to their new company. Lou Levy lost out. And to add insult to injury Lunceford demanded a cut-in.

It was a lesson well learnt, and thereafter every song Sammy and Saul wrote went into Leeds Music no matter what other publishers offered.

Leeds was typical of the youthful new companies starting up. Driven by optimism and energy, when they found their route to success obstructed by an annoying music-business institutions like ASCAP or MPPA or the Hollywood Studios, these young guys weren't bothered, they found a way round it.

Finding a way round being tied to Warner for five years, Max Dreyfus had sent his brother to England to buy Chappell. Now, with his barring clause ended, he opened a Chappell office in New York and focused on what he knew best – Broadway shows.

Brother Louis was doing the same in London, investing in West End productions of shows from Broadway, and originating shows in London to ship back to America. With Max back in action, the two brothers set about their plan of making Chappell the world's number one music publisher.

They were now well off. Max had made money from Warner and Louis was making money from Chappell in the UK, but they were careful how they spent it. Max took a pokey little office in a building on 45th Street. Lyricist Edward Eliscu complained about the size of the lift. "The building had a tiny elevator, so small that it could hardly accommodate four songwriters." Yet on some days those four songwriters might be George Gershwin, Cole Porter, Vincent Youmans, and Jerome Kern.

All Max's 'boys' came back to him. They knew they would get better deals with him than anyone else. Even Irving Berlin had become part of Max's circle having assigned Chappell the overseas rights to his songs. Berlin even had his own office in Chappell's London building for which Max and Louis charged him. What Berlin didn't know was that they were also charging Richard Rodgers for the same office. Since the two of them never showed up at the same time neither of them ever found out; the staff just switched around pictures on the wall and memorabilia on the desk to suit the arrival of whoever was coming to town.

In New York, Max occasionally got visits from some of Louis' writers from London. The most famous of these was Noël Coward, whom *The New Yorker* called, "the one foreign songwriter to capture the imagination of American theatre-goers". Whenever Coward was in town, he became the centre of what screenwriter Leonard Spigelgass described as "the most exclusive club in New York... a club into which you couldn't get".

The club he was referring to included not only Coward, but Cole Porter, Larry Hart, and film director George Cukor – "that was their world... that was Somerset Maugham... that was Noël Coward... those houses on 55th Street with butlers and the carry on..."

He was talking about the still very underground club of show-business homosexuals. Max and Louis had no objections to it; they must have been pleased to see Larry Hart and Cole Porter continuing their friendship with Noël Coward. By introducing them to each other in Venice ten years earlier, Coward had given Porter the push he needed to commit himself to songwriting. Without that push, Porter might have carried on forever as the eternal dilettante.

Even so, his lifestyle still reflected his previous playboy attitude. Born into a millionaire family, and marrying into another one, money was never a worry, and throughout the Depression he wrote buoyant carefree songs and had the most shows on Broadway of any composer. He permanently occupied the presidential suite at the Waldorf Towers, maintained homes in New England and California, and employed a butler, a maid and a secretary. He wore a fresh carnation in his lapel every morning and put on a fresh pair of white socks each time he dressed. And although he was in an exclusive 'club' with Noël Coward, it was just one of three exclusive clubs of which he was a member. The second was to be, along with Noël Coward and Irving Berlin, one of the only top songwriters to write both melodies and lyrics to all his songs. And the third was to be one of Max Dreyfus's 'boys'.

In New York, when Prohibition ended, the city's principal nightlife left Harlem and moved downtown. 52nd Street became the new centre of evening entertainment, especially the Onyx club, which had previously been a speakeasy. A whole row of bars and clubs sprang up featuring music and shows, or rather sprang down, since they were all in the basements of what had once been expensive town houses.

Just across the street were both the CBS and NBC radio studios. Musicians working in them would leave their instruments in their preferred clubs rather than taking them home, then stop in for a beer and a blow whenever they felt like it. Apart from the Onyx, some of the other clubs in the street were the Hickory House, the Famous Door, the Yacht Club and Kelly's Stable. For musicians who'd spent the day playing dull sessions to make a living, these were places they could let off steam.

It was at that moment the country went big band crazy, and 52nd Street became the number one place for bandleaders to find new talent. It was famous for new musicians arriving, sitting in with the house band, and being booked into a band the next day.

One of the first bands to make their name through playing on 52nd Street was the Count Basie band. Booking agent Willard Alexander heard them in their hometown of Kansas City and wanted to showcase them on 52nd Street, but the clubs were all too small for a big band and turned him down. It was mid-summer and steaming hot so Alexander told the owners of the Famous Door, if they would book the Basie band he would pay to install air-conditioning. They accepted.

For Alexander it was the high spot of his career. "It was crazy... Those guys didn't play together. They used to breathe together... in that small place, fourteen men played as one! You could feel the pulsations inside you."

Jazz historian Charles Edward Smith was there too. "Count Basie's fourteen men playing 'King Porter Stomp' with such steam that the leader's hands dropped off the piano and he sat listening with a slight, incredulous smile."

Big bands were taking over America; every type of music was being played by them, from ballads to jazz to waltzes. It quickly became the only way popular songs were ever heard, at the local dance hall, in hotel ballrooms, or on the radio. Every restaurant or hotel lobby that once had a small musical group now had a big band. *The New Yorker*'s music writer thought that, "having a big band was a disease of the time". Jazz critic Marshall Stearns wrote, "bandleaders became as popular – and unpredictable – as movie stars".

People going to ballrooms were now paying to look as well as listen, and bandleaders became showmen. The biggest was Benny Goodman. When the Goodman band played at the Paramount theatre in New York in the winter of 1936, five thousand young people turned up at a theatre that only held three thousand. They danced in the aisles and trampled the ushers, dodged the policemen in front of the bandstand and jumped up on stage dancing the Shag, the Lindy Hop and the Big Apple – all of them imported from Harlem. The *Saturday Evening Post* later wrote, "No other band of this quality had ever had such popular acceptance. In the past year and a half it had sold more records, played longer runs and scored higher ratings than any band of its kind in the history of American popular music... If any one musician brought along the Swing age, it was Benny Goodman."

Goodman's band played with a hard drive but there were dozens of these bands around, each with a different musical nuance. The Harry James band featured lush trumpet solos; Woody Herman's, a rippling clarinet; Bob Crosby's, a hint of Dixieland; Guy Lombardo's, silky smooth saxophones. The Count Basie band was known for its relaxed propulsion, Tommy Dorsey's for swinging at a hushed volume, and Duke Ellington's for its jumpy tunes and catchy titles, like 'It Don't Mean a Thing if it Ain't Got that Swing.'

By the mid-thirties, America had 18,000 musicians on the road and dance music was grossing $80 million a year. The bands were endless, each a self-contained road show of musicians, soloists, dancers, singers... and the bandleader. And although their route round the country was dictated by the live shows they played, their value to music publishers came from their performances on local radio in each town they visited. *Variety* wrote, "Radio now is the thought by day and the dream by night of all song pluggers."

Each time a bandleader arrived at a radio station there would be a crowd of them waiting to pounce on him and offer bribes. "Flattery, cases of Scotch, cigars, and floral offerings to bandsmen's wives... all with just one purpose."

Claude Mills at MPPA decided to put a stop to it. The MPPA fine for bribing a bandleader was $1,500. Claude Mills now decided it should be lowered to $150. This, he thought, would help stamp out the practice because $1,500 was such a severe penalty no publisher would want to snitch on another. For $150 perhaps they would.

They didn't. Instead, plugging went even further out of control – gifting, bribing, cutting-in – anything a music publisher or his plugger could devise.

For bandleaders it was sometimes a risky thing to get involved in. It wasn't the fear of repercussions from the industry; it was the public. Guy Lombardo was known for never doing cut-in deals with pluggers. One night he found himself in New York sitting with bandleader Jack Denny, who'd come down from Canada to play a season at the Waldorf. Lombardo decided to test him.

"See all those song-pluggers sitting there in the back of the room," Lombardo said. "They're a pain in the neck. If they didn't cut me in on their songs, I'd throw them the hell out of here."

Denny's ears perked up and he let the pluggers know he'd be open to a few cut-ins himself. Shortly afterwards, amidst great fanfare, he opened at the Waldorf, but he was no longer playing the tried and tested songs that had made his band famous; the Waldorf customers had to listen to the junk he'd accepted from every plugger who'd promised him a percentage of the profits. And he didn't finish out the summer.

Even so, many bandleaders simply couldn't resist the temptation. A current hit song might have three different bandleaders cut in on the royalties – one working in New York, one in Chicago, one in San Francisco. Some bandleaders were on the payrolls of five or six different publishing houses, they would even boast to each other how many songs they were cut-in on each week; top bandleaders might be cut in on as many as forty songs at the same time. *Variety* reported Rudy Vallée as saying "he doesn't feature anything he's not in on and he is supposed to be the No.1 money-getter on song royalties with his earnings placed at $75,000 from that source."

Many of the publishers involved in graft objected to it yet continued paying it anyway. Edward B. Marks complained that bandleaders not only demanded $25 for each song they played on radio, they grumbled "if payment is not made pronto".

Louis Bernstein was particularly disdainful of having to pay for 'special arrangements'. "People are being bribed to perform inferior music and today some of the poorest songs on record are being dinned into the ears of the American public for this reason."

MPPA tried again. They made the fine $1,000 for a first offence, rising to $2,000 for the second, and any publisher who reported another would be paid one third of the fine imposed.

ASCAP went even further. Its publisher members unanimously passed a resolution to "curb the evil of cut-ins". Any one of them found guilty of splitting royalties with orchestra leaders, or other entertainers, would be placed in ASCAP's 'non-participating' class for six months and receive no dividends. The ban was not retroactive, so songs published with a cut-in after the date the ban started would be okay providing the deal had been made prior to it coming into force.

Variety reported that during the last week before it took effect publishers went "on a wholesale rampage of cutting-in…. one leader made no bones about telling the publishers that he is now cut-in on enough songs to carry him for two years".

And of course, the publishers who were doing this were the same ones who'd pressured ASCAP to take action against cut-ins in the first place.

In 1935, the first network radio programme to broadcast the top ten songs started, *Your Hit Parade*. Its sponsors were Lucky Strike cigarettes and the programme was run and controlled not by the network but by the sponsor's advertising agency, BBDO (Batten Barton Durstine & Osborn). Each Saturday evening, the programme presented the fifteen bestselling songs of the week, with a fanfare for each of the top three leading to the finale – that week's number one. The songs were more important than the singers, so a stable of vocalists went uncredited and were paid only $100 per programme.

Listeners were told that the order of the songs was the result of surveying best-selling sheet music, best-selling records, songs most heard on air and the ones most played on jukeboxes. In fact, the show's ad agency never revealed the exact methods they used to determine hits, and until the show was actually in rehearsal the final run down was never revealed in full, even to the show's producers. Songs to be in each week's show were phoned through to the producers a few at a time and the people working on the show only found out the order as rehearsals proceeded.

It became an obsession with most of America to know what each week's number one would be. Every publisher in the country did everything they could to get their songs in the show. From experience they found radio performances of songs during the first three days of the week had the biggest influence. For those three days, bandleaders could name their price. And the people most willing to pay it were the people who owned the most publishing companies, the movie studios, especially Warner.

There was nothing musically stimulating about this new obsession with the Top 15. Week after week the songs all sounded much the same. Meanwhile, 65 per cent of all of the money distributed by ASCAP went to just thirteen publishing companies owned by or connected with Hollywood interests. Songwriters writing for Hollywood wrote only for their monthly paychecks. There were unlikely to be any royalties because songs written for the movies had none of the traditional, simplistic elements that appealed to sheet music buyers.

Of the old time music publishers, only one consistently got his own way with the studios – Irving Berlin. In 1937, the biggest film of the year was *Alexander's Ragtime Band*, a fictional account of Irving Berlin's life, with all the songs by Berlin. The second biggest film of the year was *Snow White and the Seven Dwarfs* by Walt Disney. Amazingly, Irving Berlin persuaded the Disney Corporation to publish the music from the film with one of his companies – the Bourne Company, owned jointly by Berlin and Saul Bornstein. That year, Irving Berlin earned more money from movie music than even Warner Studios.

But the fact that he and other top songwriters were making big money didn't mean popular music was in a healthy state. The majority of people across America heard their music only from radio – live music chosen by bandleaders bribed by Hollywood studios. It became an endless repetition of the same thing. Popular music was stagnating.

Except for one small thing...

Al Jarvis, a Canadian, had quit banking in the mid-thirties to move to Los Angeles and become a staff announcer at radio KFWB. Most music on the station was by live bands bribed by Hollywood and when records were occasionally played they were announced in a monotone. Jarvis began to add chatter. For instance, he might say, "This is the new one by Fats Waller, 'Honeysuckle Rose'. A copy given to me by the artist himself. You're going to be the first people in California to hear it and Fats said to send you all his love."

Staff announcers never spoke like that. Ever!

What's more, most of the records Jarvis played on his programme were ones he'd bought and paid for himself. And to give his listeners extra information he read *Billboard* and *Variety* and invented little behind-the-scenes stories. Before long he was getting substantial fan mail and his programme, *Make Believe Ballroom*, became a hit.

A year or so into this, a visiting newsreader from New York heard his programme and decided to copy it – even down to the name. When Martin Block went back to New York he started a show called *The World's Largest Make Believe Ballroom*. What started it was when he was told to play some records between news bulletins and found the radio station didn't have any to play. He ran across the street and bought some by Clyde McCoy's band. As he played them he made out he was talking from a dance hall where the band was playing live, and he even had an imaginary chat with Clyde McCoy. Inside three months he'd acquired four million listeners and was on air for three hours a day.

Block and Jarvis had started the trend towards something entirely new – radio disc jockeys. And although it would be another twenty years before they became commonplace, some people were already forecasting that records might be the future of radio. Maybe of the whole music business.

20

Trouble in Mind
THE WAR BEFORE THE WAR

No doubt about it, ASCAP was a monopoly. It was a society of the elite – top publishers, songwriters, lyricists, and composers – coming together to demand a licence fee from every radio station and movie theatre in the country.

In most things, the world's music industries copied America. When it came to collection societies, America had done the copying. France had been first, with legislation in 1847 requiring performers of music to pay a royalty to its composers. Italy followed in 1882, and Germany in 1903. In 1914, Britain and America formed collection societies, and since then Argentina and Japan had done so too.

In all of them, it was intended that by combining publishers and songwriters into one society there would never be a conflict between the two. But in all these societies and in all these countries, membership was restricted only to top writers and publishers. The conflict was not between writer and publisher but between elite and non-elite, a conflict that mirrored society as a whole.

Of all these countries America was meant to be the most class-free, yet ASCAP only looked after the elite of its music industry. By the end of the thirties there were tens of thousands of songwriters and small publishers all across America, but ASCAP still had only 1,100 members. The society was making ever-increasing profits for its members yet it excluded three-quarters of all songwriters and music publishers in America. Writers had to prove they'd had five 'hits' before they were allowed in, and a 'hit' didn't mean a jazz, blues or country song. The five hits needed to have been mainstream popular music. Gene Autry, the songwriting cowboy movie star, couldn't get in, nor could jazz pianist Jelly Roll Morton, nor blues singer Bessie Smith.

In 1939, under ASCAP's monopoly, radio stations across America were playing much the same music as they'd been playing when radio started in 1920. Sweet, sentimental, cute, nostalgic, danceable – music from the age of Broadway, and latterly of Hollywood – Irving Berlin, Jerome Kern, Rodgers & Hart, Cole Porter, Harold Arlen. Nothing was ever heard that was edgy, risky, provocative or even mildly exciting.

Amongst broadcasters there was growing dissatisfaction with ASCAP. Local radio stations often played music that was not from writers or publishers affiliated to ASCAP. As such, the radio stations shouldn't have to be paying for it, but because ASCAP's license was based on the total number of hours during which the stations played music of any sort, they had to pay anyway. In a coast-to-coast survey *Variety* reported that radio stations saw ASCAP as "working one huge squeeze play whose only virtue seems to be that it is legal".

Not only were ASCAP seen as bully-boys, demanding ever higher license fees, it was rumoured that when its current radio licenses expired at the end of 1940, ASCAP would be doubling its fees. There was also growing resentment amongst new writers and writers who wrote outside of the mainstream of pop music. Top writers in ASCAP didn't much want new members in the society, and they certainly didn't want writers of country music and jazz. They didn't want to dilute their hold on American radio.

In the autumn of 1939, while Britain was getting itself mobilised against Germany, the owners and executives of radio stations across America, led by the two major networks – RCA and CBS – were planning a war on ASCAP. They asked Sydney Kaye, a young copyright attorney, to draw up a plan to form an alternative body. ASCAP laughed.

After the radio executives had received his plan and studied it they decided to go ahead and set up a rival performing rights organization. ASCAP laughed again and doubled its radio license fees.

The new society was BMI, Broadcast Music Industries, and on 15th February 1940 it opened an office in New York with the announcement that it had signed up three-quarters of all the radio stations in America including all the major networks. The new society's licence fees would be half of those charged by ASCAP, and the radio stations who had signed to BMI announced that from the end of the year they would not be renewing their ASCAP licenses. ASCAP still managed a giggle. As far as they could see BMI had no music to license.

But BMI had been working on that. It had persuaded two major publishers to jump ship from ASCAP and join them instead. One was Edward B. Marks, whose catalogue included a huge number of popular songs dating back to the early 1900s. The other was Ralph Peer, whose Southern Music had the greatest catalogue of black and country songs in the world, most of them never before played on radio.

Moreover, when Victor Records executives had finally fired Peer for feathering his own nest, he'd immediately set off for Latin America where he entered into joint ventures with local publishers and brought all their best material back to the USA. Through Southern Music, Peer made alliances in Puerto Rico, Mexico,

Argentina, and Cuba, signed local writers like Pérez Prado and Tito Puente, and added all the most famous Latin songs to his catalogue – 'Granada', 'Mambo Number Five', 'Perfidia', 'Besame Mucho'.

To balance that, Edward B. Marks' catalogue gave advertisers familiar music to help sell products. And on top of this, all the composers, songwriters and small publishers that ASCAP had never allowed in, now rushed to join BMI.

To call BMI's bluff, ASCAP organised a huge party at the California Coliseum in San Francisco to celebrate its silver anniversary. W. C. Handy described it as "a program that was never before nor can ever again be duplicated this side of Kingdom Come". Amongst others, people who performed were George M. Cohan, Albert von Tilzer, Jerome Kern, Sigmund Romberg, Harold Arlen, Hoagy Carmichael and Irving Berlin. Writers sang their own songs or accompanied each other and it finished with Irving Berlin singing his own song, 'God Bless America'. *The San Francisco Chronicle* said, "Hundreds started to sing with him. Then thousands. And when he came to the end of his song, 15,000 Americans were on their feet…"

But ASCAP had totally misjudged the mood of the radio stations. Two months later, when the year came to an end, almost none of them renewed their ASCAP licences. At midnight on New Year's Eve 1940, ASCAP's music disappeared from the airwaves.

For listeners there were no more songs from Broadway or Hollywood – no more music from the masters of American popular music – just a few old songs from Edward B. Marks' catalogue, and a mass of unfamiliar music from Ralph Peer's. ASCAP waited for a howl of protest but there was barely a yawn.

Marks and Peers did well out of it; they hadn't joined for nothing. BMI guaranteed the Marks company performance royalties of $250,000 a year, four times more than it had been receiving from ASCAP. And Ralph Peers, by coming in, would finally get his huge catalogue of black, country and Latin songs heard by the public. Moreover, he could now promise his black and country writers that they could join a collection society, something ASCAP had long denied them.

BMI did something else never done by ASCAP; they brought in a catalogue of classical music. ASCAP had never dealt in classical music; they'd left the individual publishers of works to sort out their own performance royalties directly with radio stations and concert halls. Aaron Copland, who headed the American Composers Alliance, had tried for years but failed to get ASCAP interested in America's top classical composers. BMI stepped into the breach. They negotiated with Boosey and Hawkes, Britain's largest classical publisher and arranged for their entire catalogue to be available for broadcasting in America.

For almost a year BMI music dominated radio throughout America. It was difficult to believe that until now blues and country music had hardly been heard. Network radio had been the personal domain of songs from Hollywood films and Broadway shows. Although big bands had taken over in over the last five years their music was mainly from the movies with film studios paying graft to the bandleaders. Now the music heard on the radio was entirely different and listeners didn't seem to care.

BMI-affiliated radio stations had to take special care to avoid legal action. Since they didn't have ASCAP licenses there had to be absolutely no ASCAP music on their airwaves. If a jazz group was playing live on radio, they had to write out their solos in advance and submit them to the station supervisor to make sure none of their improvised phrases contained hints of ASCAP melodies. It made radio jazz a little less flowing than usual but there were also some benefits.

Billy Strayhorn, Duke Ellington's arranger, had never been allowed into ASCAP, but he now became a member of BMI. With no ASCAP songs allowed on radio, there wasn't a single thing in the Ellington catalogue the band could play on their weekly radio show, not even their signature tune. When the ASCAP ban started, Billy Strayhorn and Ellington's son Mercer had just one week to produce enough new compositions to fill Ellington's next weekly radio show. Mercer went through the trash can and found a song Strayhorn had thrown away because he thought it sounded too much like Fletcher Henderson. It became the band's new signature tune – 'Take the "A" Train'.

By the end of the year ASCAP was defeated. The entire old guard of the song business – writers and publishers – the biggest names in American music were simply not being heard. More importantly, the film studios couldn't get the music from their new films on radio. For six months they'd been storing new productions waiting for a settlement, but when it didn't come they threatened to form new publishing companies and affiliate them with BMI.

So ASCAP caved in and offered new radio licences at rates below their previous levels. It meant most radio stations would now be paying for two licences, one to each society, yet the combined cost of both was less than the increased fee ASCAP had originally been planning. And radio stations now had double the amount of music available to them.

While it was true that BMI's formation had been entirely due to the biggest broadcasters wanting to increase their profits, it also provided access to the American music market for thousands of writers and musicians who had previously been denied it. It was the usual music industry syndrome – greed bred progress.

ASCAP's capitulation was not the beginning of peace. In endless court cases over the next twenty years, ASCAP would present itself as being on the side of traditional values – 'the good old America we once knew' – and BMI as delinquent – 'destroying all that was good in the country'.

It seemed absurd that such rhetoric could fly across courtrooms based on nothing more than the business surrounding popular songs. But plenty of good came from it. The war between these two societies was the stimulus that caused royalties for songwriters to improve out of all recognition. It made songwriting a career that anyone could choose. It liberated black music. It opened the door to rock 'n' roll. And it provided a basis for a new international music industry.

First, though, there was a small problem to deal with....

Another world war.

21
New World Coming
SECOND WORLD WAR

When the war began, people in Britain wanted to hear popular songs more than ever but the BBC continued to relegate them to late evening. Seizing the opportunity the Nazi war department broadcast popular records from its radio station in Yugoslavia. When British troops started listening, the BBC was forced to change its policy. It introduced *Music While You Work*, a twice-daily medley of currently popular tunes played by a palm court orchestra. The troops still didn't listen, but factory workers had the programme played to them over loudspeakers while they worked.

British troops mainly made their own entertainment, singing currently popular songs for themselves. The ones they liked most were a mix of music hall humour, disdain for Germany, and huge optimism. 'Hang Out Your Washing on the Siegfried Line' had foreseen British troops getting quickly to the German border, not being forced into the sea at Dunkirk, paddling up to their necks, thumbing a lift home.

Once back, they found Ivor Novello had done it again. For the second world war running he'd got himself a hit musical. This time it was *The Dancing Years*, a best-selling show he'd written and was starring in. Professor Eric Brown, a flying officer in Coastal Command, saw it the night a bomb dropped outside the theatre.

The place shook, dust showered down, the orchestra stopped, and the lights went off, then back on. The audience just sat there, then the orchestra started playing, just as it had been 25 seconds before, as if nothing had happened.

The show ran for 969 performances and only came off when theatres were ordered to close because Hitler started sending over doodlebugs. However, towards the end of its run the British government put Ivor Novello in prison. It was nothing to do with the quality of his performance; it was because he'd taken to ostentatiously driving round London in his Rolls Royce picking up young men, something that was still very much against the law. The government made a private deal with him. He could be imprisoned for homosexuality, or for filling his Rolls Royce with petrol bought on the black market. He chose the black market offence and got two months.

On the evening he returned to the show, it started and finished with a standing ovation. Whether it would have done had he chosen to plead guilty to the other offence is another matter. Either way, Novello remained sensibly unashamed of his sentence and regained his good standing with the British public by volunteering to entertain troops on the front line. His *pièce de resistance* was to bring five thousand war-weary soldiers to their feet to join in the chorus of 'We'll Gather Lilacs'.

Entertaining the troops was equally important to Americans. At some time or other during the war, almost every top performer from Hollywood and Broadway flew to Europe or the Far East to perform in front of their servicemen. Yet there was one area that was a disgrace.

There were not many black troops in the US military. They were not called up for service and could only volunteer if they had special qualifications, like being able to fly a plane. And once in the forces they were not treated equally. When they watched entertainment, they had to sit apart from the white troops in a segregated area. Singer Lena Horne refused point blank to perform.

The US generals fooled her. They gave her an apparently integrated audience, but what she didn't know was – the area where the black troops were sitting, apparently mixed with white troops, was their normal segregated area. And the white faces mixed up with them were German POWs, commandeered from the local prisoner of war camp.

Back home in America, New Jersey Congressman J. Parnell Thomas announced, "What America needs today is a good 5 cent war song... something with plenty of zip, ginger and fire... like 'Over There', 'Keep the Home Fires Burning', or 'Pack Up Your Troubles In Your Old Kit Bag'..."

The poor fellow didn't realise that two of these songs came from England.

The US government then formed the Office of War Information (OWI) to instruct the music publishing industry on the sort of songs it was expected to produce to help the war effort. *Variety* published the OWI's requirements.

Songs should avoid talking about the end of the war in terms of returning to 'peace-and ease' because it might sap the morale of the people to have these thoughts in their mind. Songs about the enemy should not belittle its size and power. The armed forces should never be depicted as out to 'conquer' but to 'liberate'. There should be more fighting songs and less boy-and-girl roseate stuff. The wrong kind of slushy stuff should be kept in the publisher's safe until after the war as a matter of patriotism.

THE BUSINESS

During the summer of 1942, William B. Lewis, radio chief of the OWI, lobbied Washington on the importance of militant war songs as an "aspect of psychological warfare". During a congressional debate Senator Charles O. Andrews stressed the need for "a fresh crop of stirring songs that would intensify the war effort". The OWI then came up with a new idea – a special dance "with spirited, military steps".

One song the OWI particularly liked was, 'God Must Have Loved America'. To extend its life by not being over-played, radio stations were asked "to limit its use to no more than once every four hours".

The OWI's second choice was for anti-Japanese songs. Some of them had humour: 'When Those Little Yellow Bellies Meet the Cohens and the Kellys'. Others were plain vicious: 'We're Gonna Have To Slap The Dirty Little Jap' (with sheet music printed on yellow paper). Yet others offered thanks to God for the bloody mess he'd got everyone into: 'Praise the Lord and Pass the Ammunition'.

American music publishers, tired of the OWI's endless directives, hit back by forming their own Music War Committee with Oscar Hammerstein as chairman. They vowed to write the definitive war song but could only come up with a comic one, about a soldier who guarded the cookhouse. When it flopped, they gave up. And the music business went back to running itself as it had always done.

In the end, on both sides of the Atlantic the biggest songs were love songs, made more poignant by a backdrop of war, 'Give Me Five Minutes More' from America, and 'We'll Meet Again' from Britain. But the OWI disapproved of these because they might "soften the morale of the fighting men". Dance halls were warned that soldiers were bound to be a trifle homesick. "We don't want them to be made worse by some teary tenor or soulful soprano singing about home and mother."

The list of banned songs included 'Dear Mom', 'Miss You', and 'My Buddy'. Bandleader Woody Herman, appearing at The Stage Door in New York, was told by the venue manager that 'White Christmas' had also been banned. "It makes the boys too nostalgic".

For New York's jazz musicians, nostalgia was off the menu. They were living strictly in the present.

52nd Street was even more buzzing now than before the war, it had become the jazz centre of New York, where musicians came after hours to sit-in with one another. Amongst the old time greats were tenor player Coleman Hawkins and trumpeter Roy Eldridge, but it was a new generation of musicians that were attracting most attention, like Charlie Parker on alto, and Dizzy Gillespie on trumpet.

There were servicemen too, often in uniform, many of them black. And from this intermixing of ages and backgrounds a new form of music began to evolve which became known as bebop. It threw away the conventions of classic chord structure and harmonised in altogether new ways. For many people it was a mystery how it started, for Dizzy Gillespie it was simple.

There were always some cats showing up there who couldn't blow... on afternoons before sessions Thelonius Monk and I began to work out some complex variations on chords and the like and we used them to scare away the no-talent guys... as we began to explore more and more our music evolved.

Bebop was the re-blackening of jazz. The music that had once come from New Orleans had been largely taken over by white big bands and sold to America as the country's basic popular music. Now, black servicemen, sobered by the experience of fighting in a racially segregated military, returned from overseas to be reminded of their problems back home. Many were virtuosos on their instruments and once they got to 52nd Street they were no longer hired talent or smiling entertainers, they were true artists.

It was referred to as cool, but emotionally it was nearer cold. It wasn't just the starkness of the harmonies; musicians played without vibrato, expressing themselves through technically testing phrases, sometimes of breathtaking length and complexity, often finishing in mid-air like so many of life's experiences rather than finding a tidy end.

Bebop wasn't the joyful jazz of old; it was something more suited to the times – war, loneliness, despair – black Americans still suffering from rejection and segregation.

But it was doubtful many of them thought of it that way. More a matter of going down to the street for a blow.

Just round the corner from 52nd Street was Broadway, carrying on as if the war didn't exist. *Oklahoma* was a fine example, a romantic comedy about cowboys. In Britain, putting on something so lavish and irrelevant during the war would have been frowned at. But in America the war seemed far away and life was expected to remain as normal as possible. Besides, one of the writers was Oscar Hammerstein who had shrewdly got himself elected as president of the Music War Committee, which put him beyond criticism.

Richard Rodgers, his co-writer, was even shrewder. Usually roles in musicals were filled by actors who could sing. Rodgers suggested they worked the other way round and use singers who could act. Being a known Broadway star would come second to being a singer. The result was a cast with a slightly utilitarian look, just right for wartime. People flooded to Broadway to see it and there was little criticism of its lavishness.

Before *Oklahoma* opened, Richard Rodgers became so convinced of its success that he persuaded Oscar Hammerstein they should publish it themselves. "We went up to Bronxville, where Max Dreyfus lived, to discuss the matter with him, since he'd been Oscar's publisher as well as mine during most of our careers."

Max did what any shrewd publisher would have done. He told them it was a brilliant idea and he would organise it for them. He then set in motion a procedure that would soon become standard for established writers and their publishers. He formed a new company, half-owned by Rodgers and Hammerstein and half-owned by Chappell, who would charge a percentage to administrate it. To Rodgers and Hammerstein it meant they were now publishers. To Max it meant nothing had changed – a slightly smaller percentage, that's all.

Jean Aberbach was an employee at Chappell. He watched the way Max had dealt with *Oklahoma* and decided he would build a whole company the same way, offering writers joint publishing companies right from the outset. But for the moment he put the idea on hold because he'd just found an extraordinary writer whom he was sure would come up with a hit, and Max Dreyfus agreed to form one of these joint companies with him to promote any songs this new writer came up with. He was Igor Stravinsky.

In 1940, the year he premiered his 'Symphony in C' to huge acclaim, Stravinsky met Leo Feist (not the Leo Feist who once sold corsets and then became one of the first great music publishers, but his son, who had now taken over the family business). Listening to young Leo talk about the popular music business, Stravinsky admitted that more than anything else in the world he would like to write a hit song. Jean Aberbach, a friend of young Leo, told Max Dreyfus about this and Max proposed they form a joint company to promote Stravinsky's songs – Jean Aberbach and Leo Feist on one side, Chappell on the other.

For a couple of years Stravinsky frequented smoky music clubs in New York hoping something would sink in. But it didn't. Try as he might, Igor Stravinsky was hopeless as a writer of popular songs. For him to try, considering his fame as a serious composer, was surprising. For him to fail was proof of the unique talent required for writing hit songs. Jean Aberbach and Leo Feist junior were surprised. Max Dreyfus said he'd expected it.

In London, brother Louis was having trouble with the Germans. He lived on a farm in Surrey with horses and livestock just at the point where German bombers flying towards London liked to test a bomb or two as they approached. He decided to move to his flat in the centre of London where he stayed for the rest of the war. Being there gave him the idea of organising free concerts for Londoners and through Chappell he funded a symphony orchestra to play at Queen's Hall with no admission charge.

As the Nazi bombardment grew heavier, Louis worried that a bomb might fall on Queen's Hall with three thousand people in it. Through family contacts, he managed to contact Ralph von Siegel, an old friend in Germany who'd been appointed by Hitler to cleanse the music industry of Jewish influence in conquered countries. Since it was common knowledge that Hitler passed his evenings in private showings of Hollywood musicals, most of them written and composed by Jews, Siegel ignored his instructions and simply travelled around neutral and conquered countries assuring music publishers that when the war was over everything would be as before.

Louis Dreyfus asked Siegel if he could persuade the Luftwaffe to exempt the Queen's Hall from its list of targets, but it was wishful thinking. Siegel took the request from Dreyfus no more seriously than he'd taken the request from Hitler. Besides, Queen's Hall was in Langham Place, directly across the road from the BBC, a target at the top of the Luftwaffe's list. Nevertheless, Louis reassured everyone they would be safe and the concerts went ahead – until an incendiary bomb burnt the hall to the ground.

Fortunately that evening's concert had finished and the hall was empty.

Across the road from Queen's Hall, the BBC remained curiously safe from the bombing. The only explosions came from within.

Wartime graft was reported to have assumed "tremendous proportions" and Sir Valentine Holmes was appointed by Parliament to investigate. Despite charges of bribery, corruption, and favoritism amongst the BBC staff, when he reported back to parliament he said the allegations appeared to be without solid foundation. He found no staff at the BBC guilty of accepting 'gifts' except one – Mrs. D. Nelson, who unsurprisingly was head of the dance band section. Sir Valentine was quick to add that he didn't think she'd been influenced in any way by receiving them.

As a result of this report the BBC and the Music Publishers Association held a series of meetings at which they hammered out an agreement. It called for the BBC "to ban for life from its airwaves any artist proved guilty of accepting payments and to ban for two years the entire catalogue of any publisher similarly proved guilty". The BBC expected this agreement "to terminate once and for all the plug bribery that has been rampant here for years". Strangely, they continued to allow publishers to pay bandleaders up to £5 for making 'special arrangements' of songs. Not surprisingly, a few notes in nearly every song were changed a little each time they were played.

Bigger money than that was behind a problem brewing in the USA.

Although James Caesar Petrillo was president of the American Federation of Musicians, his real claim to fame was the fine repertoire of expletives he used before and after every word he spoke. But in the summer of 1942 he managed a complete sentence without one, "From August 1st no AFM members will record, or contract to record, any mechanical music."

The three biggest recording companies were Victor, Columbia and Decca. Decca was the only one of the three not owned by a larger company. Victor Records had been owned by RCA Broadcasting since the late 20s, and Columbia Records had been bought by Columbia Broadcasting System in the late 30s. So the two biggest broadcasters owned the two biggest record companies.

James Petrillo objected to records being played on the radio because it took work away from musicians who played live music. His solution was to enforce a new contract for recording. As well as increasing the fee to musicians who played on records, record companies would have to pay a percentage of record sales to a union fund. The record companies refused point blank and Petrillo ordered the musicians to strike.

But record companies had stock piled large numbers of new recordings. In the first twelve months of the strike they experienced their best sales in ten years. After fourteen months Petrillo admitted, "They've got us on the floor. They've got us punch drunk."

Even so, he didn't give in. And nor did the record companies. When their stockpile was finished they recorded artists with choirs or doo-wop singers. For over a year no records were made with musicians.

For radio stations nothing changed much, they used live radio bands as usual. Songwriters and music publishers weren't affected either because using radio bands was how they'd always promoted new songs. It was only the musicians who depended on recording sessions that suffered. And some people actually benefitted.

The Mills Brothers were a black singing quartet who had been popular throughout the thirties. They'd had their own radio shows, recorded for Columbia, and made Hollywood movies. In 1935 they'd become the first black Americans to play a royal command performance, playing for King George and Queen Mary in London. When the war broke out they were again in London and had to leave quickly. Herbert Mills explains what a bad effect this had on their career. "The only boat we could get was to Australia... so we didn't get back till 1941... In the meantime the Ink Spots were coming up and people had sort of forgotten us."

But when they did finally get back, because of the musicians' strike Columbia was pleased to have a self-sufficient vocal group available. They immediately sent the Mills Brothers into the studio to record *a capella*. One of the songs they recorded was 'Paper Doll', which became the biggest selling record of the war

– six million copies. The group presented James Petrillo with a copy of the gold record they received as thanks for his contribution to making it happen. They should also have given one to Edward B. Marks, the song's publisher.

In 1930 Marks was brought the song by Johnny Black, who'd written it in 1915 and was still trying to get it published fifteen years later. Marks hated the song and told Black to go away. He did. But he came back half an hour later with a violin and a pet canary. He stood in Marks' office playing and singing the song over and over again with the canary on his shoulder joining in the choruses. Marks finally gave way and agreed to publish it.

Claude Mills, the much-disliked head of the Music Publishers Protective Association had now reached retirement age. Everyone thought he would quietly fade away. Instead, he suddenly switched sides and got himself appointed as general manager of the Songwriters Protective Association.

Mills liked confrontation, and by switching sides from the music publishers to the songwriters, he was in a perfect position to provoke it. And he did.

He wanted to rectify the one thing that all songwriters most resented about the music publishing business – the granting of ownership in their songs to the music publisher. Two centuries earlier, it was this very thing that triggered the beginning of the music industry. Everything that had taken place since then had been based on publishers being the actual owners of the copyrights they promoted. But now, with the music industry's working processes accepted, and with its infrastructure for collecting royalties in place, there seemed no reason why this gross unfairness should continue.

In France and Italy, the law had long ago declared that copyright belonged to the person who created it and could not be transferred to anyone else – only the 'right of exploitation' could be assigned. Mills proposed that American songwriters too should retain ownership of their copyrights and assign only the right of exploitation. He also proposed that songwriters receive two thirds of all performance and synchronization royalties, as they did in France, rather than the fifty-fifty division they received in America.

Mills was immediately accused of "trying to upset the ASCAP applecart". Music publishers warned songwriters that if Mills and his followers persisted, the society would boycott music by members of the Songwriters Protective Association and look to new and more grateful writers for future material.

Sigmund Romberg, the president of the songwriters' society that Mills now managed, hailed his proposals and said the society was "ready to go to war". But pressure from ASCAP's most powerful publisher members foiled them. The board voted to extend all ASCAP memberships for an additional fifteen years, which meant that even if Mills pushed this through it couldn't take effect until then. So Mills resigned his short-lived job and the Songwriters Protective Association went back to the inaction that had previously been its defining quality.

Towards the end of the war Germany had some bad luck. Their biggest hit of the war got pinched by Edward B. Marks.

It started out as one of Hitler's favourite poems, 'The Song of a Young Sentry' by Hans Leip, a minor German poet. It was spotted by Norbert Schultze, a composer who'd written the music for a toothpaste commercial and wanted to turn it into a song. He combined his music with Leip's poem and recorded it, naming it after a girl mentioned in the poem, 'Lili Marlene'.

In 1939, when it was first released, the record flopped and only sold a few copies. But when the Germans overran Yugoslavia, the officer commissioned with setting up a military radio station there, found it in a job lot of records he bought from a second-hand shop in Vienna and started playing it.

Field Marshal Rommel, with the Afrika Korps in the Libyan Desert, liked it so much that he requested it be played nightly and the song became Radio Belgrade's sign-off tune. But it wasn't only the German army that was listening, it was the British army too, and they improvised English words to it.

Goebbels, the Nazi Party's propaganda minister, hated the song and tried to have it banned, saying it would sap the morale of fighting men, but its sheer popularity overcame his objections. The British government weren't happy with it either. They didn't want their troops singing along to a song in German so they asked for an English lyric to be written and commissioned film director Humphrey Jennings to make a twenty-minute documentary called *The True Story of Lili Marlene*. It was for use by the Ministry of Information in both Britain and the USA and would contain footage of British troops in Africa, a mass rally for Hitler, and the Battle of Stalingrad. Because of the war, the German publisher of the song, Apollo Verlag, couldn't be dealt with, so Marius Goring, a well-known actor and film star, and the person in charge of BBC's overseas broadcasts, wrote English lyrics for use in the film.

The film made an impact in America and because it was a German copyright it was effectively up for grabs. Shortly before the film was first shown, Chappell Music published the song with a different lyric from the one Marius Goring had written. But J. J. Phillips, head of the British company Peter Maurice Ltd, decided both the previous lyrics could be improved on and asked songwriter Tommy Connor to come up with something better.

Peter Maurice Ltd omitted Norbert Schultze's name from the credits and plugged their version of the song harder than Chappell were plugging theirs. For America, they gave it to Edward B Marks Inc., now being run by his son Herbie, and wrote him a letter saying that Peter Maurice Ltd was the one and only genuine publisher of it, which was a bit of a whopper. "Dear Herbie, don't worry about any other versions that are around... the War Office only last week ordered 1,000 orchestrations for the troops in North Africa...".

Edward B. Marks Inc printed the letter on the back of the sheet music in America. On the title page they printed, "The only authentic Peter Maurice version of the famous international hit." (Well, that was true, it *was* the only authentic *Peter Maurice* version.)

Chappell in America also published the song, omitting Schultze's name but adding Phil Park, who was actually lyric-writer Mack David. The song was then recorded by Marlene Dietrich, a German living in America, which further insulted the Nazi Propaganda Ministry, and then by Perry Como with yet another new lyric.

All the American publishers of Lili Marlene printed the same note at the bottom of the page: "Published & distributed in the public interest with the consent of the Alien Property Custodian under License". In other words, the song had been appropriated as enemy property.

In Berlin, the German Propaganda Ministry were so piqued by Norbert Schultze having written a hit song for the enemy that they ordered him to write an anthem for the German Air Force. It was another big hit, but this time only in Germany, 'Bomben auf Engelland'.

After the war Schultze was apologetic, "You know, I was at the best age for a soldier, 30 or so. For me the alternatives were compose or croak. So I decided on the former."

By the time the American musicians' strike ended the public's taste had begun to change. Listening to *a cappella* records had got people used to hearing songs without a big band. But one singer continued to use one.

When the war started, Frank Sinatra was in his early twenties and singing with the Tommy Dorsey Band. At his military medical, the doctors classified him unfit for service due to a perforated eardrum. Sinatra took advantage of not having to serve by leaving the Dorsey band and becoming resident singer on *Your Hit Parade*. And because the show had a live orchestra, he got the same big band backings he was used to.

The show was aimed mainly at housewives aged twenty-five to fifty, but after Sinatra started singing on the show the producers noticed more and more teenage girls turning up at the studio each week. Popular music had never been aimed at a teenage market, and still wasn't, yet here were hundreds of adolescent girls, all dressed in the latest teen fashion of white socks rolled down to the ankles, coming to the studio to mob Sinatra.

In 1942, at New York's Paramount Theatre, he played his first solo concert. 'Bobbysoxers' turned out in droves and he walked out on stage to a cacophony of shrieks and screams. "Absolutely deafening... a tremendous roar... five thousand kids, stamping, yelling, screaming, applauding. I was scared stiff. I couldn't move a muscle."

Thousands of bobbysoxers had been waiting outside since the break of day in lines that circled the block, fainting on the sidewalk, waving undergarments, shouting "Frank–eee!!"

One girl wore a bandage for three weeks on her arm at the spot where "Frankie touched me". Another went to fifty-six consecutive performances. And after each show the Paramount Theatre was drenched in urine.

This was a whole new market for popular music and marketing men took note. No singers had ever been screamed at that way before and advertisers had never thought much about the buying power of teenagers. Yet here, in the middle of a war, teenagers were showing themselves as a viable purchasing force. If they could buy tickets to a Sinatra concert, what else might they buy?

22

She Wears Red Feathers
FROM MITCH MILLER TO ROCK 'N' ROLL

In Britain at the beginning of the fifties there was no rock 'n' roll, the word teenager didn't exist and British pop music was trash.

Post war Britain was gloomy. There was rationing, unemployment and bad housing. More than half the homes in Britain had outdoor toilets and almost none had central heating. There was no entertainment for young people and over and over again they had to listen to their parents say, "We fought the war for you."

The music industry was still focused on selling sheet music. People bought the latest pop song and struggled through it on the piano at home. Broadcasting was controlled by the BBC and because of an agreement with the musicians union there were only ten hours each week during which pop records could be played. Listening to the current hit records meant staying awake till 11pm on a Sunday night when the Top 20 was broadcast by Radio Luxembourg, fading in and out from 208 on the medium wave.

It wasn't aimed at teenagers; it was aimed at young marrieds. Radio Luxembourg's Top 20 was sponsored by Horace Batchelor, a man with a droning West Country accent who guaranteed listeners they could win the football pools if they followed his system. But here's the point – Horace Batchelor had picked the Top 20 for his hourly week of advertising, yet the football pools were forbidden to anyone under twenty-one. That summed up pop's target audience – twenty-one to thirty-five. The songs were dreadful, with corny melodies and excruciating lyrics. And they nearly all came from America.

For America, the end of the war had meant the start of television. Its programmes projected a country of extraordinary conformity. Everyone wanted social cohesion, especially advertisers. For them, a perfect society was a homogenous one and advertising agency J. Walter Thompson led the way by using *7up* ads that played on people's fear of rejection and their desire to fit in. "You like it – it likes you".

The images were of smiling welcoming people; society, they told us, was one big happy family. But since the family projected was totally white and middle-class, it was difficult for anyone who wasn't one of those two things to see where they fitted in.

To frighten them into trying anyway, and to induce even greater conformity, Americans were told they faced a common enemy in communism. The country was liable to attack at any minute; underground air raid shelters were built at schools and students were drilled in what to do in case an atom bomb was dropped. Then along came Senator McCarthy.

McCarthy was intent on branding as many people as he possibly could as 'commies'. He ran Senate investigations on anyone he could get his hands on, from show-business stars to average office-workers, searching out anyone who might once have had left-wing sympathies. For seven years Americans conformed, afraid not to do so. And conformity included popular music.

The singers were Guy Mitchell, Frankie Lane, Jo Stafford, Doris Day and Patti Page. The songs were 'Mule Train', 'She Wears Red Feathers', 'Ghost Riders in the Sky', and 'Shrimp Boats is-a Comin''. They were cheesy and crass; popular music had never been more unlistenable. Even so, some songs managed to sound worse than others, and if they did they were probably by Bob Merrill. His hits included 'If I Knew You Were Coming I'd Have Baked a Cake', 'She Wears Red Feathers' and 'How Much Is That Doggie in the Window'. Bob Merrill had a magic touch for the truly appalling.

So did Mitch Miller, head of A&R at Columbia Records. Miller had been an oboe player, a conductor, a choral director, and a school friend of Goddard Lieberson, Columbia's new president (who liked to sign his letters 'God'). Lieberson had put Miller in charge of Artists & Repertoire, making him the man who chose the artists and the songs they would sing. And Miller's taste was pure kitsch. He was also Columbia's chief record producer, and therein lay the problem, because his productions were horrendous.

Since its invention the microphone had been like an 'audio camera' capturing magic moments of sound – a great performance by Caruso, a brilliant improvisation by Charlie Parker, a perfect rendition of a ballroom performance by the Glenn Miller Orchestra. It was a musical snapshot of what you would have heard had you been there. But Mitch Miller didn't use the microphone for capturing magic moments; he used it for creating them.

Miller's records were not recordings of a performance, they were original works in their own right, works that didn't exist before he created them in the studio. "To me, the art of singing a pop song has always been to sing it very quietly… in other words, the microphone and the amplifier made the popular song what it is – an intimate one-on-one experience through electronics."

The way he describes it makes it sound as if his records were wonderful when in fact they were the record equivalent of plastic gnomes in the garden. Despite that, he has to take credit for inventing the modern pop record – a unique work of art created in the studio.

Mitch Miller made the recording process a new creative art. There was the song, the arrangement, and the vocal interpretation. Now there was also the recorded sound, quite different from how it would have sounded had you been there. Quiet instruments became loud, loud ones became quiet, and sound effects were added – whips, cowboy whoops, bells or animal noises. The end result was not so much an arrangement of a tune, but an aural representation of the story of the song, which might have been wonderful if Mitch Miller had possessed the merest hint of good taste. Instead, everything he touched became truly abysmal.

Music critic Will Friedwald summed it up perfectly. "Miller chose the worst songs and put together the worst backings imaginable – not with the hit-or-miss attitude that bad musicians traditionally used, but with insight, forethought, careful planning, and perverted brilliance."

Another person who hated Mitch Miller's production style was Frank Sinatra. "Before Mr Miller's advent on the scene I had a successful recording career which went into decline."

Miller had signed Sinatra then fallen out with him. Sinatra had stormed out of the studios and left the label, saying Miller was taking bribes to use BMI songs, and as a result was choosing inferior material. It wasn't true that Miller was giving preference to BMI songs, but it was certainly true his productions weren't right for Sinatra.

Each time Mitch Miller stepped out of his office at CBS he would find himself on 52nd Street. For nearly ten years it had been the home of bebop. From end to end, the street was crowded with clubs and musicians. Charlie Parker, one of bebop's originators, said, "Music is your own experience, your thoughts, your wisdom – if you don't live it, it won't come out of your horn."

If the music that came out of Mitch Miller's horn was a distillation of his life, it must have been a sad one indeed. And that was the problem. His records were nothing to do with his life. He was a classical musician and when asked to produce popular music, he did it with disdain. He was equally disdainful of Frank Sinatra. "Take away the microphone and Sinatra and most other pop singers would be slicing salami in a delicatessen."

It was difficult to put a finger on what made everything he touched so resoundingly awful, but there's a surprisingly good quote from Miller himself that perfectly describes his productions – "musical baby food… the worship of mediocrity".

Unfortunately, that's what he himself said ten years later about rock 'n' roll.

Despite Mitch Miller's dominance of post-war popular recording, there was one new singer who managed to squeeze into prominence without being subjected to his awful productions. He was Johnnie Ray, who recorded for Okeh Records, the label that released 'Crazy Blues' by Mamie Smith in the 1920s and launched Ralph Peer on his path to success.

Johnnie Ray took over Frank Sinatra's mantle as the frail male that teenagers wanted to mother. In 1951 he had a hit with 'The Little White Cloud That Cried' the mainstay of which was his ability to cry real tears as he sang it. It was a double 'A' side. And with the other side titled quite simply 'Cry', there was a second helping of tears when he sang that one. By the time the record had been up the charts and down again, Johnnie Ray was the biggest new star in America and teen mania was back.

In the fifties in Britain, although the BBC still wouldn't play popular records, it now had programmes of live music in which different bands and singers performed currently popular songs. British teenagers needed someone of their own to scream at and they latched on to the singers in these bands.

When they were not on the radio, band singers like Dickie Valentine, David Whitfield or Frankie Vaughan appeared at variety theatres on a Saturday evening. It was a pale imitation of the hysterical adulation Johnnie Ray was receiving from teenagers in America. After the show, when the singers came to the stage door to sign autographs, the screams were almost polite. So were the singers.

"I want to leave them happy," said Frankie Vaughan.

"If you're swollen-headed they know it," said Dickie Valentine.

"It gets you a bad name," agreed David Whitfield.

Teenage boys in Britain were uninterested in popular music. They had more disposable income than the girls but little to use it on. Some had taken to dancing to trad jazz played in pubs by revivalist bands but mostly they spent their money on dressing up as 'Teddy boys'.

The centrepiece was a 'drape' – a long knee-length, single-breasted wool jacket, with narrow contrasting lapels and cuffs of velvet or satin. With it went drainpipe trousers, brocade waistcoats, stiff shirts, shoestring ties, suede shoes and hair slicked back with Brilliantine into what was known as a Duck's Arse.

This Edwardian suit was for nothing more than looking cool in on the street corner. For the moment, at least, there was no specific music to go with it.

It was during Mitch Miller's reign at CBS that the balance in the music industry finally tipped in favour of record companies over publishers. The deciding factor was the introduction of long-playing records. Both CBS and RCA had been developing them for years. RCA had come up with a viable system as early as the 1920s but had decided the time wasn't right and shelved it. When technology moved onwards, instead of going back to what they already had, they looked for something new. But CBS beat them to it.

In 1948 the decision to launch long-playing records was taken not at record company level but by William Paley, overall owner of Columbia Broadcasting. The record people thought LPs might kill the single market but Paley wanted to get into the market before David Sarnoff, his rival at RCA. Paley asked Sarnoff over for a meeting and Sarnoff only listened for ten seconds before accepting defeat. "I want to congratulate you and your people, Bill. It is very good."

Sarnoff immediately ordered his own engineers to come up with a matching system but they came up with something rather different. Instead of a long playing record that played twenty minutes a side at 33 revs per minute they come up with a smaller disc – seven minutes a side at 45 revs per minute. CBS's product was perfect for classical music; RCA's system was perfect for pop. Instead of competing, the two companies took their new technologies in different directions – CBS into the world of highbrow, and RCA into low, with 45s getting an extra boost when they became the standard for new jukeboxes.

These two new formats helped pushed record sales to a new high. Sales from them, and royalties from ASCAP for radio plays, now became the main source of income for publishers. And sheet music sales collapsed.

Many of the old time publishers were in difficulties, even Irving Berlin. "Without ASCAP's performance revenue I couldn't survive," Berlin told *Variety*. "I would have to close shop and see my 30-year-old organization go down the drain…"

In fact, the real reason behind his company not doing so well was something he didn't care to speak about. It was to do with Saul Bornstein, the unlikeable bully who had been the mainstay of running Irving Berlin Inc since its formation over thirty years earlier. Bornstein had turned out to be a crook – not a major one, just a typical music industry sleazebag.

In the beginning Irving Berlin had thought he needed someone like that to watch out for his company's interests, and it was true the company had done well, not just with Berlin's songs but with other songwriters too. But while doing some filing, Berlin's secretary Mynna chanced on some things in the safe that shouldn't have been there. Glancing through a stack of documents she discovered that for over 20 years the company had been paying out advances to non-existent songwriters for non-existent songs. Bornstein had been inventing these songwriters and pocketing the money the company supposedly advanced them. Mynna removed the documents from the safe and gave them to Berlin.

Later, when she was taking dictation from him, the door flew open and Bornstein stormed in bellowing, "Where did you get these papers from?"

Berlin stood up nose to nose and berated him. "Don't you dare insult her. I've been suspicious for many, many years. I needed proof and now I've got it. Goddammit, you and I are through."

Then he offered Bornstein an extraordinarily generous deal. Berlin would retain the copyrights to his own songs; Bornstein could take the copyrights to all other songs. It was a huge catalogue, worth millions. And Bornstein was given it for absolutely nothing.

He also retained the company's plush new offices on Seventh Avenue and Berlin moved back to the company's old offices at 1650 Broadway taking his most trusted employees with him. They separated but Bornstein saved face.

Maybe Berlin felt he had no choice. Bornstein was the treasurer of ASCAP – a position that required huge trust from members. He'd only been elected to that position because he worked with Irving Berlin, whom everyone respected. For Bornstein to be revealed as a cheap crook would do harm not just to ASCAP but to Berlin too. He'd always known what Bornstein was like. He should never have allowed him to climb so high in the ASCAP hierarchy.

The point was – if you use a cheap crook to help you further your aims, doesn't that make you a cheap crook yourself?

It was a question the music industry had all too often avoided.

23

Brothers in Arms
THE ERTEGUNS

In the same way that Max and Louis Dreyfus had dominated the era of music publishing, another pair of brothers arrived on the scene as the music business changed itself from a publishing industry to a record industry.

Ahmet and Nesuhi Ertegun were Turkish. In 1944 they were studying in Washington when their father, the Turkish ambassador, died. The Ertegun brothers were sophisticated, educated and exceptionally good with crossing the borders of different strands of society. They decided to stay in the USA and indulge their passion for black music.

Nesuhi went to LA and got into recording jazz. Ahmet, with the idea of recording the new style of black music that was becoming popular on the East coast, formed a record company in New York, Atlantic Records.

For some black Americans the Second World War had been a benefit. Because they hadn't been conscripted into the military they were given the opportunity to move into middle-management jobs vacated by whites who had. This caused a boost in the numbers of middle-class blacks and they were now enjoying more disposable income than ever before.

One of the things they most liked to spend their money on was music, and by the beginning of the fifties black Americans were buying enough records to spawn a whole host of new record companies catering specifically for them. The new style of music they liked was neither jazz nor pop, but funky and raunchy, and great for people to dance to.

Billboard wouldn't put these records into their Hot 100 chart even when they outsold other currently popular records. To get into the Hot 100, records had to be played on radio stations listened to by the mass audience – the white audience. Black music was played by black radio and black records could only appear on the 'rhythm & blues' chart, a name coined by the man who compiled the *Billboard* charts, Jerry Wexler.

"I could no longer stand to hear the term 'race records'," he explained.

Initially, Atlantic was a partnership between Ahmet Ertegun and Herbert Abramson, a professional dentist and an amateur jazz record producer. When

Abramson was called up for the army he left his wife Miriam behind to look after his side of things. Ahmet invited Jerry Wexler to come in as the company's record producer. Wexler refused unless he could become a partner. After talking with Abramson, Ahmet offered Wexler 13 per cent of the company for $2,063. Wexler didn't have it but offered his pick up truck instead. Ahmet valued it at $1,000 and agreed he could pay the balance later.

Ahmet and Wexler knew next to nothing about recording black music but between them they learnt by trial and error. "The truth is," Wexler said, "there was no state of the art in record-making at that time."

For two years Atlantic grew steadily. Along the way Herbert Abramson divorced his wife and gave her his shares and position as company director. She was a nightmare. Wexler would be tying up a deal; Miriam would crash through his door waving a piece of paper. "Who the fuck okayed three thousand freebies for these guys?" When Wexler persuaded Ahmet to buy her out, she stormed off shouting, "I give you assholes six months."

Eighteen months later Atlantic was the number one black record company in America. It was after Nesuhi Ertegun came back from LA to help run things and became the third partner in the company. Many people put Atlantic's success wholly down to Ahmet, or to the arrival of Jerry Wexler, or others who came later. But these were people who stimulated Ahmet's dreams and helped him fly. Nesuhi was the person who made sure he always came safely back to earth. The relationship between them was what Herb Abrasom called "the Turkish nitty-gritty". More disciplined than his brother, and more of an administrator, Nesuhi freed up Ahmet to focus on finding artists and making hits. Frustratingly, though, however many records the company sold they were unable to get into the national charts. Whenever the company had a new hit, the major record companies rushed to make cover versions of it; softening it up; fronting it with a pretty white girl or clean-cut white boy, aiming it at the mass market.

It made Ahmet furious. "White stations would play cover version of our records but refused to play ours. They'd say it wasn't 'their' type of music. But the cover versions they were playing were exact copies."

It was these white copies that went into the *Billboard* Top 100. The original black versions couldn't get there even when the records sold a million.

At King Records, they were also finding it impossible to get black records onto white radio. But King made white records too.

The company was started by Syd Nathan in his hometown of Cincinnati. Nathan was born to a poor Jewish family and grew up suffering from asthma and bad eyesight. During the Depression he worked at anything he could get – drummer in a local speakeasy, pawnshop clerk, shooting gallery owner, wrestling promoter, radio salesman, and jukebox supplier. During the war he ran a shop selling second-hand records, and when the war finished he decided to make new ones. He started out with hillbilly and his first hit was 'I'm Using My Bible as a Road Map'.

King Records was unique amongst independent record companies in that Nathan kept the entire production process in-house – recording, mastering, printing, pressing and shipping. It meant he had complete control of the whole operation and didn't have to depend on anyone else. Moreover, no artist could ever find out how many records had been shipped and sold, which helped the cash flow greatly.

Nathan was a short man with a big presence – fat, bald, big-nosed, gravelly voiced, with thick black-framed glasses and a permanent Churchill cigar in his hand, usually with his shoes off too. He had loudspeakers installed throughout the offices and factory so he could sit at his desk and yell orders for all to hear. He could be reduced to tears by a sentimental ballad but would regale his staff with the differing techniques of English and French prostitutes.

Any time someone stood between him and what he wanted, Nathan shouted. If they shouted back, so did he, and he always shouted longest and loudest. He operated his business frugally, saved money by recycling vinyl, and claimed the reason he wouldn't join the RIAA was because he didn't want to pay their annual fee, though the real reason was he didn't want to reveal sales figures. As a result, at King there were no RIAA-certified gold records.

As an employer he was an innovator, He was happy to hire blacks and put them in important positions in the company and the company's job application form asked applicants if they would object to working with someone of a different race, nationality, or religion. Because Nathan believed prejudice was rooted in fear of the unknown he sometimes hired the people who answered yes, thinking their prejudice might be overcome by mixing with members of other groups.

He set up his own distribution system and his fifty or so salesmen sold records from their car trunks. He was also the first record company to employ a full-time six-days-a-week studio rhythm-section to churn out new records by the hour.

He wasn't generous with his artists. Grandpa Jones made a record for King that did well, 'It's Raining Here This Morning'. But Jones had wanted a record contract so badly he'd signed what Nathan put in front of him, giving him a royalty of just 5/8ths of a cent. Even that was enough to get him a cheque for $1,000 after three months sales, which meant Nathan had made that fifty times over.

Cowboy Copas, one of King's most successful country artists, told Nathan he'd refused to pay $50 for the rights to a song he was offered on one of his scouting trips. Nathan told him, "You did the right thing, Copas; ain't no song in the world worth fifty bucks." But there was. It was a rough version of the song that later became 'Tennessee Waltz', offered to him by Jimmy Wilkinson, the bass player in Pee Wee King's Golden West Cowboys. When Copas turned it down Wilkinson sold it to Pee Wee instead. And when it went to number one, Pee Wee made two thousand times the money he'd paid.

Eventually Nathan found his black records selling more than his country ones so he signed some star black names – guitarist John Lee Hooker, who continued to record for other labels under names like John Lee Cooker – sax player Earl Bostic, who for commercial records made his alto sound like a dozen kazoos but was actually one of the best jazz players in America – and doo-wop singers the Swallows, who fired their lead singer then re-hired him as their valet. Nathan also signed country singer Wynonie Harris, negotiating with him in a hotel room in front of three naked ladies with Harris wearing nothing but pink satin underwear.

To produce his black records Nathan hired Ralph Bass, a white producer. To make country records he hired Henry Glover, a black trumpet player. Glover liked the way Nathan thought of music. "He perceived this wonderful notion of American music as not being segregated into different styles, but one big cross-ethnic whole."

Another company making records for the newly emerging black market was Chess, owned by Leonard and Philip Chess, Jewish immigrants from Poland. At first they had a liquor store and Leonard's son Marshall worked there.

My father didn't like working for anyone. He soon discovered how black people love to have a good time, that they bought a lot of liquor, so he sold the liquor store and in the same neighbourhood opened a corner pub that had a jukebox, which in turn gave him his first experience of knowing what a hit record was!

The Chess brothers then opened the Macomba Lounge, an after hours club that became a hangout for jazz players. Aristocrat, a jazz and blues record label, approached the brothers about recording some sessions there, which gave them a new idea. Shortly afterwards the club burnt down and with the insurance money they bought out Aristocrat and renamed it Chess.

The brothers got the hang of things quickly. Their first big artist was Muddy Waters; then they picked up Howlin' Wolf, and to top things off they discovered Chuck Berry while they were vacationing in St. Louis. Eventually Leonard Chess made enough money from the record business to build a large house in Chicago and invited Syd Nathan of King Records to visit. Nathan arrived to find a black workman painting the outside of the house, and singing. When Nathan asked if he'd ever thought of making a record, the workman told him he was Muddy Waters.

If you wanted to stay on the payroll at Chess Records, work was whatever you were asked to do.

There were several other small record companies, and dozens of other black rhythm & blues artists, and from them a new style of music began to coalesce. The most important person behind promoting it was Alan Freed, a radio disc jockey on Cleveland radio WJW. Somewhere in the process of popularising this new form of black music, he coined the phrase rock 'n' roll.

It may have originated from a record by Trixie Smith in 1922, 'My Man Rocks Me With One Steady Roll'; or it could have been from a Boswell Sisters record in 1934 simply entitled 'Rock and Roll', which referred to the sway of a ship on the sea; it may even have had something to do with the most popular jukebox in America in the 1930s, the Rockola. Either way, once Alan Freed started using the name on his radio show his listeners began using it too.

Rock'n'roll was rhythmic black music and Freed was playing it for a young white audience. Rather than cover versions by white artists, he always chose to play original songs by black artists – Chuck Berry, Fats Domino, Earl Bostic, the Drifters, and Louis Jordan.

Freed called his show 'The Moondog House' and billed himself as 'The King of the Moondoggers'. He'd had an operation on his larynx and his voice had a raspy deep sound which he used to sound as black as possible. His on-air manner was busy but buttery. His audience were told they were part of a hip new sect, 'Evangelicals for Black Music'. When he organised 'The Moondog Coronation Ball' at the Cleveland Arena the audience that turned up was beyond the arena's capacity. The concert was stopped, the roads were blocked, Freed was blamed, and his show was offered syndication on New York radio.

Before long the phrase 'rock 'n' roll' was known nationwide.

In Memphis there was a vibrant African-American community but it was nothing like Cleveland – this was the segregated south. There were black lawyers, dentists, doctors, surgeons and university professors, but like everyone else who was black they had to use separate schools, bathrooms, drinking fountains, park benches, churches and restaurants. And on buses they had to sit at the back.

Just down the road from the black community's 2,000-seater auditorium on Beale Street was Sun Records, owned by Sam Phillips, a white man. Like many other young southern whites, Phillips had been drawn to black music's rhythms. In the early 1950s he'd chosen the black area of town to open a small recording studio where he recorded local blues singers and leased masters of them to labels across the country.

Phillips' recording method was simple; he cut a song several times and kept the version with the most feeling. Amongst his successes were B B King, whom he leased to the RPM label, and Howlin' Wolf, whom he leased to Chess. But by 1952, the labels to which he was leasing his records were coming to Memphis and signing artists for themselves. In order to survive, Phillips decided to sell records through his own label, Sun.

Phillips was the son of a poor white tenant farmer. When he was eleven his family had taken in an old blind black man named Silas Payne from whom Phillips learned the art of imagination, "a belief in things that are unknown to you". He got on well with the local black musicians who were from much the same background. He'd talk to them about the sounds of his childhood, "the sound of the sharecroppers working and singing in the fields, the sound of a hoe striking the ground, the sound of the silences in between".

Sam Phillips wasn't making records to exploit the artists he recorded; the poor black community was his market as well as his source of artists. In the studio he knew just what he wanted from them. "My mission was to bring out of a person what was in him."

Back in New York, Atlantic now had America's definitive roster of R&B artists, among them Joe Tex, Solomon Burke, Ray Charles, Mose Alison, and the Drifters. But it had been Joe Turner who'd tipped things over the edge.

Ahmet and Nesuhi Ertegun had gone one night to the Apollo Theatre in Harlem to see Count Basie's band. There was a new singer replacing the Count's longtime blues man Jimmy Rushing. They signed him on the spot – Big Joe Turner.

Atlantic went on to have three hits with him, all of which went to the top of the R&B chart, though some radio stations wouldn't play them because of the sexual innuendo in Turner's grunts and shouts. Then came 'Shake, Rattle and Roll' and the cat was really out of the bag. This wasn't innuendo – shake rattle and roll meant just one thing, and it wasn't dancing.

With this record Atlantic became the hippest record company in America and it attracted the attention of CBS records. They sent two of their executives to offer Ahmet a deal:

> *They offered to take over our label and distribute it for us. I said, "Really? What would you give us for that?" They said, "Five per cent royalty." I said, "What about the artists?" They said, "You're not paying niggers royalties, are you?" I said, "Yes we are." They said, "Well, you're going to spoil the whole business for everybody."*

24
Hound Dog
ROCK 'N' ROLL IN BLACK & WHITE

At the end of the war, when Frank Sinatra was selling ten million records a year and bobbysoxers were screaming and swooning, *Newsweek* wanted to know, "If fans never screamed at singers before, why Sinatra?"

They decided his look of innocence and vulnerability set off a "sublimated maternal instinct" that caused "mass sexual delirium". Conservative newspapers called the girls teenage delinquents. The music industry called them a new market.

Delinquency and teenage marketing finally dovetailed when Bill Haley had a hit with Joe Turner's 'Shake, Rattle and Roll'. The Bill Haley version was the first white rock 'n' roll record, a mixture of Joe Turner's bawdy blues, country twang, and black shuffle. The Bill Haley band was signed to Decca and produced by the company's A&R man, Milt Gabler. He made them copy one of the black swing bands of the forties, Louis Jordan's Tympany Five. "We'd begin with Jordan's shuffle rhythm and we'd build on it. I'd sing Jordan's riffs to the band; that would be picked up by the electric guitars and tenor sax."

Haley's 'Shake, Rattle and Roll' was a hit all over the world. Whether rock 'n' roll had needed a white face to sell it, or whether it had just needed to be calmed down a bit, was unclear. Either way Bill Haley became an overnight star. A movie company picked up his next record and made it the title theme of a new film, *Blackboard Jungle*. The song was 'Rock Around the Clock' and the film was about delinquent schoolchildren. It instantly became a worldwide call to arms for rebellious youth, which meant more or less anyone under twenty-one. Later, Frank Zappa wrote in *Life* magazine about the first time he heard it. "When the title flashed Bill Haley and His Comets started blurching... It was the loudest thing the kids had ever heard at that time." Bill Haley was playing the teenage National Anthem – 'Rock Around the Clock'.

Columbia Pictures grabbed Haley and made a couple of cheap musicals with him. Their success swept round the world. From Rio de Janeiro to Hamburg to Tokyo, teenagers filled cinemas. 'See You Later Alligator' sang Bill Haley from the big screen, and the kids jumped out of their seats to join in.

Nowhere did it make more impact than in Britain. All those Teddy boys hanging around on street corners suddenly found the music they'd been waiting for. They flooded into the cinemas with flick knives and while Haley sang 'Rip It Up', they tore up the seats. Britain was frightened by this outpouring of teenage energy it was difficult to see how it could be put to good use, but when Teddy boys started dancing they found an outlet for it. Bill Haley's music, recreated by local bands in every town, rejuvenated Britain's dance business. And with the BBC still not playing records, dance halls once again became the place for publishers and record companies to plug their product, but this time it was aimed squarely at under-twenties.

In just twelve months the emphasis of popular music had switched from Hollywood glitz and Mitch Miller gimmicks to adolescent dreams and teenage rebellion.

Seeing white musicians take rock 'n' roll and make it their own, some of the black record companies fought back. Little Richard came out with a track that made 'Shake, Rattle and Roll' look like a kiddie's song. 'Tutti Frutti' was a song he'd been performing on the gay club circuit. At Speciality Records, producer Bumps Blackwell knew at once it was a hit, though it needed some spring-cleaning. It started with a scat intro of *'a-wop bop-a loo-bop, a-wop bam-boom'*, and that was acceptable. But the lyrics of the verse were, *'If it don't fit, don't force it. You can grease it, make it easy'*. So they were changed to the ultra boring, *'I've got a gal, named Daisy. She almost drives me crazy'*. But Little Richard sang it with exactly the same raunchy innuendo he'd used when it was about shoving your cock up someone's ass. And off it went, zooming to number one on the R&B chart, but still not the Hot 100, not for something as far out as this.

Little Richard was manic. He wore a hugely baggy black suit with two-foot wide trouser bottoms, had make-up on his face, mascara'd eyes, even lipstick, and a daft little moustache. On stage he went wild.

In the southern states, concert venues were still divided into separate 'white' and 'colored' areas. Little Richard's audiences would begin segregated but with his encouragement start to mix once he was onstage. The North Alabama White Citizens Council put out a statement on television warning that "Rock 'n' Roll is part of a test to undermine the morals of the youth of our nation. It is sexualistic, unmoralistic and… brings people of both races together."

Apart from CBS, which was still mired in the mulch of Mitch Miller, the other record companies could clearly see that rock 'n' roll, if it was combined with the right white artist, could produce something huge. They were searching for a white singer who could adapt black rock 'n' roll the way Bill Haley had, but was younger and good looking. Bill Haley's records sold well, but not as well as Frank Sinatra's had done ten years earlier. Nobody screamed at Bill Haley, he was in his thirties, he looked like a paunchy uncle entertaining kids at a children's party. Remembering the extraordinary reaction Frank Sinatra had elicited from teenagers, record company executives were asking, Where can we find the Sinatra of rock 'n' roll?

At Sun studios in Memphis, Sam Phillips had a clever trick. He hired the studio by the hour to people who came in off the street to make demos for themselves; he not only earned money from it, he used it as a way of auditioning all the emerging talent in town. Several times he told friends, "If I could find a white man who had the Negro sound and the Negro feel, I could make a billion dollars."

In fact that person had been around for a while, but hadn't yet been noticed. In August 1953, Elvis Presley had come to the offices of Sun Records and booked half-an-hour of studio time to record a couple of songs for his mum. After he'd recorded them, Sam Phillips, asked the receptionist to make a note of his name and address. Six months later he called Elvis back and provided him with two musicians. "I called Scotty Moore, told him to get Bill Black and come in and work with Presley," Phillips said. "I told him: 'I've got a young man and he's different. He's nervous and timid and extremely polite. Work with him and see what you can do'."

Out of the session came 'That's Alright', which Phillips released on Sun. He then booked Elvis to do a live show supporting country singer Slim Whitman. Trying to move to the rhythm and frightened by the large crowd, Elvis's legs shook with fear beneath him, which was emphasised by his wide-cut pants. A few girls screamed and Elvis took note and put it in his act. But he was no overnight success.

From there Phillips put out four more singles and Elvis toured the southern states billed as the 'King of Western Bop'. Not instantly, but bit-by-bit, he began to click with young kids. Then quite suddenly he took off. It was only in the south-east, but the kids went wild for him. Shy, polite Elvis was turning into a raucous sensation.

Sam Phillips, in urgent need of operating capital for the studio, wasn't sure how much bigger it would get. So as Presley's fame with the young southern audience spread, he decided to offer Sun's contract with him to a major record company for $35,000, a whopping high price for a performer with only local appeal.

By now Presley had a manager, a Dutch born southern booking agent who called himself Colonel Parker. He was in favour of Phillips selling his contract with Elvis to a major label and helped hype the price. Ahmet Ertegun saw Presley's talent at once and offered $25,000, which was all the money he could get together. He told Nesuhi, "All those cover versions everybody does of our black records, this boy is a cover version of all our black artists rolled into one."

But when RCA offered the $35,000 Phillips had asked for, that's where Elvis went. And Colonel Parker, who had played a large part in persuading RCA to pay that much, now introduced Presley to two friends of his in music publishing, Jean and Julian Aberbach.

A few years earlier, Jean Aberbach had left Chappell, where he'd learnt the publishing business from Max Dreyfus, and set up his own company, Hill & Range. He built its catalogue by forming joint companies with each songwriter he met. But Elvis didn't write songs, which for a publisher was something of a setback.

Aberbach came up with an unusual arrangement. He formed Elvis Presley Music, a joint company between Elvis and Hill & Range. If a songwriter wanted Elvis to sing one of his songs, he would have to donate one third of it to Elvis Presley Music. If he refused, Elvis would sing something else.

To help persuade Elvis this was a good deal, Aberbach came up with some cash. "I gave Elvis a check for $2,500, an advance against the royalties of his stock ownership and he promptly went to the Cadillac dealer and got a pink one."

To find suitable songs, the Aberbachs employed their cousin, Freddy Bienstock. Bienstock was born in Switzerland and raised in Vienna. For the last few years he too had been working at Chappell. He wore monogrammed shirts, carried a monocle on a silk chord, and had never lost his German accent. He considered the deal his cousin had made with Elvis to be a fair one. "If Elvis liked the song, the writers would be offered guaranteed sales of a million records…"

For the chance of an Elvis recording, songwriters would do anything Bienstock asked. And as far as Freddy Bienstock was concerned, so long as one third of the song was assigned to Elvis Presley Music, the song was good.

Songwriters called it 'the Elvis tax'.

Elvis changed everything. Writers no longer had to care about the old 32-bar format, or middle-class sensibilities, or family values. It was music for the young and no one else.

The older generation hated it. After a show in La Crosse, Wisconsin, an urgent message from the local Catholic newspaper was sent to FBI director J. Edgar Hoover warning that "Presley is a definite danger to the security of the United States."

The *New York Daily News* said his act had "reached the lowest depths of 'grunt and groin'".

When Colonel Parker booked him into Vegas, a middle-class middle-aged audience gave him an ice-cold reception – "like a jug of corn liquor at a champagne party", said *Newsweek*.

A car showroom in Cincinnati advertised they would break fifty Elvis Presley records with each car sold. And sold five in a day.

Even Frank Sinatra threw himself into the controversy, saying, "This rancid-smelling aphrodisiac, I deplore."

Elvis replied, "I admire the man. He has a right to say what he wants to say. He is a great success and a fine actor."

Presley's success had been due entirely to the emergence of BMI. It had opened the music industry to new writers and the airwaves to new music. ASCAP, totally misjudging the direction music was taking, took sides with conservatism. There was a new civil war in progress – youth against age, students against schools, liberals against right-wing fanatics, and ASCAP against BMI. High schools and government bodies were printing pamphlets denouncing rock 'n' roll as evil and obscene. ASCAP decided to use the courtroom to do the same.

Arthur Schwartz wrote 'Dancing in the Dark'; he was also a lawyer and an ASCAP member. He was obsessed with the idea of destroying BMI. What had set him off was having one of his songs rejected for a TV show by an RCA executive who chose a BMI song instead.

Schwartz didn't understand that most TV producers preferred BMI music because it was more current than ASCAP music. He thought rock 'n' roll and Elvis were the work of the devil. He believed TV companies had an inherent preference for BMI music because most them owned stock in the society. So Schwartz bought an action against "all those others who have directly and indirectly injured writers by placing American music in a strait jacket manipulated through BMI".

After much expensive arguing, ASCAP's lawyers had to listen to the judge find against them. Undeterred they tried again, this time through a friend of the society in Congress, Emanuel Celler, the chairman of the House Judiciary Committee. To get himself elected he'd declared he was dedicated to "breaking the power of the broadcast networks". As soon as he got into the senate he ordered hearings by the Antitrust Subcommittee about "the involvement of radio and television networks in music publishing and promotion".

A past president of ASCAP set the tone of the agenda when he told the committee that the radio networks, by being "arbiters of the audible and viceroys of the visual" had sought to control "the faucets through which music flows".

But it was songwriter Billy Rose who bought the thing down to basics. "It's the current climate on radio and TV which makes Elvis Presley and his animal posturing possible.... not only are most of the BMI songs junk, but in many cases they are obscene junk, pretty much on a level with dirty comic magazines."

The author of a recent best-selling exposé of Madison Avenue's advertising techniques was produced as a star witness and asserted that a "gross degradation in the quality of music supplied to the public over the airwaves" was taking place, due to BMI's use of the "cheapest types of music" – hillbilly and rock 'n' roll.

In defence of BMI, Senator Al Gore read a telegram from the governor of Tennessee saying remarks of this type were "a gratuitous insult to thousands of our fellow Tennesseans both in and out of the field of country music".

Gene Autry, a singing cowboy movie star, told the committee it had been easier for him to get an invitation to the White House than to get into ASCAP.

In the end, the general opinion of the committee fell in line with the judge's summing up in the original Schwartz versus BMI case. "Never in my experience have I seen such sweeping charges made against so many people with such flimsy evidence… They have made the most slanderous kind of charges against a whole industry… and they have failed to substantiate these charges with the slightest shred of evidence."

25

American Pie
COUNTRY BECOMES MAINSTREAM

In the 1950s, Nashville was just getting started. In another ten years it would become the American music industry's third major hub. For the moment, though, northerners still thought of country music as hillbillies dancing to violins in cowboy movies.

Now and again there had been country hits. Jimmie Rodgers' songs in the twenties, and Gene Autry's in the thirties, sang from the back of his horse in Hollywood westerns. But until BMI opened the airwaves in 1939, national radio in America had played almost no real country music.

The one exception was *National Barn Dance*, a programme started by a Chicago radio station in the twenties to cater for the city's white southern immigrants. But it didn't have the credibility of being broadcast from the place where the music originated.

Grand Ole Opry did. It was started in 1925 as a copy of *National Barn Dance* and was broadcast locally from the radio station of a Nashville insurance company. That first year the star was a seventy-seven-year-old fiddler called Uncle Jimmy Thomson. The following year the organisers did it again, then came up with the name *Grand Ole Opry*. In Nashville it became a much-loved annual event.

Further afield it was little known but when BMI began so did national broadcasts of the *Grand Ole Opry*. In 1939 it was syndicated on NBC's 'Red Network' and broadcast nationally for the next seventeen years. By the mid-fifties *Grand Ole Opry* had become an accepted piece of Americana – a star-studded three-hour annual celebration of country music listened to by millions of people, most of whom didn't listen to another note of country music until the following year.

Another boost for country music came when Patti Page had a national hit with 'Tennessee Waltz'. The writer was Jimmy Wilkinson, a Nashville musician who played bass with Pee Wee King and his Golden West Cowboys.

Short of ready cash, Wilkinson sold the original version of the song to his bandleader for fifty dollars. Pee Wee King tarted it up, registered it as his own and published it with local publishers Acuff-Rose. Because the original version was a favourite of her father's, Patti Page got to know it well. Page was one of Mitch Miller's top acts at CBS, and when he called her into the studio to make her annual Christmas record she asked if she could put 'Tennessee Waltz' on the 'B' side.

With 'Boogie Woogie Santa Claus' as the 'A' side, it wasn't surprising that DJs preferred 'Tennessee Waltz'. It went to number one in *Billboard*, the first country song ever to do so.

Acuff-Rose, the song's publishers, were another by-product of BMI.

Roy Acuff had been a singer and guitarist with The Smokey Mountain Boys, but then he put together a songbook of his favourite country tunes. Frustrated by a lack of interest from established music publishers, he purchased fifteen minutes of advertising time on a local radio station in Nashville. The next week his songbook sold 10,000 copies, and another 100,000 in the following month. Hooked on the quick money of music publishing, Acuff quit playing in a band and looked for a partner to team up with.

Fred Rose had lived up north during the twenties and thirties and written popular songs for Paul Whiteman. After having hits like 'Honest and Truly' and 'Deed I Do' he was allowed to join ASCAP, but he never rose above a 'Category 4' writer and was mostly paid just $200 a year.

In 1940, when he teamed up with Roy Acuff, he stayed faithful to ASCAP and requested an advance for the new company. ASCAP had no interest in country music and turned him down, so Rose went to BMI who gave him $2,500.

Ten year's later the Acuff-Rose catalogue was bulging. The company was BMI's top performer; and the company's top writer was Hank Williams.

Williams came from a poor white family and started out aged fifteen singing in the street in Montgomery, Alabama. A producer at a local radio station liked what he heard and told him to come to the studio. Next thing, young Hank was given his own show – fifteen minutes twice a week, with a fifteen dollar salary to match. It was enough to start his career, but alcohol was enough to finish it. Roy Acuff told him, "You've got a million-dollar voice, son, but a ten-cent brain."

By the time he'd drunk himself to death aged twenty-nine, Hank Williams had written a stack of hits, including 'Hey Good Lookin', 'Your Cheating Heart', and 'Jambalaya' – all with contracts safely tucked away in Acuff-Rose's safe.

What finally put Nashville on the map wasn't really country music, it was the music of artists who broke away from it. When Elvis Presley appeared on the *Grand Ole Opry* in 1954, the traditionalists didn't approve one bit. The audience may have reacted politely but the organisers told him he should go back to truck-driving in Memphis.

Another southern singer they disapproved of was Jerry Lee Lewis. His parents mortgaged their farm to buy him a piano, then sent him to bible college in Waxahachie, Texas. He was thrown out for playing a boogie-woogie version of 'My God Is Real' at church assembly. After that he took to playing things like 'Whole Lotta Shakin' Goin' On' and 'Great Balls of Fire'.

Lewis tried to be as manic as Little Richard but couldn't get it right. He wore black slacks and a striped ivy-league shirt with white belt and shoes and looked like a college kid doing holiday work in a drug store. Onstage he kicked the piano and warned the audience his music would lead them to hell. "I have the devil in me," he told them.

Perhaps he had, because he then married his cousin who was just thirteen. He was blacklisted from radio right across America and overnight his asking price for performances fell from $10,000 a night in concert halls to $250 a night in beer joints. Falling from grace was a family trait. His cousin, Jimmy Swaggart, was a television evangelist who got caught with prostitutes. On national television he wept and ranted to the Almighty, "I would ask that your precious blood would wash and cleanse every stain until it is in the seas of God's forgiveness."

A third performer from the region who was not strictly country was Carl Perkins, the singer Sam Phillips was left with once he'd sold Elvis to RCA.

Perkins was no Elvis but he didn't do badly; he wrote and recorded 'Blue Suede Shoes'. It reached number two in the Hot 100 but was kept from number one by Elvis's 'Heartbreak Hotel'. In the middle of a tour to promote it, Perkins had a road accident, smashed himself to bits and ended up in hospital. Elvis very kindly offered to help out.

He recorded a cover version of the song so it would go on selling and Perkins could continue to earn money from it while he was recuperating. But what at first looked like heart-warming generosity turned out to be less so when Elvis demanded his usual 30 per cent tax on it. He then also took 30 per cent on the version Carl Perkins had recorded.

As these singers emerged from the south, more and more owl-eared executives from the north came prowling to Nashville and Memphis, looking for opportunities. Nashville music people, knowing that the best local artists were already signed up, went looking further afield, travelling south. And it was on just such a trip that a Nashville agent found himself at a Bill Haley gig in Lubbock, Texas, where he saw a singer he felt lukewarm about – just enough to tell people in Nashville it might be worth giving him a listen. They did, and signed him up.

Buddy Holly became the link between Elvis Presley and the generation of artists who followed – the singers who wrote their own songs. He was the one person on the chart who was different from all the others. His success only lasted a year and-a-half yet he was described by critic Bruce Elder as "the single most influential creative force in early rock and roll".

Critics have written pages of analysis about Holly's music trying to justify that influence, but in terms of his musical style there wasn't much that was new. It was his understatement that did it. Most whites played rock 'n' roll by pushing it as hard as they could, Holly did the opposite. Music critic Greil Marcus wrote, "Buddy Holly shied away from the violence implicit in rock 'n' roll... looked for space in the noise..."

While there's no doubting the influence he had on subsequent generations of rock musicians, Holly's life was so unremarkable that biographers have been forced to fill pages with such things as the serial number of a dollar bill found in the wallet he lost while water-skiing. Holly won a singing contest when he was five; learned to play piano, guitar, and violin; performed harmony duets at talent shows and sang in the high school choir. After he left school he was signed as a solo artist by Decca in Nashville and recorded four singles, two of which were released but got nowhere.

Decca blamed his glasses. They said he looked like the class swot rather than a rock 'n' roll singer, so they dropped him. They also barred him from re-recording the songs he'd recorded for them.

Holly then met Norman Petty, a country musician and religious zealot who had a recording studio in New Mexico. Petty required his artists to pray to God before each take to ensure a good performance, and afterwards, if it turned out well, everyone in the studio had to hold hands and thank the Lord. He became Holly's record producer, publisher and manager, and recorded him singing 'That'll Be The Day', one of the songs Decca had barred him from re-recording.

When Coral Records showed interest, Petty, hoping Decca wouldn't realise it was Buddy Holly, signed the track to them under the name 'The Crickets'. It was an unnecessary ruse. Coral was funded by Decca and when the song became a hit there wasn't a problem. It reached number one on both sides of the Atlantic and was followed, first by 'Peggy Sue', and then by two albums – one for Coral as The Crickets, and one under Holly's own name for Decca.

Norman Petty's passion for prayer was nothing compared with his passion for money. He not only signed all Holly's songs to his own publishing company, but also demanded a cut-in for his production work in the studio.

In due course, Holly hired a lawyer and tried to get out of the contract but ran out of money before the dispute could be settled. To put himself back in funds he accepted an offer of a well-paid tour with Ritchie Valens, Dion, and the Big Bopper. When the tour bus broke down in Clear Lake, Iowa, Holly and some of the others chartered a light airplane to take them to the next stop on the tour and his career ended with a plane crash one hour later.

Short but sweet, but he'd changed pop music. On stage, he'd projected self-doubt, sincerity and innocence. His songs were simplistic, and he had the personality of the guy who never gets noticed.

"An obvious loser," British writer Nik Cohn called him, "the patron saint of all the thousands of no-talent kids who ever tried to make a million dollars."

26
Hallelujah
PAYOLA

On Broadway there were still musicals and the Dreyfus brothers still hogged the publishing. But they were now in their eighties and beginning to seem irrelevant to an industry that was breaking new ground. As did Broadway shows.

People enjoyed them and the best shows ran and ran, like *The King and I* and *West Side Story*. But although they drew people, made money, and created royalties for songwriters and publishers, so too did the amusement park on Coney Island. Broadway shows were old-time stuff; the music industry had moved on. Strangely, where it had moved to was right there in the middle of theatre-land, two buildings almost the same size and shape as each other, 1650 Broadway and 1619 Broadway.

1619 was known as the Brill building. It was named after its original owners, a men's haberdashers called Brill who initially occupied the ground floor and bought the building intending to develop it. Foiled by the Depression, they turned the upper storeys into tiny offices – mere cubicles – and rented them out to whoever came, mostly people at the bottom end of the music business. Then slowly, over the next twenty years, some of the top end moved in too.

The upper storeys housed hopeful publishers and fading songwriters, refugees from the old Tin Pan Alley. The cubicles were topped with frosted glass, but not quite to the ceiling, so all the noise from next door came in.

In 1958, there were ninety music publishers listed as having premises there, including two of Sinatra's favourite songwriters, Johnny Burke and Jimmy Van Heusen. Irving Caesar was there too, the man who once wrote George Gershwin's lyrics and used to go to the races every Friday with Max Dreyfus. Even Charles K. Harris's company had an office there, long after the ball was over.

On the lower floors were proper offices, some of them even with a touch of class. Alan Freed, radio's number one rock 'n' roll DJ, had the lushest one. Jerry Wexler, producer of every black Atlantic recording star, visited him each Friday with a bag of cash – $600. "Purely a defensive move," he insisted. "The baksheesh didn't guarantee play for any particular record; we were only buying access."

Morris Levy was also at the Brill. Levy was Alan Freed's manager and owner of Birdland, New York's top jazz venue. He was also the only music publisher with enough gall to cut himself in on songs by his own writers, taking a cut of 'Why Do Fools Fall in Love' by Frankie Lymon and the Teenagers. He had Mafia connections but was proudly Jewish, with photos of his children's bar mitzvahs on the walls of his office. Whenever artists asked Morris about royalties, he yelled at them, "Royalties? Try Buckingham Palace."

Most of the publishers lunched at Lindy's, over the road. Wexler described seeing them there, dressed in "double-breasted gabardine suits, wide white-on-white collars and big-knotted hand-painted ties... always a smile, always a story to tell and a song to sell".

The Brill was halfway between seedy and happening. Many of the tenants were old-time ASCAP songwriters still rhyming moon with June and thinking the reason they couldn't get their songs recorded was due to a BMI plot. Some, though, were currently successful, like Burt Bacharach and Hal David. They met every weekday at 11am in one of the small upstairs cubicles, writing songs like 'Magic Moments' and 'Another Time Another Place'. Real old-fashioned ASCAP hits.

1650 Broadway was the rival building. Almost identical in style but different in tenants. Here they were younger, some just teenagers, many of them Latino or black. It could have been called BMI House.

Built in 1922, it was a decade older than the Brill Building and a couple of storeys taller. It had been built with a recording studio in the basement in the days when New York had a by-law saying musicians couldn't enter buildings by the front door. So the entrance was round the corner on 51st Street.

In 1958, there were sixty-six music publishers listed as having offices there including W. C. Handy. Many tenants were still under twenty-one, too young to buy a drink so they used the soda fountain at Hanson's Drug Store on the corner of 51st and 7th. Like the Brill building, in the offices and cubicles of 1650 you could find publishers to buy a song, arrangers to spruce it up, musicians and singers to record a demo, and a machine that would cut acetate copies for sending to A&R men.

1650 was the hip building. The Aberbachs' company, Hill & Range, was on the top floor, complete with cousin Freddy searching out material for Elvis.

Jerry Leiber and Mike Stoller were there too. Leiber and Stoller were Jewish from Los Angeles but caught up in black culture. They had a knack of writing songs that black artists felt comfortable with. Their first big chance had come in 1952 when Big Mama Thornton liked a song they'd written called 'Hound Dog'. At the recording session the drummer wasn't up to scratch so Leiber and Stoller suggested the producer play drums instead. They then stepped in and produced the session.

When Leiber made suggestions to Mama Thornton about how she should phrase their song, she bellowed, "White boy, don't you be tellin' *me* how to sing the blues."

The scolding was worth it. Mama Thornton went to number one in the R&B chart.

With that success under their belts, Leiber and Stoller decided the next step should be New York. There, they started making mock black records. Using white singers with black sounding voices they had a hit with 'Riot in Cell Block 9'. But at Atlantic Records, Nesuhi Ertegen had the idea of doing the same thing in reverse – produce black artists and make them sound more white.

Leiber and Stoller went into the studio with the Drifters, who had twice put out records that were banned on radio because of their sexual innuendo. They toned down their lyrics, softened their sound and added strings. Jerry Wexler loathed it. "Get that out of here, I hate it. It's out of tune, and it's phony, and it's shit…" But Leiber and Stoller had just invented 'soul music'.

'There Goes My Baby' by the Drifters was the first R & B record to go into *Billboard*'s Top 100. It was rhythm & blues with soft production.

Leiber and Stoller then made 'Yakety Yak' with the Coasters, and for rhythm & blues that was the final breakthrough – number one in the *Billboard* Hot 100.

The Aberbachs persuaded them to form a joint publishing company with Hill & Range. The Aberbachs were getting more and more people to do this. Piecing together a publishing empire by forming joint companies with anyone who came along with a song. They'd say, "Look, we're being honest with you – publishing is a bit of a racket, money for old rope, so we'll let you in on it. Instead of us publishing your songs we'll form a joint company with you, so it'll be *you* publishing your own songs. We'll just run it for you."

Leiber and Stoller had learnt their production from Mitch Miller, but only in terms of the producer being the creative force of the record. They ditched all the bad taste aspects of Miller's productions and replaced them with black rhythm sections, subtle strings, and songs as skilfully conceived as the best of 1930s Broadway.

Their productions for the Drifters and the Coasters took Atlantic Records to a new place. Jerry Wexler was an old-fashioned producer; he left the band to rehearse, then had them play. But Leiber and Stoller were involved in everything – the placing of microphones, the sound quality, the balance of every note of the record. Wexler didn't understand all that. When they asked him for a producer's credit, he was scornful. "What the hell do you want your name on the label for? Your name is on the label as writers. How many times do you want your name on the record?"

They won that battle then asked for royalties. This time the fight turned nasty, but in the end they won again, and another aspect of the business changed forever.

Even though Atlantic was considered a company where black artists got a fair royalty, payments were usually made with a moderate amount of improvisation. So Leiber and Stoller asked for an audit of the records they'd produced with the Drifters. When it revealed a deficit of $18,000, they demanded to be paid. Jerry Wexler re-named them "Mr Greed and Mr Avarice".

In other matters, Atlantic could be surprisingly casual with money. Wexler recalls being in Chicago when they had to pay an R&B disc-jockey to break a Joe Turner record. In the hotel room they spread out piles of twenties and fifties and Ahmet said, "I think we need three inches of money."

ASCAP and BMI members were at each other's throats again. ASCAP banned its writer members from co-writing songs with BMI members. BMI, in order to help ASCAP writers co-write with its members, said if they did so it would pay the BMI member not just his own share of the royalty but his ASCAP co-writer's share too, which he could then pass on.

ASCAP said anyone found writing with a BMI member under an assumed name would suffer a year's deduction of royalties. This left the residents of the two Broadway music buildings, 1650 and 1619, like opposing armies in their castles. But in one of the camps there was rebellion within too.

Many ASCAP writers were resentful of the games their society was playing. They were also upset about the weighted vote system. Voting rights were vested in only 5 per cent of the writer members and 15 per cent of the publishers. They told the ASCAP board they would "take it to Washington" for a showdown, and supporting them were some of the ASCAP publishers who were not in the society's inner sanctum. Now ASCAP was not only at war with BMI, it was fighting its own members.

A congressional committee was instigated with four days of hearings and ASCAP counselor Herman Finkelstein started the proceedings by proudly announcing that the society had "little or no rock 'n' roll" in its catalogue.

Fred Fox of Sam Fox Publishing criticised ASCAP for punishing him with a royalty deduction because he'd claimed extra money for works lasting more than four minutes.

Hans Lengsfelder, a spokesman for the smaller publisher members, complained that the board had not informed members about its hiring of a Washington attorney for $350,000.

Hal David, a comparative newcomer to writing hit songs, objected to ASCAP's method of payment which gave writers no royalties on a new song until it had been continuously successful during four consecutive three-monthly distribution periods.

ASCAP was reported to be spending over a million dollars fighting its own members in public, and the members were spending plenty too. Top music attorney

Lee Eastman represented ASCAP's currently successful writers and claimed the payment method discriminated against them. Charles Horsky, a Nuremberg Trials prosecutor, presented the grievances of the lesser writers and attacked the society's lack of democratic procedures. This was washing dirty linen in public.

While ASCAP suffered publicly at the hands of its own members, BMI was celebrating its seventeenth anniversary with the most hits in its history – six in the top seven of 'Your Hit Parade', and the entire top ten in *Variety*'s 'Top Record Talent and Tunes'.

The ASCAP board could only hope BMI might bankrupt itself with the high payments it was making to its writers, paying them in accordance with the number of radio plays each song received. ASCAP's press office activated every bit of bad publicity that could be dug up to malign its rival; in particular, they tried to link BMI to rock 'n' roll. In a magazine interview, Frank Sinatra obliged them with a suitable definition, "the martial music of every side-burned delinquent on the face of the earth".

In the *New York Herald Tribune*, Oscar Hammerstein wrote that BMI's close connections with owners of radio stations gave it "an interest *beyond* giving the best music to the people". And in a Senate debate Senator Goldwater quoted Hoagy Carmichael as saying "the airwaves of this country have been flooded with bad music since BMI was formed". There was even serious consideration given to the possibility that rock 'n' roll might be a communist plot.

In which case, the commies were taking over the Brill building.

The Aberbach brothers, flush with money from Elvis's continuing success, and with a host of country music publishers signed up to fifty-fifty partnerships, now moved into the top floor of the Brill building. Becoming a little flash, they turned it into one of the best penthouse suites on Broadway and filled it with pictures from Julian Aberbach's private collection, artists like Bernard Buffet and Edward Burne-Jones.

Cousin Freddy was still around, still searching for songs on which to levy the Elvis tax, enjoying his daily banter with the endless flow of songwriters.

A songwriter might start on the penthouse floor where we had our office and if we didn't take his songs, he would go to the 11th floor and so on until they found a home... Walter Donaldson, who was always betting on racehorses and always needed money, would sell a song like 'My Blue Heaven' to three different publishers and then they would have to sort out their interests.

Leiber and Stoller, now one of Aberbach's joint companies, also moved in, bringing two more writers with them, Doc Pomus and Mort Shuman ('Viva Las Vegas' and 'Save the Last Dance for Me').

Doc Pomus complained about the large new room they were given. He didn't like the grand piano and deep pile carpet. "We never did a bit of work... we had to get another office... just a small piano and two upright chairs..."

People from 1650 Broadway were like that; they didn't feel comfortable being posh.

In the old building a new company replaced the Aberbachs as top dog – Aldon Music, which belonged to Donnie Kirshner and Al Nevins.

Kirshner was the son of a tailor who had a shop in Harlem that counted Pearl Bailey and Dinah Washington amongst his clients. But Kirshner himself grew up in the Bronx. The only thing he'd ever shown any flair for was basketball, but he had an ear for good songs.

When he was eighteen, he became friendly with an amateur singer he met in a candy store, called Robert Casotto. Kirshner decided they should work together writing songs for Casotto to sing. To make ends meet, they went door to door, offering to write commercials for shops and businesses. Casotto then changed his name to Bobby Darin and got himself a hit on Atlantic with a song he wrote in ten minutes, 'Splish Splash', Atlantic's first ever hit with a white artist.

Kirshner realised he either had to face failure or give up writing songs. "I don't have the talent myself," he admitted, "but you know... I'm the man with the golden ear."

It was then he met Al Nevins who'd written a few small hits including songs for Doris Day and Jimmy Dorsey's band. At the time they met, 'Twilight Time', one of Nevins' small hits, had just been re-recorded by the Platters and gone to number one. Nevins felt flush with funds and was ready to put his money into something. And the thing he chose was Don Kirshner.

They formed Aldon Music and took an office at 1650 Broadway. While they were unpacking the furniture two writers stuck their heads round the door looking for a deal, Neil Sedaka and Howard Greenfield. They'd already had some songs recorded but hadn't had a hit. Kirshner and Nevins had even less to offer – a new company, an empty office, and not a single song in their catalogue.

Kirshner bluffed the two hopeful songwriters into singing him some songs and immediately offered them a long-term contract. Sedaka said Kirshner should prove himself first and gave him eight songs for a three-month period. If one of them charted they would sign.

When Kirshner had been writing advertising jingles for shops with Bobby Darin, they'd once used a girl singer from New Jersey to sing on one, Concetta Franconero. She was now known as Connie Francis and had a Top 40 hit with 'Who's Sorry Now'. So Kirshner put Neil Sedaka in his car and drove him over there.

Thinking she would want a song similar to her hit, Sedaka sat at the piano and played a string of old fashioned ballads. Concetta didn't like a thing she heard, so out of desperation Sedaka played 'Stupid Cupid', a silly rip-off of Jerry Lee Lewis. Concetta loved it, and two months later it was in the Top 20.

Kirshner and Nevins were now hit publishers. They persuaded Sedaka to write some songs for himself. He did, and got a hit with 'Oh! Carol'. Pleased with his new publishers, he introduced them to the song's inspiration, his friend Carole Klein. She changed her name to King, started writing with her boyfriend Gerry Goffin and wrote a hit for the Shirelles, 'Will You Still Love Me Tomorrow'.

Kirshner built a row of writing cubicles, each with a standup piano, and filled them with all the young songwriters he could find for $150 a week. Soon he had eighteen writers aged nineteen to twenty-six. They composed eight hours a day then cut acetate demos of the songs they'd written and played them to each other in the evening, making comments and suggestions. Kirshner oversaw the meetings and had the final say. From a cold start, in just one year he became America's most successful publisher of current hit songs.

American Bandstand was the first rock 'n' roll TV show in the USA, though perhaps the description 'rock 'n' roll' was overdoing it. If rock 'n' roll was Bill Haley and Elvis, this was just slosh. It was the sort of song Don Kirshner's writers were turning out at the Brill building, music for white teenagers – good tunes, sharp lyrics, and just a hint of rock 'n' roll rhythm. Cute enough, but never daring.

With the help of American Bandstand, that's what rock 'n' roll became. Dick Clark, the show's host, was known as the man who made rock 'n' roll acceptable. He reassured the nation's parents that rock 'n' roll wasn't so bad after all.

The show was shot in a studio filled with dancing teenagers. The boys dressed like kids in a high school dance and the girls all smiled liked Doris Day. The camera angle was always from above, so to an adult turning on it looked safe, like opening the door at a party for twelve-year-olds and seeing all the cute young things one foot below your eye-line. It was a brilliant move. The camera never got among them, never showed a pelvic thrust or a wiggling boob. Eighteen-year-olds looked like they were five years younger, dancing mechanically, expressionless, bobbing up and down like sexless zombies. Yet young people watched right across America. They had no choice – there wasn't another show on TV that played their sort of music.

Black artists sometimes appeared but were kept under tight control so the programme still felt white. Advertisers were afraid of their products becoming connected with blacks and this often made the music industry look more segregated than it really was. Jerry Wexler complained that whenever Atlantic's artists appeared on the show, the man from the advertising agency would be there, pushing them to behave like blacks in a Hollywood movie, dancing with cute steps and flashing big smiles. "They were Jim Crowing the business. They controlled what could sell in a white market."

The show's host, Dick Clark, was of course up to everything a man in that position could be up to. The competition amongst record companies to get their songs on the show was huge. But Clark didn't take bribes Alan-Freed-style in brown paper bags; he took them in the more sophisticated form of shares in music-related companies. Later, when he was dragged into trials investigating illegal practices in the music industry, Clark's name became synonymous with payola – record plays obtained through bribery. He testified under oath that he'd never received a thing. But an investigation of his books revealed he'd made half a million dollars in twenty-seven months from music publishing, talent representation, record pressing and distribution.

Singer Orville Lunsford said his song 'American Boy' was played on every show after he'd ordered 50,000 records from Clark's pressing plant. The investigative panel found Clark had cut himself in on every possible source of revenue. He had shares in six publishing companies, three record labels, a record pressing plant, a record distributor and a firm that managed singers.

And the conclusion? The district attorney stated publicly that Clark was innocent of payola.

It was a thank-you from the American establishment for his having so brilliantly castrated rock 'n' roll.

Payola first became a big deal when it was rumoured TV producers were rigging popular quiz shows, in particular *The $64,000 Question*, which led to an investigation of all bribery in broadcasting.

It turned out TV producers were asking music publishers for a 30 per cent cut on theme tunes for shows. A theme tune played on a regular morning chat show on NBC or ABC would earn ASCAP or BMI royalties. Guests to these shows had once been introduced with a drum roll. Now it was a copyrighted fanfare, with the show's producer as a 'co-writer'.

If a publisher could persuade a TV producer to let him supply all the musical content for a morning show on one of the networks, it would earn $4,000 a week. On TV in 1958 theme and background music amounted to six million dollars of ASCAP's distribution. There were now 'brokers' to whom TV producers gave notice of vacancies for upcoming music. The brokers went round the publishers taking bids. The producers of *Twenty-One* set up their own publishing company and made themselves $100,000 a year from ASCAP payments. But it wasn't the small publishers who were cashing in on this; it was the ones at the top. Of 272 musical selections used on twenty-one shows in a single week in 1959, 70 per cent were owned by Warner Bros publishing.

As for radio, top DJs earned between $25,000 and $35,000 a year from their radio stations. Besides that, every new record arrived from the record company with money attached, at least fifty of them every week. DJ Martin Block said his involvement with payola had never gone beyond receiving "a $10 bill attached to a new disc". This was contradicted by a distributor who said it wasn't worth them sending records to Block because "$20 was our top price for getting the record played". Block said these amounts were like giving a head-waiter a tip for a good table and couldn't be considered a bribe.

Being an election year, President Eisenhower chipped in and called payola "an issue of public morality". But Stan Richard, a DJ from radio station WILD in Boston, disagreed. "This seems to be the American way of life, which is a wonderful way of life. It's primarily built on romance – I'll do for you, what will you do for me?"

However these comments were interpreted one thing became clear – radio DJs were less concerned with pleasing their listeners than pleasing the record companies and music publishers who paid for their drinks and drugs and nights out on the town. To stop this, Top 40 radio was introduced and the DJ no longer got to choose the records. But the bribes didn't go away. They just went to the radio station's senior producer instead, to influence his choice of records for each week's Top 40.

During the course of these payola investigation, Alan Freed refused to sign an affidavit stating he had never received bribes. As a result he had to resign from his radio show. He didn't get much sympathy, least of all from Jerry Wexler who'd given him all those $600 paper bags week after week.

Sometime after that paper-bag period, Atlantic Records had been through a bad patch. In the office, the Erteguns were so broke they sometimes had to share a hamburger for lunch and Jerry Wexler simply couldn't deliver his weekly bag of money. "When hard times set in for us, I felt sure Alan would be sympathetic… 'I'd love to, Wex, but I can't do it,' he said. 'That's taking the bread out of my children's mouths.' With that memorable declaration, he took us off the radio."

As a result of these congressional hearings, paying for a record to be played became illegal with a possible jail term and a $10,000 fine. The conclusion of the Federal Communications Commission was, "payola is just a symptom of the disease – the disease itself is the involvement of the entire broadcasting industry, networks and local stations, in a deliberate and successful distortion of music programming for their own financial gain."

Really, these payola investigations were laughable. The history of the music business was well documented, going right back to England in the mid-nineteenth century when Chappell bribed Dame Clara Butt to sing their ballads at her concerts.

Nothing had changed. The music industry was, always had been, and always would be, the payola industry.

27

Please Please Me
BRITAIN COMES TO LIFE

People in Britain liked rock 'n' roll, even adults. It was lively, and Britain needed livening up.

The fifties had started out as dreary as could be. When rock 'n' roll arrived from America it was an evangelical call to arms for every teenager. When Bill Haley sang *'Let's rip it up... I'm gonna rip it up at the ball tonight'*, it was the best thing kids had ever heard. Whether it was really a cry to rip things up or just meant "let's have some fun" made little difference. It united the younger generation all over Britain. Surprisingly, rock 'n' roll was given a TV show of its own that was the complete opposite of *American Bandstand*'s emasculated presentation. On British TV rock 'n' roll was solid gold excitement.

The British rock 'n' roll show was *Six-Five Special*. It had come about because of the Musicians' Union ban on the BBC playing records on radio. There were only ten hours a week when the BBC could play records of popular music, and those were mostly request programmes playing sentimental ballads. Rock 'n' roll didn't get a look in. But TV was different. On television, artists could mime to their records and be paid as if they were performing live. Since they were being paid, the MU didn't care if they mimed or not, or perhaps they thought they were actually playing live. Either way, television was the way forward for rock 'n' roll.

The person behind the show was Jack Good, a bespectacled ex-drama student from Oxford University who had been planning a career in Shakespearean theatre. By chance one afternoon he wandered into a cinema in London and found himself watching Bill Haley and his Comets in *Rock Around the Clock*. "I'd never heard rock 'n' roll before. But when I saw those kids bopping up and down in the aisles, I was converted like St Paul on the road to Damascus."

The BBC was planning a youth oriented show. They chose Jack Good to produce it partly because he was the youngest person in the building and partly because he spoke with a posh accent, which led them to think he would treat teenagers in a suitably patronising manner. The result was the most anarchic show British TV had ever seen.

Jack asked if he could have teenagers dancing and was told, "Certainly not."

So he ordered conventional scenery but put it on rollers. BBC executives inspected it before the show but as soon as they'd gone Jack wheeled it away and waved the teenagers onto the set.

"I decided that rock 'n' roll wasn't the music itself, it was the *response* to the music – it was a riot! The head of Light Entertainment came up to the control room in the middle of the show and said, 'You can't do this!' I said: 'I'm doing it. Cut to Camera Five.'"

Act after act belted out rock 'n' roll with all the raunch they could give it, including American acts who'd never been allowed to do it on TV back home – Little Richard, Joe Turner, Gene Vincent. Rock 'n' roll in Britain didn't mean prissy teenage songs from the Brill building; it was music on the edge, with young people letting off all the steam they'd been holding in for the previous seven days.

After a while, Jack Good got fired and things quietened down. He did another show for ITV, the rival channel, but it was never as hot as the original one. But the show had served its purpose. Suddenly, all across Britain there were kids who wanted to be rock 'n' roll stars.

A sharp young guy from Essex had seen this coming. Larry Parnes was the owner of a women's dress shop; he was Jewish, homosexual and a bit of a loner. When rock 'n' roll first hit Britain, Parnes saw an opening for himself and found a London boy he reckoned could be Britain's answer to Elvis, Tommy Steele.

Tommy Steele was no Elvis, but he was twenty-one and fresh-faced, and played the guitar. With some songs by Lionel Bart, who would later write the musicals *Oliver!* and *Blitz!*, Parnes pushed Steele to stardom with PR and hype. On stage he wore a pale blue page-boy suit. Really, it was pantomime stuff, but British kids wanted a rock 'n' roll star and Tommy Steele was all they had.

Not satisfied with just one star, Parnes looked again and this time found Cliff Richard, who was nearer the real thing. Born in India, he had a mysterious skin colour and a brilliantly sulky pout. But Parnes' contract wasn't tight enough and Richard moved on, allowing his new advisors to turn him into an 'all-round entertainer'. Soon Cliff Richard was singing happy summer songs and appearing in jokey movies. Worse still, he caught religion and exchanged his tight bulgy jeans for something baggy, without a glimmer of excitement round the crotch.

Parnes didn't give up. With rock 'n' roll exploding all around him, he realised he'd found the perfect excuse to surround himself with just the type of young men he fancied. He tightened up his contracts, and tightened up his young stars' trousers, giving each one a new image and name: Marty Wilde, Vince Eager, Billy Fury, Georgie Fame.

Soon he had a dozen artists and they all had hits. He created a special niche for himself within the music industry and totally controlled his boys. He moved them into a house together, monitored their private lives, kept them off drink and drugs and made them go to bed before midnight, sometimes, it was rumoured, with himself.

Around this time the word 'pop' started to be used to define popular music. Once someone had said it for the first time it quickly became the word everyone used. From the mid-fifties onwards, pop and the culture that surrounded it was the new teenage obsession; rock 'n' roll was just a part of it.

With the new word came a new chart. The Top 10 in Britain changed from being the Top 10 songs assessed by the sale of sheet music, to being the Top 10 best-selling records. It was rock 'n' roll that had done it. Sheet music alone couldn't represent what was heard on a rock 'n' roll record. Records were now all-important and the charts followed suit.

With the chart based on the singer not the song, music publishers now had to reverse their position with regard to getting cover versions. A publisher had to make absolutely sure that only one singer recorded each song otherwise the sales would be split between different versions and there would be less chance of a high chart position.

The same changes were happening right across Europe. Each country was finding itself swept up in rock 'n' roll madness. Just as Britain had Cliff Richard and the boys from the Larry Parnes stable, European countries too had rock 'n' rollers – Johnny Hallyday from France, Tommy Kent from Germany, Little Tony from Italy – they all found themselves with a recording industry that had suddenly slewed towards a teenage market, selling music that the older generation frowned on. And although many of the top people in recording and publishing companies came from that older generation, if they hated rock 'n' roll they at least loved the profits.

British teenagers were now spending £500 million a year, a great deal of it on records. The BBC finally recognised that things were changing and started the first radio programme aimed at teenagers and their music, *Saturday Club*. Then followed it with *Pick of the Pops*, a run down of the week's Top 20 records. At the same time, always keen to educate, the BBC hit on the idea of an evening radio show of black American rhythm and blues. Teenagers, they decided, should be listening to the real thing, not a commercial copy of it, and they got round the Musicians' Union ban on playing records by claiming the music was serious, ethnic and educational. Surprisingly, they got it right. The programmes attracted a substantial audience of young people who'd never had the opportunity to hear this type of music before.

Until then, the only guitar group to become famous was the Shadows, the group that had originally backed Cliff Richard. But they weren't young. The reason was

National Service, a two-year sojourn in the army between the end of school and the start of work. Any time teenagers got together and tried to form a pop group, as soon as one of them reached eighteen their call-up papers would arrive.

But in 1959 compulsory conscription was abolished. A year later there were young groups all over Britain playing music based on what they'd heard on BBC radio, not white rock 'n' roll from the American charts but the original black music that had inspired it – Bo Diddley, Muddy Waters, T-Bone Walker, and the like. As a result, what they were playing was raunchier and more authentic than what was coming from the commercial music industry in the USA.

With the end of National Service, these new groups at last had a chance to make a name for themselves and break into the big-time. But first they needed managers. Larry Parnes' success as a manager had given encouragement to many people like him. Homosexuality was still illegal and remained underground. The only careers that allowed gays to be themselves were hairdressing or the theatre. Encouraged by Larry Parnes' success with rock 'n' roll singers, many young gays decided pop management might be a good profession to try.

So just when dozens of teenage guitar groups, freed from the tyranny of National Service, began looking for suitable managers, a host of gay entrepreneurs began searching for musical talent. The first one to hit the jackpot was surprisingly similar to Larry Parnes – provincial, Jewish, homosexual and a shopkeeper – Brian Epstein. And the group he found became the biggest British act ever.

In Britain, on New Year's Eve 1962 there was a blizzard that left snowdrifts twenty feet deep across the country. It then froze and stayed that way until March. Night frosts produced temperatures of minus fifteen and birds dropped out of the trees. In the midst of it, in mid-January, the Beatles had their first big hit, 'Please Please Me', which went to number two. For anyone who'd failed to notice their arrival, they came back in March with a number one, 'From Me to You'. And in August, 'She Loves You' also went to number one.

Their next single, 'I Want To Hold Your Hand' was released simultaneously in the USA and coincided with the assassination of President Kennedy. America, in search of something to help deal with its loss, became as besotted with the Beatles as Britain. Five months later the group occupied the top five positions in the *Billboard* Top 100. But it wasn't only due to America's emotional vacuum, it was also the group's brilliant songwriting.

Even William Mann, the classical music critic for *The Times*, was impressed. "One gets the impression that they think simultaneously of harmony and melody, so firmly are the major tonic sevenths and ninths built into their tunes, and the flat-submediant key-switches."

The Beatles based their music on what they liked best from the USA – black pop. They messed around with the harmonies, added strikingly non-black backing voices and played their guitars in a folksy style that took the music far from its American roots. It was glorious hybrid pop. In one year they went from being unknowns to the biggest British artists ever. But not everyone approved.

Writing in the *New Statesman*, Paul Johnsons said, "Those who flock around the Beatles… are the least fortunate of their generation, the dull, the idle, the failures… a fearful indictment of our education system…"

Beatlemania opened a new outlet for all creative young talent in the UK. Everyone wanted to be a pop star; pop was the new bible of youth culture. Record companies worshipped it too; they couldn't get enough of these new artists. They loved the way that a quick signing followed by some well-chosen songs could make a penny's worth of vinyl worth a pound.

The music business exploded with new names, new faces and especially new groups – the Rolling Stones, the Yardbirds, the Animals, the Moody Blues, the Tremeloes, the Kinks, the Hollies, the Troggs – all of them given confidence by the Beatles' success, trying to make music in their own style rather than copy the sound of America.

The story of the Beatles' climb to fame was endlessly told in the popular press. Brian Epstein, a Liverpool record shop owner, saw them in a local club, signed them for management, polished up their image, made some demos, and set off for London to get a deal. Decca turned them down, EMI signed them, George Martin produced them, George Harrison didn't like his tie, the original drummer was replaced with Ringo (who George Martin thought was no good). And their deal with EMI was terrible.

What was less known about was their publishing deal.

After the group got a small hit with 'Love Me Do', Brian Epstein, knowing nothing about music publishing but needing to do something about it, asked George Martin who he should speak to. Martin gave him two names. The first was David Platz, who ran a company called Essex Music. After making an appointment and waiting fifteen minutes in his office without him showing up, Epstein moved on to the second, Dick James.

James was amiable and paunchy with horn-rimmed glasses and a smile like a sideways half-moon. He'd started out as Richard Vapnick, son of a Polish immigrant butcher in the East End. When he was seventeen, he started singing at the Palais de Danse in Cricklewood and after a stint in the army during the war he ended up as a solo singer and changed his name to Dick James. He made several records and had one hit, 'Robin Hood'. It was released on Parlophone, an EMI label, and produced by the company's youngest producer, George Martin.

As his singing career began to fade Dick had set up as a publisher but so far hadn't had a hit and was running his office on a shoestring. When Epstein came in, James listened to 'Please Please Me', liked it and offered to publish it on a normal deal – a fifty-fifty split of income from records and performance royalties, plus 10 per cent of the selling price of sheet music.

To encourage Epstein to agree, Dick James phoned an old friend from his singing days who now produced a TV show broadcast from Birmingham, *Thank Your Lucky Stars*. His friend listened to the song down the phone and agreed to give the group a slot on the show. That swung it for Brian and he agreed that Dick James Music could publish the song.

James paid no advance but he gave Epstein tea and biscuits.

Later, people told Epstein he'd made a bad deal. Songwriter Mitch Murray disagreed. "Dick wasn't unfair – it was just normal practice – like it used to be normal to send small boys up chimneys."

Not so normal was what Dick James did next. After just one hit with the group he decided to do what Max Dreyfus had done with Rodgers and Hart, and what the Aberbachs had done to build their publishing empire, he offered to form a joint company with Lennon and McCartney.

Dick James would divide his publisher's share of the income with the two writers, but he would take 10 per cent off the top for 'administration'. Brian Epstein would be paid his management share directly rather than taking it as commission. And the end result was Northern Songs Ltd.

From the money it took in, Dick James would get 32.5 per cent; Lennon and McCartney, 29.25 per cent each; and Brian Epstein, 9 per cent.

Because they were getting a share in the company, Epstein persuaded Lennon and McCartney it would be all right to sign for another three years. Paul is still upset today that nobody tried to help them understand it better. "We were in a little mews house in Liverpool one morning and there was this lawyer, who we later found out was sort of ours. He didn't look like ours, and he certainly didn't do a deal like he was ours."

In fact, by the general standards of the music publishing business at the time, it was an extraordinarily fair deal for a new writer to be given. But that wasn't due to Epstein's skill as a manager. He was so ignorant of the value of publishing that when Dick James, quite correctly, offered to assign the copyright of 'Please Please Me' into the new joint company, Epstein told him, "No, keep it for yourself as a thank-you for making it a hit."

When McCartney met Lennon one morning and suggested, "Let's write a swimming pool," he showed a much greater understanding of a song's value than his manager had done.

28

The Times They Are a-Changing
ALBERT GROSSMAN

Woodie Guthrie never wanted a swimming pool. And he never much cared about money. He frequently performed with the slogan *This Machine Kills Fascists* displayed on his guitar. He was loosely called a folk singer, but he wasn't really. He'd traveled with migrant workers from Oklahoma to California, learned traditional folk and blues, and written songs about his experiences during the Great Depression. But he was never interested in making money from them. In 1935, in a songbook distributed to listeners of an L.A. radio show, he wrote, "This song is Copyrighted in U.S., under Seal of Copyright # 154085, for a period of 28 years, and anybody caught singin' it without our permission, will be mighty good friends of our'n, cause we don't give a dern. Publish it. Write it. Sing it. Swing to it. Yodel it. We wrote it, that's all we wanted to do."

In 1965, Guthrie was fifty-three, but his lyrics were full of the ideas young people thrived on. If he'd been twenty years younger he would have written a dozen best-selling albums. Instead, in the new age of long-playing records, Bob Dylan arrived to do it for him.

Dylan first listened to Guthrie in 1959 and fell head over heels in love. "It was like the record player itself had just picked me up and flung me across the room."

Dylan, too, didn't give a toss for swimming pools. He wrote about his feelings, his frustrations, and the changes he felt were coming. Suddenly that's what every other young person wanted the freedom to write about. If you were young, and in a group of musicians, you no longer wanted to sing songs created for you by Brill building rhyme-merchants – songs that Dylan called, "I'm hot for you and you're hot for me, ooka dooka dikka dee" – you wanted to tell the world what you thought about it in your own words.

Bob Dylan didn't just slide right in and claim Woody Guthrie's crown. He hung around New York for a year, played small gigs in bars and eventually got noticed by the son of John Hammond, who mentioned him to his dad.

John Hammond was the great-grandson of William Henry Vanderbilt and for most of his life had been besotted with jazz. In the early 30s he'd set up one of the first regular live jazz programmes on radio and wrote regularly about the racial divide. "To bring recognition to the negro's supremacy in jazz was the most effective and constructive form of social protest I could think of."

Now Hammond had become a record industry executive and thrown in his lot with the commercial world of Columbia as a specialist producer. He was finding it difficult to raise enthusiasm for the artists they wanted him to record but young Bob Dylan's Guthrie-esque quality appealed to him and he agreed to cut a few tracks. First, though, Dylan was sent to meet Hammond's friend Lou Levy to work out a publishing deal.

Lou Levy, top man of Leeds Music Publishing company, took me up in a taxi to the Pythian Temple on West 70th Street to show me the pocket sized recording studio where Bill Haley and His Comets had recorded 'Rock Around the Clock' – then down to Jack Dempsey's restaurant on 58th and Broadway, where we sat down in a red leather upholstered booth facing the front window.

Levy introduced Dempsey who gave Dylan some advice, "Don't be afraid of hitting somebody too hard."

"He's not a boxer, Jack," Levy said, "he's a songwriter and we'll be publishing his songs."

Back at the office, Lou, puffing on a cigar, got Dylan to sign away all his songs for the next three years on a straight fifty-fifty basis for $1,000 advance.

John Hammond seemed more sensitive than Levy. He'd recently brought Pete Seeger to Columbia and told Dylan he understood his sort of music. That was what Dylan wanted to hear. "John Hammond put a contract down in front of me – the standard one they gave to any new artist. He said, 'Do you know what this is?' I looked at the top page which said Columbia Records, and said, 'Where do I sign?' Hammond showed me where and I wrote my name down with a steady hand. I trusted him. Who wouldn't?"

Dylan then went to meet the company's PR guy who annoyed him by asking a lot of silly questions, like, "Where are you from? What type of music do you play? What did your father do?"

Dylan started off answering politely, then snapped when the PR guy asked how he'd come to New York. He said he'd ridden a freight train when actually he'd come in a '57 Chevy. The freight train remark was just what the PR guy wanted. Dylan's image was off to a good start.

What Dylan didn't tell anyone at Columbia was that a few months earlier he'd signed a five-year management contract with a guy called Roy Silver who managed up-and-coming comedians. At the time he'd seen it as a way of getting some gigs, nothing more. But now John Hammond had signed him to Columbia he attracted the interest of Albert Grossman, a more important manager.

Grossman looked after a folk group, Peter Paul and Mary, and had his own folk club in Greenwich Village. He was a bit of a rogue but not altogether bad – somewhere between a fraudster and a caring elder brother. What attracted him most to Dylan was a song he'd heard him playing at his little gigs around town, 'Blowin' In the Wind'.

To get rid of Roy Silver, Grossman paid $10,000. To get rid of Lou Levy, he gave Dylan $1,000 and sent him to ask for his contract back. "I did that and Lou was only too happy to oblige. 'Sure son,' he said. He was still smoking that damn cigar. 'There's something unique about your songs, but I can't put my finger on it.' I gave Lou the $1,000 and he gave me the contract back."

For Grossman, the next move was CBS. He went with both his lawyer and Dylan to see John Hammond. Dylan, he pointed out, had signed the agreement as a minor without legal advice, so it was invalid.

Since he'd signed it, Dylan had turned twenty-one, so Hammond simply handed Dylan a pen and asked him to re-sign the agreement there and then in front of his manager and his lawyer. Dylan wavered. Grossman knew they were going to need CBS and wanted to avoid too serious a confrontation, so he eventually agreed to let Dylan sign but with improved terms. Then they went to see a new publisher.

Recently, Warner Bros had dug into their closets and found an old company they'd forgotten about, one they'd bought thirty years earlier during their spending spree at the end of the 1920s – Witmark, the company that had once published George M Cohan and Vincent Herbert. Because of the old hits in its catalogue, it was self-funding, so Warner hired a guy called Artie Mogull to re-launch it. Dylan liked the idea of being signed to a company that had once published legendary songwriters, so when Grossman said, "Sign here," he agreed.

As with Dick James and the Beatles, Artie Mogull proposed forming a joint company that would split the publishing money fifty-fifty. But that wasn't what Mogull proposed for Dylan, it was what he proposed for Grossman. When the new company was formed Mogull authorised $100,000 to be paid into it with which Grossman could find and sign new writers. So by signing Dylan, Grossman was making himself $89,000 ($10,000 having been paid to Roy Silver and $1,000 to Lou Levy).

With this joint company in place, Grossman would now split the publishing income with Witmark as well as taking his 25 per cent management commission from Dylan's writer share. It meant on each song written by Dylan, Grossman would end up with 37.5 per cent of the total income, the same amount as Dylan.

Grossman was also manager of Peter Paul and Mary, who recorded for Warner Records. From Warner, he had negotiated a kickback of 25 per cent of the group's recording income. So if Peter Paul and Mary were to cover a Dylan song, Grossman would get half the publishing money from Witmark, 25 per cent kickback on record sales from MGM, 25 per cent management commission from Peter Paul and Mary's earnings, and his 25 per cent management commission on Dylan's writer's share of the song royalties. Quite a packet!

And surprise surprise! The next thing he did was to suggest that Peter, Paul and Mary should record a song by Dylan.

They did. It was 'Blowin' In The Wind' and it went to number one, taking Dylan with it. At that year's Newport Folk Festival he was introduced as the greatest folk artist in America. And by the following year Grossman had made his first million.

It was the same old story – Grossman's greed had created Dylan's success. The desire to make money had always been the music industry's principal driving force, so what was there to complain about?

Nothing really – except that Dylan knew nothing about Grossman's double-dealing.

29

Come Together
RECORD COMPANIES RE-GROUP

At the beginning of rock 'n' roll the music business tilted in favour of record companies. By the mid-sixties they'd taken over completely. The success of the Beatles pushed records to the forefront of everyone's consciousness. Sales of recorded music increased by five times and the music industry was now being referred to as the record industry.

Even before the Beatles, by1963 EMI was already the biggest record company in the world. Its best-selling acts were a strange bunch – Cliff Richard, pretty face and nice thighs; the Shadows, the gangly group that backed him; Matt Monro, a ballad-singing ex-bus-driver; and Frank Ifield, a yodeller.

Amazingly, this strange quartet sold more records around the world than anything American companies could come up with, including Elvis.

Yodeller Frank Ifield was the biggest act in Britain and toured in 1963 with the Beatles as his support group. (Later, when the Beatles made it in the USA, Vee Jay Records released an American album of the tour with tracks by both artists. The liner notes contained a misprint. "It is with a good deal of pride and pleasure that this *copulation* has been presented.")

In building their world market, EMI had been stealthy and focused. It sold its records everywhere – only America was missing. So for $8.5 million EMI's boss Joe Lockwood bought Capitol Records, now the USA's third biggest record company, and in one job lot picked up Frank Sinatra, Nat King Cole, Peggy Lee, and the Beach Boys.

Joe Lockwood had done a great deal for EMI since becoming its new chairman in 1954. He'd changed management structures, reduced rivalry between the two labels, HMV and Columbia, and in particular made sure that EMI's record stores all over Britain, which were known by the name HMV, changed their policy of stocking only records from EMI's two labels and started selling records from all British record companies. He also allowed EMI records to be sold in any other outlet in Britain that sold records. This meant EMI records could now be bought in WH Smith, Britain's top stationers with stores in every single main street in the country. EMI's success in the domestic market was fantastic. In 1964 a combination of eight EMI artists held the No.1 position in the UK charts for forty-one of fifty-two weeks.

The other three record companies in Britain were Decca, Pye and Philips. Decca's sales looked as dismal as EMI's looked dazzling. Edward Lewis was now Sir Edward – the title a gift from the nation for investing the money from the sale of American Decca into developing radar during the Second World War. But he'd become old and quirky.

Apart from loving classical music, he also loved cricket. During the winter months, when cricket wasn't played, most of the top teams laid-off their players rather than pay them, so Sir Edward gave them temporary winter jobs at Decca. It was charmingly charitable but didn't do much to improve the company's profits.

Sir Edward hated the new beat music that young people were buying and most of all he hated Decca's own most successful act, the Rolling Stones. Having turned down the Beatles it was almost inevitable Decca would sign the next group that walked through the door, and they did. Not that they chose badly. But whereas the Beatles were as charming and polite as Brian Epstein himself, the Rolling Stones' manager, Andrew Loog Oldham, had bestowed on them an image of malignant surliness.

For the market Decca was aiming at, signing the Stones was spot on; records poured out and they became almost as big as the Beatles. But when it came to discussing album covers and press photos, the Stones and Decca were at war. Word got round and other groups didn't want to go there.

Rather than replace his senior staff with some in-the-know young men, Sir Edward preferred to keep the people he knew and trusted, most of them old and dying. Mike Smith wasn't one of them.

Smith was in his twenties, the company's most successful pop producer. While he was making an album with Brian Poole & the Tremeloes, one of the group's most successful acts, he discovered he was earning less than the group's van driver. He went to Dick Rowe, the head of A&R and asked for a raise.

"You can't have one," Rowe told him, and also refused him a royalty.

So Mike Smith left.

Perhaps that's what Rowe wanted; his reputation had suffered greatly because of Smith. On New Year's Day 1962 the Beatles had auditioned at Decca Studios in West Hampstead and the person producing the audition was Mike Smith. When he'd finished with the Beatles, Smith auditioned another group, Brian Poole & the Tremeloes.

Afterwards he took the tapes of both groups to Decca House and played them to Dick Rowe. "I was told that I could take one and not the other."

Smith chose Brian Poole & the Tremeloes. He thought they'd been better in the studio and would be easier to work with since they lived in London. But it was Dick Rowe who was forever blamed for the decision. And Decca.

Philips were Dutch and had their eyes on the world market. To the public they were known for toasters and television sets.

The company had been founded by a Dutch cousin of Karl Marx in 1891. In 1950 they'd spotted records as a growth industry and started a record label in London as a step towards world domination. The new British office did a deal with CBS America for the rights to all records from the Columbia label and throughout the fifties released all Mitch Miller's hits. At one time they held the number one position in the charts for twenty-eight consecutive weeks. There was an underlying seriousness at Philips about how they tackled the British market. They had long term plans in place, and were following them. Their target was the world rather than just Britain.

Pye was Britain's fourth record company and like Philips were principally a manufacturing business – TVs, radios and gramophones. Their chairman, Louis Benjamin, loved show business and was a shareholder of the London Palladium. He presented the annual Royal Variety Performance but his idea of pop was girl singers like Petula Clark and Sandie Shaw; he hated groups and refused to let his A&R people subsidise them with equipment.

The furthest Pye had gone towards compromising with new styles of pop was to sign the Kinks, but Benjamin didn't like them either. He didn't think artists should be messing around with guitars; they should be standing at the microphone singing. Peter Prince, an A&R man at Pye, recalled, "We signed a couple of groups, and like all groups they came to the record company for help to buy equipment for touring. Louis Benjamin had never heard of such a thing. He was incensed. He banged the table and screamed 'NO AMPS!'"

In America, at the end of 1964, the whole music industry was in shock.

In December 1963, having previously refused to release them, Capitol released a first single by the Beatles, 'I Want to Hold Your Hand'. One year later, the American record industry had seen something that staggered them. There had been four Beatles albums released during just twelve months and they'd all gone to number one except one, which was stopped from getting there by one of the others. At one time the *Billboard* singles chart showed the Beatles at numbers 1, 2, 3, 4 and 5, with seven other songs also in the Hot 100.

One of the biggest winners from all this was BMI. 1962 had already been its best year ever with 78 per cent of *Billboard*'s Hot 100, 92 per cent of its Top Country Hits, and an unbelievable 100 per cent of the Top R&B Hits. But the real boost came at the end of 1963. Through Northern Songs, BMI had the Beatles' publishing, and the society finally reached parity with ASCAP in the amount of money it was collecting for its writers.

The success of the Beatles was impossible to compete with. Record executives, other than those at Capitol, simply felt like giving up. There was an immediate realisation that record companies would have to defend themselves against something like this ever happening again. And the answer was consolidation. They needed to come together and amalgamate, making their companies larger, and with a bigger pool of artists. They needed to diversify too.

Even Atlantic, whose speciality was black music, had felt the pinch. Jerry Wexler said, "If you didn't have the Beatles in 1964, you didn't have anything… it was a difficult year… Solomon kept us going."

'Solomon' was Solomon Burke, who'd given Atlantic their biggest selling album to date, *Rock 'n' Soul*. It was this album that finally pushed black music into the mainstream of American pop culture. But in view of what they'd seen happen with the Beatles, the Ertegun brothers decided on two things; they would sell the company to a larger record company, probably CBS or RCA, and they would turn their focus towards white artists. They'd already had hits with Bobby Darin, Don Kirshner's old songwriting partner, and in 1965 had signed Sonny and Cher, who immediately had a number one with 'I Got You Babe'. The company now signed another act from the same managers, Buffalo Springfield, a white Californian folk group featuring guitarist Stephen Stills and singer Neil Young.

By 1967 RCA were ahead of CBS and were confident of weathering the Beatles storm. With their signing of Elvis ten years earlier they'd thrown off years of stuffiness and entered the new age of rock 'n' roll, enhancing their image as a dynamic company. The arrival of 45rpm singles had also helped, making RCA seem more in touch with young people than CBS whose album sales focused mainly on Broadway shows and classical music.

Between 51st and 52nd streets on the corner of 6th Avenue, CBS had a new building. It stood 38 stories high and was instantly nicknamed Black Rock due to its dark granite cladding and tinted windows. The company thought its new headquarters would move it into a modern age but on the floors housing the record division there was still a distinct smell of mildew left over from the Mitch Miller era.

Although the company already had Bob Dylan, when it came to being current and in touch, things stopped there. However, the elderly chairman, Goddard Lieberson, took to heart the lesson the Beatles had given the industry – that pop music was a serious business – and decided to step down. In his place came the company's personable in-house lawyer Clive Davis whose job would be to rejuvenate the artist roster with acts that appealed to a new and younger audience.

In June 1967, Davis went to the Monterey Pop Festival where he had a Damascus moment and arrived back at the office wearing a flowered shirt with a necklace of love beads. Thereafter he refocused the A&R department, signing Scott McKenzie, Donovan, Laura Nyro and Blood Sweat and Tears.

CBS's market share shot up. Once more it was the number one company. But when the next challenge to its supremacy came, it wasn't from its old rival RCA, or from a new Beatles, but a completely unexpected direction.

Jack Warner, old and in decline, decided it was time to dispose of everything he owned. Having made the decision he sold out to the first offer he got, from a company called Seven Arts, asset-strippers who were rumoured to have Mafia connections. They had no knowledge of films, records or music publishing, but once in at the deep end they decided to splash out. When they heard rumours that Atlantic might be for sale, they bought that too. At $17.5 million, it was the best offer the company had received. Wexler and the two Erteguns took a vote. Wexler wanted some cash in the bank for the future. This was his opportunity, so he said yes. Ahmet was enjoying life in New York and liked his independence, so he said no. Nesuhi, as was his nature, thought more broadly. He was worried that the boom in soul music was coming to an end; to survive Atlantic would need to be part of something bigger, so he too said yes.

Warner Music Group, in which Atlantic Records became a new division, had a few successful artists, among them Peter Paul and Mary, and the Grateful Dead, but under Jack Warner's ownership the company had grown tired and needed re-structuring. It already had two record labels – Warner Records and Reprise Records, which Jack Warner had set up for Frank Sinatra some years previously to tempt him into making some movies. The man running Warner Records was Joe Smith, an ex radio DJ. And the man running Reprise Records was Mo Ostin. The Ertegun brothers got on well with both of them.

Overseeing Smith and Ostin, was the head of Warner Music Group, Mike Maitland. The Erteguns took an instant loathing to him. But that wasn't their only problem. Jerry Wexler, now a director of the company and their chief record producer had upset an organisation called The Fairplay Committee.

The Fairplay Committee wasn't a toothless government organisation as its name suggests, but a ruthless gang of black street-thugs who might twist off your testicles and shove them down your throat if they thought you'd offended the dignity of Afro-American artists. Some people thought they were seriously trying to better conditions for black people in a white-run record industry. Others thought they were simply trying to become a central bank for the receipt of payola payments to black DJs all over the country. Either way, they announced, "Anyone who works for Atlantic Records is not welcome at any black radio station."

Wexler's three sins were – to be one of the three partners in Atlantic Records, none of them black – to be one of its two record producers, neither of them black – and to be attending that year's conference of the National Association of Television and Radio Announcers in Miami, which had been hijacked by the Fairplay Committee.

During the three-day event he was hanged in effigy. He responded by calling the Fairplay Committee, "con men, street-smart guys, extortionists, and racketeers".

Maybe – but they were pretty scary. Enough to persuade the Erteguns not only to pay them off with a substantial contribution, but also to start moving away from black music. So with the additional funds available from having sold out to Seven Arts, Ahmet Ertegun turned to signing white British groups instead.

The first was a newly formed supergroup, Cream, which featured Eric Clapton on guitar, previously of the Yardbirds; then two years later, Blind Faith, with Stevie Winwood on vocals, previously of the Spencer Davis Group.

Seven Arts then announced they were through with asset-stripping the film company and were going to sell it, together with the record company, to the highest bidder.

The company that got it was Kinney, whose background was in car parks and funeral parlours, with another slight whiff of Mafia connections. They paid $400 million, giving Seven Arts $350 million profit on their total outlay.

The boss was Steve Ross, and Ahmet Ertegun went to meet him intending to give in his notice. But Ross had prepared well for his meeting, taking lessons on the current music scene from his teenage son. He floored Ahmet when he managed to name all the members of Blind Faith; he also said he had no intention whatsoever of interfering in the running of the record division. As long as it made a profit he would stay away; he was more interested in the Warner film company.

Ahmet persuaded Ross to change the music division's name from Kinney back to Warner and to fire Mike Maitland. He then settled down to become a good corporate game-player and set himself a target – he would sign the Rolling Stones to Atlantic when they left Decca.

The Warner Music Group now had three labels – the Erteguns with Atlantic, Joe Smith with Warner, and Mo Ostin with Reprise. Although each of them would put their own labels first, they agreed to work together to build Warner into the number one music group, so they started to look for other companies they could bring into the fold. There were several worth considering.

Apart from the two majors, and Capitol, there were four second-tier companies that were close to being majors. MCA Entertainment Inc, the world's largest talent booking agency, had merged with Decca in 1962 and created MCA Records. Another label, MGM, was originally set up by MGM Studios for the release of movie soundtrack albums but had expanded into pop and jazz. Mercury Records, until 1962, had been the biggest record company in America not affiliated with a larger company but was then bought by Philips as their first foothold in America. And ABC Records was a company owned by the ABC broadcasting network and included Paramount Records and Dunhill Records. But none of these companies were small enough or entrepreneurial enough to be of interest to a company structured like Warner. If the company was going to expand as separate divisions – like Atlantic, Warner and Reprise – then each addition would need to bring another key label boss with it. Warner would expand by buying up record entrepreneurs.

The companies in America most suitable for combining with Warner's structure were Motown and Elektra.

Motown was Atlantic's principal rival for recording black artists. Like most of the old-time publishers, its owner, Berry Gordy, had started as a songwriter. He'd written songs for local acts in Detroit, where he lived, but when his song 'Lonely Teardrops' became a hit for Jackie Wilson, Gordy found he received almost no royalties from it. He knew for sure someone somewhere was getting the money so he decided in future it would be him. He found songwriters and singers and formed a company with a $700 loan from his family. He'd wanted to name it 'Tammy', after the hit by Debbie Reynolds, but the name was taken so he called it Tamla, and the Motown was added later.

Since the twenties, black music had moved a long way – from being a background influence to being the principal influence on all pop music. Even Mitch Miller had done his bit, releasing Johnny Mathis on a par with his white artists and pushing him into the top ten of the *Billboard* Hot 100 with every release, refusing to define him as rhythm & blues just because he was black. The down side had been that Johnny Mathis had to record sentimental songs almost as bad as all the others Mitch Miller put his name too. But as a boost to black artists in general, his success had been tremendous. Gordy now wanted to do this with all the music on his label. He wanted an across-the-board market for black music. Motown's records were not aimed at the rhythm & blues charts, they were made specifically for the Top 100.

Since the war, white record companies had been taking black hits and whitening them up for the mass market. Gordy decided to do the same, but keep the artists black. The company's first act was Smokey Robinson and the Miracles and their first hit was 'Shop Around'. The music sounded less black than regular rhythm & blues, but there was no compromise in the colour of the artist who performed it.

After that, Gordy found hit artist after hit artist – The Temptations, Mary Wells, the Marvelettes, Martha and the Vandellas. The trick was to give them a production as slick and white as Leiber and Stoller had done for the Drifters at Atlantic. So, like Syd Nathan at King Records, Gordy hired a full-time group of musicians who clocked each morning at 9am and worked till 6pm – six days a week, one track an hour. The sound they created was black pop, and it sold around the world.

Initially it was done on a shoestring, his artists didn't get advances and they did as they were told, which sometimes meant doing thirty or forty takes to get a song just right. Not so much artistic perfection as commercial – the company simply couldn't afford flops.

Motown's accounting methods were even less refined than Atlantic's. Ahmet Ertegun pointed out that in its early years, like at King and Chess, Tamla Motown artists never received gold records. "Motown wouldn't let the RIAA look at its books so Motown could never be awarded a platinum or gold record... even though they sold millions."

For Warner, that presented a problem. With nobody allowed to look at Motown's books, it was hard to put a value on the company. But there was another reason for Warner not to buy Motown. Ahmet Ertegun, the most persuasive voice, at Warner Music, felt there was a trend away from pop music. The Supremes and Smokey Robinson were not going to fit well with the Grateful Dead. Nobody trendy or forward-looking wanted to be associated with pop anymore, and although Atlantic Records had gone some way towards white pop with Sonny and Cher, by the end of the sixties Ahmet was focused on something tougher.

Rock was the new chic word. And California rock was developing a musical ethic of its own – more laid back than on the East Coast, more outside the general run of American society. For groups that evolved in the canyons of Los Angeles, signing with a West Coast company was the natural thing to do. For Warner to be able to pick up these groups it needed to brand itself as different from East Coast record companies like RCA and CBS; it needed to expand by bringing in other companies based in California. And the obvious one was Elektra.

Jac Holzman started the company in 1950 specifically to sign non-mainstream artists. The first Elektra LP was a collection of *Lieder* and similar 'art' songs which sold almost nothing. During the fifties he concentrated on folk music and in 1964 signed Tom Paxton, another of Bob Dylan's early influences. Holzman then changed direction and signed a couple of groups – the Doors, and Love.

Like most of the other owners of small record companies, Holzman liked artists for what they were – self-obsessed and irrational. When he signed Love he gave them a $5,000 advance. There were five of them, all living together in a single hotel room and they needed transport to get them to gigs with their equipment. They took his money and went to buy something suitable. An hour later they came back with a gull-winged Mercedes sports car capable of taking two. Holzman shrugged and shelled out again, this time for a van. At a major company no one would have done that.

Elektra not only had the right look for local musicians looking for the right company, it had the right look for Warner too. It would make an excellent new division, and Ahmet Ertegun and Mo Ostin both sent memos to Steve Ross suggesting he buy it.

He did. And from then on Warner Music was known as WEA – Warner Elektra Atlantic.

30

Shape of Things to Come
ROCK WITHOUT THE ROLL

In 1966 the British music press started drawing a line between pop and rock. Two years earlier the word rock, without the roll, had never been heard, the trendy word was 'pop'. By 1968 'rock' had become the new thing.

The differences were vague. Pop was the instant hit, formulated, tidy like a snapshot. Rock was disorganised, less packaged. Pop was conformist. Rock was anti-social. Pop was a song. Rock was a lifestyle.

Several groups previously known as pop were now thought of as rock. Mostly, they were groups who had been influenced by the BBC's 'educational' rhythm & blues show. As a result, British rock had a decidedly black tinge to it.

But while British rock music was evolving from groups playing black American folk music, American rock was evolving from Bob Dylan's love of white American folk music. It finally morphed into rock when Dylan met with the Beatles while they were on tour and was persuaded to start using an electric guitar in his act. The resulting hybrid music – half folk, half pop – became the template for rock music American style. British rock arrived by a different route.

In May 1966, the *NME* Poll Winners Concert at Wembley Arena was the last time the Beatles played a live show in the UK. The last three groups on the bill were the Yardbirds, the Rolling Stones and the Beatles – the best finale anyone could have dreamed of. But these big concerts were not as good as people nowadays think they were.

The sound was downright terrible. Insufficient amplification and far too much screaming. Groups were unable to hear themselves play. There was no way of balancing the sound at live concerts; there were no mixing desks and the size of the vocal amplifier was chosen according to the size of venue – medium for Hammersmith Odeon, large for Wembley Arena, gigantic for Shea Stadium. The amplification of the guitars and keyboards had to be built up to match, so amps were piled one on top of the other in a towering stack. Then you couldn't hear the drums.

At the previous year's poll-winners concert, the Rolling Stones' manager, Andrew Loog Oldham, had decided the group couldn't be televised. There was no good reason why; he just wanted to be bloody-minded like managers sometimes should be. Brian Epstein took note of what he did and this year did the same for the Beatles and refused to let them be televised.

With Oldham repeating his bloody-mindedness of the previous year and Epstein playing copycat, it meant the last act to be televised would be the Yardbirds, who were actually third from top of the bill. For viewers at home they topped the show, and the Stones and the Beatles were nowhere to be seen.

It was a strange bill; a mixture of what we would now call rock with other things that were very much pop – Dusty Springfield, Herman's Hermits and Dave Dee, Dozy, Beaky, Mick and Tich. And if that sounds like an odd collection of acts, it was because people hadn't yet started using the word rock. All this music was still called pop.

Andrew Loog Oldham was now the person with the greatest influence on youth culture in Britain. His father was an American airman of Dutch descent who'd been shot down and killed during the war before Oldham was born. Oldham was his mother's maiden name but the word 'Loog' was Dutch. Translated into English it meant caustic, and Oldham did his best to live up to it. He was the first manager to turn against the music business establishment. He taught the Rolling Stones the importance of fighting with the record company and being rude to anyone who annoyed them, and in doing so he created the basic image of British rock.

The music the Stones played wasn't pop, nor was it called rock, it was rhythm & blues, with clever compacted arrangements for singles, and longer laid-back versions for live performances.

The Beatles still played pop. When they performed on stage, they performed in the old pop tradition, dressing neatly, talking politely to the audience, and bowing at the end of songs. At the 1966 *NME* Poll Winners Concert they did just that, and for people who'd seen them before it seemed to be just one more Beatles performance. In reality, it was a historic occasion, and it certainly *should* have been televised and recorded because it turned out to be their last concert ever in Britain.

John Lennon felt uncomfortable continuing to play pop songs to an audience of teenagers. He wanted to write songs that contained socially important messages and he'd been greatly influenced by meeting Bob Dylan. Afterwards, he even started singing in a more nasal way.

The meeting had taken place in 1964, when the Beatles were on tour in the USA. Dylan and Lennon had got on rather well, which seemed strange, because they existed in totally different areas of the music business. Dylan attracted politically inclined college kids while the Beatles' audience was screaming teenagers. But while their audiences were different their attitudes were less so.

Later, during his UK tour in 1965, Dylan spent time at Lennon's home in Kenwood. At that time, Dylan's music was still not unique. He was playing music derived from his folk singing heroes, acoustic and old-fashioned. But after spending time with the Beatles, he admitted, "They were doing things nobody was doing. Their chords were outrageous, just outrageous, and their harmonies made it all valid... but I just kept it to myself that I really dug them... I knew they were pointing the direction that music had to go."

Back home, he started experimenting with electric guitar, encouraged by record producer Tom Wilson who had produced his first two albums. Wilson was a black record producer working with white folk-rock acts at CBS, not just Bob Dylan, but Simon & Garfunkel too. In both cases he influenced them to dilute their purist acoustic approach with electric instruments.

By the time of his next album, *Blonde on Blonde*, Dylan had developed a sound of his own and a personality to go with it. Australian critic Jack Marx called it "the arrogant, faux-cerebral posturing that has been the dominant style in rock".

What Dylan had come up with was rock without the roll, the industry's principal money-making product for the next four decades. And there was more to it than just the music. In order to be considered rock, the personal style of the person performing had to be just right too.

In Britain, once the word started to be used, many groups who were previously deemed 'pop' deliberately altered themselves to justify the name rock. It was good imagery – it separated them from the traditional image of pop stars as stupid and manipulated. If they became rock instead of pop, they crossed the line from entertainer to true artist.

To do it, they toughened up their music, ran their songs longer when they played live, behaved in a more anti-social manner, were rude to anyone who offered advice, and told journalists to fuck off. The Rolling Stones was the group everyone modelled themselves on.

The Stones had made their transition to rock by Mick Jagger being arrested and displayed handcuffed to the public before being sent to jail for nothing more than buying four legally available airsickness pills at Rome airport. The authorities' obvious delight in managing to imprison a Rolling Stone immediately promoted the group to the top spot in the new rock hierarchy. But it was their music too. The singles were cleverly compressed into three minutes, but when the group played live, songs like 'Satisfaction' and 'Get Off Of My Cloud' hit a groove and sometimes ran for seven or eight minutes.

Kit Lambert, the Who's manager, watched the Rolling Stones and followed suit. He had a renegade soul. Anarchy was in his blood and he pushed Pete

Townshend to smash his guitar on stage and Keith Moon to throw his drums into the audience. The music on the singles was still pop but when they played gigs the group became violent and threatening.

The Yardbirds like the Rolling Stones started by playing harmonica blues but that was too far from what was required for pop singles. In order to get hits they compromised, but kept clear of the normal sounds of pop. Instead they made their singles sound strange; adding chants, switching tempos in mid-song, even coming to a complete halt in the middle. In live performances they continued to play blues but with a heavier sound – the lead guitar playing the riffs that had originally been played on harmonica. The sound grew heavier still when the group bought in a second lead guitarist, Jimmy Page. He stood front-stage left, with their other guitarist, Jeff Beck, standing front-stage right, playing all the solos in unison.

Another route from pop to rock was through drugs. Pop groups mostly used 'blues', amphetamine pills prescribed by doctors for weight loss. From the mid-sixties onwards there was also LSD. Spacey and hallucinogenic, it was totally unsuitable for listening to pop singles which were simply too short. Groups who wanted to shake off their pop image and root themselves in rock let everyone know that LSD was their preferred drug. It pushed them towards something more substantial than just three-minute tunes; the Moody Blues made an album that was continuous, with orchestral links between the different tracks. On LSD musicians created music that drifted, flickering with unreachable fantasies, which helped boost the sale of LPs. So record companies were delighted and became rather drug supportive.

In Britain, 1964 and 1965 had been the glory days of pop. First the Beatles explosion, then pirate radio stations. These were set up on ships moored beyond territorial waters, broadcasting American-style non-stop pop twenty-four hours a day. The essential style of pirate radio was copied from American Top 40 radio, and even included payola.

Being outside territorial waters, pirate radio stations were also outside the laws of graft. For plays on Radio Caroline you simply phoned Phil Solomon, the man who owned it, and told him what you wanted; for instance, fifty plays on a new record, half in prime time, half in non-prime. He told you the price and you sent him the cheque. Easy as that.

On Radio London there was a different method. You phoned the man who ran the radio station's publishing company. If you agreed to give him your 'B' side, Radio London gave your 'A' side thirty plays.

In 1967, after four years of this, the government finally banned off-shore radio. By then its popularity was such that they only dared to do so by promising the public a similar pop music programme from the BBC. Under government pressure the Musicians' Union, having always refused to allow the BBC to play records of popular music for more than ten hours a week, finally relented. The BBC would open its own Top 40 radio station playing non-stop pop music for eighteen hours a day.

There was, and always had been, a great snobbery at the BBC against currently popular music. In the 1930s it meant popular songs of the day played by a dance orchestra at the Savoy Hotel, and it could only be broadcast after 10pm. During the war the BBC introduced 'Music While You Work', a half-hour medley of currently popular songs played live by a small orchestra in the BBC studios. This was intended to help workers in factories be more productive, but therein lay the snobbery – the concept that popular music was for working class people. There was a patronising element within the BBC that thought the lower classes should be taught to like something more intellectually challenging. And amongst the BBC hierarchy there was horror that they were required to open a non-stop programme of pop music.

Part of the BBC's new arrangement with the musicians union was that a large amount of music on Radio One would not actually be records but would be songs re-recorded in the BBC studio by groups whose records were currently in the charts. Obviously this gave a substantial advantage to those groups who could play well and whose records weren't manufactured with the help of session musicians. In the main this meant the sort of groups that were currently being labeled rock. Groups that played music based on Southern blues, or rhythm & blues, or even on American white folk music, were regarded by the snobbish commissars at the BBC in a better light than those who played parochial pop. A pop star was the brainless tool of the entertainment industry, doing as he was told. A rock star was a true artist, creating his own work.

By aligning themselves with this concept of rock, the powers that be at the BBC managed to persuade themselves that Radio One had a higher purpose than just replacing pirate radio stations.

So the BBC gave rock music its blessing.

By the beginning of 1968 the divide between pop and rock was clearly defined. With the help of live sessions for Radio One, the last few stragglers from the pop era had rebranded themselves with the more credible term rock – the Animals, the Small Faces, the Pretty Things, even the Troggs had managed to cross the line. Only one major act had been unable to make the transition – the Beatles. And it bothered them hugely. Even though they did their share of drugs their music stayed resolutely pop. Their songs were just too perfect, too rounded, too cheerful.

In March 1968 there was an anti-Vietnamese war rally in Trafalgar Square. The leader of the movement, Tariq Ali, tried to persuade John Lennon to come along but he excused himself saying he had to go to India for meditation with the

Beatles' guru, the giggling Maharishi. The real reason, though, was that Brian Epstein had warned him his American visa might be refused if he attended an anti-war protest. So Tariq Ali asked Mick Jagger to come instead, and he agreed.

In Trafalgar Square 100,000 people high on pacifist passion listened to speeches by religious and political leaders. Afterwards, the younger part of the crowd, about 10,000 of them, headed towards Grosvenor Square to enjoy themselves hurling insults at the American embassy. They were met by mounted police and a cordon of regular police that they managed to break through. They ran towards the embassy with police horses charging behind, caught up in a Sunday afternoon revolution.

Most of them were clueless teenagers, some carried North Vietnamese flags. A young Malcolm McLaren was there too.

We rolled hundreds of marbles along the floor at the mounted police. Suddenly it looked like these horses were on an ice skating rink, and then, like Agincourt, we ducked down and people behind us had catapults and started firing gobstopper marbles at the windows of the American embassy.

Keeping Mick Jagger at his side, Tariq Ali stood atop a pillar and waved his troops on like Achilles at the gates of Troy, using Jagger as his icon of cultural revolt.

After the riot Jagger suggested the whole thing was the fault of the authorities. "They never ought to have had police there… If they had no police there, there wouldn't be trouble…"

But the riot had impressed him. Back home, he started on a new song. And when 'Street Fighting Man' came out in August, it was the Stones' toughest single yet. Jagger had moved the band to a new place – rock stars could be revolutionaries.

John Lennon came back from India feeling left out. To be ranked as less of a revolutionary than Mick Jagger was galling. He tried to get on top of things by writing 'Revolution', but there was a line he couldn't finish. *'When you talk about destruction don't you know that you can count me…'* What?

He couldn't decide if it should be 'In' or 'Out'. And so as not to commit himself he made a version of each.

The *Black Dwarf* newspaper didn't rate his song. "No more revolutionary than *Mrs Dale's Diary*."

Lennon wrote back, furious. "Who do you think you are? What do you think you know? I don't remember saying Revolution was revolutionary – fuck Mrs Dale…"

But it wasn't the words that were wrong. It was simply that 'Revolution' was a pop song. 'Street Fighting Man' was rock. The difference was intangible; something Jagger could feel and Lennon couldn't.

Lennon was jealous of the Stones' streetwise image. He'd struggled to move in a more credible direction by writing 'Revolution'; now the Beatles tried again by forming their own company, Apple Corps. But their next album, *The White Album*, released in 1968, took them right back to the world of pop tunes for young girls, 'Ob-la-di, ob-la-da' and 'Sexy Sadie'.

A short while previously, Brian Epstein had misjudged the number of pills he needed for a good sleep and was now no longer around to offer them a steadying hand. Without his modifying influence, the Beatles poured millions into a four-floor building on Baker Street which they filled with non-music business characters – drug pushers, eccentric inventors and people to cook them nice lunches.

They started their own record label and immediately got a number one, 'Those Were The Days', by Mary Hopkin, as pop as the Beatles themselves.

They tried again, grew their hair long and stopped washing it, filled themselves with drugs and stopped being nice to everybody. John even stayed at home in bed for a couple of months doing heroin with Yoko Ono, but they still couldn't hit that rock nerve. All they managed to do was change from being cute Beatles to grubby ones.

By 1969, Apple Corps was spending millions, signing anyone who walked in the door, especially if they had some drugs in their pocket. So they tried a new manager.

Allen Klein, like Dick James, was the son of an Eastern European immigrant butcher, but American. A couple of years earlier he'd bought Andrew Oldham's share of the Rolling Stones management. When Brian Epstein died, Mick Jagger suggested that the Beatles should consider Klein as a possible replacement. The group discussed it but couldn't agree. Lennon liked him; McCartney didn't. Eventually they let him come and run Apple but McCartney refused to sign an agreement with him.

Klein was an Albert Grossman duplicate – Jewish, American, brash, blunt, and none too honest. He had a way of ripping through niceties and was uncaring about any gentlemanly traditions the British music business still clung too. On his desk he kept a framed quote from the bible, modified, "Though I walk in the shadow of the valley of evil, I have no fear, as I am the biggest bastard in the valley."

To start with Klein did well for them. He brought Phil Spector to London to work on tapes for the new *Let It Be* album. He re-negotiated their contract with EMI, getting them the highest royalties ever paid to an artist at that time, with 69 cents per album for the USA. In exchange, EMI was allowed to repackage earlier Beatles material as compilations, which Brian Epstein hadn't permitted. But despite Klein's efforts, he was only re-packaging and re-marketing what was already there. The Beatles weren't breaking new ground and weren't likely to. They'd been too hugely over-publicised to now be able to blur their image into something new. And they knew it.

As a group the Beatles were trapped in the imagery of five years previously, the imagery of pop. And more than that, the supreme pinnacle of pop. Nor was it just the imagery; it was their music too. As musicians they'd grown together, matured together, written together, and produced together. They'd set themselves in an unbreakable mould, and now the world had moved on. The Beatles were pop in an age when everything hip had become rock. The only solution was to end it.

On a grey day in January 1969, the Beatles lugged their instruments up five floors to the rooftops of Savile Row and set up their amps amongst the chimneys. It was cold enough for Ringo to have to borrow his wife's red plastic raincoat and Yoko Ono's fur.

Over the previous months there'd been increasing bitterness between them, mainly stirred up by Yoko pushing her way into the group and getting John hooked on heroin. But once the music started the bitterness faded.

Taking their lunchtime break in the street below, businessmen in pinstripes and secretaries in mini-skirts stared up at the figures on the roof. People gathered at windows and on neighbouring rooftops to watch the four men who had changed the world of pop. They hadn't played live in the UK since the *NME* Poll Winners Concert in 1966 and the people watching thought this might be a sign they were going to start performing again.

After eight songs a roadie shouted up from the street below that the police were threatening to shut down the show.

"We're not stopping," Paul shouted back.

But Police Constable Number 503 of the Greater Westminster Council climbed five flights of steps, made his way to the back of the rooftop and pulled the plug.

Five minutes later they were all downstairs in the street, standing in the cold January drabness. Although they would record one more album, this was their last live performance. The era of classic pop had ended and the era of classic rock had begun.

The Beatles had failed to cross the divide.

Rock was more than a new music; it was a new lifestyle, the new creed of young people as they went into the seventies. Music publishers had always judged a songwriter's ability by the catchy quality of his songs, and record companies by an artist's ability to perform. Now both publishers and record companies had to rethink their strategy for selecting new artists. Songs no longer had to sell themselves, instead they had to sell a group's beliefs, or image, or lifestyle, which was the real product on sale. The music was simply its packaging. Publishers and record companies had to make decisions on whom to sign from a whole new list of criteria.

In America, Frank Zappa was one of the new rock performers who got signed and did well. But who could have guessed in the beginning that he would have hits? He started in 1964 by joining a band called The Soul Giants as a guitarist. He persuaded them to change their name to Mothers Of Invention and to play songs he'd written himself.

Producer Tom Wilson spotted them and signed them to Verve, which was part of MGM. Wilson knew he was sticking his neck out; the songs were pure politics.

Zappa pushed Wilson as far as he could.

> *The first thing that we recorded was 'Any Way the Wind Blows,' and that was okay. Then we did 'Who Are the Brain Police?' and I saw him through the glass and he was on the phone immediately to New York going, "I don't know!" Trying to break it to 'em easy, I guess… He laid his job on the line by producing the album.*

The album was *Freak Out*, an attempt to capture the Los Angeles subculture of anti-government revolution and drugs. Yet Zappa himself was no freak. He never did drugs and called people who did, "assholes in action".

Zappa's audience saw him as part of the sub-culture his record revealed, in fact he was no part of it, he was simply a commentator. But he knew how to wind people up. At a show in New York he persuaded some US marines, fresh from Vietnam, to come up on stage and dismember a rag doll by pretending it was a 'gook' baby. "We're satirists," he explained. "And we are out to satirize everything."

So how was a music publisher or record company meant to make a decision about signing a group like that?

For the publishers it was particularly difficult. To survive, they had to pre-empt record companies and catch these songwriting artists before the record companies got hold of them. If they waited until acts had made successful records before they signed them, they would have to pay through the nose.

It meant making judgements of songwriters not on their ability to write hits but on their ability to create a social niche and find a group of fans who liked their look, their nihilsm, their outrageousness, their politics, or their sexuality.

The songs were just backing tracks to the personality of the artist. So publishers struggled.

Rock had stood the music business on its head.

31

We Will Rock You
STADIUM TOURS AND MANAGERS

Rock now stood live music on its head too.

Concerts had always been the preserve of the promoter. He found the money, made the deal, named the times the artist would perform and stayed tightly in control of every aspect of the event. Even the biggest stars were subject to the promoter's control. But when rock music went on tour things began to change.

"Fifty thousand people at worship in a stadium. People aged twenty-six aren't equipped for that. That's like Hitler."

The words of Tony Bennett, a starchy old singer, past his sell-by date. Poor old thing – what would *he* know? The young are equipped for anything.

Hitler's rallies were no more than rehearsals for what was to come in the seventies. A decade of stadium rock – the Nuremberg experience conveniently brought to your home town for twenty dollars a ticket. Storm-trooper security-teams, foot-soldier roadies, the musicians as superstar generals, and the Führer – Mick Jagger, Roger Daltrey, Robert Plant, or whoever else owned the microphone. All the fun of the rock 'n' roll circus.

The groups were endless – the Rolling Stones, Deep Purple, Pink Floyd, Status Quo, Wings, Jefferson Starship, The Who, Lynyrd Skynyrd, the Eagles, Crosby Stills and Nash, Led Zeppelin, and at least forty more.

To reach this level of stardom, a new group – mild, modest and eager – had to pass through the jaws of the record company machine (the lobby) and get its tape on the right desk upstairs. The path to success was almost identical in each case. Approved, auditioned, produced, plugged and promoted. Demeaned with dumb promotional ideas, sent round radio stations saying daft things to daft DJs – and finally touring.

With enormous luck and perseverance, after two or three albums and four or five years of constant touring, one group in a thousand might come out somewhere near the top. Feeling pleased with themselves its members might become a little arrogant. Sometimes even a touch out of control.

Led Zeppelin went berserk.

Surrounded by their manager's thugs, Zeppelin became thugs themselves, condoning what went on, even joining in. Consuming drugs by the bagful, their minds scrambled in a morass of music, violence, sex and fan worship, they broke every attendance record in stadium after stadium, took the most money ever per gig, and performed shows up to three hours long, playing every song differently every night, their music constantly evolving.

The images that flowed from their tours were plastered across the media. Flying into town on their private 747. Limo'd to the gig with police escort. John Bonham's thundering drums. Robert Plant's skintight jeans. The tour manager roaring down the hotel corridor on a Honda CB450. Jimmy Page strutting in his white linen suit, shooting his guitar at the audience like a gunfighter. John Paul Jones falling asleep with a joint and setting fire to the hotel. Their manager's multi-ringed fist smashing into a roadie's face at a gig in San Francisco. Security guards scouting the audience for fifteen-year-old girls for after-gig partying.

Heroin, champagne, whiskey, cocaine – rooms smashed, groupies fucked, televisions slung out of windows, and the whole thing repeated tomorrow night and every other night for five months. Like this, Zeppelin became the defining group of seventies rock.

Buddy Holly showed a generation of young hopefuls that anyone can pick up a guitar and write a hit; the Beatles gave the world a template for pretty pop groups; but Zeppelin delivered a prototype for touring excess. Bob Dylan had the concept, the Rolling Stones the attitude, the Yardbirds the blues-riffing style, but it was Zeppelin who wrapped it all up in a package and said this is the real, unadulterated, big-balled bazooka – 100 per cent double-distilled rock.

Actually, most people preferred it as a cocktail – slightly less extreme. There were fifty or so other rock circuses crisscrossing America throughout the seventies, each one a vehicle for selling between three and ten million albums every eighteen months, which is why the music industry had so happily jumped on the rock bandwagon. The money was flowing in like a cash tsunami. Rock groups could have and do whatever they wanted.

Van Halen smashed up the entire backstage area in the university hall in Pueblo, Texas – over $100,000 of damage – simply because there were brown M&Ms in a plate of candy in the dressing-room when their rider said there shouldn't be. Newspapers were full of questions for the band. What was the meaning of doing something like that, they wanted to know.

"Why should rock 'n' roll be meaningful?" Alex Van Halen asked.

There were those who thought it should be. Bruce Springsteen never thought otherwise. He put seriousness into his every moment on stage. Standing silently, moodily between numbers, fingering his guitar. But was it really thoughtfulness, or just a pose he'd come up with that he knew would work? Was there any real feeling left after playing five hundred stadiums? Maybe! At least, it seemed so.

He always found emotion when he needed it. Night after night, he spat out the chorus of Badlands with the same fury, anger consuming him, hands crashing onto the guitar strings.

Yet there was something odd about pumping out those angry words and smiling happily at the end when people applauded. The words were too meaningful; rock anger was better as an act.

Mick Jagger found the balance perfectly. He knew anger was something a rock audience wanted, but they didn't want a political lecture; they wanted anger for anger's sake. So he gave it to them and was able smile happily at the end of the song because there was no residual message to be digested. When he asked who shot the Kennedys in 'Sympathy for the Devil', it wasn't a real question; it was just the usual two fingers up at an establishment that had no connection with ordinary people.

Rock critic Greil Marcus said, "People hear what they want to hear."

Lou Reed agreed. "I'm very good at the glib remark that may not mean something if you examine it closely, but it still sounds great."

Jagger accepted that violence was inherent in rock. "Violence and energy... *that's* really what rock & roll's all about... it's inevitable that the audience is stirred by the anger they feel... but if it's contained within a theater and a few chairs get broken... so what?"

Sometimes, though, it wasn't contained. And shortly after Jagger's blasé pronouncement, violence on another level altogether erupted at a Stones concert.

At the end of 1969, the Rolling Stones had just completed a long, well-organised tour of the USA during which they'd been criticised for high ticket prices and great attention to profit. The shows had been good and no audiences had complained, but stung by criticisms in the media, Mick Jagger announced that the group would finish the tour with a free show.

Together with the Grateful Dead, the Stones organised a one-day festival which would include Santana, Jefferson Airplane and Crosby Stills Nash & Young. It was originally intended to be held at the Golden Gate Park in San Francisco, then changed to Sears Point Raceway, and finally switched to Altamont Raceway just two days before the event, which caused some problems.

The stage had been pre-fabricated and was only thirty-nine inches off the ground, which would have been fine at Sears Point Raceway because the location sloped from one end to the other and the stage was intended for the high end. But at Altamont, which also had a slope, it had to be set up at the low end. This meant the stage could easily be climbed onto by concertgoers, and more importantly the general weight of the crowd would push down the hill towards it rather than up the hill away from it.

There was no security arranged for the event, but because the stage was too low and the crowd would inevitably be pushing forward down the hill, the local chapter of Hell's Angels were asked if they would sit in front of the stage to dissuade the audience from clambering onto it. For doing this they would be paid with $500 worth of beer, which was delivered in a truck and sent to them at the front of the stage.

Three hundred thousand people turned up.

The drugs being taken that day were split between methamphetamine and LSD. When an audience is divided between two drugs of such different effect, there's no way they're going to be able to mix amicably – their minds will have been transported to totally different places.

With the natural slope of the arena pushing people forwards, it was difficult for them to push their way out of the crowd to go to the toilet – even more difficult to get back again. As the day progressed people got hungry, and uncomfortably full of urine. They got into arguments and there was lots of pushing and shoving. At the front, several people tried to jump on stage and were shoved back (not gently) by the beer-swilling Hells Angels, now as drunk as the audience was high.

Rock Scully, the Grateful Dead's manager saw the situation worsening and told his group to leave. They wouldn't be playing. That meant, between the group who played before the Rolling Stones and the beginning of the Stones' performance there was going to be a long gap, made even longer when Bill Wyman missed the helicopter bringing the group to the gig.

In the audience there was some bad-tempered fighting and as the Rolling Stones began their set, a group of about 5,000 fans pushed forwards to the very edge of the stage, some trying to climb onto it. Mick Jagger broke off the song to tell them, "Just be cool down in the front there, don't push around." But within a minute of starting the third song, 'Sympathy for the Devil', a fight erupted in the front of the crowd and the band stopped playing.

Jagger again appealed for calm and for the next half hour he got it. But as the group started to play 'Under My Thumb' some Hell's Angels got in a scuffle with an eighteen-year-old black guy, Meredith Hunter.

When he attempted to get onstage, one of the Hell's Angels punched him and chased him back into the crowd. But he came right back again. Rock Scully was sitting on top of a truck by the stage. "I saw what he was looking at, that he was crazy, he was on drugs, and that he had murderous intent. There was no doubt in my mind that he intended to do terrible harm to Mick or somebody in the Rolling Stones, or somebody on that stage."

The show was being filmed and footage seen later showed Hunter in a lime-green suit drawing a long-barrelled revolver from his jacket. One of the Hells Angels, Alan Passaro, had a knife and ran at Hunter, parried the gun and stabbed him. The other Hells Angels joined in the stabbing and Meredith Hunter died.

America saw the event as a black day for rock music. But similar things had happened before, and have since. It was the presence of the film crew that turned it into the 'black day' it became known as. At least concert promoters now had an excuse for not getting involved in free shows. *'No thanks. I'll charge for admission, make good money and organise the thing properly.'*

Four months before Altamont, the other great rock concert of the sixties had already confirmed that "profit is best".

Woodstock was set up as a normal profit-making event intended for an attendance of 200,000, to be held in August 1969. With three weeks to go the venue had to be changed from an industrial park in Wallkill, New York, to an area of fields in Woodstock, New York. The organisers sold 186,000 tickets in advance at $18 each, a total of $3.3 million, which at today's rate of inflation would be over $13 million. Because far too many people turned up, at the suggestion of the police the organisers cut the perimeter fence and allowed the extra numbers in free. Because of that it was often referred to as a free concert, which it wasn't.

The festival ran for three days and featured thirty-four acts including The Who, Arlo Guthrie, Creedence Clearwater Revival, Jefferson Airplane, Crosby Stills Nash and Young, and Jimi Hendrix. It had been raining for days beforehand, leaving the fields muddy. There was insufficient sanitation and too few food facilities, but the atmosphere was peaceful and the drug of choice amongst concertgoers was LSD.

When the movie of Woodstock was released, the high spot was the music, but behind the scenes there were also a couple of deaths. One was from an overdose of heroin; the other was due to a concertgoer sleeping in the long grass in a nearby field being scooped up and turned into a bundle of hay by a combine harvester. Apart from those two people, and despite the rain and mud, the crowd left the event happy. It was considered a triumph for the new age of reason and peace. And for LSD.

In fact, the event's peaceful conclusion was nothing more than an amazing piece of good luck. Because no major accident happened, Woodstock was turned into a piece of rock folklore and the more than healthy profit the organisers made was hardly ever commented on.

For better or worse, these two events in the sixties, together with the earlier Monterey Pop Festival, triggered the eruption of rock touring that took place in the seventies. Stadium rock tours became an integral part of the overall business of music. Each tour coincided with the release of a new album, with intensive marketing in each city and the group doing promotion on arrival, meeting DJs and record store owners and recording interviews for TV and radio, sometimes willingly, sometimes less so.

There were new mammoths of rock coming up all the time – David Bowie, Queen, Metallica, Aerosmith, Jefferson Starship, Little Feat, Alice Cooper, Blue Oyster Cult – all of them with the same style of rock circus, all of them running round America in a continual spiralling loop of excess, though the excesses weren't always violent. Elton John's excess was in his theatrical exuberance. He started his show like a Broadway finale, then built further – eight grand pianos, fifty dancing girls, thirteen changes of costume.

But whatever the differences in their stage shows, when it came to drug-taking every group told the same story. After being onstage and getting sent sky-high by the intense release of adrenalin it produced, rock performers found they couldn't come down when the show was finished. The periods between performances became an intolerable vacuum. People thought it was all parties, but it wasn't; it's just that the parties were what people remembered. Mainly it was boring. Waiting. Staring blankly at TV. Ordering room service.

For all rock artists the problem was the same; when the audience wasn't in front of them the emptiness was all-consuming. And usually there was just one answer. Drugs.

"Fucking rock-star ridiculousness..." said Butch Trucks, the drummer with the Allman Brothers "...the cocaine was *pouring*... you would go backstage and there would be a line of thirty dealers waiting outside."

"Hangers-on came backstage with piles of drugs like 'the three Kings off to see Jesus in his stable'," said Robert Greenfield in his book on touring with the Stones.

Steven Tyler of Aerosmith believed, "anything that was worth doing was worth overdoing".

Musicians did drugs to have fun, to pass time, to kill the craving for being on stage, to obliterate themselves – going up, coming down.

Brian Jones told friends it was like being dead in an elevator.

The person who had the real power in all this was not the record company but the manager. Powerhouse rock managers were a new music industry phenomenon, born in the sixties, rising to absolute power in the seventies.

Peter Grant of Led Zeppelin was the archetypal manager, demanding 90 per cent of the gate money and refusing to pay for advertising when a couple of announcements on local radio would be enough to sell out the gig. He had good business logic but a bullying belligerent face.

Promoter Bill Graham loathed him. "He was a dictator with this little army... They fucked with promoters by cutting costs and cutting corners... They surrounded themselves with physical might... They were ready to kill at the slightest provocation."

Albert Grossman was generally considered the first great American rock manager. In his initial dealings with Bob Dylan perhaps he'd been a little sharp in making money for himself, but once he had it, he changed. He started demanding that his artists should really be treated as artists; he got top money for everything they did and was totally protective of them.

Music writer Fred Goodman put Grossman's success down to one characteristic over everything else: "his great business lesson – appreciate, empower, and follow the artist…"

But Jerry Wexler thought he was a fraud.

He had people buffaloed. He would talk in tongues. He had a habit of going on and on and not saying anything. And cryptically he'd look at you. The suggestion was that if you're a cogent-enough person, you'll understand what I'm getting at. If you don't dig me, you're some kind of insensate asshole.

Either way, he was sometimes put in his place. In 1968, when he was already worth millions, Bob Dylan made Grossman write to Clive Davis at CBS asking for a free set of backyard toys from the CBS Creative Playthings catalogue for his two-year-old son Jesse.

The fact was, for a manager, it was a wildly up and down occupation. Standing at the top of a stadium looking down on a hundred thousand people stomping and cheering at his artist, or popping another million dollars into the bank account, or being hailed as the Svengali behind the new icon of youth culture – it felt good. But when his nitwit rock-star, out-of-his-head on drugs or drink or self-admiration, told his manager to cancel the gig with a stadium full of expectant people waiting for the first chord, or woke him in the middle of the night with a call from Rio de Janeiro to say he couldn't go on stage because he had no clean socks – it felt less so.

In Britain during the sixties, three managers had been pivotal figures in their groups' development – Brian Epstein with the Beatles, Andrew Oldham with the Rolling Stones, and Kit Lambert with The Who. But none had the staying power to deal with where the music business was heading.

Epstein, desperate to have the Beatles as friends, styled them nicely enough to meet his mother and hit on the look that sold them. Oldham, filled with angst and revolt, persuaded the Stones to behave outwardly the way he felt inside, thereby creating the image of rock as a whole. Kit Lambert, spilling over with creativity and subversive wit, gave The Who pop art clothes, violence on stage and access to the New York Metropolitan Opera House.

But drugs did for all of them. When the Stones got too heavily involved in them Andrew Oldham ran for the hills. Brian Epstein and Kit Lambert chose differently; they joined in the drug-taking, matching their groups sniff for sniff, pill for pill, hypodermic for hypodermic. Epstein died, Lambert carried on, but in both cases the effect was much the same – neither was in a fit state to deal with what was needed in the seventies.

In the seventies, management took an altogether new stance. Managers became five star generals, holding the group together and setting out their plan of attack. Everyone else in the team was less important than they were – producers, promotion people, stylists, designers, choreographers – all of them could be temporarily employed, then dumped, according to evolving circumstances.

It wasn't long before the manic world of rock touring began to influence the previously staid world of recording companies. Record executives took note of the swash-buckling lifestyles enjoyed by rock managers and decided to give themselves some of the same.

32
Light My Fire
EXECUTIVES BEHAVING BADLY

Whenever a rock singer experienced success the ambition lobe in his brain seemed to develop a permanent, painful erection. Now it started happening to record executives too. Walter Yetnikoff's ambition lobe leapt right out of his trousers.

When Yetnikoff was made head of CBS records he decided to re-invent himself. "I was intent on making noise. As a label honcho I needed an identity."

The identity he came up with was a raging bull. He would go to war with Warner.

"War required a battle cry, so I had banners printed at our annual convention with slogans that couldn't be faulted for their subtlety. They read, 'Fuck Warner. Fuck the Bunny'."

Yetnikoff had got the job as company boss because his predecessor, Clive Davis, had encountered some bad luck. Davis had been bought into CBS in the late sixties and done astonishingly well. He'd been clever with his new signings and clever with the more conventional side of the CBS catalogue – old recordings, classical music, LPs of Broadway shows, things that could support him if some of his new signings foundered.

But bit-by-bit, as more and more money went into promoting records, laws began to be broken. Payola was paid out and drugs were distributed to DJs, with everything done in cash – vast sums of it.

The whole point of doling money out in cash was so it couldn't be properly accounted for and traced to anything illegal. And of course, with a lot of cash passing through your hands there might be a temptation to use a bit of it for something other than what it was meant for – re-decorating your home, paying for your children's bar mitzvah parties, that sort of thing. And because it had all been in cash, when various people in the company who didn't like Clive Davis decided they'd like to get rid of him, he didn't have a leg to stand on.

Anyone who really knew how the record business worked would have let something like that go unnoticed. Davis was doing a great job and the record division was prospering. But the stiff-collared conservatives in the broadcasting division couldn't wait to see the back of him. They thought he was too full of himself so he was dispatched to the wilderness.

For a year, Goddard Lieberson came back as a caretaker CEO, then it was given over to two lawyers from the business department, Walter Yetnikoff and Dick Asher. Asher, who was cautious, would oversee international; Yetnikoff, who wasn't, would run America.

His principal strategy would be his war on Warner. To give the conflict even more focus he decided the first person in the firing line should be Mo Ostin, now promoted to President of Warner Bros Records. Yetnikoff had already made banners saying 'Fuck Warner' and 'Fuck the Bunny.' To these he now he added, 'Fuck Mo Ostin!'.

While the American record industry went to war with itself, British rock groups invaded its stadiums and cleaned up. But back home, UK record companies were finding the search for new artists less easy. The seventies proved nowhere near as fertile as the sixties.

At the beginning of the decade glam rock had swept in and created two huge stars – David Bowie and Marc Bolan. Bowie transformed himself into the fantasy character from his album *Ziggy Stardust* and zoomed off to America to join the British invasion of stadiums. Bolan, after trying painfully hard to capture the American market, failed, and sank into a cocaine-fuelled wasteland. So Britain turned to punk.

British punk was not as nihilist as the punk ethos actually dictated; British punks liked to be successful and earn money. But it was a localised fad, not bound for world domination, and not likely to give British record companies big artists with which to face the future. Of all the companies who fell flat on their faces, EMI did it best.

The problem started when the company signed the Sex Pistols. Their manager, Malcolm McLaren, was an anarchist through and through. He wanted to sabotage world order with his group and rehearsed them to be a bunch of foul-mouthed yobs. On a promotion trip to Europe, Johnny Rotten arrived at the airport somewhat worse for the previous evening's wear. "Hey Malc," he told his manager. "I've got to find the toilet quick."

Malcolm held his arm tightly and headed for the gate.

"But Malc, I'm going to vomit."

Malcolm wouldn't let him out of his grip and eventually the vomit arrived with Malcolm still walking him to the boarding area. As a result, the vomit got spread around a bit – into every newspaper in Britain. 'Vile Sex Pistols', 'Disgusting Punks', 'Teenage Filthies' all the usual sort of stuff.

At this time, EMI were more than just a record company. During the Second World War the company's manufacturing arm had helped develop radar and after the war had started producing broadcasting equipment, including the BBC's first television transmitter. They'd then moved into photomultipliers, brain-scanners and kidney dialysis machines and were planning a merger with Thorn Electrical, one of Britain's biggest electronics companies. EMI Records had become just an offshoot of all this and the powers-that-be at the top were in no mood to suffer problems with the company's image.

When a couple of days later the Sex Pistols said 'fuck' during a live TV interview, it was too much. The A&R department tried in vain to explain that it was like the early days of the Rolling Stones, or Elvis – a little shocking at the start but with big money to be made later. But it was hopeless. EMI dropped the group just a few weeks after signing them.

The scandal it caused in the press froze EMI's A&R team into inaction. For the rest of the decade they were afraid to sign anything and EMI propped itself up on classical music and the Beatles back catalogue. The company's only new success was Queen, whom they'd signed before the Sex Pistols debacle. Other than that, EMI's record division spent the rest of the decade demoralised – cutting costs, losing staff, putting out discount albums, re-promoting Cliff Richard – and as a result of this self-inflicted wound from the boardroom, EMI had its worst decade ever.

This over-cautious attitude ran through all British record companies, even when their top executive happened to be American, like Maurice Oberstein at CBS. His skill was to run the company in a very British way.

CBS did well in the UK because Oberstein refused to be pressured by edicts from America. When it was suggested he might chase after the Sex Pistols he refused to consider it. It wasn't that he objected to the group's music or morality but because the British market was more parochial than the American and splashing out big money to sign a controversial rock group was too risky. In the UK, a company's profits depended on every act being capable of hitting a national nerve and selling across the board. Because of that, pop played a more important part in the British music industry than in the American.

Although Britain had been the birthplace of rock the British saw its imagery as theatrical rather than serious. The British loved rock but took it with a pinch of salt. In the end they were more inclined towards pop music and pop imagery, and Oberstein, an American living in London, could see this more clearly than most.

In the early 70s New York suggested we push the British company's output towards rock to match its American image – Bob Dylan, Janis Joplin, Paul Simon. And what happens? Our biggest hits of the year were Benny Hill singing 'Ernie the Milkman' and Clive Dunn singing 'Grandad'. Then we had the Wombles, for heaven's sake – furry animals singing children's songs.

While the British industry wombled, the American industry got on with its civil war. At CBS, Walter Yetnikoff mentioned his attack plans to Nat Weiss, the lawyer for James Taylor, one of Warner's top artists. Weiss said Taylor's contract with Warner was about to expire, perhaps if CBS would guarantee a million dollars an album, he would change labels. Yetnikoff jumped at the opportunity and added a 2.5 million advance to go with it. Taylor had never really wanted to leave Warner, he was happy with them and Warner begged him not to go. So having already told CBS he would sign, Taylor changed his mind. Yetnikoff called him to a meeting, locked the door and argued with him for ten hours until he agreed.

A little later, Mo Ostin got a chance to sign Paul Simon, one of CBS's longest serving and most valued artists. Yetnikoff had been unnecessarily brusque with him and when Ostin heard about it he made an offer. Paul Simon swapped sides and the war was on for real. Yetnikoff announced he would destroy Paul Simon's career.

When Rod Stewart's contract came up for renewal at Warner, his manager, Billy Gaff, leaked a rumour that Walter Yetnikoff had called him. When he walked into Mo Ostin's office he was offered $20 million before he could open his mouth – ten albums at $2 million a piece.

Nobody was balancing the budget. Established artists like these were meant to provide the profits needed for financing fledgling acts. Paying too much for them was unwise. In the end they'd all reach a point where they no longer got any more hits – it was like buying a coal seam without checking how much had already been mined. Sometimes you hit lucky, sometimes you didn't.

Ahmet Ertegun had hit lucky – that's what started the whole thing off. At the beginning of the seventies he'd developed an obsession with signing the Rolling Stones to Atlantic. It had taken him a long while. First he'd waited until the group fired Alan Klein as their manager, then he'd made himself the Stones' best friend, partying, drinking, drugging, and travelling with them.

In 1971 they were finally able to leave Decca and Ahmet signed them, giving them their own label. The result was a Rolling Stone renaissance. The group sold more records than ever before and Ahmet got the credit.

In fact it wasn't quite as clear-cut as that because the group had wanted to sign with Atlantic all along. But the chase – Ahmet's ability to keep up with their partying, his prodigious drinking and drug-taking, and his eventual signing of them – made him into a rock 'n' roll businessman hero. Other executives started courting the same sort of adulation but with less justification. Living the high life and massaging the executive ego was becoming the norm in the new record industry.

Jac Holzman was from the old record industry.

When Holzman started Elektra he told his friends he wanted to make a million dollars having fun. Warner and Atlantic offered him ten million dollars to forget the fun and merge his company with theirs. By bringing Elektra into the fold Warner Music got a new name – WEA – and three top artists: The Doors, Tim Buckley, and Love.

The first new act Jac Holzman picked up as part of WEA was Queen. He grabbed them from CBS just as they were about to sign. The thing that swayed them was the no-nonsense contract Holzman handed them – how many years, how many albums, what royalty, who had artistic control, but nothing more. Holzman explained, "The CBS standard contract was a thing of wonder for CBS, but for artists it was desperation – thirty pages or more, the first sixteen protecting CBS and on page seventeen a tiny paragraph about what the artist might receive if all the planets were properly in conjunction."

However, once Elektra was part of Warner there was pressure on Holzman to start using a contract not dissimilar to the lengthy CBS one. It was one of many things that began to needle him.

Another was David Geffen.

Before he'd gone chasing after the Rolling Stones, Ahmet Ertegun had made another shrewd deal. He'd financed David Geffen, the manager of the Eagles, to start a label, Asylum Records. Geffen had grown tired of being a manager. He didn't like the midnight calls and being so closely involved with personal lives and he threw himself wholeheartedly into running his new label.

It did superbly. Soon it not only had the Eagles, whom Geffen managed, but Linda Ronstadt, Jackson Browne and Joni Mitchell, so Atlantic bought out Geffen's label for $7 million and Geffen became a fully-fledged record executive at Warner Music. He gave up managing the Eagles and gave control of his old management company to the people who'd helped him run it.

Jac Holzman didn't like Geffen, he wasn't a team player and his method of working was provocative; "hurrying in with a raincoat over his head to avoid being seen... behind closed doors on the phone shouting... suddenly coming out and screaming at someone... psychiatrist making house calls at the office... insecurity rampant in the corridors".

Having Geffen around the building was enough to make Holzman decide it was time to go. He wanted to retire to his house in Maui and was by his own admission 'burnt out' after twenty years in the business. What he disliked most was seeing new people around the office that he knew had been hired for just one reason – to supply drugs. If this was corporate America rock 'n' roll style, Holzman wanted out. So he left.

The next person Geffen upset was Jerry Wexler. There was already jealousy between the two men arising from their relationship with Ahmet Ertegun.

Ahmet was a great spotter of talent, not just musical or creative talent, but business talent too. Ahmet had seen Geffen as having dynamic business qualities and got him into Warner. He befriended him and travelled with him, and Wexler who'd always seen himself as Ahmet's special relationship, felt pushed out. At a Warner social event in front of all the other executives, Geffen and Wexler lost control. Geffen sneered across the table and called Wexler a washed-up has-been. Wexler screamed back, "You'd jump into a pile of pus to come up with a nickel between your teeth."

Ostensibly, the row had been about Bob Dylan. When Dylan's deal with CBS had come up for renewal, both Geffen and Wexler had chased after him for their respective labels and Geffen had got him – an enormous coup at an enormous price. But it was wasted money. After just one album Dylan fell out with him and went back to CBS.

"Geffen was just interested in being a celebrity," he said.

After seeing Dylan leave CBS for Asylum, Walter Yetnikoff took no risks when Paul McCartney's contract came up for renewal. He gave him everything he wanted. McCartney still hesitated, saying perhaps he should check around a bit first.

Since this could only mean going to Warner, and knowing McCartney's passion for music publishing, Yetnikoff threw in a publishing company owned by the CBS publishing division, Frank Music. Its catalogue included all the songs of Frank Loesser, who wrote *Guys and Dolls*, and hits like 'Baby, It's Cold Outside'. When Yetnikoff bought the catalogue for CBS, he'd promised Loesser's widow it would be the 'jewel in the crown' of the company's publishing, now he was giving it away for nothing.

McCartney accepted at once, as Yetnikoff knew he would. But it was pure financial vandalism – Frank Music was worth at least ten million, almost double the money McCartney was getting from the deal. It wasn't like giving away a free tank of gas with a new car; it was like giving away three cars for the price of one.

Spending at Warner and CBS was going out of control. The money they were paying out would have to come from somewhere, and many of these artists, however big, were not going to sell enough albums for the companies to recoup. The point was – these executives weren't just naughty kids playing games – this blustering warlike power-game was the new image of the music industry.

Walter Yetnikoff wasn't a normal chief executive, he liked to stay up all night drinking vodka and whiskey; he cheated on his wife with his secretary, then cheated on his secretary with one of his artists. He tried to get CBS TV's top investigative journalist Mike Wallace fired for investigating the music industry. He loved socialising with Morris Levy, the Jewish mobster who owned Roulette records. Yetnikoff called him Moishe and they laughed about "fucking the artist" and doing "ball-shattering deals".

Ahmet Ertegun wasn't much different; he drank even more than Yetnikoff and could stay up all night partying and still be at a 9am meeting if he was needed. He was obsessed with parties; if there wasn't one he would invent one. And he loved mixing with the stars from his label. Some of the best parties had been at Sonny and Cher's house, but they'd now separated, with Cher retaining the house. Of late, she'd started an affair with David Geffen, who'd moved in with her.

Ahmet had dinner one night with a European countess and Bianca Jagger. Tom Dowd, one of Atlantic's producers, was there too. "We finish dinner at one o'clock – by which time they're sweeping the floor of the restaurant and putting the chairs on the tables. Mick Jagger's joined us by then, and Ahmet says, 'There's got to be a party somewhere'."

A waiter brought a phone to the table and Ahmet called Bette Midler. "Hello Bette, what are you doing? There's a party going on at Cher's – we'll pick you up on the way there."

It was now 2am. Cher, still at the romantic stage of her affair with Geffen, would almost certainly be in bed. Ahmet called her anyway, "I'm with Tom and Mick and Bianca and Bette – we'll come over for a nightcap."

When they got there, Cher had managed to get herself together and was wearing a gold lamé dress. David Geffen only had on shorts and tennis shoes. Mick Jagger sat down at the piano and Ahmet told Cher to get out the champagne. But it turned out there wasn't any in the house.

Ahmet turned to Geffen with a frown. "We never had that problem when Sonny was here."

33

All Around the World
GLOBILITY

In the early sixties, the Beatles gave the world a template for teenage success – four boys, fashionable clothes, pretty hair, clean skin, big smiles – just add good songs. In Spanish, French, Japanese, Malay, Serbo-Croat, or Thai. There was nowhere this formula didn't work. The Beatles were an instruction manual to the world's record companies on how to tackle the teen market and get rich. There wasn't a country in the non-communist world where every local record company didn't have at least one copycat Beatles. By the time the fad began to wear thin, there was a truly global music industry.

Then came rock! Drums, guitars and attitude. Any group of young musicians, anywhere in the world, any clothes, any hairstyle, no need to smile, good skin optional. The popular press saw this as a *social* phenomenon; for the record industry it was a *financial* phenomenon. The teenagers' own ambition drove them into the record companies' arms. A demo tape left at reception would find its way to the big box upstairs that contained dozens. From there it was just a matter of selecting the right groups and sending them off to the recording studio.

Rock created an endless, inexhaustible, self-delivering supply of raw material from which the music industry could multiply itself one hundred-fold. Which is exactly what it did.

Before the Second World War, the American and British music industries were domestically oriented. Practically all revenues came from the home market. Foreign revenue was a small extra profit on which American and British music companies were not dependent. The foreign markets didn't offer enough return to justify modifying British and American music to suit foreign tastes, nor to maintain elaborate organisations overseas.

But by the end of the sixties the situation had changed. The British music industry in particular had begun to derive a substantial part of its income from foreign markets, and now the Europeans were getting in on the act. Philips, operating from the Netherlands, had already bought Mercury in America. Now it merged its entire record division with Polydor, operated by the German company Deutsche Grammophon, owned by Siemens, a multinational engineering and electronics conglomerate.

The new company was called PolyGram and opened offices in London with a German managing director. But it kept the separate identities of the Phillips and Polydor labels.

PolyGram became the number two record company in Britain, with EMI number one. Pye and Decca were now struggling to keep afloat, while the American companies – RCA, CBS and Warner – were only just starting.

Things moved quickly. Five years later, in the mid-seventies, CBS, RCA, Warner, EMI and PolyGram, had local offices in every non-communist country in the world. These regional offices of major companies were mainly there to sell the local population product from the company's home territory, but they also functioned as a local record company, signing and developing artists. But not with a view to promoting them outside that country.

From the head office's point of view, promoting foreign artists outside their own countries was too expensive and had no good benefits. They didn't travel well; they spoke strange languages and needed visas; they were strictly for local consumption. On the other hand, if there was competition in signing one from the half dozen other local companies, the local office of a major record company didn't hesitate to play their winning stroke, "Sign with us and you get a shot at the world market".

In fact, the very opposite was true. The people running these local offices were never allowed to forget that their primary purpose was to promote the company's British or American product. In 1973, Maurice Oberstein was head of CBS in the UK.

> *After we'd sold every last copy we could of it, we were told to throw more promo money at Bob Dylan's new album. It was ridiculous. We'd done what was needed and a few extra sales wouldn't justify the expense. All of us running offices outside of America preferred to invest in local acts – they gave us a bigger return – but the CBS rule was, US acts first, UK second. To retaliate, I pushed some of our international offices to put extra cash behind the Wombles. It amused me – Dylan/the Wombles – our most credible act versus our most non-credible. And in most places the Wombles did best.*

Despite the major companies' lack of interest in promoting artists from non-English speaking territories, by the mid-seventies foreign hits were beginning to creep into the British and American charts anyway. From the Netherlands came Golden Earring, a rock group. From Greece, Demis Roussos, an oversized tenor in a kaftan. Tangerine Dream was synthesiser rock from Germany. And from Brazil came Morris Albert's 'Feelings', which went to number one in America.

With these international successes, major record companies began to realise artists who were not from Britain or America might occasionally be worth promoting. And as their record executives started for the first time to move around the world, they came across an essential travel companion.

In the sixties Phillips had developed a four-track mini-cassette tape. It was put on the market in 1963 and sales had been growing ever since. In 1972, Sony bought out a high quality stereo version that ran on batteries and fitted into a briefcase size bag together with two speakers. More importantly you could plug in earphones. And since the machine itself was only the size of a large hardback novel, it wasn't long before it caught on with travelling executives and rock stars who would pack it in their carry-on bag together with a good pair of headphones and a selection of cassettes. Surprised by its success, Sony set about developing a smaller version.

Six years later they had it – the *Walkman*. Half the size of a paperback, it would fit into a jacket pocket and was listened to through ear-pieces. Over the next twelve years 100 million of these *Walkmans* were sold, each one creating an estimated fifty cassette sales – a total of five billion cassettes.

With their personal stereo, Sony had discovered the future of the music industry.

Meanwhile, the US government had discovered its past.

Since the first recordings of it started to find their way overseas in the 1920s, jazz had become *the* international music of the twentieth century. The music industry in America had been slow to latch onto its international possibilities, which was understandable. American record companies saw jazz as *commercial*, just one more product to sell. It was less profitable than pop or rock, but a steady seller nonetheless. The rest of the world saw it as *cultural*.

It was the US government rather than the music industry that first noticed how the rest of the world felt about jazz. In the USA, the likes of Duke Ellington, Lionel Hampton and Benny Goodman had seen their best days during the big band boom of the thirties. They'd been the pop stars of the moment and jazz was the music they'd played. Now we were in the era of youth and rock.

But in the rest of the world they were treated with reverence.

Seeing the respect with which jazz was regarded outside of America, the government recruited all its greatest living proponents and paid to send them round the world, plugging America, "advertising its core values of non-racialism and fairness".

The US government hoped to offset what they perceived as European and Soviet superiority in classical music and ballet, while at the same time shielding America's Achilles heel of racism by demonstrating racial equality in action.

THE BUSINESS

It was a crafty ploy. Send ageing jazz musicians to communist countries to win converts to 'the American way of life'. Then later, when capitalism arrived, the locals would buy American records. Music industry executives should have thought of it for themselves.

Willis Conover, for forty years the announcer for the Voice of America's nightly hour-long jazz programme to Eastern Europe, believed that people who were denied freedom in their political culture could detect a sense of freedom in jazz. "Jazz is a cross between total discipline and total anarchy. The musicians agree on tempo, key and chord structure but beyond this everyone is free to express himself. This is jazz. And this is America. That's what gives this music validity."

It was certainly true that the music was appreciated everywhere. The US government sent Benny Goodman to South East Asia at a time when the region looked likely to fall prey to communism. Each country he visited tried to do outdo the others in how it honoured him. In Phnom Penh, Cambodia's King Norodom decorated Goodman with the order of the Chevalier de Monisa Raphon. In Kuala Lumpur he was made honorary governor; in Bangkok, honorary mayor; in Singapore, honorary fire chief.

But there was a false facade to these tours. Black musicians met foreign dignitaries at embassy parties in Istanbul or Moscow and praised the equality of American society. Charlie Parker, Dizzy Gillespie, Miles Davis and Oscar Peterson were amongst those who helped spread the word, yet back home there were jazz clubs in the southern states where they still had to enter through the back door. On one occasion, Alvin Ailey, the choreographer for a dance troupe that joined one of the tours, was grabbed by police in the street in Washington DC simply for being there and being black. He was handcuffed, thrown in a cell and beaten and kicked. When the police found his passport and saw who he was, they let him go. Two days later he rejoined the tour in Athens, attending the usual embassy parties, selling the USA, advertising its core values of non-racialism and fairness.

But what these jazz musicians suffered from most was the lack of professionalism shown by the government in making tour arrangements. When an American consul in Germany forgot to get Dave Brubeck the correct visa to cross over from West to East Berlin, he suggested Brubeck hide in the trunk of his car to get across.

Duke Ellington's musicians were flown on a ten-hour flight to Kabul in Afghanistan in a converted cargo plane. Ellington was furious. He couldn't believe the State Department would have flown a classical orchestra in such conditions and dubbed the plane "a cattle-car for Negroes". No rock group would have stood for it, which proved perhaps that market forces work best.

Playing for profit was better than playing for propaganda.

34

Into the Groove

DISCO

The Peppermint Lounge was a dump. Adjoined to the Knickerbocker Hotel, off Times Square, it was a grubby gay hustler joint with a long mahogany bar and a tiny dance floor at the back where a band played at weekends. Full house was just 179 customers – rent boys, sailors, transvestites, lowlifes and street toughs. It was classic sleaze, one of the gungiest dives in town, worth adding to a conducted tour of the city for that reason alone. Which is why Hollywood actress Merle Oberon – now fifty-ish and a bit of a fag hag – popped in one Saturday night in the early sixties with her new toy boy Prince Serge Oblinski. They stayed ten minutes and danced the twist, the smart new dance imported from Harlem, played at the Peppermint Lounge by the weekend group, Joey Dee and the Starliters, unknowns from New Jersey.

Next day, gossip columnist Earl Wilson wrote that Merle Oberon and Prince Serge Oblinksi had danced the night away. That evening so many people went to the club that police had to put up barricades. Within weeks, the people who had been seen dancing the twist at the Peppermint Lounge sounded like a red carpet awards ceremony in Hollyood – Judy Garland, John Wayne, Jackie Kennedy, Nat 'King' Cole, Shirley MacLaine, Tennessee Williams, Truman Capote, Marilyn Monroe, Shelley Winters, Richard Burton, Elizabeth Taylor, Norman Mailer and Liberace. There wasn't a single celebrity in America who didn't want to go along to the Peppermint Lounge and be seen dancing the twist.

Author Tom Wolfe wrote,

> *Elsa Maxwell, Countess Bernadotte, Noël Coward, Tennessee Williams, and the Duke of Bedford – everybody was there, and the hindmost were laying fives, tens, and twenty-dollar bills on cops, doormen and a couple of sets of maitre d's to get within sight of the bandstand and a dance floor the size of somebody's kitchen.*

The *New York Times* reported, "Cafe society has not gone slumming with such energy since its forays into Harlem in the Twenties."

"Even Greta Garbo", *Time* magazine reported, "hauled herself out of her myth-lined cocoon and appeared – lank-haired and bone-pale, to snap her fingers and smile."

'The Twist', the hit record that triggered it all, wasn't by the group at the Peppermint Lounge, it was by Chubby Checker. It first came out in 1960, did quite well in the USA, but didn't spread overseas. When the Peppermint Lounge hit the headlines towards the end of 1962 it was re-released and went round the world like a storm, nowhere more than Britain.

The twist took off in Britain like no dance fad had since the Charleston. Between Christmas and New Year 1961 it spread through the South and started heading North. On 12th January, the Highland Lass Darts Club in Strathpeffer, advertised Scotland's first twist contest at the Pavillion Ballroom. "Sweeping the South. Now for the first time in the North. Come to the Pavilion Ballroom and try it for yourself."

Soon, the same thing was happening all over Britain. 'Rock 'n' Roll' nights became 'Twist Nights'. And by February a new word was appearing; the weekend dance was now called the 'Saturday Twistacular', which was quickly followed by Monday to Friday twistaculars.

Even BBC TV's *Television Dancing Club* joined in. Normally the home of the foxtrot and waltz played in strict tempo, bandleader Victor Silvester arranged an old Gershwin tune for the new dance, 'Fascinating Rhythm Twist'.

The movements were explained with great seriousness in the BBC dance manual. "Stand up on the balls of your feet. Stay on the balls of your feet as you twist your body round from side to side… Hold your arms above your waist with the elbows bent and as your body twists one way, your arms twist the other."

Chubby Checker described the same movements more vividly. "It's like putting out a cigarette with both feet while wiping your bottom with an invisible towel."

Even in Victor Silvester's sanitised version of the dance there must have been some hint of sexual danger. The BBC fielded complaints from all over the country. In particular people disliked the Twist not being a 'couple dance'; they thought it would change the nature of dancing if people could do it by themselves.

They were right. Dance halls would never be the same again; it changed everything that had gone before. No longer was the Palais de Dance a source of embarassment between the sexes, with girls sitting around like wallflowers and blokes standing in a group at the bar, discussing the girls but never daring to talk to them. Either sex could now dance in any combination they liked.

Girls danced with their girlfriends. And blokes, instead of having to suffer the embarrassment of asking a girl to dance, could twist together, hanging onto their pints, puffing on their cigarettes, losing none of their masculine reference points. Little did they realise they were dancing the way the queers did in Harlem, and black ones at that. (Well, not exactly! When gays danced together in Harlem it was pure sex.)

It was from Harlem gay bars that the dance had spread to the Peppermint Lounge. And it arrived in Harlem from the Caribbean where people had danced that way for years. Since they didn't have to touch in order to do the twist, gay men could dance together while staying on the right side of the law. In fact, the beauty of the twist lay in the act of *not* touching each other. The trick was to writhe snake-like between each other's bodies – legs between legs, arms between arms, lips a teasing half-inch apart, crotches even closer.

But the British tabloids never mentioned that. They talked about twist marathons on Brighton pier, of models twisting on the catwalk at the Dorchester Hotel, or Princess Margaret doing it in a Mayfair night club. With the buzz it created, Britain's seedy Palais de Danse and Locarnos, which had fallen on hard times in the fifties, burst back into bloom. Lifeless resident bands that had only just mastered rock 'n' roll now had to come to grips with the twist. But soon a new trend sprang up – record nights.

It had never happened before, but songs like 'Let's Twist Again' demanded it; they sounded so much better from the record than from the ageing musicians in the dance hall bands. So the hall owners reached an agreement with the Musicians' Union; if the musicians could have the night off on full pay, records could be played. And dancers turned up in their thousands.

The same things happened in smart places too, like London's Ad Lib club. Up a private elevator to fur-lined walls, black mirrors and beautiful people – the Stones, the Beatles, Richard and Sybil Burton, Julie Christie, Laurence Harvey, Shirley Bassey – dancing till 3am.

Soon people moved on from the twist and danced in another new way. Still not touching, they stood rooted to the spot like Paul and George singing falsetto 'ooohs', waving their arms to the beat.

The twist's big moment was 1961. By the middle of the sixties the music being danced to was Motown, easy to move to because it was played with four even beats to the bar, the snare drum crashing down on each one of them. But the twist had done its job – dancing had changed forever.

Dancers stood apart and didn't touch.

In 1964, Richard Burton walked out on his wife Sybil in favour of Elizabeth Taylor. Sybil went to New York and opened a bar called 'Arthur' whose clientele was much like the Ad Lib in London – film and music celebrities, anyone in town who was anyone. The newspapers ran an opening night picture of Sybil dancing with Rudolf Nureyev.

In most clubs where people danced to records, the person who chose them was the club manager, or even the girl from the cloakroom. The person who played them was faceless and uninspired; waiting for each to fade-out before putting on the next.

At Sybil's, the guy hired to do it was Terry Noel. He used two turntables so the end of one record flowed into the next, and he built a speaker system that could swirl the sound around the room. He chose records that lifted or calmed the mood and he held dancers completely in his sway. He didn't play records; he delivered a sound-show. Sybil Burton's connections got people to the club; Terry Noel got them onto the dance floor. He was the first club DJ.

After Sybil's, the next step forward was the Sanctuary, a gay club located in a former Baptist church on 43rd Street. Its DJ booth was set up where the altar used to be and the DJ was Francis Grasso. Music writer Albert Goldman wrote,

> *Grasso invented the technique used by every DJ ever since of holding the record he was about to play at the precise point he wanted it to start playing, while a felt mat underneath it revolved on the turntable. Then letting it go, to make a seamless connecting point between two pieces of music.*

Grasso's other speciality was to play two tracks at the same time mixing heavy drums from one with a chorus from another – a stomping drum intro from Led Zeppelin under a soulful chorus from Gladys Knight. According to Goldman, Grasso didn't just play records, he "reinvented them out of their composite parts, the top end vocals and the bottom end rhythm".

While he did this, fifteen hundred gays stuffed with drugs and testosterone turned the place into a dance orgy – half dance, half sex, half crazy. By the time the place was closed down, it had been copied by similar clubs in other cities – Philadelphia, Pittsburgh, Detroit, Chicago. But for this sort of party music to spread to the straight world, something simpler was needed. There wasn't going to be a Francis Grasso in every dance club; normal DJs would need to receive their records ready-Grasso'd, with a thumping bass-drum pounding through them.

At the beginning of the seventies, the music most played in regular dance places in America was the Philadelphia sound – Barry White's 'Love Theme', George McRae's 'Rock Your Baby', Van McCoy's 'The Hustle' – a style first created by producers Kenny Gamble and Leon Huff. These records were pop songs with a black sensibility – subtle but slightly complex rhythms – great for dancing if your body flowed naturally but not much use for lumbering Europeans, shy of stepping onto the dance floor.

British DJ Pete Waterman had been looking for an answer to Europeans' lack of dancing ability. In 1975 at Midem, the annual Music Industry conference at Cannes in France, he heard a song that was startlingly different. "The track was called 'Save Me' and it was released under the name Silver Convention... It was like the old Motown sound except they'd replaced the snare with the bass drum played on every beat of the bar."

Waterman immediately bought the rights to the record, took it back to London and remixed it. "We changed the song around and made it into more of a pop song. That record became the catalyst for every four-to-the-floor dance record that ever followed, which means almost every dance or dance-pop record made since."

In Munich, an Italian record producer, Giorgio Moroder, also heard the Silver Convention record. He used the four-to-the-floor bass-drum for a record he was making for Hansa Records with a black American singer who lived in Germany, Donna Summer. Hansa took it to America and played it to Neil Bogart, owner of Casablanca Records in Los Angeles. Bogart asked if it could be extended to twenty minutes. Moroder did as he suggested and the record took off.

The new beat changed America. The twist had taught people to stand apart, the four-to-the-floor drum told them when to move their feet. You simply stomped them in time with it. And that was disco.

French producer Jacques Morali and songwriter Henri Belolo had an idea for an all-American, all male, all macho, disco group. They went to New York, found the guys they wanted and released them as the Village People, again with Casablanca. When Village People went to number one with 'YMCA' the entire music business jumped on the bandwagon.

From Germany came Boney M, four black artists from Aruba, Florida, Montserrat and the UK. Produced by German producer Frank Farian, they had worldwide four-to-the-floor hits with 'Ma Baker', 'Rivers of Babylon', 'Brown Girl in the Ring', 'Sunny' and 'Rasputin'.

Sweden came up with Abba; white silk pants, ostrich feathers, and soaring synthesisers. 'Dancing Queen' was Euro-disco personified and was Abba's first number one in America.

Rod Stewart did a four-to-the-floor remix of 'D'ya Think I'm Sexy', another Number One for disco. And even the Rolling Stones jumped on the bandwagon, thumping away on all four beats with 'Miss You'.

Four-to-the-floor disco music was now the sound of dance all over the world. PolyGram saw it as the driving force of a new international music market. Most people in the American record industry thought of PolyGram as a dusty, stiff, out-of-touch company, from another planet, barely literate in the ways of entertainment. But more than anyone else, the company's Dutch-German owners understood that the record business was about gambling and that Americans did it best. The company's attitude was, "If we let the Americans do it for us, it's a gamble, but we might get a big win. If we lose, well… it happened far away across the ocean. It won't affect our core shareholders in Europe. We'll survive."

So PolyGram moved into America in a big way. They'd already bought Mercury; they now bought a 50 per cent stake in Casablanca with an option to buy the rest if they chose to, then set up offices on 8th Avenue and put in Dutch and German managers, somewhat insensitive to their new surroundings. One German executive, Kurt Kinkele, liked to introduce himself to his American staff by telling them the first time he saw America was through the periscope of a German U-boat.

Was it meant as a joke, or a warning shot across the bows of the American music industry? No one was sure.

Buying Casablanca had been something of a bargain, giving PolyGram not just Donna Summer and the Village People but also the rock group Kiss. They now bought RSO, the record company owned by Bee Gee's manager Robert Stigwood, and gave him $5.5 million a year to develop movies. With the cost of record promotion soaring all over America, PolyGram realised that a hit movie with new songs in it could save millions on the plugging bill.

Stigwood had bought the rights to the movie *Saturday Night Fever.* He now put the film into production with the Bee Gees writing five songs for it. When the Gibb brothers' strange falsetto harmonies were laid over a four-to-the-floor dance track, it became the sound that broke all sales records for the decade – over thirty million albums worldwide. In 1978, the RSO label topped the US album chart for twenty-four weeks with three number one disco singles – 'How Deep Is Your Love', 'Stayin' Alive' and 'Night Fever'.

On the strength of the film's success, Robert Stigwood made a follow-up movie, *Grease*, based on rock 'n' roll dancing at the end of the fifties. In the current mood for dance, it was another wild success, and again the soundtrack album sold thirty million. Meanwhile, Casablanca had a huge album with Giorgio Moroder's soundtrack music from the film, *Midnight Express.*

With both Casablanca and RSO a part of PolyGram, the company's sales of recorded music for 1979 came to $1.2 billion. No record company had ever before topped a billion in annual revenues.

PolyGram now considered itself a full-fledged American record company. Its market share had risen from 5 per cent to 20 per cent; it was up there with CBS and Warner. The company exercised its option and bought the rest of Casablanca. But in their excitement at adding up the year's figures, the company's accountants had failed to notice that if you took away the two big soundtrack albums, the U.S. operation was no more profitable than it had been in previous years. Though PolyGram's market share was way up, it was entirely due to the two thirty-million selling albums, something PolyGram was never likely to repeat again, leave alone every year.

Worse than that, Casablanca had gone out of control. The company held a daily drug binge with a half kilo of cocaine being sent in every afternoon and secretaries joining executives, sniffing their way through meetings in which nothing was ever resolved. Important decisions were made without the slightest attempt to be clear-headed. Neil Bogart issued four Kiss albums at once, each a solo effort by one of the group's members. They sold around 600,000 each, which would have been fine if he hadn't shipped three times that amount. And now the returns were coming in.

The same was happening at RSO. Robert Stigwood decided to make a movie of the Beatle's *Sergeant Pepper* starring the Bee Gees and Peter Frampton. It was a box-office disaster. *Rolling Stone* magazine voted its two-record box set the worst album of the decade. Even so, it sold around three million records. Not too bad – except Stigwood had insisted on shipping eight million.

The record industry had never imposed limits on the number of records stores could return. If a company insisted on shipping more than were needed, dealers didn't care; they just sent them back again. The five million leftovers of *Sergeant Pepper* were eventually sold to a 'cut-out' distributor for 25 cents apiece, a quarter of their actual production cost.

Worse than that – in the excitement of having had a billion-dollar year, PolyGram had upsized its distribution network so it could handle the same volume of sales the following year. But the following year there was no *Saturday Night Fever* and no *Grease* and the distribution depots lost $7 million a month.

At Casablanca, with everyone coked to their eyeballs, no one noticed that the disco market was shrinking. They continued to sign acts as fast as they could find them. In 1979, their never-to-be-heard-of-again signings included Angel, Brooklyn Dreams, Bugs Tomorrow, Eclipse, the Godz, Love and Kisses, Mizz, Paris Connection, 707, Space, and Trigger. And that was just the beginning – there were over one hundred of them. Each at a signing cost of around $100,000 before promotion. So that was another ten million loss.

The Dutch and German bosses at Polgyram decided to bring in a new head of the company. They employed Harvey Schein, an expert on corporate law but not a good people-manager. Schein's way of dealing with problems was to yell at people. He had no interest in the day-to-day running of PolyGram's American office so he brought in someone else to actually run it and promoted himself to CEO. But the person he bought in to run it had no experience at all of running a company; David Braun, a music business lawyer who had previously represented Bob Dylan.

As problem piled on problem Braun realised what a mistake he'd made. "There were things I did not know about running a big company and Harvey was never there to help."

Schein was equally disappointed with Braun. "He wanted all the candy, not the spinach."

The Dutch and German owners of the company appeared unconcerned by the friction, they seemed to enjoy seeing their senior executives argue with each other. At a meeting attended by PolyGram's European bosses Harvey Schein had a yelling fit, screaming at two of David Braun's employees over a bookkeeping error. Braun shouted back. "Enough! This is not Nuremberg."

While PolyGram lost hundreds of millions, Warner and CBS watched with delight, congratulating themselves for not having jumped too heavily into dance music.

Outside of America the world kept on dancing. But in the USA, disco was a dirty word.

35

Signed, Sealed, Delivered
MUSIC PUBLISHING

Who, in their right mind, if they had just written a novel, would sign the rights to a publisher who agreed to neither print the book nor market it, yet demanded half of any money it might make if someone else did?

By the beginning of the 1980s, that's what music publishing had become.

Fifty years earlier, a writer would give a publisher a song because the publisher promised to print the music, make it a hit, and sell thousands of copies. Providing the writer hadn't sold the song to the publisher outright, he would then receive a royalty. But by the 1980s, music publishers no longer did this. They simply acted as bankers.

An aspiring pop singer or rock group, short of money at the beginning of their career would go to a music publisher and ask for an advance. The publisher would give it to them in exchange for three or five or ten years of all the songs the writer would write in that time. The writer would receive as large a percentage of the royalties as he could negotiate. The standard split was fifty-fifty, but by the 1980s, a writer sometimes was able to get as much as 60 per cent, or even 70 per cent.

The publisher then did nothing. The writer had to find himself a record deal, and the record company, by releasing the record, would effectively publish the song. If it became a hit, the publisher wouldn't necessarily print sheet music but might assign the right to do so to a company who specialised in it.

More and more often writers were heard complaining – what does the publisher do other than collect a percentage of the money that should be mine? And more and more often the answer was – nothing. Moreover, for doing absolutely nothing, music publishers were about to make more money than ever before.

The CD had been invented. The whole world was off to its local record store to re-buy its record collection on hiss-free scratch-free CDs. What's more, they were being charged a higher price than for regular albums, and best of all for the record companies, the stores were sending very few back. Dave Glew, head of WEA distribution, had never seen a money bonanza like it before. "Selling something at sixteen ninety-eight with no returns... the windfall profits were absolutely amazing."

None of the record companies had seen it coming and most of them had been against it. Walter Yetnikoff had told everyone at CBS the CD was just a gimmick and wouldn't last. When he was taken to see the new CD factory CBS had invested in he left saying, "Ten million fucking dollars for this?"

How wrong could he get! The ten million CBS invested in that plant would turn into ten billion. CD sales gave record companies profits beyond their wildest imagination. But music publishers, too, joined in the bonanza.

In America the statutory rate per recorded track had increased enormously. By 1990, it was eight cents a song. In the UK it was 8.5 per cent of a CD that would sell for a wholesale price of £8. For an American publisher, if a group had written all the songs on their album and there were ten songs on it there would be a total 40 cents per record for the publisher, $2 million if the album sold five million copies, and the same amount for the group. In the UK, it was even more.

Not bad for doing nothing. Which is why record companies started buying up publishing companies.

Private individuals were buying them too, including Paul McCartney.

Back in March 1969, two months after the Beatles' final concert on the rooftop at Savile Row, John Lennon was in the middle of a bed-in with Yoko Ono at the Amsterdam Hilton when a journalist handed him an English newspaper. Dick James and his accountant had sold their shares in Northern Songs to ATV giving the Beatles no notice and no chance to buy them out first. John let the world know he was upset. "I'm sick to death of being fucked about by men in suits sitting on their fat arses in the City!"

He called Paul and suggested they send in their American manager Allen Klein to try and stop the deal, but Paul insisted his side of things be dealt with by his wife's brother, John Eastman. Without the full backing of both writers, Allen Klein couldn't overcome the financial clout of Lew Grade, who was their adversary in the bidding war. So the copyright in Beatles songs passed to Grade's company, ATV.

Of all the Beatles, Paul was the most upset. He responded by going into publishing himself, buying up other catalogues, just as the Beatles catalogue had been bought up. Paul grumbled to journalists about not owning his own songs, but at the same time he would rave about the benefits of buying other people's. He was doing to other writer's catalogues exactly what had been done to his. "The music publishing I own is fabulous. Beautiful. I owe it all to Linda's dad Lee Eastman and her brother John. Linda's dad is a great business brain."

Linda's dad suggested he buy the Buddy Holly catalogue. The fact that Paul still complained about the deal he got with the Beatles publishing in no way made him think he might like to call the people receiving money on behalf of Buddy Holly's estate and offer them better terms on the publishing. And although his biggest worry about the Beatles catalogue was that ATV might license the songs for use in television commercials, he went ahead and licensed Buddy Holly songs for exactly that.

The old story of the abused becoming the abuser.

In 1985, Elton John sued Dick James. The contract in question was one signed by Elton John and his songwriting partner Bernie Taupin in 1967.

John had received an initial fifty pounds advance and a weekly fifteen pounds guarantee against the royalties allotted him in the agreement, and seventeen-year-old Taupin, three years his junior, was paid ten pounds a week. Dick James had signed the songs for 'life of copyright' – which meant until fifty years after Taupin and John were both dead. But the real bone of contention wasn't that, it was America.

Dick James's UK company sub-published to an American company on a fifty-fifty basis. The American company remitted only 50 per cent of what it collected, and the UK company then paid John and Taupin 50 per cent of that. So from America they got only 25 per cent.

But the company Dick James sub-published to in America was Dick James USA. So Dick James, through companies in the UK and USA, received a total of 75 per cent while John and Taupin received only 25 per cent. And it wasn't just in America, it was the same in almost every country in the world.

The judge decided Dick James could keep the songs but made him back-pay the royalties his American company had kept that should have gone to the writers. James could well afford it. He was now a rich man, richer than Elton John, and richer than any of the Beatles except the one who had joined him as a music publisher, Paul McCartney.

By the end of the eighties, most small publishing companies on both sides of the Atlantic had been bought up by the major record companies. It meant there were four super-sized publishing companies, each affiliated to record companies – EMI, Warner Chappell, Universal Music and BMG. But there were still one or two independent ones, like SBK, which belonged to Charles Koppelman.

Koppelman had started as a publisher with Don Kirshner in the early sixties, and had been steadily building his company since then. Inexplicably, in 1986, CBS Records agreed to sell him its publishing company, April Music. There seemed no good reason why CBS should sell, except they could put the sale price in their annual accounts and make it look like an exceptionally good year.

SBK though, had a great reason to buy. With the company nicely enlarged, Koppelman sold it almost at once to EMI, the largest music publishing deal ever made – $295 million. Koppelman did well from the deal, but EMI did even better. It made them the world's biggest publishing company.

But not for long.

Someone else still wheeling and dealing in publishing was the Aberbachs' cousin, Freddy Bienstock. A few years earlier, in return for all the work he'd done for them, the Aberbachs allowed cousin Freddy to buy the UK rights to Hill and Range, the publishing company that contained almost everything they owned, including the Elvis Presley company. Bienstock then moved to London and set up a company called Carlin.

Having the UK rights to the Presley catalogue was enough to make Bienstock rich for life; having the rest of the catalogue made him super rich. But he wanted more. He wanted to buy Chappell.

In 1968, the widows of the two Dreyfus brothers had sold their shares in Chappell to PolyGram, who combined it with their other publishing company, Intersong. In 1984, PolyGram, still smarting from its disco experiences of the late seventies, was losing $300,000 a year. To patch up the leaks they decided to sell Chappell, and cousin Freddy put together a consortium to buy it. The consortium, including a company run by the heirs of Edward B. Marks and another by the heirs of Rodgers and Hammerstein, paid $100 million. And since cousin Freddy had the biggest chunk of shares he took control of the company.

Having started his career at Chappell, Freddy Bienstock felt particularly good about buying it. But he couldn't run it the old-fashioned style of the Dreyfus days; it was far too big. After EMI, it was the world's second largest publishing company holding 400,000 song titles and netting $30 million profit annually on gross revenues of $80 million.

Modern music publishers had little or nothing to do other than sign up songs that couldn't fail to be hits, and Freddy decided to operate the modern way – paying huge advances for huge acts.

"I became aware of U2 and I started to negotiate with their management... a three-album deal for $5m... we were getting 50 cents an album and within eight months, 'The Joshua Tree' had sold fourteen million albums and we had $7m back..."

Some people thought less of Freddy than he thought of himself.

Some years before, songwriter Artie Wayne did him a favour.

The Jackson Five abruptly left Motown and was short on cash. I helped a grateful 'Papa' Joe Jackson get a $25,000 advance for the group's world wide sub–publishing rights from Freddy... A few years later when the world-wide sub-publishing hadn't paid off for Freddy, he blamed me for wasting his $25,000. Then when Michael explodes, Freddy claims all of the mega-songs *that Michael has written fall under his contract! Now I had a once grateful 'Papa' Joe mad at me for helping him get "a paltry $25,000.advance", and Freddy whom I expected to be grateful, never returns any of my phone calls ever again.*

For Bienstock, the thrill of owning the company he'd once worked for soon diminished. The administration work was huge. In America, 65 per cent of the company's total income came from only the top 500 songs; in Britain, 90 per cent came from the top 2,700 songs. But there were another 397,300 songs that had to be administered for almost no income at all. So in 1987 Bienstock gave up running Chappell, made an agreement with the other shareholders, and sold the lot to Warner for $285 million

Warner Chappell became the number one publishing company, which meant EMI fell to number two. But the truth was – not much of this was about publishing music; it was about trading in copyrights. And getting rich.

36

Shine On You Crazy Diamond
MICHAEL JACKSON AND MADONNA

You'd have to be blind to human nature not to have seen from the start that Michael Jackson had a screw loose. In the music business, you don't talk in that daft lady's afternoon tea-party voice, and pretty-up your face the way he did, and wrinkle your nose at swearwords as if you've smelt a poo, unless you're at least a tiny bit potty.

Like every great artist, Jackson was brilliant, and brilliantly flawed. Everything that happened to him – success, downfall and eventual glorification – was totally in keeping with all the other great, strange, original artists in history. Most good artists are halfway to being nuts, which doesn't much matter, because the saner they are the less likely they are to deliver anything worthwhile. Nutty or not, though, many of them show an extraordinary ability to plot and manipulate and get what they want.

Jackson was no exception. He used the media as a part of his image building so skilfully that seeing him on stage or on video, or hearing his records, became just one small part of the overall experience of knowing him. Interestingly, the eighties threw up another artist of almost equal ability at self-promotion across the full spectrum of media, Madonna. Had Jackson not been around, Madonna would certainly have taken centre stage. But against him it was impossible. In the eighties Michael Jackson reigned supreme.

At the 1980 Grammy awards Michael Jackson sat with his producer, Quincy Jones. Their album *Off the Wall* had sold over six million copies in the USA. That made Jackson the biggest black artist America had ever seen. He fully expected to be nominated for the Album of the Year and Record of the Year awards, for both of which he'd received nominations. But he missed out on both. Record of the Year went to *What a Fool Believes* by the Doobie Brothers, one of the few non-disco number ones on the *Billboard* chart during the previous year. Album of the Year went to Billy Joel for *52nd Street*, rocked-up pop and not really qualifiable since it was released in 1978.

Jackson was shattered. He felt it was totally unfair. And he told the people he worked with that it would never happen again.

Maybe he thought it was because he was black, but it was unlikely. Stevie Wonder had won top awards for records in every category. It was simply an industry backlash against disco and dance. In Chicago, radio DJ Steve Dahl hated disco so much he'd raised a 'disco destruction army'. His followers rallied around the slogan 'Disco Sucks'. Dahl ranted on radio, "Disco is a disease. I call it disco dystrophy."

In July that year there'd been a joint promotion between the Chicago White Sox and Dahl's radio station, the all-rock WLUP. Anyone who deposited a disco record in a garbage can at the turnstile got a reduced price entry. More than 10,000 disco records were collected and at half time Dahl them put in a container mid-field and blew them up. The disco Ku Klux Klan invaded the pitch, set fires, dug up the turf and chanted "Kill disco".

Since then 'Kill Disco' had become the most popular car sticker in Middle America. The music industry knew that for any sort of a dance-connected record to win the Grammy's would be a bad idea. Billy Joel's record was really a leftover from the previous year, but at a stretch of the imagination it could be called rock – so it won.

Michael Jackson saw it differently. He suspected a conspiracy. He decided there and then when his next record came out it would be a perfect balance of everything that anyone could want to listen to. And he wouldn't be black.

In 1980, when *Off the Wall* came out, Michael Jackson was twenty-one and his skin colour matched his brothers'. Two years later, when *Thriller* came out, he was twenty-three and his skin was cappuccino. Pepsi announced they were going to feature him in their biggest campaign ever and to prepare for it Jackson straightened his nose and put a dimple in his chin.

Thriller had been carefully designed with crossover audiences in mind; 'Billie Jean' was for the dance crowd, 'Beat It' for white rockers. And when Jackson gave the songs from the new album their first public performance, it was astonishing. The routines on the *Thriller* songs had leapt forward a million miles from his old sexless routines. When he spoke between numbers, Jackson's high-pitched, over-polite voice made him sound like a pansy, but when he danced he looked as raunchy as Jagger, as delicate as Nureyev, as footsure as Sammy Davis Jr.

No question about it, he was horny. There was no point critics suggesting anymore that he was probably asexual. He was telling us point blank that he wasn't. His dancing, his movements, his crotch jerking, his grunting – he could never have projected sexuality so overtly without knowing personally what it was about. But there was something odd too; certain gestures that weren't normally seen in pop and rock stars. When he jerked his crotch, he didn't thrust it towards the audience like Jagger or David Lee Roth, he thrust it upwards towards his face and sometimes brushed his hand across it, like adolescent sex in the bedroom mirror. He enjoyed feeling his bottom too.

There was no doubt about it – Michael Jackson's generous use of make-up was part of what kept his face in front of the public. At the same time, it was something he could hide behind. Because of it many people saw him as an actor playing a part. If he acted daft and fell in love with a chimpanzee or cavorted with little boys, couldn't that be just an affected image? Something to gain notoriety?

Sensible observation said no, yet the staginess of his make-up did somehow lessen the impact of the daft things he did, suggesting they were all part of a game. When he went home and we couldn't see him, surely he took off his make-up and relaxed – no more chimpanzees, no more little boys.

The surprising thing was how easily the public accepted the make-up in the first place, and for that Jackson could thank MTV.

Between the release of *Off The Wall* and *Thriller*, MTV started. It was launched in 1981 and in an extraordinarily short time became the central promotion mechanism of the American record industry. It then launched in Europe and Asia where it quickly gathered similar promotional importance. Its launch coincided with substantial improvements in colour TV technology and at the beginning of the eighties there was a substantial increase in the number of colour TV sets being sold.

Hoping to benefit from this, MTV executives insisted that everything the channel showed should contain maximum colour. Pop stars who wanted their videos shown had to throw out their blacks and greys and come up with colour. Not just clothes, but faces too, which brought gender-bending back into fashion, perfect for Britain's New Romantic movement.

In London, the eighties had bought a new fashion trend centred round a West End club called Blitz. There the clientele dressed to kill, mainly in copycat clothes of cinema icons of the past – Bette Davis, Marlene Dietrich, Clark Gable, Errol Flynn. The two leading members of the movement were gay, Boy George and Steve Strange, but although both went on to make hit records, being gay wasn't essential. The next wave of Blitzers were straight – Spandau Ballet, Duran Duran, Eurythmics, Depeche Mode. They enjoyed wearing make-up and didn't give a hoot about the traditional separation of male and female fashion. Eurythmics singer Annie Lennox wore men's clothes and dyed her crew-cut hair bright red. Which was the colour of Boy George's lipstick.

The colours of pop androgyny were a perfect match for the new television technology, so MTV jumped on the British bandwagon. Very soon for a male entertainer to be wearing colourful make-up seemed totally unsurprising. And once people got used to men wearing make-up in videos, it was only a small step to get used to them wearing it elsewhere, which made Michael Jackson seem much less odd than he might have been otherwise.

Yet Jackson himself was missing from the videos that filled MTV's screen each day, and when CBS executives asked why, they were told, "His music's not rock."

Well, nor was Boy George's, nor the Eurythmics', nor even Duran Duran's.

MTV argued that rock nowadays could mean pop providing it wasn't trite or trashy. In which case why wasn't Michael Jackson being played? Was it because he was black?

Absolutely not, said MTV.

Walter Yetnikoff decided it was. He became enraged because MTV refused to play Jackson's videos. "I said to MTV, 'I'm pulling everything we have off the air, all our product. I'm not going to give you any more videos. And I'm going to go public and fucking tell them about the fact you don't want to play music by a black guy'."

MTV relented and played 'Billie Jean' in heavy rotation. Afterwards, the *Thriller* album went on to sell an additional ten million copies.

From thereon MTV opened up for similar artists, all of them with Jackson and Yetnikoff to thank for fighting their corner.

MTV should have thanked Yetnikoff too. Opening up to dance and black acts doubled its audience and by 1985 they had twenty-five million paying subscribers.

Exactly two years after the release of *Thriller*, Madonna had her first big album, *Like a Virgin*. It was mostly dance, but the industry was still shying away from using the word. Even so, the two most-played singles, 'Like a Virgin' and 'Material Girl' were danced to across America and around the world. Onstage Madonna seemed as keen as Michael Jackson to thrust herself sexually into the audience.

Her mother had died of breast cancer when she was four. Before it happened, unable to bring herself to explain to her daughter that death was creeping up on her, she would cry and Madonna would respond by wrapping her arms around her mother. "I remember feeling stronger than she was. I was so little and yet I felt like she was the child."

Before she died, Madonna never really understood what was happening to her mother.

There was so much left unsaid, so many untangled and unresolved emotions, of remorse, guilt, loss, anger, confusion... I saw my mother, looking very beautiful and lying as if she were asleep in an open casket. Then I noticed that my mother's mouth looked funny. It took me some time to realize that it had been sewn up. In that awful moment, I began to understand what I had lost forever. The final image of my mother, at once peaceful yet grotesque, haunts me today also.

Child abuse doesn't have to be inflicted with intent; it's sometimes inflicted by circumstance. After her mother died, Madonna, terrified that her father could be taken from her as well, refused to go to sleep unless he was next to her. When he married the family's housekeeper and had two children by her, Madonna loathed him forever after and thought she was utterly alone. At school she did anything she could to put herself at the centre of attention; did cartwheels in the hallways between classes, swung by her knees from the climbing bars in the playground, pulled up her skirt in class so boys could see her panties.

Which was exactly what Michael Jackson seemed to be doing onstage when he handled his crotch and touched his bottom. It was exquisite, the greatest dancing anyone had ever seen, but disquieting at the same time – like a disturbed thirteen-year-old in a roomful of adults, playing with himself to provoke a reaction. Anyone who knew a bit about his background must have realised, sooner or later things would go wrong.

Jackson's father had not only beaten him but verbally abused him too, saying he had a fat nose and was ugly. So Jackson had grown up hating his own appearance. He recalled how his father sat in a chair with a belt in his hand as he and his brothers rehearsed. "If you didn't do it the right way, he would tear you up, really get you." His father admitted he regularly whipped Jackson as a child. And Jackson admitted he often cried from loneliness and would vomit on the sight of his father. It was the classic artist's training, child abuse turning people into stars; Eva Tanguay, Ethel Waters, Bessie Smith, Billie Holiday.

It came across again in Jackson's songs – not all of them, just the ones he'd written himself. 'Wanna Be Startin' Somethin' was unhinged – he'd become a weird fruit that was being devoured for its strangeness. 'Beat It' was pure fury – at what, it was difficult to know. 'Billie Jean' was more controlled but just as angry, spat through the teeth rather than shouted.

The album supplied *Billboard*'s Top 10 with seven singles, something no album had ever done before. At the 1984 Grammy Awards Show, Michael Jackson captured eight awards, including Best Album and Best Record of the Year. For 'Beat It' he even got 'Best Rock Vocal'. Extraordinary when you thought back two years to his whimpering vocal on 'You're Out of My Life'.

His tally for *Thriller* was eight Grammys. An industry apology, perhaps, for 1980.

Madonna never got an apology for *Like a Virgin* being passed over. Like Jackson's *Off the Wall* it drew a complete blank. She was as hurt as Jackson had been. "I was surprised by how people reacted to 'Like a Virgin' because when I did that song, to me, I was singing about how something made me feel a certain way –

brand-new and fresh – and everyone interpreted it as – 'I don't want to be a virgin anymore – fuck my brains out!'"

Family organisations complained that the song and its accompanying video promoted premarital sex and undermined family values. Madonna responded by promoting outrageous fashion items – lace tops, skirts over hot pants, fishnet stockings, and jewellery bearing the crucifix.

The album *Like a Virgin* sold twenty-one million copies worldwide but Madonna was never going to get a Grammy. On the industry disapproval list, a girl lying onstage faking masturbation was near the top. Even the usually liberal *Village Voice* called her 'whorish.' They may have been right. Ninety years earlier Eva Tanguay put a hint of orgasm into her interpretation of songs but at least suggested some sort of sexual communion with the audience. It wasn't clear what Madonna's purpose was in lying on the floor between songs raising her crotch to the heavens other than to raise an equal amount of objection from the media. Which it did.

After *Thriller*, Michael Jackson was rich. From it he'd made nearly $100 million and half of it he spent on an excellent investment.

A year after *Thriller* was released he'd agreed to be featured on a song called 'Say, Say Say' from McCartney's album *Pipes of Peace*. Jackson stayed with the McCartneys during the recording sessions and one evening at dinner Paul brought out a booklet displaying all the songs for which he owned the publishing rights. He explained that music publishing was a way to make big money. Jackson told Paul that one day he would buy the Beatles' songs.

Paul laughed, "Great. Good joke."

Sometime afterwards an Australian businessman, Robert Holmes à Court, bought ATV Music Publishing and Pye Records and started asset-stripping them. He then put ATV Music up for sale, including Northern Songs and the Beatles catalogue.

When Michael Jackson's attorney told him the Northern Songs catalogue was for sale Jackson told him to check first whether McCartney or Yoko Ono wanted to buy it. Yoko was afraid of conflicts with McCartney and bad press from the tabloids – "They'll say the dragon-lady strikes again". And on behalf of McCartney, a message came from his business advisor John Eastman that the catalogue was "far too pricey for Paul's interest". So Jackson's lawyer went ahead and bought ATV Music complete with the Beatles catalogue for $47.5 million, just half the money Jackson had made from *Thriller*.

McCartney appeared to be livid. He said he was afraid Jackson would give permission for the use of Beatles songs in TV advertising, which is exactly what Jackson proceeded to do. He licensed 'All You Need is Love' to National Panasonic and 'Revolution' to Nike.

Perhaps the real reason McCartney didn't buy the Beatles catalogue was because he was following the advice of his father-in-law, Lee Eastman – "only buy copyrights of dead composers". McCartney said he was annoyed Jackson hadn't asked the Beatles' permission before allowing their songs to be used for advertising. Yet he'd done the very same thing with the Buddy Holly songs he controlled, licensing 'Oh Boy' to General Motors for a campaign called 'Oh Buick'.

When questioned about it, he said, "One thing I can't do with Buddy is ask him."

Later, he said it was a pity Jackson hadn't contacted the Beatles and offered them an improved deal on the songs. But had McCartney bought the catalogue with his own money, would he really have offered to increase the royalties going to Ringo, George and Yoko?

Michael Jackson spent the other half of his *Thriller* money on something less sensible.

He bought 'Neverland', a vast Californian home where he constructed both a funfair and a zoo. At weekends Jackson welcomed coach loads of children to come and enjoy the place and from them he chose favourites, whom he would invite to stay-over in his warren of luxury suites. To most people it looked obvious – that daft Lady Veronica voice and his obsession with young boys, coupled with the regular dribble of gossip that leaked out – it was Vesuvius with the lid on. Throughout the eighties it was the principal job of his various managers to keep that lid from blowing off.

To run 'Neverland' Jackson employed courtiers, cooks, accountants, cleaners, lawyers, zoo-keepers, and bodyguards. Paying his large staff was expensive and eventually the money began to run short. Laying a few off was a risky option; with journalists hovering, disgruntled staff were a worry. So at the beginning of the nineties a new tour was organised to bring in some much-needed funds – the *Dangerous* tour.

Halfway through it, the lid blew off. One of the boys who'd stayed over reported that besides playing video games and watching TV, they sometimes drank wine and took drugs. Worse still, they did what many thirteen-year-old boys do together – they played around sexually. The trouble was, one of the thirteen year olds was over thirty.

Just before a show in Bangkok, these sexual accusations were broadcast worldwide. For two days Jackson lay sedated in bed, the concert postponed, his brain brought to a standstill. He tried to cancel the show but because an estimated thirty thousand ticket-holders had come from the provinces and were sleeping rough waiting for it to take place, the government refused him permission to leave Thailand until he'd performed. So he did. A halting, tearful, pitiful performance done under the influence of tranquilisers. Then he fled back home.

To fight the case, plans were made, lawyers hired, and money raised. Sony, watched nervously, afraid they were about to lose their biggest artist to a scandal from which he would never recover. But they hedged their bets brilliantly. They gave Jackson the money he needed to fight the case in exchange for a 50 per cent share in ATV Music, Jackson's biggest asset, including all the Beatles songs. With guaranteed income from music publishing Sony would cover themselves from loss of income if Jackson's record sales slumped; moreover they were ensuring he had the necessary money to possibly escape unscathed.

Then came an article in *Vanity Fair*. The thirteen-year-old accuser recounted how he lay naked on the bed while Jackson made him come, then licked it off his tummy. No libel action came from the Jackson camp, just a twenty million offer to withdraw the accusations.

It was accepted. And somehow the lid stayed on.

The music industry's take on all this was what it always was in these situations; Jackson's guilt or innocence would be decided by just one thing – could he still sell records? If he could, then he probably didn't do it.

He sold a few, but not as many as before. Not enough to be conclusive either way. The jury was still out.

37

Money, Money, Money
CONSOLIDATION

At five foot four, Irving Azoff was short. Because of this he sometimes suffered snide remarks comparing him to some of history's diminutive tyrants, Napoleon for instance, or Genghis Khan. But there was one big difference. Azoff had a sense of humour.

It wasn't to everyone's taste. At his own wedding he picked up the cake and pushed it into his mother's face. And he once sent booking agent Mike Lipman a boa constrictor in a box for his birthday. With Azoff, people tended to take sides. They loved him or hated him. David Geffen was one of the haters. "I don't wish to have him in my life, even for a second."

Azoff had worked as a booking agent with David Geffen's management company, Geffen-Roberts. When Geffen moved to WEA to set up his record label, Irving Azoff became the Eagles' manager. Although Azoff had a reputation for being abrasive to everyone, the Eagles got on well with him. And because the Eagles were the most important act on David Geffen's label, Geffen had to get on with him too.

There was no doubt about it, Azoff was a good manager; he looked after his artists' interests ferociously. And unlike some other managers he always travelled with them.

Most managers hated being on the road and avoided it as much as possible. They hated waiting around at airports and concert halls and hotels. They hated the endless burgers and brain-deadening repetition; the sound-check, the press conference, the performance, the all-night party, the hangover, and the early morning start. Azoff loved all of it.

He carried the band's drugs in his shoe and took a large wad of $100 bills with him at all times. He enjoyed pushing the group to be destructive in hotels, and in this he led the way. If the hotel didn't have a suite for him, he'd create one – take two rooms and smash the wall down, then peel off the requisite number of $100 bills to pay for the damage. For every television set one of the group threw out of a window, Azoff threw two. But his favourite trick was to 'quarter-jam' hotel doors, slipping 25 cent coins soaked in hot glue between the door and the floor, one at a time. Eventually the door would be lifted just enough to stop the bolt sliding back. Someone from the hotel would have to smash the door with a fire axe – and out came the wad of $100 bills. Azoff liked to tell people, "I never met an asshole in the music industry I didn't like."

After Irving Azoff had been managing the Eagles for five years, Lew Wasserman, the owner of MCA Entertainments, decided he would be the perfect person to run MCA's record company. Azoff did well, he turned it round and made it profitable; he let go all but five of the forty-six acts on the roster and did a deal to distribute Motown Records, which at that time was having success with Stevie Wonder and Lionel Richie. And he broke a multi-platinum teen act, Tiffany, by having her do promotion in shopping malls.

Under Irving Azoff, profits at MCA rose to tens of millions, as opposed to losses when he moved in. He used $61 million of the profits to buy out Motown completely; then he bought Front Line, his own management company. When MCA first employed him he'd kept control of it. Now, as MCA's CEO, he authorised its purchase with $15.7 million of their money paid into his own bank account.

David Geffen complained to *Billboard*, "For MCA to be in the management business – it's shocking. They'll be dealing out of self interest!" The music press agreed with him.

Azoff called them 'small-minded'.

Five years earlier, David Geffen had retired from Elektra. He'd been diagnosed with bladder cancer and stayed home quietly waiting to die. To help him deal with life he collected antique tea cosies. After a couple of years, realising he was still alive, he got a fresh diagnosis and was told there'd never been anything wrong with him.

That was his story. But many people thought Geffen had suffered a nervous breakdown. Worried that it sounded too un-macho he'd decided on bladder cancer instead. Either way, after a three-year break, fired up with fresh energy, he went back to Warner and got himself a new deal. A good one too! Warner would provide 100 per cent of the finance for a label that Geffen would own.

It wasn't long before he was upsetting people again. As before, Ahmet Ertegun smoothed things over and was right to do so; for although Geffen could be obnoxious, back-biting, dishonest, and neurotic, when it came to business he delivered the goods. However, he could also be traitorous.

When Walter Yetnikoff heard Geffen hadn't yet tied up the foreign distribution for his new label, he made him an offer – for $17 million CBS would buy the overseas rights. Geffen accepted. For him it was a pile of cash out of the blue and would give him some extra leverage with Warner. For Yetnikoff, it was a stab in the back to Warner and some extra leverage with Geffen if he ever happened to need it. Neither of them were thinking first and foremost of the value of the overseas rights.

Yetnikoff and Geffen sometimes said they were friends and sometimes said they were enemies. The real truth was – seven years earlier when Geffen stole Dylan from CBS and Yetnikoff stole him back again, both men enjoyed the jousting so much they hardly knew whether they liked each other or not.

By coincidence, at the very moment they were doing the deal for Geffen Records' overseas rights, Dylan's recording contract came up for renewal again. A few years after he'd left Asylum Records and gone back to CBS, Dylan had switched faiths, going from Jewish to born-again Christian. He made two albums filled with songs to God but because they didn't sell well CBS hadn't rushed to offer him a new deal. But now, with David Geffen back in the picture, Walter Yetnikoff was eager to tie up a new deal quickly.

Because it would cost a lot – and because it might prove disastrous if Dylan continued to sing religious songs – Yetnikoff gave the job of re-signing him to Dick Asher, who agreed the money but laid down stringent conditions. "No fucking religion!"

When Dylan tried to argue Asher exploded.

I'm telling you Bob, there'll be no fucking religion – not Christian, not Jewish, not Moslem. Nothing! For God's sake man – you were born Jewish, which makes your religion money doesn't it? So stick with it for Christ's sake. I'm giving you twenty million bucks – it's like baptising you, like sending you to heaven. You want twenty million bucks from us? Well you gotta do what we tell you. And what we're telling you is… No Torah! No Bible! No Koran! No Jesus! No God! No Allah! NO FUCKING RELIGION. It's going in the contract.

So no artistic freedom at CBS if you wanted twenty million up front.

Shortly afterwards, Dylan re-signed and Asher got his notice. He'd only been kept on at CBS to solve the problem of Dylan's new contract. If his next album had bombed like the previous two, Walter Yetnikoff would have said, "It wasn't me who re-signed him – it was Asher."

With Asher out of the way Yetnikoff had CBS to himself. And if his war with Warner was madness before, it now went beyond insanity. He constantly referred to Mo Ostin as a "short little Jew".

His friends remonstrated. "But Walter, you're just a taller Jew. What sort of talk is this?"

Yetnikoff wouldn't relent. "We're going to bury those people. We're going to have the leading market share."

When *Thriller* arrived, they got it. No wonder CBS had insisted there should be no God on Bob Dylan's new album. At CBS there was only room for one God, and it was Walter Yetnikoff. He liked to claim he was the company president who cared most about his artists. He claimed he had a personal relationship with each of them and could banter with them any time he wanted. And he loved to tell everyone about each little banter.

When Jackson finished recording *Thriller* he delivered it to CBS and Yetnikoff was delighted. "You delivered! You delivered like a motherfucker!"

It was a word Jackson didn't much care for, "Please don't use that word, Walter."

Yetnikoff relented. "You delivered like an angel. Archangel Michael."

"That's better. Now will you promote it?"

"Like a motherfucker."

Together with cocksucker, motherfucker was Yetnikoff's favourite word. He had a pet lawyer. If there was an artist CBS was about to sign, Yetnikoff told them, "Go hire Allen Grubman."

Grubman was fat and slobby, worked with his shoes off, had smelly feet and a bulging belly; he charged his clients the earth and swore like Yetnikoff. They loved negotiating together, calling each other on the phone all day, cursing back and forth.

"You're busting my balls!"

"Schmuck!"

"Cocksucker!"

"Putz!"

"Motherfucker!"

In 1986 RCA Victor, America's oldest and most venerated record company, was sold to Germany. It was bought by BMG – the Bertelsmann Group.

The man behind it was Reinhard Mohn whose great grandfather, Carl Bertelsmann, established the company in 1897 in north-east Germany to sell hymn books and religious material.

During the Second World War, the company was the biggest single producer of Nazi propaganda and both Reinhard and his father were members of the SS. At the end of World War II, the publishing house was closed for a while for illegal paper-trading. Reinhard wanted nothing more to do with it but his father persuaded him publishing was in the family blood, so Reinhard persevered.

Because he couldn't find funding, he got his own employees to each fund a small bit, which led to him being known as 'Red Mohn'. Then he had the idea of a book club. By joining the club, customers could buy books at a discount, but they had to agree to buy books on a regular basis. Salesmen went door to door and sometimes Mohn joined them, making sales himself. Within four years it had over a million subscribers. He then added a record club, and in 1962 launched it in Spain and South America, then France. At their height, the book and record clubs had over twenty-five million members around the world by which time Mohn had started a record label too, Ariola.

The different companies were all lumped together under Mohn's grandfather's name, Bertelsmann. And in 1979 they began their move into the USA by buying Arista, the company Clive Davis had formed when he was pushed out of CBS.

Bertelsmann then took over RCA and renamed it BMG – Bertelsmann Music Group. There was a certain lack of sensitivity about the take-over. The RCA building on 6th Avenue had a new sign over its entrance saying BMG, and the floor where the top executives had their offices rang to the sound of German. When you went to the canteen for lunch, hamburgers had been replaced at the top of the daily 'specials' with *Sauerklopse mit Kartofflen*.

To seal their move to the top of the American music business, Bertelsmann moved Clive Davis' company, Arista, into the main building on 6th Avenue. It was the most successful label in the group, doing better than all the rest of RCA put together. The Germans called Clive Davis 'The Jew in the Crown'.

This consolidation of one company with another had reduced the number of major record companies to six – CBS, BMG, EMI, MCA, Warner and PolyGram. And there were only four major publishing companies left, each affiliated to one of the record companies – EMI, Warner Chappell, PolyGram, and BMG. Something else surprising was that only half of the six record companies were American owned – CBS, Warner and MCA – and soon there would be none. The first to go was CBS.

Laurence Tisch, the man who owned it, wasn't really interested in popular music. He'd made money from the Loews' chain of movie theatres. He'd bought CBS for its broadcasting licenses – radio and TV – and wanted to find a way to dump the record company, along with Walter Yetnikoff's fits of craziness.

Yetnikoff couldn't stand Tisch and did all he could to rile him. Yetnikoff's employment contract was extraordinarily detailed and outlined every last thing to which he was entitled including his right to first class travel, to stay in a five-star hotel, to eat in the best restaurants and have a full American breakfast.

One time, he and Tisch were together in Los Angeles and had a breakfast meeting at the Beverly Hills Hotel. All Yetnikoff wanted for breakfast that morning was a bagel. But when he ordered one Tisch pointed out it wasn't authorised in his contract. He would have to pay for it personally.

After that Walter never travelled anywhere without a bagel in his briefcase. Any time Tisch was present, whether it was in a CBS board meeting, at a negotiation in another company's offices, or sitting next to him in first class on a flight, Walter would put his briefcase on the table in front of him and place the bagel on top of it.

Eventually Tisch could no longer put up with Yetnikoff and the problems the record division gave him. He decided to sell and accepted an offer of $1.4 billion from Triangle Industries, a company that made copper wire and slot machines.

Walter Yetnikoff hit full flame.

Tisch backed down and made a proposal. If someone could match the copper wire company's offer in cash, they could buy the record division.

Yetnikoff went to Sony. For twenty years Sony's record label in Japan had been a joint venture with CBS. With the success of the CD and the Walkman, Sony were in search of software to go with their hardware; they needed CBS, and knew it. Akio Morita of Sony agreed to fund the deal. When he did, Laurence Tisch immediately increased the price by six hundred million. Morita swallowed hard and agreed.

The deal was finalised in February 1988, ninety-nine years after Columbia had been established; CBS Records was now Sony Records, owned by the Japanese. Yetnikoff made $23 million out of the deal and was put in charge of the new company worldwide. To run the lesser things he previously ran, he bought in Tommy Mottola, a former artist's manager.

Yetnikoff then retired to his new office on the 51st floor where he feasted on cocaine and vodka and ranted at the world down half a dozen telephones.

The sale of CBS to Sony and Walter Yetnikoff's $23 million pay-off, hit a nerve with David Geffen who felt it was time he did something similar.

When he'd made his comeback deal with Warner Music Group, he'd negotiated cleverly. Although Geffen Records was financed and distributed by WEA, it was wholly owned by Geffen himself. In the eight years that followed he'd done brilliantly. Geffen Records had rock acts Guns N' Roses, Whitesnake and Aerosmith; pop acts Elton John, Kylie Minogue, and Cher; and old favourites Asia, Neil Young, and Peter Gabriel.

By 1989 the company's annual revenue was nearing $175 million, but when WEA announced it was going to merge with Time to become Time Warner, Geffen was worried there would be less focus on the record business. He decided it was time to sell his company and pick up his rewards. He had his eye on doing a deal with MCA but with his old enemy Irving Azoff in charge there wasn't a hope. He needed to get Azoff out of the way, so he persuaded Mo Ostin to offer Azoff a 'dream deal', a record company of his own at Warner. Azoff took the bait and left MCA to run his own label, Giant Records.

Geffen then sold his company to MCA for $545 million in shares. Although the money thrilled him, the loss of his company seemed to mean nothing, "I don't like the music and I don't like the people."

At MCA, while he continued to oversee it, he also moved into movies. His first was *Days of Thunder*, which he thought would look nice with a title theme by Michael

Jackson. Because he occasionally received business advice from Geffen, Jackson allowed him to use an outtake from his last album, a cover of John Lennon's 'Come Together'. That meant the song would end up on the movie's soundtrack album and need a clearance from Sony, which meant Walter Yetnikoff.

When Geffen called him, Yetnikoff refused. Not only that, he suggested Geffen's chances of getting permission might be improved if he were to give Walter's girlfriend lessons in sucking cock. Since David Geffen was gay, this seemed rather more insulting than Yetnikoff's normal tossing around of the world cocksucker. And Geffen took offence. He persuaded Michael Jackson to fire his long-term lawyer, who was friendly with Yetnikoff, and hire a new one – then to re-negotiate with Sony for a higher royalty.

Jackson already had the best record deal the industry had ever known – 41 per cent of the wholesale price of every record sold plus an eighteen million advance for every album he delivered, three million of which was non-recoupable even if the album didn't sell a single copy. To ask for more was ridiculous, so Yetnikoff knew at once it was Geffen who'd put him up to it. Worse still, Geffen now appointed Allen Grubman to be his own personal attorney.

When Yetnikoff called Grubman to say it was treachery, Grubman told him, "Geffen's a gentleman."

"And Hitler's in Heaven."

"You better get wise," Grubman warned.

But Yetnikoff didn't. He retired to his office and exploded in all directions, screaming obscenities down the phone at anyone he could get hold of. In the music industry, David Geffen was known as something of a gossip; it was said the three quickest ways to spread news were telephone, television and tell Geffen. But Yetnikoff could run him a close second, and he now did so, calling everyone in his phone book, tongue-lashing the world. "If he called me a pussy lapper I wouldn't get upset… If he thinks I'm gonna stop calling him a cocksucker, he's wrong."

It was more than his Japanese bosses could take. Yetnikoff was replaced with Tommy Mottola, the man he'd brought into the company to be his second in command. The dismissal was carried out by Norio Ohga, Yetnikoff's old friend, the man at Sony who'd made the deal to buy CBS. Yentikoff was told to leave by a side door accompanied by a guard.

If Geffen felt good about Yetnikoff's demise, he felt even better four months later when the Matsushita Corporation of Japan bought out MCA and paid him $800 million in cash for his shares – another $250 million profit.

Geffen had now despatched both Irving Azoff and Walter Yetnikoff and made more money than either of them.

38

Fly Me To The Moon
DRUGS AND DJS

Anyone who's been around the music business knows the ins and outs of artists on drugs.

Marijuana is the commonest – harmless, but it can slow people down, as can downers like Ketamine or Xanax. People doing acid should be kept away from windows and rooftops in case they feel a sudden urge to fly. Heroin, while having the worst name, is comparatively harmless so long as the person taking it doesn't overdose or get himself arrested while trying to get hold of some.

Worse than heroin is methamphetamine. Hitler was injected with it twice a day throughout the Second World War. People who take it get paranoid and see conspiracy theories in every corner. Guitarists think roadies are deliberately handing them untuned instruments to make them sound bad. Roadies think guitarists are plotting their dismissal so they hand them them untuned instruments.

By far the worst drug is cocaine. People using it turn into neurotics when they can't get hold of it. When they can, they become positively brainsick.

Mostly, drugs and music have gone well together. They've been a staple part of the musician's diet since the New Orleans exodus to Chicago, when Prohibition gave a boost to marijuana. Even so, drugs rarely had any influence on the actual music, only on the ambiance in which it's played. But on three occasions they were closely involved with musical trends.

In the late forties and early fifties, amphetamine tablets were widely used in the USA by long-distance truck and bus drivers to keep themselves awake. Soon they became a staple diet for country musicians in the south-eastern states. A young Johnny Cash, playing in the Nachez Club in Memphis, used to receive Benzedrine tablets as tips. Soon he was taking his music at faster tempos. And Jerry Lee Lewis's searing piano playing was also developed with the help of a good dose of amphetamine. Amphetamine was one of the major influences on country music's evolution into rock 'n' roll. Presley himself said, "My stuff is just hopped-up country."

In the sixties, acid influenced the switch from singles to albums. If you were floating in a hallucinogenic haze, a three-minute single was an annoyance. Between 1966 when the LSD craze started and 1969, when it waned, the principal product sold by the music industry changed from a three-minute song to a forty-minute album. LSD made record companies a fortune. They did nothing much to promote it, nor did they produce music especially for it; they simply rode their good fortune and pumped out LPs to fill the demand.

In the seventies amphetamine returned as sulphate, a powder to be sniffed. It was behind the hell-for-leather tempos used by seventies punk bands, both British and American – the Ramones, the Sex Pistols, the Jam. But the drug itself was vile. *NME* critic Charles Shaar Murray likened it to "sniffing powdered razor blades off a toilet floor… for two hours you'd have a post-nasal drip of foul tasting mucous flowing down the back of your throat".

Despite these drugs influencing the evolution of a musical style, the music industry itself played little part in promoting their popularity. Until the 1980s.

Ecstasy was different. Chemically it was MDMA – *methylene-dioxy-meth-amphetamine.* It had first been synthesised in 1914 and the drug's ability to bond people in friendship made the CIA think it could be an aid to interrogation. It came in the form of a small white pill and was as easy to take as an aspirin. Journalist Peter Nasmyth related his first time with it. "Suddenly I knew I could trust her with my closest secrets… strange because half an hour before I wouldn't have cared if I never saw her again in my life."

In the mid-eighties, smart young New Yorkers were taking Ecstasy on holiday with them to Ibiza for their summer vacations, using it at dance raves. Ecstasy had been used to treat broken marriages and soldiers in shell shock; now it revolutionised dancing. It endeared trust in strangers, even instant affection. In a room full of users, smiles became infectious; everyone was in the same great mood; people became part of a whole, not individuals. A tab of ecstasy not only created empathy and affection for all those around you, it delivered six hours of dance energy. It wouldn't let you lie back on a sofa with fantasies swirling over you; it made you leap into the middle of your dreams and start dancing. The whole dance floor became a party. It was like midnight on New Year's Eve every night, all night long.

Brits in Ibiza on holiday soon latched on to it and started buying as much as they could from Americans to bring back home at the end of their holidays. But it wasn't the drug alone that made the party atmosphere work, it was the style of music too.

It had originated in Chicago, a stark rhythm-heavy style. It used a new Roland drum machine, the TR-808, pumping out a heavier bass beat, keeping the tempo going between records, allowing the DJs to make smooth transitions, switching the pitch to hold the tempo, mixing one song over the other. With Ecstasy, it wasn't the songs that made the atmosphere, it was the emphasis on rhythm, and repeated snippets of melody that cropped up within it, over and over again, like well-timed hiccups.

A song's hook no longer had to be its chorus, it could be nothing more than a weird laugh. New sampling machines made DJs creative as never before. The samplers could take a word or a sound and regurgitate it on the beat every bar, or every four bars. The DJ would record a short burst of sound and programme it to be replayed whenever and wherever he wanted it. "Oooh, George" goes a giggly girl on the off-beat, and four bars later, there she goes again. "Oooh George", on the off-beat – "Oooh George", on the off-beat – "Oooh George", on the off-beat.

Back from Ibiza after the summer of '87, DJ Danny Rampling decided to open a new club specially for the new music, and the new drug too. It was in Southwark, a fitness centre with mirrored walls and space for 200 people, and he called it Shoom. He got hold of the right records, the right equipment, and made sure his 200 clientele got hold of the right drug to go with them.

In no time the new music had been dubbed Acid House. Rampling had flyers made for the club saying, "Can You Pass the Acid Test?" a copy of a flyer given out in California in the sixties by the Merry Pranksters, a group of pagans who turned people on to LSD. Shoom's small size meant people had to be turned away, but Rampling went for a balanced clientele – from pop stars to labourers, even a few football hooligans. A year earlier they'd been cutting up rival football teams' fans with flick knives. Now they held hands with strangers and danced in a circle as Rampling watched in amazement. "This thing united everyone together. The way I was feeling at that point was the golden age was dawning."

One night, dancers full of ecstasy and adrenaline were turned out of the club at 6am but continued to dance in the street. When a police car raced up with its siren wailing, they all burst into song *'Can you feel it? Can you feel it?'* The siren was the hook of the song they'd just been dancing to inside the club.

In London, 'E' clubs boomed – Rampling moved Shoom to bigger premises. At Heaven there was Spectrum with room for 3,000 people; there was also The Dungeon, Clink Street and The Trip.

In Manchester, the use of Ecstasy spread through the city's clubbing scene in just two or three weeks. The Hacienda, modelled on big clubs in New York got so full that people had to dance on the stairs and in the toilets. Ecstasy made people want to congregate in bigger and bigger groups and dance the night away. Entrepreneurs emerged who set out to promote 'raves' for thousands of people at a time, initially using film studios, empty warehouses or unused aircraft hangars – £15 to enter, £15 for a tab of Ecstasy.

Then they hit on the idea of using the open countryside. For a rave called Sunrise Mystery Trip, coaches were laid on to take ravers to an equestrian centre at Iver Heath in Buckinghamshire. In his *book Altered States* Matthew Collin wrote that "Flares burned along the wooded approach road, and as the coaches drew nearer, lasers flashed into the sky." At the height of the evening, dry ice flooded the dance floor, and as the sun rose people were collecting wild flowers to thread through each other's hair.

Another rave was a gatecrash of the Glastonbury Rock Festival. Set up in a car park adjacent to the festival, it started at 3am, stealing thousands of rock fans from the tents in which they'd just gone to sleep, tempting them to revive the day with a tab of 'E'.

Author Sheryl Garrett says, "A lot of the people involved in this did think it was going to change everything ... the Berlin wall *did* come down, Nelson Mandela *did* walk out of prison ... There were huge changes going on in the world which felt like a part of it. It was a very euphoric time."

Major record companies were caught on the hop. It was obvious that drugs had become a new and most efficient plugger of their music. Without the record companies intending it, the drug was already being harnessed to record promotion.

Singles had all sorts of drug references slipped into the lyrics that those not in the know missed. The BBC found itself plugging the English football squad's 'E for England', written by the ultra-druggy group New Order. And the very week the BBC announced a 'Drugs alert' campaign, the Shamen's song 'Ebeneezer Goode' went to number one with a chorus that appeared to blare out the message "E's are good".

Moving with the times, the record companies realised the moment had come to make themselves more aware of drug trends. If drugs made young people want a certain type of music, they'd better supply it to them. They commissioned remixes of songs directed specifically at certain clubs according to their drug use. 'E' mixes – sparse and specific in their hooks. Marijuana mixes, more floating and spacey, with sounds spinning round the dance floor. Coke and amphetamine mixes, with driving tempos and heavily repeated hooks. The companies employed young people in A&R chosen specifically for their knowledge of the drug scene.

This wasn't to say the record company executives themselves were completely ignorant of it, but for most of them cocaine was all they knew. Copious amounts of it, sniffed from morning to night, messing up their judgments, firing up their aggression, screwing up the company's success rate, but no more than the companies they were competing with, where just as many people were doing the same thing.

By the end of the eighties, drugs were an integral part of the popular music industry, part and parcel of creativity, performance, marketing, artist relations, and executive privilege. In America, in Britain, all over Europe, drug scandals rose and were suppressed, or sometimes leaked out. Like the multi-track tape, urgently needed by EMI's managing director, which the security guard opened to find stuffed with plastic bags of white powder. Like Walter Yetnikoff, sitting in the CEO's office at Sony America, pouring sachets of coke into his vodka. Like Warner, with employees specially hired to make sure the cocaine turned up on time each day.

Moreover, most of the plugging at radio stations was being done with drugs. In America cocaine had to be purchased by the hundredweight and shipped off to 5,000 radio stations round the country in weekly packages.

In the twenties, when Leo Feist was a top publisher, his organisation had printing presses in every major city in the USA with local agents visiting vaudeville performers in each city, persuading them to sing Feist songs. Sixty years later, the local agents of record companies in each area were suppliers of drugs.

By the late eighties, the Ecstasy rave scene in Europe was unstoppable. Factories were pumping out tablets in their millions. A 'Mistubishi' was the best, produced near Maastricht, home of 'The Treaty of Europe', centre of the European Union, which seemed just the right place for the headquarters of 'acid house', a truly European phenomenon.

In the early nineties, the British government, lobbied by alcoholic drink manufacturers (who were losing out badly), finally stepped in and passed a law forbidding large-scale unlicensed dance events. In the resulting bill, the definition of music was "sounds wholly or predominantly characterized by the emission of a succession of repetitive beats".

With the country's youth hooked on huge raves, alternatives had to be found, and the obvious answer was big clubs built in warehouses. It didn't take long for dancers to decide they preferred warehouses to muddy fields – the underground scene had become legitimised.

The people who got there first were the owners of three industrial buildings; in London, Ministry of Sound; in Liverpool, Cream; in Birmingham, Q Club. They didn't have to do much to them. So long as the kids who turned up had already taken an E, they would have a great party. A sound system and a few lights were enough. A bar helped, but wasn't essential, and perhaps a few sofas to collapse onto between dancing.

The major record companies wanted to cash in on this new dance market but didn't know how. The answer was compilation albums. But who would compile them? While they were pondering on that, the biggest of the new clubs, Ministry of Sound, started doing it themselves. In just a few months they became the country's biggest independent record company, selling millions of dance compilation albums, with tracks linked together by leading acid house DJs.

Desperate to compete, the major record companies hired DJs. Judge Jules, formerly a law student, then a club DJ, landed his own label at PolyGram Records. Other DJs did remixes of current Top 10 singles for majors wanting to sell them in the dance market – stripping out the vocals and all the bits that were normally considered the essential ingredient, boosting the bass and the rhythm, finding one little element to repeat endlessly every four bars – a musical phrase or a few words – like Marrs' 'Pump Up the Volume'.

With the major companies now pushing the dance craze, clubs proliferated. And so too did DJs. Clubbers, high on dancing and drugs, needed the music played just right to suit their evolving mood. If the DJ got the mood right, he got the praise. Soon he was the centre of the evening. Magazines started writing about DJs as if they were stars. *Mixmag* put one on its cover "Sashamania – the First Pin-up DJ".

During the seventies disco craze, the majors had got burned. They hadn't understood how quickly dance tastes shift and change. After getting it wrong once, they were shy to try again. But as DJs became the medium's stars, record companies started paying them for the use of their name and photo on compilation albums made up of songs by a variety of producers and artists. The albums were a continuous run of music, the tracks mixed in and out of each other by the DJs whose face was on the sleeve. For the DJ, it was easy work. For a couple of hours in the studio he could earn a £50,000 fee with royalties to boot. For the record companies there was big money too. For each 500,000 albums Ministry of Sound sold in Britain, they allotted £800,000 for TV advertising yet still made £1 million profit.

The cult of the DJ took over the dance market. A well-known one might earn $100,000 for nothing more than playing records for a few hours. Ecstasy, which had set the whole thing in motion, was less predominant. Clubs were one again as they'd always been – lush, comfortable, and sexy, with alcohol flowing freely and a whole range of drugs to augment it. Teenagers had become drug literate. A report commissioned by the Joseph Rowntree Foundation said, "young people who use drugs are as sociable, sensible, and morally aware as others of their age". Mostly, they now saw drugs as a normal part of everyday life, using the right drug for the right mood; amphetamine for late night swotting, a joint for an evening listening to music, Ecstasy or cocaine for Saturday night clubbing. Teenagers in general found their view of drugs much like Keith Richards', "I've never had a problem with drugs. I've had problems with the police."

As drug-taking came of age, so did electronic dance music. EDM spread the new dance culture to every country in the world except the USA. From Rio and Buenos Aires to Beijing and Tokyo, electronic dance became the backing track to young people's lives. But America remained unconvinced. It preferred something much more insidious.

39

Fuck tha Police
RAP

Rap began when Kool Herc, a West Indian DJ resident in New York, started toasting his friends in the audience over the breakdown section of records he was playing.

"Yo, this is Kool! Kool Herc saying my mellow-ski Marky D is in the house."

Intimate and friendly, that's how it started.

When Kool Herc first moved to New York from Jamaica in the late sixties, no one liked the reggae records he played back home so he shouted his little messages to the audience over the locally popular dance records, which only ever had short breaks in them. To do so he had to extend them, using a double turntable and an audio mixer with two identical records from which he continuously replaced the desired segment. Sometimes when he shouted over the instrumental break, someone in the crowd would shout back, sometimes with a little rhyme, "Davey D is in the house, an' he'll turn it out without a doubt."

The trend grew fast, the breaks got longer and more frequent, the improvised rhymes more complex, and in 1979 came the first hip-hop rap record; it was by King Tim III and the Fatback Band. A couple of years later came the first rap hit by a non-black artist, Blondie's 'Rapture'. After that the Beastie Boys, white, and Run DMC, black, sold rap to audiences all over the world. Soon, any kid speaking any language, even if he didn't sing too well, could be a pop star by taking up hip-hop and rapping. And the strange thing about rap was, it always had underlying humour. Even when it was angry and violent, there was usually some sly wit in it. And though it seemed like a fad that would eventually die out, it just kept on and on evolving until it finally came of age.

'Fuck tha Police' was a five-and-a-half minute rap musical written by Dr Dre for his group Niggaz With Attitude, a court case with a full range of characters – judge, attorney, accused and defendant. With just a hint of Gilbert & Sullivan, the rap lyrics rhymed wonderfully, and at the end of the song 'Judge Dre' delivered his verdict with masterful understatement: *'The jury has found you guilty of being a redneck, white bread, chickenshit, motherfucker.'*

One of the group's rappers was Ice Cube. "Rap music is funny," he proclaimed. "But it's not funny if you don't get the joke, then it's scary."

Kids got the joke. Their parents didn't.

After Michael Jackson tried to make himself as white as possible, a new generation of American blacks decided to re-establish the image of the black man as bad, and made themselves as black as possible. It was a repeat of the 'coon craze' one hundred years earlier – let the white man have the black man who fits his preconceptions. Stylists were employed to design rappers in the image of the white man's worst fears – tough, broad shouldered, big-handed, gold-decorated, tattooed, profane and belligerent. Gangsta rap was hip-hop plus violence, sex, homophobia, racism, rape, street gangs, shootings, thievery, drug dealing, and materialism.

But there was one thing most whites seemed to miss about rap – even when it sounded violent it was still underlined with humour. And for young people it was fun.

There was nothing inner-city kids of any colour enjoyed more than yelling "fuck tha police". Niggaz With Attitude's white manager, Jerry Heller, recounts the first time they played the song live in Los Angeles. "Every member of the audience had felt the heavy hand of the LAPD come down on them. When Cube hit the chorus, the crowd unleashed their pain and anger into a deafening unison chant...

"Fuck tha police".

In due course the inevitable letter arrived from the Department of Justice warning the group's management against inciting violence. And when the group was due to play in Detroit's Joe Louis Arena in November 1989, the local police threatened not to police the event if the group sang the song. Since insurance for gigs was only obtainable with a guarantee of proper policing, Heller asked the band, just for one night, to drop the number from their set. And they agreed.

Heller signed a letter to the police stating "N.W.A., absolutely, categorically, unconditionally, guarantee it will not perform the inflammatory anthem, 'Fuck tha Police' at the Detroit concert."

In return, the Detroit police department agreed to provide their services as normal. But when the group arrived at the appropriate moment in their set they just went straight into it as usual. Jerry Heller was on the phone from California at the time. "Two things happened at once. The crowd went wild, and undercover police officers set off M-80s to simulate gunshots. Then they jerked their badge-wallets out of their shirts and rushed the stage. I was on the phone with Gary Ballen when it happened. 'The cops are charging us!' he shouted".

As the cops climbed up the front of the stage, the band kept singing 'Fuck tha Police'.

The album sold three million. *Newsweek* called it "gangster mystique that pays no attention where criminality begins and marketing lets off". *Time* ranked it as one of the 100 greatest albums of all time.

After a couple more albums, Dr Dre moved on. He formed a hip-hop company called Death Row, financed by Interscope, which in turn was financed by Atlantic. After hits with Snoop Dog, Tupac Shakur, and white rapper Eminem, he sold out to Interscope for $52 million. Then went into business with Interscope's chairman, Jimmy Iovine, to make headphones called Beats.

If sociologists were right and rap was a repeat of the coon phenomenon of a hundred years earlier, with black Americans painting themselves in the image of white people's preconceptions – murderous, profane, and promiscuous – one new talent they were displaying removed them even further from such imagery. The modern black American was proving himself to be very savvy at business.

The next joke in the rap repertoire was more difficult for the elder generation to take. And it upset the police no end.

Rapper Ice-T formed a group called Body Count that came up with a song called 'Cop Killer'. It wasn't regular rap music, it was rock. White kids loved it, and when their parents complained, Ice-T told them, "If you took your kid and you put him in jail with a microphone and asked him how he feels you'd get Body Count – 'Fuck that. Fuck school. Fuck the police…' You'd get raw anger… Through rock 'n' roll I injected black anger into white kids."

Body Count were signed to Seymour Stein's label, Sire, which was part of Warner. When Stein first heard a demo of Ice-T, he told people, "He sounds like Bob Dylan." But what 'Cop Killer' really sounded like was the best of British rock circa 1966. A guitar-driven, drum-thrashing, chorus-throbbing super-smash. Which, of course, is what upset all the parents so much. It wasn't just a pushy nigga telling their children to kill cops – he was doing it with *their* music. Body Count was a band of black guys playing white rock better than any white rockers ever played it. That's what the row was really about. As the backing track to his profanities, Ice-T had stolen the older generation's music.

Warner took a battering. The American Police Federation dug up one of Warner's most famous shareholders, Charlton Heston, head of the gun lobby, the American most in favour of allowing everyone to carry arms. They persuaded him to go to a meeting of Warner shareholders and stir them up by reciting Ice-T lyrics. Outside, pickets carried signs saying things like "Time Warner Puts Profits Over Police Lives."

Warner stood by Ice-T and its spokesman defended artistic freedom. But the pressure was too great and eventually Ice-T himself agreed to pull the record, though not before it had gone gold. "I called a meeting with Body Count and said, 'This record is out of control… Our fans who wanted the record have already bought the album… All the new people who are buying it are just snooping assholes… So let's pull it and tell them to shut the fuck up.'"

Ice-T didn't suffer much. He released his next album with Priority Records, the independent distributor that had released Niggaz With Attitude. He wrote more albums, made movies, did TV, and ended up like everyone who's successful in the record industry, heading for the mainstream – teaming up with Tupperware to throw a party for charity, then making a reality TV show with his wife, *Ice Loves Coco*.

Ice-T's benign nature did little to influence the new angry brigade. Rappers spread across the world like Beatles imitators had done twenty years earlier. They came in every shape and size, and every degree of humour and anger: some were big and brutal, some were almost jolly. Ja Rule, Lil Wayne, 50 Cent and Usher – in some ways totally different, but in others exactly the same – all with their pants hanging down (to empathise with Niggaz Behind Bars, who had their belts confiscated on entry), and all making hand movements so stereotyped that every rapper became a choreograph twin of every other. Some were downright amusing, some were even musical; others were bullying brutes.

These American rappers provided a template for copycat rappers across the world, but kids on other continents copied only certain aspects. American black guys dressed like hoods and lambasted the police with obscenities. But rap felt different when it was done by an eighteen-year-old teenager in Tokyo rapping about family life in the suburbs. Overseas rap became cute and lost its anger.

In America, it didn't.

By the 1990s, East Coast rap was ready to challenge West Coast. And the principal challenger was Sean Combs.

Rapper, record company owner and music publisher, Combs was first and foremost a businessman. He was born in Harlem in 1969 and got a job as a publicist with Uptown Records while still studying. In college he ran an oversold gig at which nine people were crushed to death when a stairwell door was shut and blocked with a table to stop people getting in. Following this he got fired by Uptown Records and set up his own company, Bad Boy Records. The first release was by The Notorious B.I.G., a group led by rapper Biggie Smalls.

On the West Coast, one of Dr Dre's artists on Death Row Records was Tupac Shakur. He accused Biggie Smalls and Sean Combs of setting up a robbery against him in which he'd had jewellery stolen and got shot. In his next record he sneered at them demeaningly and it started an East–West hip-hop feud, Bad Boy versus Death Row, Shakur versus Smalls.

Sometime later Tupac Shakur was shot and killed by persons unknown. With one less rapper on the scene, Sean Combs decided it would be a good moment to move himself from behind the scenes and into the forefront. He recorded a rap under the name 'Puff Daddy'. When it was released, it stayed at number one for six weeks. Shortly after it fell out of the chart, Biggie Smalls was shot and killed by an unknown assailant in a drive-by shooting in Los Angeles. Puff Daddy's next single was in memory of him, 'I'll Be Missing You'. Again it went to number one. So did his first album, *No Way Out*. A little while later, while out with his girlfriend, actress Jennifer Lopez, he was arrested on a shooting charge himself.

The music industry took no view on any of this other than a sales one. If this stuff sold records, it was good. And it did.

40

I'll Be Missing You
END OF CLASSICAL AND EMI

The last few years of the eighties was a period when the unthinkable happened, not just once but repeatedly. The Soviet Union voluntarily dissolved itself. White South Africa freed Nelson Mandela from jail and announced the end of Apartheid. East and West Germany knocked down the Berlin Wall and headed towards re-unification. And in the music industry, CBS Records sold itself to Sony. Now it was Warner's turn.

Steve Ross, the man whose Mafia-tainted car-park company had originally bought the Warner Group of companies from Jack Warner, decided the time had come to sell Warner Communications, the huge corporation he'd built it into. Or rather, he decided to merge it with another company of equal size, Time Inc.

At Warner Music the changes started when Nesuhi Ertegun, CEO of WEA international, one of the most senior positions in the group was made to step down, ostensibly to concentrate on producing jazz records, in fact to fade away and die. Ahmet Ertegun was then forced to give up his position as head of Atlantic and made to share the top job with Doug Morris, the man previously below him. Other Warner Music executives also felt the ground shift beneath them.

Steve Ross stayed firmly in charge of everything and followed his goal single-mindedly. The only opposition to the proposed merger came from straight-laced executives at Time who'd heard of his Mafia past. But Ross sold himself and his company well, making sure that those who had to vote for the merger would receive substantial benefits in bonuses or shares.

Time Warner Inc would be a cumbersome conglomerate dealing in a wide-range of media and communications businesses. From the beginning it would be saddled with debt, much of it due to the money being raised to pay five hundred Warner executives an average of more than a million dollars each for their shares. For everyone who'd worked at Warner Music it was the end of everything they'd ever loved about the company. It was that which had prompted David Geffen to sell his company to MCA, saying, "We're at the end of an era... all the companies have put these numbers guys in charge."

Worse still, these 'numbers guys' at the top, mostly accountants and lawyers, continually chopped and changed the people running the music divisions. Ahmet Ertegun almost walked out.

They kept putting up people to run it who were non-music people... they would never take somebody from the cable division and let them run the movie division...: but they would take anybody and let them run the music... there was no leadership from the top... it was everybody fighting everybody else...

It wasn't only Warner that was caught up in this type of arrangement, there were now just six major record companies, all of them owned by similar holding corporations run by lawyers and accountants. Ed Bicknell, manager of Dire Straits, said that dealing with this sort of situation at PolyGram altered his whole personality. "You sometimes do things you wouldn't do to a mate. I had no compunction in screwing a corporation. I got through sixteen or seventeen managing directors... they're incredibly inefficient and absolutely hopeless to deal with... it was a farcical way to run a business."

This dismal new situation filtered down to the A&R departments too. Artists and record companies were locked together in mutual disrespect. Warner's biggest selling artist, Prince, tried to terminate his contract and refused to use his name any more, calling himself 'The Artist Formerly Known as Prince'. At Sony, George Michael also tried to get out of his contract.

It was rumoured to have been triggered by George overhearing the company's new president, Tommy Mottola, referring to him as a 'limey fag'. If a regular employee of Sony was referred to by his boss in the same way the company would probably end up in court and be fined. But an artist was not an employee, he was just an ingredient to be used in the making of hit records.

Some people thought that an artist who could sell millions of albums for the record company, and was locked into a five-year contract, should be able to demand that the company deals with him in a proper manner, not with insults. But George Michael didn't sue them on that basis. Instead he claimed his contract was invalid. It didn't win him the case but it at least allowed the public to learn a great many things about the record business they hadn't previously known. And much of it dated back to the fifties when Don Kirshner ran his successful song factory in the Brill building.

Prior to that, when they signed artists, record companies paid the costs of recording and gave the artists a royalty of 1 cent per record. Kirshner started something new. He made finished records and licensed them to the record companies. Because they wouldn't have to pay any recording costs they gave him four or five thousand dollars for each master tape, and five cents royalty. And they only started paying him his royalty after enough records had been sold at five cents each to repay the advance of four or five thousand dollars. Which meant, so long as the record sold enough copies, the record company would effectively pay nothing for the cost of recording it.

Because record companies enjoyed not paying the cost of recording, they started doing the same thing to artists signed to them on the normal 1 per cent royalty basis, refusing to pay the 1 per cent royalty until the cost of recording had been recouped.

In the case of Don Kirshner's records, after fifteen or twenty years, the rights in the master recordings were returned to him. For other artists, those rights stayed forever with the record company. It seemed absurd – the artist was now paying the cost of making the records but the record company owned them. "The bank still owns the house after the mortgage is paid," is how Senator Orrin Hatch described it.

Encouraged by the financial benefits this gave them, record companies then started finding more ways of not paying artists the royalties they'd been promised. If a record company shipped more records to the stores than were sold, no royalty was paid on 'returns'. If a store was sent twice as many records as it needed it would send half of them back. Because these were technically 'returns' no royalty was due on them, so the record company shipped them off 'royalty-free' to other record stores.

Artists had to pay a packaging deduction of around 15 per cent of the retail selling price. This, despite the fact that packaging rarely cost more than 5 per cent. The remaining 10 per cent was enough to pay the record company's entire cost of manufacturing the record.

All in all it meant an artist who sold 200,000 copies of a first album would still be in debt to the record company despite the record company having made a million dollars profit.

In creative matters too, the record companies kept the upper hand. An artist might ask for an equal say in selecting songs for his album, or in choosing his record producer. On the front page of his recording contract it would state that the choice of songs and record producer was to be made jointly by the artist and the record company. But on page 59 or 60 of the contract, in small print, it would say, "in the event that the record company and artist cannot agree on anything hereunder, the record company's decision will be final".

Following the time-honoured tradition of the insurance industry, the record industry decided that what the large print promised the small print should take away.

But the worst thing about being signed to a major was that you lost the freedom to run your own life. It put you totally out-of-control of your own career. And though top artists could sometimes re-negotiate an unfair contract, it soon became clear that in the music business you didn't get out of an unfair record contract to get into a fair one, you got out of an unfair contract to get into another unfair one, but with slightly better terms.

All this was laid out for the public to learn as a result of George Michael's court case with Sony. Eventually the two sides settled out of court. George Michael was free to take his recordings wherever he wanted but Sony would still receive a royalty from them.

At the same time as the George Michael case was being settled, Sony was suffering in a quite different department, not brought on by a difficult artist but by a difficult executive – the one at the very top, Norio Ohga.

Before Sony had taken over CBS, classical music had been a bad word. Despite its importance in the history of record companies, Walter Yetnikoff had been commercially practical and given it only the funding it deserved from a commercial point of view. Which had slowly sunk to almost nil.

But Norio Ohga, the man at Sony with whom Yetnikoff did the deal to buy out CBS, was a classical fanatic and an amateur singer and conductor of a high standard. He was determined that some of the company's profits should be ploughed back into classical music and told everyone that Sony would be "the most important classical label by the end of the century".

To make it that way Yetnikoff was told to hire Gunther Breest, former head of the world's most respected classical label, PolyGram's Deutsche Grammophon. Breest immediately moved Sony classical's headquarters from New York to Hamburg.

Actually, Sony's classical label, *Masterworks*, hadn't been doing too badly and had managed to win *Billboard*'s top classical music award in six of the last seven years. Nevertheless, Breest fired most of the US staff and set about running things from Germany, hiring in people from other companies and over-paying them to make sure they came.

Breest put image before practicality, paying top conductors like Claudio Abbado to give Sony some small part of their output just for the prestige of it. Deutsche Grammophon still had first refusal on everything he recorded. Sony just got the leftovers.

Breest then paid a vast amount to steal Vladimir Horowitz from Deutsche Grammophon, but he died after making just one recording.

Despite his big budget bravado, Breest was beginning to look like a loser. Still, he managed to bring in the Boston Pops Orchestra and a few more big names and a great deal of recording took place. Unfortunately it involved a great deal of spending, and this triggered other companies to do the same.

After a few years of this the world became flooded with high priced classical recordings for which there was insufficient market. Between them, Norio Ohga and Gunther Breest had almost bankrupted the entire classical recording industry.

Meanwhile, in Hong Kong, one man had found the secret to selling classical music at a profit.

Klaus Heymann, a German living abroad, had a local record distribution business. As a result of various business deals, he accidentally found himself the owner of some classical master tapes. At the time there was a drop in CD manufacturing costs so he decided to try and market them. "I couldn't sell them at full price because these were unknown East European orchestras, although the performances were not bad. I had to put them out on a budget label. That's how Naxos Records was born."

At a price of $6, Naxos were the cheapest classics by far, a third of the price of a premium album from a major company. In 1987 they sold across Asia, then in Woolworth's in Britain and in petrol stations in the north of Europe.

Soon, Heymann was selling more classics in Britain and northern Europe than all the majors put together. In three years he notched up four million sales. By 1994, adding the US and Japan to his markets, he sold ten million, with an annual growth of 50 per cent. In 1996, one in six classical records sold anywhere in the world was a Naxos.

Heymann was not on an artistic mission; he was simply a businessman who liked classical music. "I sat down with a catalogue and marked everything that had more than ten recordings. That was our initial policy: record the hundred most recorded things in reasonably good quality, reasonably good sound, and make them available."

He did this mostly in Eastern Europe where rates of pay for orchestral players were cheap and conductors and soloists got a flat fee with no royalties. The records weren't sold on the name of the performers but on their musical content and reasonable price. And Heymann spent nothing on publicity.

Before long Naxos had offices all over the world, most of them making recordings with local orchestras, but never top ones. In Britain, the Bournemouth Symphony rather than the London Philharmonic. In the USA, the Buffalo Philharmonic rather than the New York Symphony.

Ten years after Sony's purchase of CBS and Norio Ohga's instruction to lift the classical division company to the top level, the glut of expensive recordings triggered by Gunther Breest's extravagance, and the cut-price competition created by Klaus Heymann's Naxos label, had caused the market for top price classical music to collapse. Sony classics were losing so much that Ohga had to be confronted. When he learned of the lack of return from Breest's mad spending, he fired him and allowed the classical division to move back to New York.

The department was taken over by Peter Gelb, previously Breest's right-hand man. Gelb's plan was simple – stop recording classics. Instead he would release film music.

To get him off to a good start he received an extraordinary gift. Sony had bought the soundtrack to *Titanic* including the theme song performed by Celine Dion. Tommy Mottola, intent on giving Sony a new hip look, refused to release it on Epic or Columbia. His other label bosses followed suit and turned up their noses at it. So it came to Gelb.

He accepted, and *Titanic* became the best-selling soundtrack of all time, racking up twenty-five million CDs and giving Gelb the aura of a financial genius. He immediately lectured the industry on how it should be done. "I believe in great music," he told a classical music conference, "I just don't want to record it."

The demise of classical music was helped further by Edgar Bronfman Jr's arrival on the corporate stage. Bronfman was a member of the Seagram family, owners of one of the world's biggest drink companies. With the family money he bought MCA Records.

In the music business, everyone laughed. They said he was the spoilt son of a rich man. But what they laughed at most was that he wrote songs – not great ones, but he'd managed to get a couple recorded, including one by Dionne Warwick. The very same people who for ten years had been raising their hands in horror because the industry was being run by lawyers, now piled opprobrium on Bronfman because he aspired to be a songwriter. Yet the entire American music industry had been built by people exactly like him – Leo Feist, Harry von Tilzer, Edward B. Marks, even the great Max Dreyfus, had all started out wanting to be songwriters.

There was only one other person at the top of the industry who had started out writing songs and that was Doug Morris. After helping Warner remove Ahmet Ertegun from the top spot at Atlantic, Morris had been fired. So Bronfman brought him into MCA as president. That meant, at MCA records, both the owner and the person running the company were people who'd once written songs. But there was a difference. Doug Morris had been running record companies for thirty years, Bronfman had never run a record company in his life.

He'd never run a film company either, yet part of what Bronfman had bought was Universal Film Studios whose name he now used for MCA, re-christening it Universal Music Group. On an unstoppable spending spree, he next bought PolyGram from Philips Electronics. The combined company became the world's biggest music company, with a vast catalogue of classical music as well as a thriving film division.

When they still owned PolyGram, Philips' company slogan had been 'Let's make things better'. Once they were out of the music business, they changed it to 'Sense and simplicity'.

Bronfman showed neither. His wheeling and dealing had put him in control of some of the most famous record labels the industry had known – A&M, PolyGram, Island, Geffen, Interscope, and Motown, were just a few. He fired 980 PolyGram employees and cut 200 acts from its music roster, closed fifty-three-year-old Mercury Records and merged Geffen and A&M with Interscope.

Through his purchase of PolyGram, he also had control of the world's two greatest classical record companies, Deutsche Grammophon and Decca. With Sony having stripped back its investment in classics, the future of high quality classical recording was now largely in Bronfman's hands. He decided to copy Sony and cut financing to the minimum, which meant an end to classical music's elite position in the industry. In future it would be seen as just one more category, to be judged solely on its ability to turn a profit.

Classical's death knoll coincided closely with EMI's, the company that had made the first recordings of Caruso and was once the largest record company in the world.

Despite having success with the Spice Girls in the mid-nineties, the company had never really recovered from the decline that started with the Sex Pistols in the seventies. Finally, in 1996, EMI's shareholders made the worst decision they could – they voted to separate from Thorn Electric.

For the first time in its history, EMI was on its own. As part of the Thorn group EMI had not been subject to having its shares bought and sold. But it now became the only major record company in the world not owned by a larger corporation and would be re-evaluated daily on the stock exchange at the whim of the charts or the sales of its latest releases.

Even so, things didn't look too bad. Apart from the Spice Girls there were also two world renowned rock groups, Radiohead and Coldplay, and solo singer Robbie Williams. The company also had Paul McCartney and the Beatles' back catalogue. Skilfully dealt with it should have been able to survive and thrive. But the days of a major record company being skilfully dealt with were long gone.

EMI was no exception. Within the company there were constant changes at the executive and management levels – newcomers made statements about changes to be made, then departed without making them, only to be replaced by new newcomers making new statements, with subsequent new departures. Confidence dropped, share prices fell, artists complained, and the staff were demoralised.

EMI's biggest problem had always been that it focused too much on Britain. The power-centre of the music market was America. All the other major companies, whatever nationality their owners, operated their head offices out of America. EMI's head office was in London. Worse still, its main office in America wasn't even in New York, it was in far away Los Angeles, a round building built to look like a pile of records. Journalist Emmanuel Legrand thought the roundness of the building was the cause of EMI's problems. "I have a theory that when you have a circular building then you never see the angles and never have a straight view of anything – I believe that does affect your psyche."

In November 1999, in their year-end fiscal report, ABN Amro's monetary experts put it less whimsically. EMI, they said, was a "low growth consumer cyclical". Their advice to shareholders was to sell.

They did. And EMI ended the decade with its share price at rock bottom.

41

Mad About the Boy
BOYS AND BILLIONS

Lou Pearlman managed two boy bands – Backstreet Boys and 'N Sync. When he announced plans for a third one, a journalist asked him weren't two boy bands enough?

Lou Pearlman thought not. Boy bands will only stop being popular, he said, "when God stops making little girls".

Actually, the demise of boy bands would be more likely if God stopped making homosexuals.

It seems obvious – if an entrepreneur is able to view young men from the same sexual vantage point as the young girls who buy records, he's going to choose the right boys to go into the group. A straight man is likely to choose the sort of boy he would like his son to be; a gay man, the sort of boy he'd like to have sex with. There have been a few straight managers of boy bands, but not too many, and it's the gay ones who come up with the winners, time after time.

The UK has done well at producing them. Bay City Rollers dominated the seventies; Bros and Take That, the eighties; Boyzone and Westlife, the nineties. All with gay managers.

Then there's Menudo who came from Puerto Rico; their ages were from thirteen to sixteen, and the group kept going for over twenty years. There were five of them. Each time one reached the age of sixteen, he was kicked out and a new thirteen-year-old came in.

It was the brainwave of Edgardo Diaz, as was the choice of boys. They had success all over South America and were the training ground for Ricky Martin who had a number one as a solo artist in America with 'La Vida Loca'.

When parents of some of the boys tried to bring a sexual abuse case against Edgardo Diaz, he re-located to Miami and continued to run Menudo from there.

But the country that has done best at marketing pretty boys for young girls is Japan.

Johnny Kitagawa was born in the United States and went to high school in California. In the early 1950s, he traveled to Japan to work at the United States Embassy. While walking through Tokyo's Yoyogi Park he encountered a group of boys playing baseball and recruited them to form a singing group. He named them, 'The Johnnies', and mixed their attractive looks with easy songs and crisply coordinated dance routines. When it was successful, he repeated it. Endlessly.

For forty years he has manufactured group after group. All the boys in his groups are referred to by the Japanese press as 'Johnnies'. There have been over fifty groups and half-a-dozen of the best known are Four Leaves, SMAP, Tokio, V6, KinKi Kids, and JUMP.

They've always come in two age-widths – Junior Johnnies, 10–14; and Senior Johnnies, 14–18. They do TV commercials, sell products, make movies, and occasionally go on to be solo artists. One band, KinKi Kids, released twenty-five consecutive singles that debuted in the charts at number one. By the end of the 1990s, Kitagawa's company, Johnny and Associates, was generating annual profits of nearly three billion yen and Johnny himself had become one of the richest men in Japan.

Kitagawa recruited his boys at ten years old, kept them in a company-run hostel, made them sleep in company dormitories, and had them attend the company school. He also got to know them in a way that wouldn't have been universally approved of had it been known.

In 1999, *Bunshun Weekly*, a Japanese tabloid, interviewed a boy from one of Kitagawa's most successful groups.

Mr. Johnny loved to shout at someone from the bottom of his lungs, "YOU!!" Normally it was, "You!!! Come here!!" Then you had to go with him to the dormitory restaurant and eat together. Another time, he'd yell at a boy, "You!! Get into bed!" That's the one nobody wanted to hear… Once, I was in my bed when he suddenly burst into the room… He got in close behind me… I was so frightened I couldn't turn to look. It hurt – hurt awfully.

There followed a libel case that Kitagawa won. But at appeal, *Bunshun Weekly* were exonerated.

In court, Kitagawa's explanation of his actions was bizarre. "I didn't intend to abuse anyone sexually. But my boys were so lovable, we were so much like one big family, it was horrible to think we weren't actually related. By having sex with them, I was trying to reach across that divide…"

The statement released by the National Police and Welfare Ministry seemed equally confused. "The acts could not be considered child abuse because Kitagawa was neither parent nor guardian to the boys in his employ."

If this sounds strange to Western ears, bear in mind that homosexuality is not illegal in Japan and the age of consent is thirteen. For the police, the only question would be – was it consensual?

The American music business was always nervous of anything that might be seen as gay. It was never comfortable with boy bands, just as it wasn't with disco. For five years after the Monkees, a sixties manufactured version of the Beatles, there was nothing until the Osmonds, who looked like something from a church, then later the Jacksons, who looked like something from a circus.

When boy bands did materialise in the USA, unlike Europe and Asia which specialised in boy bands with soft looks and pretty faces, in America they tended to follow the Hollywood ideal of male youth – muscled and masculine. Lou Pearlman thought there was a market for a European-style boy group, but he needed to find a record company executive who agreed.

Clive Calder was not gay and not American; he was born in South Africa. In his teens he was in a group, then progressed to promoting groups, then to recording them. At every turn he came up against Apartheid. He liked black music and black people and couldn't live within the restrictions so with his business partner Ralph Simon, and another friend, record producer Mutt Lange, he went to London. There, while Lange went off to do his own thing, Calder and Simon set up as music publishers under the name Zomba (the capital of Malawi where tribal members are said to have superior hearing).

Their company's first success was to pick up the British sub-publishing for the Village People. Simon Draper, a co-founder of Virgin Records, recalls that Clive Calder didn't quite fit in to the London scene. He was "slightly off the pace, a little uncool, didn't dress quite correctly, hadn't exactly got the tempo". But he was good at networking and clever at making money.

Mutt Lange quickly became a big-time producer, working with the new wave band, Boomtown Rats, and then producing AC/DC's album, *Highway to Hell*. Calder and Simon used Lange's connections to meet producers and songwriters, and got Lange to ask every performer he met to come to Zomba for their publishing deal.

They did well, and in 1977 opened an office in New York. One of their British writers was also a singer, Billy Ocean, who became the first British black artist ever to have hits in America. As its American publishing income began to exceed its British, Zomba built a studio in New York and expanded into a gospel label. They also expanded into marketing, distribution, and music equipment, and in 1990, just fifteen years after Calder and Simon set off from South Africa, Zomba was worth $225 million.

At that stage Calder did a deal with BMG. He sold them 50 per cent of his publishing company and 20 per cent of his record company. Additionally, if at any time before 2002 Calder requested them to, BMG would be obliged to purchase the balance of his shares in both companies for three times the profit of the previous three years. And Calder could choose the date from which the previous three years would be assessed.

Clive Calder continued to build the company and dabbled for a while in hip-hop but was looking for something bigger, something with which he could dominate the American market. And then he met Lou Pearlman – fat, jolly, double-chinned, balding, and sociable.

Pearlman was a juggler – he threw companies in the air and talked up profits that didn't really exist. He got people to invest in one company, bought assets with the money invested, then borrowed against them to finance the next company. By doing so, he'd managed to build up a group of companies that had air blimps and hired them out for events. He also said he had an airplane hire company, with over 400 planes. One way or another he conjured up enough money to live like a millionaire, and by doing so conjured up more.

Pearlman liked boys. None of his friends knew that, so when he told them he was thinking of putting together a boy band, it seemed surprising and out of keeping with his other businesses. He did auditions at his home in Orlando, Florida, and eventually found five boys age twelve to fourteen. He called them Backstreet Boys and started to coach them. Soon, wherever they played they attracted an audience of young teenage girls who went crazy over them.

One of Clive Calder's A&R men introduced him to Pearlman. Calder knew it was logical for there to be a huge market for a boy band in the USA. If there was an audience for boy bands in every other country in the world, why not America too? So he signed them. He sent them to Sweden to record and when they came back he thought they had a smash hit song.

But radio stations wanted rock music, with older people playing it. So Calder sent the group abroad, first to Germany where radio stations were used to playing songs by boy bands, and then to Asia where a friend, Stuart Watson, organised a promo tour for them in shopping malls across South East Asia – Thailand, Malaysia, Taiwan, Japan – and in all those countries the band became famous.

By the time they got back to the USA, they could sing and perform well, and had learnt how to deal with people at radio and TV stations, and they didn't look quite so young either. This time, when Calder sent them off for a promo tour, they got good reactions. If a radio station was putting on a local promotional event, it needed a band that would turn up on time and be polite. Backstreet Boys did just that, so they started to get their records played. They were cute and fun and could dance! Every radio station wanted them to show up for their birthday bash, their Halloween party, their Christmas show, whatever.

Soon Calder had got them away. He now wanted a young girl to push to the same audience as the Backstreet Boys. One of the boys in the band had been a Mouseketeer in the Orlando Mickey Mouse Club and knew a girl who might be right, Britney Spears.

She sent in a demo, and although it wasn't good the accompanying photos were cute, so Calder agreed a deal and again recorded her in Sweden. She came back with 'Baby One More Time', and thirty days after it was released it was number one.

The Backstreet Boys and Britney Spears had exactly the same audience. Promotion and marketing could be dovetailed. Sales of both grew.

Meanwhile Lou Pearlman's millionaire lifestyle had gone through the roof. He gave up his blimp and airplane companies and focused on management.

He now lived in a $12 million mansion in Orlando with another mansion on the shore of nearby Lake Butler where he kept boats and jet skis. He rode in a blue Rolls-Royce with a chauffeur, made political contributions to the local Republican Party, owned a piece of the local football team, the Orlando Predators, and continually held auditions of thirteen- and fourteen-year-old boys for groups he gave names to but which never actually materialised.

Eventually, though, he became serious about having a second one. "You can't make money on an airline with just one airplane," he told the *Los Angeles Times*. So he put together 'N Sync.

This time he signed the group to RCA. Bob Jamieson, the head of the company at the time, found Pearlman strange. "He was arrogant and thought he was the smartest guy in the room, but he could be very charming. But there was always an element of him that made you second-guess. You felt uncomfortable."

Some of the kids in the group felt uncomfortable too, especially when Pearlman showed them pornographic movies or jumped naked onto their beds in the morning to wrestle. Steve Mooney worked for Pearlman as an assistant; he lived in his house and saw what went on. "There was one guy in every band – one sacrifice – one guy in every band who takes it for Lou. That's just the way it was."

But once these annoying preliminaries were over, there was fame and fortune to look forward to.

With 'N Sync, Pearlman copied everything Clive Calder had done with Backstreet Boys. He first sent the group to Germany, then to Asia. And soon the group took off in just the same way.

The Backstreet Boys didn't like their manager having a second hit group. They turned up for a meeting with Pearlman with their lawyers. First they complained that the new group was taking too much of Pearlman's attention; then they moved on to financial matters. They'd sold millions of records and still had very little money. Pearlman, who called himself Big Papa, was living like an emperor. Where was their money?

"It would be nice to have them as my five sons," Pearlman said (reminiscent of Johnny Kitagawa seeing his 'boys' and him as one big family). "Instead," Pearlman complained, "it's five sons with lawyers in between."

The Backstreet Boys left and went with another management company. But Pearlman still had 'N Sync who were now selling the same amount of CDs and concert tickets as Backstreet Boys had been. But 'N Sync soon had the same complaints. They hired lawyers who found they'd signed a contract that allowed Pearlman to take 50 per cent of all their merchandise income and 30 per cent of their touring income. They called a meeting with him to negotiate a new deal. It lasted all day and one by one the members of the band walked out.

A few days later RCA received a letter from 'N Sync's lawyers saying they'd left Pearlman. And since their recording arrangement with RCA was through a contract signed with Pearlman rather than directly with RCA, the group's lawyers maintained they were no longer under contract with RCA.

Overseas their records were released in a similar way, through a deal Pearlman had made with BMG in Germany. So with a new album just finished and a potential to sell twelve million or so albums, the group were out of a recording contract.

The group's lawyer started talking to several record companies, but presumed the group would not want to be on the same label as Backstreet Boys. When Clive Calder heard about it he rushed to persuade them otherwise. Zomba's experience with the Backstreet Boys, he said, would make them the perfect label for 'N Sync.

The group signed, but before the album could be released RCA sued. They claimed their contract was still valid. The case took three months but finally went against RCA. Immediately, in January 1999, Zomba released 'N Sync's new single, 'Bye Bye Bye'.

The sales were huge, and the album that followed, *No Strings Attached* was the group's biggest yet.

For the previous five years, Calder had been working towards just one objective – to enforce the clause in his contract with BMG that required them to buy the balance of the shares in Zomba at a time of his choosing. Since the buying price was based on Zomba's previous three years' profits, Calder had been manipulating everything towards creating a best-possible three-year result. He was almost there. All he had to do was to estimate the time when three years of profit from album sales by the Backstreet Boys, Britney Spears and 'N Sync would hit its highest level.

But after hanging on till just the right moment he was almost foiled by the events of 9/11. 'N Sync's *No Strings Attached* came out in 2000 and sold eleven million copies in the USA alone. Calder then set the release of Britney Spears' new album for the autumn of 2001. The attack on New York's 'Twin Towers' came in September and in its aftermath record sales in the USA dropped to nothing. America wasn't in the mood for pop records and Calder had to hold his promotion campaign as long as possibble, hoping things would improve. They did. The album was released at the beginning of November and by June 2002 Britney Spears, 'N Sync, and the Backstreet Boys had each set international records for album sales. During the three previous three years Zomba's publishing and record companies had made average annual profits of $913 million. Clive Calder called BMG and told them he wanted to sell.

Meanwhile, Lou Pearlman ran out of money and did a bunk overseas. *Vanity Fair* ran a piece called *Mad About the Boys*, and the truth was out. It turned out Pearlman had been financing his millionaire lifestyle not just from the two groups but also from a Ponzi scheme, using the glamour of the music business to attract investors whom he then defrauded.

When he was finally tracked down, Pearlman's reward for being mad about the boys was twenty-five years in jail.

Clive Calder's reward for being mad about the very same boys was $2.74 billion, which put him in the Top 200 richest people on the planet.

BMG's reward was a loss of two billion dollars. None of the artists they got from Zomba ever had big sales again.

42

Everybody's Doing It
DOWNLOADING

Records were selling less and less. Profits were down and the major record companies blamed downloading. But that was rubbish.

The problem was not the downloading itself, it was that record companies hadn't foreseen it, nor moved to be a part of it. A record company's purpose had always been to make recordings and supply them to the people who wanted to buy them. If they were unable to do that, what was the purpose of their existence? It was a question to which they needed a quick answer.

The downslide had started in earnest when American record companies decided they didn't want to release singles. Singles! Anyone could have told the record companies they were acting like fools. Certainly the people in any of the publishing companies that the record companies owned could have told them. The music business was about hit songs.

For record companies, hit singles cost the same to press as an album, the same to package, the same to ship, and the same to bribe stores to stock and display. But when they were sold, the mark-up on the costs was just a quarter of the mark-up on an album. So record companies decided to cut them out; plug the album by supplying DJs with special copies of the best song to play on air, get music fans hooked on the song but make them get it by buying the album. It meant a lot more money to the record companies who rationalised that music fans would be just as happy buying albums instead.

Partly, they were right – music fans did buy the albums, because it was the only way to get the songs they liked. But they weren't happy about it; they preferred to buy singles. So when another way of getting them came along, they grabbed it.

Downloads were set in motion by several things. Around the world various technical people had been working since the eighties on a new method of compressing music files so they took less space and could be sent by email. A 'wav' file – a full quality file of recording studio quality – took hours to upload and download, but by the beginning of the nineties a new compressed file was being used on the internet. An mp3 file could be sent in a few minutes, even over a slow old-fashioned phone connection it could be sent to a friend in fifteen minutes. So if you had a friend who'd bought an album by Linkin Park on which there was one song you particularly liked, and you had a Coldplay album with one song your friend particularly liked, you both copied your albums into your computers, pulled out the song your friend wanted, converted it to mp3 and sent it by email.

Record companies knew nothing of this. The top executives as ever were mainly interested in jostling for positions at the top, living on expenses and leaving everything creative or inventive to people lower down the chain, who anyway were mostly doing much the same thing.

In 1999, Shawn Fanning, a nineteen-year-old student, came up with a piece of software called Napster, like a dating agency for people looking for music. Within a year there were twenty million users, all swapping songs with each other. You went on line, went to Napster, registered all the music you owned and gave them access to it. This in turn gave you access to the music all their other members owned. You could then download everything you ever wanted. The obvious thing for record companies to do was to start their own Napsters and charge an item-by-item fee. But they dithered.

While they dithered, Apple brought out the iPod. Basically it was a tiny *Walkman* that played mp3s. Then, without waiting to consult anyone, Apple went ahead and built the software that was needed by the major record companies if they were going to sell their product as downloads on the internet. Apple then managed to persuade the major record companies to let it sell single tracks for them at 99 cents each.

It was mainly a matter of arm-twisting. Apple was putting its iPod on the market. If the record companies didn't quickly release their product for sale on the internet at a reasonable price the iPod was going to increase free file-sharing by 1,000 per cent. Ninety-nine cents was an attractive price for record-buyers and good for advertising; it had a nice ring. And although the last time record companies had released singles they'd sold them at $3.99 as CDs, that price had also covered pressing and distributing. Now there was nothing to do except collect the payments. One by one the majors succumbed to Apple's pressure and agreed.

Apple took over the record business at 99 cents a shot. The record company got 77 cents and had to divvy it up between songwriters, publishers, artists and themselves. And with 200,000 songs on sale when the service was launched, there were almost as many iPods sold as recordings. The record companies had helped Apple make a monster profit.

And sales of CDs plummeted.

As far as the public were concerned, the music business seemed to be booming. New technology made music sound better and more vibrant than ever before.

In the charts, pop, rap and rock mixed together on equal terms and most young people stopped buying albums and instead downloaded just the songs they liked. If record sales suffered, who cared? Only the people who had bought it on themselves – the major record companies.

Their grip on things was going fast. Each week brought more gloom. CD sales were down on last year, which were down on the year before, which were down on the year before that. Out of spite for their demise, record companies started suing anyone who'd downloaded from Napster. Their trade organisation, RIAA, chased the general public in all directions – pensioned grannies and underage children ended up with fines way beyond their ability to pay. But when researchers looked further they found that the people who did the most file sharing were also the people who bought the most albums from record stores. And to top it all, while members of the public were still being sued, BMG issued a statement saying, "Napster has pointed the way for a new direction for music distribution." Then bought it for $85 million.

So the other companies sued BMG.

The major record companies were incapable of thinking and acting as one. For years they'd attended RIAA meetings and come up with new rules for chart returns, then rushed back to the office to discuss with their staff how to bypass the very rules they'd just made, exactly as the music publishers had done sixty years earlier as members of the Music Publishers Protective Association. How could companies that behaved like this be expected to come up with a coordinated plan for selling music over the internet? From BMG the other majors demanded damages, and got them – $60 million to Universal and $110 million to Warner Music.

The record industry had shot itself in the foot and no one was sympathetic. For Ed Bicknell, who'd spent the previous twenty years as manager of Dire Straits, it was a pleasure to see. "The record industry, particularly the monoliths and their predecessors, has since the 1950s fucked the talent completely. Even the successful talent has been fucked. It's all done in this backslapping 'Isn't it great, guys – we're all at number one' manner."

Artists started looking back at past royalty statements, demanding audits. Irving Azoff, once a manager, then a record company executive at MCA, then owner of his own label, changed sides yet again. He became the head of the American Artists' Association, which started suing all the major record companies on behalf of its artists, from Led Zeppelin to the Eagles, from Elton John to Sheryl Crow.

Azoff talked about 'time-honoured' accounting traditions, by which he meant decades of record companies cheating their artists out of royalties. And having been head of his own record company at Warner, and the CEO of MCA Records before that, he spoke with authority.

Everyone had the same story, "systematic thievery", which were the words used in the Dixie Chicks writ against Sony claiming under-payment.

Irving Azoff was pessimistic about the Artists' Association winning much. He thought the majors were too far in the red. They'd rushed in and bought all the artist-friendly labels like A&M, Island and Chrysalis, basing their purchase prices on record sales that no longer existed. Now they were licking their wounds.

Meanwhile more mergers took place. Edgar Bronfman decided to sell Universal to a French water supply company, Vivendi. It bought Bronfman's family a total of thirty-five billion dollars, and left them the biggest single shareholders in the new company. Bronfman agreed to continue running it under the overall control of the French company's CEO, Jean Paul Messier. But Messier turned out to be an egomaniac, intent on buying up the world in the name of Vivendi. In no time he'd reduced a company valued at fifty billion to imminent bankruptcy. At the last minute he was fired by the board of Vivendi with Bronfman pushed out too.

Sony then decided to amalgamate with BMG, and top executives from the two companies fought openly over who should be made redundant.

Sony/BMG saw an immediate improvement in sales but had a disastrous set back when it attempted to stop the copying of records by putting a secret code into CDs. It had the unintended effect of making people's computers more vulnerable to viruses. And sales slumped again.

In Britain, EMI was restructured for the umpteenth time. Jim Fifield, head of the company was paid $22 million to leave, and a little while later, Ken Berry who replaced him was also fired, this time at a cost of $9 million. Alain Levy, who for years had been the overseer of PolyGram's worldwide companies, was hired and sent to America to run EMI from there. But it was too late to make much difference.

Then 'Wonder Boy' arrived. Guy Hands, with a golden coiffed hairdo. Although the tabloids made fun of him, the financial editors of the broadsheets discussed him in reverential terms, running articles about his ability to do something new and striking in the music business where others had failed.

Anyone with an eye for the ineffective could see at once he wasn't the right person to handle the situation. It wasn't really the man you had to look at, just the mop of carefully careless golden hair on top of his head. People who'd been around the music business a while had seen it all before – an executive who arrives in the industry from somewhere a good deal less glamorous and is overwhelmed by this new world of stars. Guy Hands was in love with money, perhaps, but he was even more in love with Guy Hands. He turned up full of himself and started jetting round the world attending parties with the who's who of the entertainment business, star-struck, but mainly with his own star quality.

Guy Hands had made a killing buying up motorway service-areas in Germany and installing nice bathroom facilities, something they'd always lacked. The bathroom facilities at EMI weren't too bad, so looking for ways to improve things he said the company would no longer accept being bullied by its artists. If they were unhappy they could leave.

Radiohead left. And Paul McCartney followed. Mr Hands shrugged it off and said the company would invest in finding new talent.

The poor man hadn't a clue. The cost of finding new artists, breaking them, and building them into guaranteed income was greater than any demand an established artist might make for more royalties. It wasn't just the cost of searching out new talent; it was the ten-to-one signing ratio needed to produce a first hit, followed by the ten-to-one ratio between those who get a first hit and those who go on to become substantial sellers of albums. One thing you never did was to let a profitable artist leave you.

The problem was – Mr Hands wasn't from the music industry, and he didn't understand the difference between dealing with ordinary businessmen and dealing with creative artists. When news leaked out that he'd authorised the sale of a million surplus copies of Robbie Williams's album, *Rudebox*, to be sold to China as material for surfacing roads, William's manager accused him of behaving like a "plantation owner".

In due course, as could be predicted, Mr Hands went a step too far. Doom arose and engulfed him, and Citibank, from whom he'd borrowed the money to buy the company, took possession of EMI.

It had all come down to pride. When he first bought EMI, Mr. Hands was shocked to discover that artists took drugs and stayed up late. They weren't interested in the difficulties of running a record company; they only wanted higher royalties. When he met them and complained they gave him shit.

His reaction to their attitude caused his downfall. Installing new toilets to make money from service stations had taught him that shit was best flushed away. But anyone who dealt regularly with artists could have told him – sometimes it's better swallowed. First he lost the artists; then he lost EMI.

And so did Britain.

43

I've Got a Great Idea
NEW DIRECTIONS

The twenty-first century cried out for new ideas for the music industry. Record sales were dwindling but live music was as popular as ever. Because downloading allowed people to buy just one single track, the industry had gone back to its original idea of a hit song being the best promotion tool. Which posed the same old question. How best to plug a song?

In America at the end of the eighties two unfamiliar names had hit the headlines, Isgro and DiSipio.

Joe Isgro was described as being a pleasant enough fellow – your average ex-Vietnam purple-heart record promoter. In a drawer in his desk he was said to keep a box of photographs of all the Vietcong he'd killed during his time in the Vietnam war, but only his best friends got to see that. When he visited WEA, the company's vice-president Stan Cornyn reported, "Isgro shone, with shirts of black silk and jewellery of gold tonnage. He looked like he'd seen *The Godfather* once too often."

Fred DiSipio was described by Cornyn as "nerdy, nasal and short". DiSipio had been blown out of his ship during the Second World War and afterwards became tour manager for Al Martino. Then he became a record promoter and now he owned racehorses and had the biggest bodyguard the music industry had ever seen, Big Mike. "When he went into a restaurant," Cornyn said, "they didn't give him a menu, they gave him an estimate."

An NBC News investigator got hold of some video footage that connected these two gentlemen with the Mafia. Since they were also receiving brown envelopes stuffed with cash from record companies, a new payola scandal seemed set to emerge. NBC planned a programme on it; Walter Yetnikoff tried to have it supressed. He failed, and the attorney general weighed in. Eventually the record companies were forced to act in unison. "No more independent promotion," they announced.

"The end of an era of amazing grease," said Stan Cornyn.

But if payola of this sort was brought to an end, how were songs to be plugged at a time when hit singles were needed more than ever? As usual, nothing really changed. DiSipio and Isgro were replaced with a new brand of pluggers – small corporations known as 'indies'.

Of the 10,000 commercial radio stations in the United States, record companies needed one thousand to create hits and sell records. To help them get these, large independent promotion companies came into being. These companies purported to 'promote' radio stations. They would help a radio station maintain maximum listeners by advising it which were the best new records to play. And to persuade the radio stations it was worth paying attention to its advice, the company paid each one of them $100,000 a year. Once an indie had 'claimed' a radio station in this way, the record companies were advised that they would be invoiced for $1,000 each time that station added a song to its playlist.

If a radio station added four new songs a week for fifty weeks of the year that would be $200,000 worth of invoices to the record companies. Which meant $100,000 profit to the indie for each radio station.

And that was just the beginning. Next came 'bill-backs' and 'spin maintenance'.

A 'bill-back' was an extra $800 a week for the indie to continue to call a station about a record company's current song. "Yes, it's been added, but we don't want them to drop it, do we?"

'Spin maintenance' was a $4,000 per week 'spin programme' to make sure the song went into the Top 15.

For record companies, independent promotion costs were huge. Just to launch a single at radio could cost up to $500,000 in indie fees. Even if it was someone at the record company who persuaded the radio station to play it, the indie still got paid. Even if the song was a sure-fire hit and needed no promotion, the indie got paid. Yet somehow this type of promotion stayed just on the legal side of the payola borderline. And from it came a new idea.

Clear Channel, the largest owner of radio stations in the USA with 850 of them, formed an alliance with Tri-State Promotions, the largest indie plugging company which claimed to have contracts with 3,000 radio stations. This alliance greatly cut down on wastage and enhanced profits.

To benefit from this excellent arrangement, Clear Channel formed a new company, Live Nation. With record companies facing extinction, Live Nation was presented as the saviour of the music industry. The man chosen to oversee it was Irving Azoff, the hotel-smashing, door-jamming, cake in the face, snake-giving, multi-millionaire, artist manager and ex-record company executive. Not bad credentials for someone tasked with having to arrive on a white charger and rescue an industry in distress. But many people in the American music business were not sure if Live Nation was friend or foe.

The company's plan was to pay blockbuster advances to buy contracts with artists for everything that could be got from them – their recording rights, their publishing rights, their touring and merchandising rights. The money for this was sought on the stock exchange, and with the lure of star names to pull it in, it was easily found. Live Nation signed Madonna and Jay Z on staggering advances – $120 million for Madonna, and $150 million for Jay Z – and U2 in exchange for shares in the company. It then merged with Ticketmaster, the largest ticket agency in America, and became Live Nation Entertainment Inc.

Just one company now controlled the artists, their recording and touring rights, the radio stations that plugged them, and the company that sold tickets to their gigs. Was there anything missing? Yes – the venues themselves. So Live Nation started buying those too.

Still not satisfied, the company moved overseas and made joint deals with management companies around the world, ending up with twenty-seven overseas branches, from the Czech Republic to China, from Norway to New Zealand.

By the end of 2012, Live Nation Entertainment's value was quoted at around two billion dollars and the share price was rising. Yet concerts were making the company almost nothing because established artists demanded nearly all the ticket money. And though the company's annual turnover was around six billion dollars, profits were nil. So what was Live Nation's value based on?

'Mirrors', suggested equity analyst David J. Phillips when he looked at the company's books with a view to advising investors.

Wipe out the $2.46 billion in goodwill and intangibles (such as brand name and client/vendor relationships) from the asset-side of the ledger, and stated book value of $7.90 per share evaporates completely. Subtract the $64.4 million increase in accounts payable (monies owed) and the $124.8 million in deferred revenue (advances on services not yet rendered), and free cash flow of $276 million falls to $86.8 million. Given these facts, maybe Elvis was right. When it comes to Live Nation, 'Only Fools Rush In'.

So if Live Nation wasn't the future of the music industry, what was?

Perhaps this!

From Britain in 2001 came *Pop Idol*. At first glance it was just another talent contest, little different from all the other TV talent shows seen around the world since the first day television was invented. In Britain in the fifties there'd been *Opportunity Knocks*. Singers who won it and went on to have hits included Mary Hopkin, Peters and Lee and Lena Zavaroni. In America, Arthur Godrey's show *Talent Scouts* did better – it discovered Tony Bennett, Eddie Fisher, and Connie Francis. And worse – at the audition stage it turned down Elvis Presley and Buddy Holly.

With *Pop Idol* there would be one big difference. In the 1950s, shows couldn't be recorded for future use unless they were filmed. It was prohibitively expensive and to do it the show had to be rehearsed intensively, then run through without a break in order to save film and money. But we were now in the digital age.

Once you had your cameras, you could film any amount of footage absolutely free; anything could be recorded and kept indefinitely. And what didn't go into the show was still the property of the producers. In 1955, when Elvis Presley was turned down on *Talent Scouts*, DJ Bill Randle, who had arranged for him to do the show, said he'd been totally unprofessional.

Presley forgot the words, picked his nose, and was the antithesis of what Arthur Godfrey looked for in talent. He had a dirty red suit on, food all over it, and his clothing was rumpled. He had terrible acne, he just looked like a bum and he couldn't perform for them, and it was just a disaster, a real disaster.

What would it be worth today to have footage of Elvis moping around backstage having just been told that?

With *Pop Idol* all these things would be filmed and kept for posterity. Everything would be seen – the show, the rehearsals, the auditions, the queue for the auditions, the kids on the bus going to the auditions, the kids going to buy clothes the day before the auditions – go back as far as you like. Providing someone had the time to edit it, you could put it all in the show, and for the first time the public could watch the entire process.

Added to this was a bit of luck called Simon Cowell. As one of the judges, his custardy camp voice and complete lack of sympathy for anyone who wasted his time turned the show into an instant hit. Of course, those who wasted his time were as carefully chosen as those who dazzled him, all of them pre-auditioned and categorised by an experienced production team. And as the shows became slicker, so too did the contracts the contestants were asked to sign, eventually allowing the producers complete freedom to manipulate them as they pleased – "I further understand that my appearance, depiction and portrayal in the program may be disparaging, defamatory, embarrassing…and may expose me to public ridicule, humiliation or condemnation…"

With little left to chance, and everything meticulously stage-managed, *Pop Idol*'s success was repeated in the USA where it became *American Idol*, making Simon Cowell an even bigger star than he was in Britain.

The show's concept was then fought over in court, Cowell and his ex-partner, Simon Fuller, both claiming to have devised it. Fuller, who had previously managed the Spice Girls, won the rights to the name but with a proviso – Cowell could claim ownership of *The X Factor*, a different but almost identical show he'd devised.

With Cowell again a judge, *X Factor* became an even bigger hit in the UK than *Pop Idol*, though Americans could hardly tell the two shows apart. *Los Angeles Times* TV critic Mary McNamara said Simon Cowell explaining why *X Factor* was different from *American Idol* was like "watching Meryl Streep in *The Devil Wears Prada* explain to her neophyte assistant why two turquoise belts of similar width and style represent utterly distinct looks".

Undeterred, Cowell then devised a third identical show called *Britain's Got Talent*. In the *Telegraph*, TV critic Clive James described a final where "two singers called Richard and Adam were heroically battling their limitations and the rising dry ice fumes…"

Despite the critics carping, within three years of *Pop Idol* first appearing, all three concepts had swept around the world. Now there were not just British and American idols, but Bangladeshi, Armenian and Chinese ones too. The show's international success was followed by a similar global epidemic of *X Factor* and *Britain's Got Talent*.

Suddenly the whole world had talent. And more importantly, it had mobile phones. Digital cameras weren't the only new technology that made these shows possible; their success was equally triggered by mobile phones giving hundreds of millions of people easier access to a telephone.

The key factor in all of these talent shows was not so much the selling of artists as the selling of phone calls. In millions, the public voted for the winners by phoning in, and the phone calls cost them money. For 150 years the music industry had looked for ways to avoid having to pay cash to plug its music. These new talent programmes showed them how. The winning artists released recordings of songs the show had already promoted, and the show was financed by phone calls.

Instead of the record companies paying payola, the public was paying it for them. Nice work while they could get it, but by the end of 2013 the popularity of these shows was fading.

44
Where Do We Go From Here?
PRESENT AND FUTURE

Since 2014, the big word in popular music has been 'streaming'. Vast libraries of music containing every song, symphony, jam session, tune or aria ever recorded – all of them available instantly at a click to be listened to on your home stereo, iPod, computer, smartphone, TV, or car music system. No need to buy anything because it's all there, all available, all the time. And virtually free.

The first streaming service to catch on was Spotify, based in Sweden. It was quickly followed by Blinkbox, Deezer, Grooveshark, Pandora and others. But the clear winners have been Spotify, Apple, Tidal and SoundCloud.

The number of songs on these sites is vast. As of February 2022, Spotify was having 60,000 new songs uploaded each day, or 137 million a year. Its most popular songs reach up to 3 billion streams with over 150 million people listening each day. The royalty paid is complained about by artists but it's often comparable to or better than the royalty they would have earned from a single. A hit single in the old days would have been played between 100 and 500 times by its purchaser. Spotify's royalty is usually around $0.005 per play, so 200 plays will earn $1. No single ever earned an artist any more than that per purchaser. But of course, it has to be split between record company and artist. So in the end, as always, the artist's earnings depend on their deal with the record company.

To start with, record companies despaired over their loss of profit from selling vinyl at inflated prices. But now, with no manufacturing, no warehousing, no distribution and no shops to split their percentage with, they've learnt to play the system. They're making more money than before and they're more in control of the industry. That isn't to say there isn't room for independents – there are more of those than ever – but, as it always was in the past, once independents become successful the record companies suck them up; they buy them out and retain a near monopoly on the industry's power structure.

Perhaps you could say the real power is with the streaming companies, or YouTube, which remains the biggest global music force and the place where most kids still go to get their music. Or perhaps it's TikTok.

TikTok launched in 2017 and is Chinese-owned. It's now the music industry's most powerful promotional tool for selling to consumers in their teens and early twenties. It streams short clips of current music and its customers make videos to sync with them, which they upload to the app. Its biggest stars have fans in the tens of millions and are able to make themselves millionaires. Successful TikTokers can get $200,000 per post if they collaborate with big brands. Some can even charge $1 million per post. Yet nearly all of them still aspire to get a record deal, even though those record deals are as bad as ever.

As of 2022, the biggest change in the business is that back catalogue is outselling new material by 70 per cent to 30 per cent. The 200 top new tracks account for less than 5 per cent of total streams. New songs, while often reaching the top of the charts, rarely create the social impact that hits of former years did.

Record companies, benefitting from this surge in public demand for their back catalogues, are less interested than previously in grabbing hits where they can. Instead, when they invest in new artists, they are looking at them with an eye to creating a lucrative back catalogue for the future. For that reason, they're using algorithms and computers to make their judgments. But algorithms can only be programmed with information gleaned from previous hit material, so truly unique artists are finding less opportunity than ever before to present themselves through major record companies.

And why should they? Amongst the newcomers to the industry are companies like DistroKid and TuneCore, which allow new artists to upload their songs to every current streaming platform, presenting their music to the world without ever having to go to one of the industry's top three corporations. But because publicising them once they're there takes influence and investment, most new artists still aspire to sign with a major.

In New York, Sony's impressive building has a lobby with a seventy-foot-high atrium, heavy with music business *ambiance* – gold records, photographs and the 'Sony Shop of New Technology'. Upstairs, the main reception area is like the lounge of an exclusive club. Young people, dreaming of stardom, stand in wonder breathing in the atmosphere, looking at memorabilia – platinum CDs, photos of stars, framed press reports, *Billboard* charts. For a new artist or manager, just to step into the building is a thrill. The impression is of a corporation dedicated to the success of its artists, almost altruistic in its understanding of their needs.

Aspiring artists still go there dreaming of being signed though the ratio of success to failure is what it always has been – for every ten artists signed, nine will get nowhere. A contract with a major record company has always been a 90 per cent guarantee of failure and so it still is in 2022.

WHERE DO WE GO FROM HERE?: PRESENT AND FUTURE

Major record companies always had an excuse for the miserable contracts they gave their artists – the cost of production, the cost of promotion, the cost of signing ten artists to find one. Many of those costs are now non-existent but contracts remain almost unchanged. The biggest change is that instead of listening to music in order to make signing decisions, heads of A&R now look at sheets of data about which artists and which songs are picking up the most listeners on streaming services. But once they decide on their signings they still want the same substantial mark-up they used to make from vinyl, now replaced by an excessive share of the royalties received from streaming companies. And as always, until artists have repaid all their advances and recording costs, they will receive nothing more. But although record companies still use the same insidious contracts they always did, what they want from their artists has changed considerably.

Older ones, like Britney Spears, fight court cases for the rights to control their professional lives. Younger ones are industry-savvy. In her song 'Brutal', Olivia Rodrigo makes it clear that she accepts being exploited and even wants to be. Yet fans also want her to take a stand on political issues. If Britney Spears' role as a newcomer twenty-five years ago was simply to sing hits and look cute, Rodrigo's includes commenting on social issues. But has there really been an evolution in attitude at the record companies or is it simply what the record companies need these days to market artists? Could it be that the artists are as beholden to them as ever? The majors will always give customers what they want. New artists suffer as much from objectification as any of the older generation did. But now, to be worshipped by kids, they need to take a stand on women's rights, gay rights, fair play and fair pay, and myriad other social matters. Whether they want to or not is no concern of the record company – it is required of them.

For years now there have been young female stars who broke traditional moulds – Queen Latifah, Lauryn Hill, Alanis Morissette, and more recently Cardi B and Janelle Monáe. The difference is, it is now a record company requirement that their artists are seen to rebel against them. And as many other things as possible.

But the companies have to be cautious. Fans can log on to Twitter or TikTok and find out in a flash what's happening. So record companies have become more subtle; they get what they want from their artists with less overt pressure. They even employ psychologists to help them. Yet basically the artists are on the same old deals and the terms of their contracts would still not be acceptable in any other industry.

Imagine the outcry if people working in a factory were told that the cost of the products they were making would be deducted from their wages, which anyway would only be paid if the company managed to sell the products in the first place.

That's what it means when an artist has to pay their own recording costs out of future royalties. When the *Wall Street Journal* investigated the music industry it concluded that "for all the twenty-first-century glitz that surrounds it, the popular music business is distinctly medieval in character: the last form of indentured servitude."

Some things have now improved. Music publishers, for instance, regularly offer new writers contracts for a split of 75/25 compared with the old one of 50/50. And they're prepared to take ownership of the songs for just five years rather than for the life of copyright.

However, a new trend has been for publishers to buy from major writers and artists what was traditionally seen as the songwriter's pension: residual income. This is usually described in the press as buying rights to their songs or recordings but for the most part this is not what they're doing. They, or another corporation, usually have those rights already. What they're doing is buying from the seller their future share of income from the exploitation of those rights. Sting, Bob Dylan, the David Bowie estate, Bruce Springsteen and 50 Cent are just a few who have done these deals.

In the beginning, these rights to income were being bought by straightforward investment companies like Hipgnosis. Now they are also being bought by the major music industry companies – Sony, Warner, Universal and BMG. Once bought, these rights to income make the major corporations even more interested in putting resources into promoting back catalogue rather than new releases. And so the decline in creating new material continues.

Amongst other changes in the new millenium is the way Live Nation, a company that looked so shaky in its early days, has become a dominant force in globalising live music, having partnered with local promoters in almost every country. Also remarkable is the upsurge of success from non-English-speaking companies in Asia. The popularity of Korea's boy bands has amazed the linguistically prejudiced record companies in the West. To attend a gig at Madison Square Gardens in New York or the O2 Arena in London and hear English or American teenagers sing along with choruses in Korean is truly amazing.

Perhaps the biggest plus for the industry since the turn of the century has been the way American kids have taken to dancing. It was a long time coming. After decades of resistance, the USA finally succumbed to electronic dance music. The EDM that swept Europe thirty years took twenty of those years to reach North America. But now it truly has.

Huge gatherings of happy, uninhibited, young dancers – the DJs on stage worshipped like rock stars, lasers flooding the sky, dry ice flooding the dancers, everyone with their hands in the air. The European rave scene of the eighties is now a regular part of what's happening in America.

All across the USA, weekend dance festivals have become commonplace for young people. The biggest stars on stage are a mixed bunch, half from America, half from Europe – Skrillex, Marshmello, DJ Snake, David Guetta, Deadmau5, Martin Garrix – some just DJs, some musicians; some trying to re-create the original British subculture of the eighties, others presenting a show that's almost family entertainment, like Tiësto from Holland, who travels with a crew of thirty-five people and even has residencies in Vegas. There's nothing underground about this; a dance night out at one of his events is as mainstream as seeing *Cirque du Soleil*. Crowds of 30,000 are blasted by a thunderous beat that underpins music reminiscent of the movies – *Titanic* violins, *Avatar* tympani, *Psycho* string stabs, *Mulholland Drive* sex sighs, *Apocalypse Now* cluster bomb percussion. From this Tiësto earns an annual income of around $50 million – a happy man.

Dance, too, was the initial trigger for TikTok. Short, fun, crazy clips of new dances that kids watched, copied, amended, changed, videoed and uploaded back onto the app, continuing the chain process. But also continuing the switch to old music.

TikTokers are mainly young. Often they like the old hit songs their parents used to like; what they always disliked was the ancient imagery that went with it – artists in out-of-fashion clothes and videos that were ponderous and flowed too slowly. Now they make their own youthful imagery to accompany these songs and give them a new life. Some of the old songs featured in clips on TikTok are getting up to 100 million streams a day, and this causes a boom in the number of people then streaming them on Spotify and Apple. And once again, it's pushing old music over new.

As the recording industry hit the 2020s, it was showing an annual worldwide profit of $40 billion, with a further $30 billion generated by the global live music industry. Wall Street forecasts that those figures will more than double by 2030. And this is without taking into account China, the world's biggest music market, which could potentially double them again.

So where has the music industry got to?

Dance has become more popular than rock. Singles are again preferred to albums. Streaming has replaced downloading and CDs. And for anyone who wants to make their own record, the internet can be used to promote it to the world, provided a way can be found of attracting people to a streaming playlist where it can be heard. Which takes us back to the music industry's original conundrum: how to make people listen to a new tune long enough for it to stick in their minds.

The music industry, which once spent millions on radio pluggers and marketing campaigns now employs thousands of tech staff to try to penetrate and influence streaming-service playlists and artist-of-the-month selections. It pays teenage influencers huge amounts to dance to their latest releases and post videos of themselves on TikTok.

Plugging, bribing, buying influence, paying for plays, paying for kids to dance to new tunes – all of it is as intensive as it ever has been.

In 1930, music sociologist Dr Isaac Goldberg wrote, "Everything we ever sing or whistle is the end result of a huge plot involving thousands of dollars and thousands of organised agents... the efforts of organised pluggery."

Nearly a century later, nothing has changed.

ENDWORD

In 1966 I came into a business that was alive with excitement and optimism. I was one of a select group – the young managers, Brian Epstein, Andrew Loog Oldham, Robert Wace, and Kit Lambert – who'd taken over the UK's new pop groups – the Beatles, the Rolling Stones, The Who, the Kinks, the Yardbirds. We young managers were on fire. We hustled, and we were free. We weren't in any way associated; we weren't even friends, yet we knew each other from hanging out at the 'in' night clubs of the moment, the Ad Lib and the Scotch of St James. And despite differences between us, we found one thing in common – we all saw our principal job as going to war with the record company.

The first record company I ever went to was Decca in London in 1964. It was a six-storey building on the South Bank of the river at Lambeth. The inside was painted in the same colour olive green as government buildings – like the labour exchange or the tax office. With a gruff commissioner on the door, it was pure bureaucracy, the civil service of the music industry.

At Decca they didn't like visitors, but I managed to talk my way into seeing someone in A&R, a small mean-minded man who sat picking his nose while I played my record. It was a group I wanted to manage and I'd paid for them to make the recording. The man was a pedant, a killjoy. "It's dreadful!" he exclaimed. "The song's not memorable and the musicians don't catch the beat." Then, surprisingly, he agreed a deal. It was a very small one, but I was delighted – my first step into the music business. But if the record was as bad as he'd said it was, why did he give me a deal? And if it wasn't that bad, why had he said it was? I left the building thinking, "What a wanker!" And it was difficult ever after to think of A&R people in any other way.

When I took over the management of the Yardbirds I had to deal with EMI. There was an air of pomposity about the place. Artists were from the wrong class – they tended to cause problems. EMI preferred to deal with managers, especially if they were middle class and public school, and I fitted neatly into that category. The people in the business affairs department were extraordinarily pissed off when I told them I considered their contract with the Yardbirds to be invalid. They doubted I was right (and so did I), but they were afraid to challenge me in case they lost the group altogether, so they agreed to negotiate a new deal. In order to bypass the company's A&R department, I insisted the Yardbirds should produce their own records. I demanded the biggest advance any British record company had ever paid, £25,000, and the highest royalty, 12 per cent of retail. If I'd known anything about the music business, I would have known these demands were impossible, but I didn't. So I asked for them and got them. Knowing too much isn't always the great help people think it is.

To begin with I thought I'd passed my entrance exam to the music business with flying colours. I soon learned I'd failed. EMI had simply advanced the Yardbirds their own royalties, most of them already in the pipeline, and had included a host of tricky accounting clauses; for instance, the artist was only paid on 90 per cent of records sold (a hangover from the days of 78s, when records broke easily), and were not paid on 'over-pressings', although these were usually sold anyway. I asked the group's lawyer why he'd let these things pass. "If I told my clients not to sign unfair contracts they'd never get a deal."

Never mind! I'd learned the first golden rule of management – record companies are not to be trusted.

Certainly not the major record companies, which even today aren't run by young forward-thinking people; the people at the top are the same old faces who've been there for years, growing ever more wrinkled and clinging to overpaid jobs.

Being a musician was always poorly paid; being the star was what made you a fortune. And stars were the lucky ones. Not always the most talented; they were the ones who arrived at the right moment, were prepared to let the industry manipulate them, and had just enough talent to build on their moment of good fortune. And that's how it will be in the future.

New entrepreneurs will arrive on the scene with new ways of making money from music. New stars will arrive too, chosen for the same reasons they always were – talent, looks, and acquiescence with the system. Most likely they'll also be taken advantage of as before, that's simply the way of the business – new music, new stars, new hypes, new rip-offs. It should be accepted and enjoyed.

Some people take it a bit too seriously. When ex-Fugees singer Lauryn Hill walked out on her recording career in 2011, she wrote on her website, "I abandoned greed, corruption, and compromise."

She was wrong to be so dismissive. The business of popular music has always been a compromise between music on the one side and commercial interests on the other. To be 'true' artists in the purest sense of the word, singers and songwriters can go and sing in the garden. To make money from their music, they need to enter the music industry – a world of greed, corruption, self-interest and fun.

And what an excellent combination that's proved to be. Without it, half the songs we've known and loved during the last hundred years would never have been created in the first place.

Cast of Characters

50 Cent American rapper, and music entrepreneur

Abbado, Claudio Italian orchestral conductor and music director of La Scala opera house in Milan (1933–2014)

Aberbach, Jean Austrian-born American music publisher (1910–1992)

Aberbach, Julian Austrian-born American music publisher, brother of Jean Aberbach (1909–2004)

Abramson, Herbert Jazz record producer and one of the founders of Atlantic Records (1916–1999)

Abramson, Miriam Wife of Herbert Abramson, and one of the founders of Atlantic Records. Later the wife of Freddy Bienstock

Achilles Greek hero of the Trojan Wars

Acuff, Roy American country singer and music publisher in Nashville (1903–1992)

Ailey, Alvin American choreographer (1931–1989)

Albert, Morris Brazilian singer and songwriter

Alexander, Willard American booking agent (1908–1984)

Ali, Tariq British Pakistani writer, filmmaker and political activist

Alison, Mose American jazz and blues pianist

Allen, Sir Hugh English musician, academic, and administrator (1869–1946)

Alstyne, Egbert van American songwriter and pianist (1878–1951)

Anderson, G. K. American dancer who invented alternative 'Foxtrot'

Anderson, Mr Accountant at Leo Feist publishing company in the early 1900s

Andrews, Senator Charles O. Wartime American senator (1877–1946)

Antheil, George Avant-garde composer and arranger (1900–1959)

Arlen, Harold American composer and lyricist (1905–1986)

Armstrong, Lil *see Lil Hardin*

Armstrong, Louis Legendary American great of jazz trumpet, originally from New Orleans (1901–1971)

Asher, Dick Deputy President CBS Records International in the 1970s

Astaire, Fred American dancer and film star (1899–1987)

Autry, Gene American songwriter and singing star of cowboy movies (1907–1998)

Azoff, Irving American rock manager and record company executive

Bacharach, Burt American composer and record producer

Bailey, Pearl American jazz singer and actress (1918–1990)

Baker, Belle American singer and actress and Broadway star (1895–1957)

Baline, Issy *See Irving Berlin*

Barraud, Francis The artist who painted HMV's trademark of a dog listening to a gramophone (1856–1924)

Bart, Lionel British songwriter (1930–1999)

Bassey, Shirley Welsh singer now a DBE and known as Dame Shirley

Batchelor, Horace British entrepreneur who sold a system with which to win the football pools (1898–1977)

Bayes, Nora American vaudeville singer and recording artist (1880–1928)

Beck, Jeff British rock and blues guitarist

Beethoven, Ludwig van German classical composer of the eighteenth and nineteenth centuries (1770–1827)

Bell, Chichester Scottish inventor and partner of Charles Tainter (1848–1924)

Belolo, Henri French music producer and songwriter

Benjamin, Louis British head of Pye Records (1922–1994)

Bennett, Robert Russell Staff arranger at T. B. Harms c.1930 (1894–1981)

Bennett, Tony American popular singer

Berkeley, Busby Ground-breaking American dance choreographer for movies (1895–1976)

Berlin, Irving One of America's greatest writers of popular song in the twentieth century. Previously known as Issy Baline (1888–1989)

Berliner, Emile Inventor of the flat disc gramophone (1851–1929)

Berman, Pandro Temporary head of RKO film studio who commissioned movie *Top Hat* (1905–1996)

Bernadotte, Countess Swedish actress and philanthropist

Bernhardt, Sarah French stage actress in the later nineteenth and early twentieth centuries (1844–1923)

Bernstein, Louis New York music publisher in the early 1900s

Berry, Chuck American guitarist, singer and songwriter

Berry, Ken British record executive

Bertelsmann, Carl German who founded Bertelsmann printing company in 1835 and great-grandfather of Reinhard Mohn

Bicknell, Ed British manager of Dire Straits

Bieling, John Member of the American Quartet, a four piece singing group in the early twentieth century (1869–1948)

Bienstock, Freddy American music publisher who ran Elvis Presley Music (1923–2009)

Big Bopper, The J. P. Richardson, American disc jockey and recording artist (1930–1959)

CAST OF CHARACTERS

Black, Bill American rockabilly musician (1926–1965)

Blackwell, "Bumps" American bandleader, songwriter and record producer (1918–1985)

Block, Martin First American radio disc jockey (1903–1967)

Bodanzky, Artur Austrian-American orchestral conductor (1887–1939)

Bogart, Neil American record company executive, head of Casablanca Records (1943–1982)

Bolton, Guy British playwright and writer of stage musicals (1884–1979)

Boosey, John Head of Boosey publishing company in the late nineteenth century

Boosey, Thomas Cousin of William Boosey and head of Boosey Publishing Company in the early twentieth century

Boosey, William Head of Chappell publishing company in the early twentieth century, and adopted son of John Boosey

Booth, Harold Managing director of British publishing company Aschberg Hopwood and Crew in early part of twentieth century

Bornstein, Saul General manager of Irving Berlin Inc, and owner of Bourne Music Inc

Bostic, Earl American jazz and R&B alto sax player (1912–1965)

Boswell Sisters Three American sisters, Martha, Conee and Helvetia who formed a close harmony group successful in 1930s and 1940s

Bourgeois, Jeanne Real name of Mistinguett, French actress and singer (1875 1956)

Bowers, James F. President of the Aeolian Company, manufacturer of pianola rolls, in the late nineteenth and early twentieth centuries

Bowie, David British rock singer and songwriter

Boy George British pop singer, part of Culture Club

Bradford, Perry American composer, lyricist and music publisher (1893–1970)

Bradley, Josephine Irish-born British ballroom dancing champion (1893–1985)

Brahms, Johannes German classical composer and pianist (1833–1897)

Braun, David American attorney to music stars (1932–2013)

Breest, Gunther German record executive and classical music specialist

Bronfman, Edgar Canadian heir to the Seagram family fortune who bought MCA and PolyGram Record companies and founded Universal Music

Brown, Lew American songwriter (1893–1958)

Brown, Professor Eric British flying officer in Coastal Command c.1940s

Browne, Jackson American singer-songwriter

Brubeck, Dave American jazz pianist and composer (1920–2012)

Buck, Gene Second president of ASCAP and illustrator of sheet music (1885–1957)

Buckley, Tim American singer and musician (1947–1975)

Buffet, Bernard French expressionist painter (1928–1999)

Burke, Johnny American lyricist for popular songs (1908–1964)

Burke, Solomon American rhythm & blues singer (1940–2010)

Burlington Bertie One of the stage names adopted by Vesta Tilley when performing as a male impersonator in the early twentieth century

Burne-Jones, Edward British artist and designer (1833–1898)

Burton, Richard Welsh actor who married Elizabeth Taylor (1925–1984)

Burton, Sybil Welsh actress who married Richard Burton and became New York proprietress of 'Sybil's' nightclub in New York (1929–2013)

Butt, Dame Clara British opera singer in the late nineteenth century

Caesar, Irving American lyricist and theatre composer (1895–1996)

Cahn, Sammy American songwriter and co-founder of Leeds Music (1913–1993)

Calder, Clive South African-born businessman and music executive, co-founder of Zomba Records

Cantor, Eddie American comedian, dancer and popular singer (1892–1964)

Capone, Al American gangster (1899–1947)

Capote, Truman Waspish American novelist (1924–1984)

Capps, Frank Boss of Pathe Records pressing factory in New York in the 1920s

Carlisle, Kitty American singer and actress (1910–2007)

Carmichael, Hoagy American composer, lyricist, bandleader and pianist (1899–1981)

Carnegie, Andrew Scottish-American industrialist who developed the American steel industry in the late nineteenth century and became famous for his charitable works and the Carnegie Hall, named after him (1835–1919)

Carson, Fiddlin' John American country violinist (1868–1949)

Caruso, Enrico An Italian tenor, one of the all-time greats of opera and a pioneer of recording (1873–1921)

Caryll, Ivan Belgian-born songwriter involved in a number of George Edwardes' stage musicals in the early twentieth century (1861–1921)

Cash, Johnny American country singer-songwriter (1932–2003)

Casotto, Robert Original name of singer Bobby Darin

Castle, Irene One half of a husband-and-wife dance duo known as 'The Castles' in the early twentieth century (1893–1969)

Castle, Vernon One half of a husband-and-wife dance duo known as 'The Castles' in the early twentieth century (1887–1918)

Chappell, Samuel Founder of Chappell Music in the early nineteenth century

Chappell, Thomas Son of Samuel Chappell

Charles, Ray Blind American pianist and soul singer (1930–2004)

Checker, Chubby American pop singer

Cher American singing star and actress

Chess, Leonard Founder and co-owner of Chess Records (1917–1969)

Chess, Marshall Son of Philip Chess

Chess, Philip Founder and co-owner of Chess Records

Chevalier, Maurice French film star and singer (1888–1972)

Christie, Julie British actress and 1960s pop icon of Swinging London

Clapton, Eric British rock and blues guitarist

Clark, Alfred First chairman of EMI in the 1930s

Clark, Dick American radio and TV personality and businessman (1929–2012)

Clark, Petula British pop singer

Coburn, Charles British music hall singer and writer (1852–1945)

Cocteau, Jean French poet, novelist, artist, designer, playwright and film-maker (1889–1963)

Cohan, George M. American composer and theatrical producer in the early twentieth century (1878–1942)

Cohen, Sadie A character in one of Irving Berlin's songs, 'Sadie Salome Go Home'

Cohn, Nik British journalist, novelist, and music critic

Cole, Nat King American pianist and singer (1919–1965)

Collin, Matthew British author and music journalist

Collins, Arthur An American singer who recorded for Columbia c.1890 (1864–1933)

Collins, Lottie British music hall singer (1865–1910)

Combs, Sean "Puffy" American rapper, record producer and businessman

Condon, Eddie American jazz banjo player and bandleader (1905–1973)

Connor, Tommy British popular songwriter (1904–1993)

Conover, Willis American broadcaster and jazz producer for Voice of America radio station (1920–1996)

Cooper, Alice American rock singer and songwriter

Copas, Cowboy American country music singer (1913–1963)

Copland, Aaron American classical composer (1900–1990)

Cornyn, Stan Longtime American senior executive at Warner Group

Coward, Noël British playwright, composer, actor and singer (1899–1973)

Cowell, Simon English A&R executive, TV producer, entrepreneur and TV personality

Cramer, Johann Baptist British nineteenth-century classical composer and pianist (1771–1858)

Cros, Charles French inventor who conceived an idea for the phonograph (1842–1888)

Crosby, Bing American singer who invented style known as crooning (1903–1977)

Crosby, Bob American bandleader and singer (1913–1993)

Crow, Sheryl American folk-rock singer and songwriter

Crowley, Aleister British occultist, mystic, poet, mountaineer, and recreational drug experimenter (1875–1947)

Cukor, George Hollywood film director (1899–1983)

Dacre, Harry British music hall songwriter (1860–1922)

Dale, Alan Theatre critic for *The American* in the early twentieth century

Dalhart, Vernon Popular American singer and songwriter (1883–1948)

Daltrey, Roger British singer and songwriter with The Who

Darin, Bobby American pop singer (1936–1973)

David, Hal American lyricist (1921–2012)

David, Mack American lyric writer and elder brother of lyric writer Hal David (1912–1993)

Davies, Clara Mother of Ivor Novello (1861–1943)

Davis, Bette American film star (1908–1989)

Davis, Clive American head of CBS Records, New York

Davis, Miles American jazz trumpeter, composer and bandleader (1926–1991)

Davis Jr., Sammy American singer, entertainer, and tap dancer (1925–1990)

Davis, Tom British theatre producer in the early twentieth century

Day, David Founding partner in British music publisher Francis, Day & Hunter

Day, Doris American film actress and singer

de Frece, Lady The name Vesta Tilley adopted after her husband was knighted and she retired

de Frece, Walter Husband of Vesta Tilley (1870–1935)

De Koven, Reginald American music critic and composer of comic operas, early twentieth century (1859–1920)

de Martinville, Édouard-Léon Scott French near inventor of the phonograph (1817–1879)

de Reszke, Edward A tenor at the New York Metropolitan Opera House c.1900 (1853–1917)

de Sylva, Buddy American songwriter and record executive (1895–1950)

Dempsey, Jack American heavyweight boxing champion (1895–1983)

Denny, Jack American orchestra leader (1895–1950)

Deutch, Murray Vice-President United Artists Music, 1965

Diaz, Edgardo Panamanian-born Puerto Rican, manager of Menudo

Dietrich, Marlene German-born singer and film actress (1901–1992)

Dillingham, Charles American theatrical producer (1868–1934)

Dion, Celine French Canadian singer and entertainer

DiSipio, Fred American independent record producer in the 1980s

Disney, Walt Owner and founder of Walt Disney Studios (1901–1966)

DJ Kool Herc West Indian-born American hip hop DJ

Dodds, Johnny New Orleans jazz clarinettist who played with King Oliver's band in Chicago (1892–1940)

Dolly Sisters Hungarian twins Rosie and Jenny Deutsch, American vaudeville performers (b.1892, d Jenny 1941, Rosie 1970)

Domino, Fats American pianist and rhythm & blues singer

Donaldson, Walter American songwriter who wrote mostly for Irving Berlin Inc (1893–1947)

Donovan British pop/rock singer

Dorsey Brothers, The Joint bandleaders of 1930s band – Tommy Dorsey, trombone, and Jimmy Dorsey, sax.

Dorsey, Tommy American trombonist and bandleader (1905–1956)

Dowd, Tom American record producer for Atlantic Records (1925–2002)

Downes, Olin Music critic for New York Times during the 1920s (1886–1955)

Dr Dre American record producer, rapper and music entrepreneur

Draper, Simon Co-founder of Virgin Records together with Richard Branson in 1972

Dresser, Paul Partner in Howland Haviland, a New York music publisher at the end of the nineteenth century, and a successful songwriter

Dreyfus, Louis Brother of Max Dreyfus, partners in Harms Publishing Company and later in Chappell Music

Dreyfus, Max Brother of Louis Dreyfus, partners in Harms Publishing Company and later in Chappell Music (1874–1964)

Dubin, Al American composer of popular songs (1891–1945)

Dylan, Bob American rock singer

Eager, Vince British pop singer

Eastman, John American businessman and brother of Linda Eastman, who married Paul McCartney

Eastman, Lee American business man and attorney, father of Linda Eastman, who married Paul McCartney (1910–1991)

Edison, Thomas American inventor of the phonograph (1847–1931)

Edwardes, George British producer of stage musicals at the turn of the nineteenth century (1855–1913)

Elder, Bruce Canadian filmmaker and critic

Eldridge, Roy American jazz trumpet player (1911–1989)

Elgar, Sir Edward British classical composer (1857–1934)

Eliscu, Edward American lyricist (1902–1998)

Ellington, Duke American jazz pianist, arranger and orchestra leader (1899–1974)

Eltinge, Julian American stage, screen and vaudeville performer, a female impersonator (1881–1941)

Eminem American white rap artist

Epstein, Brian British manager of the Beatles (1934–1967)

Ertegun, Ahmet Turkish-born founder of Atlantic Records (1923–2006)

Ertegun, Nesuhi Turkish-born founder of Atlantic Records (1917–1989)

Fame, Georgie British keyboardist and singer

Fanning, Shawn American inventor of Napster

Feist, Leo New York music publisher in the early twentieth century (1869–1930)

Feist, Leo Son of original Leo Feist, founder of Feist Music (1911–1996)

Feldman, Bert British music publisher first part of twentieth century

Fifield, Jim British record executive and CEO of EMI from 1988 to 1998

Finkelstein, Herman ASCAP lawyer in the 1950s

Fisher, Eddie American entertainer, singer and film star (1928–2010)

Fisher, Fred German born American songwriter and music publisher (1875–1942)

Flynn, Errol Australian-born Hollywood film star (1909–1959)

Forbstein, Leo Composer and head of music Warner Bros studios (1892–1948)

Ford, Lena American lyric writer of the song 'Keep The Home Fires Burning' (1870–1918)

Foster, Stephen American writer of classic American songs in the mid-nineteenth century

Fox, Fred American music publisher and co-owner of Sam Fox Music

Fox, Harry American vaudeville performer and inventor of the 'Foxtrot' (1882–1959)

Fox, Harry Founder of mechanical collection society Harry Fox Agency in 1927

Frampton, Peter British guitarist, singer and songwriter

Francis, Connie American pop singer

Francis, Harry Founding partner in British music publisher Francis, Day & Hunter

Francis, William Founding partner in British music publisher Francis, Day & Hunter

Franconero, Concetta Original name of Connie Francis

Franklin, Aretha American gospel and soul singer

Freed, Alan Radio DJ who publicised the phrase rock 'n' roll (1921–1965)

Friedwald, Will American music critic and writer

Frohman, Charles American stage producer (1856–1915)

Fury, Billy British pop singer (1940–1983)

Gable, Clark American film star (1901–1960)

Gabler, Milt American record producer (1911–2001)

Gabriel, Peter British singer-songwriter, musician and founding member of rock group Genesis

Gaff, Billy British manager of Rod Stewart

Gaisberg, Fred The world's first A & R man (1873–1951)

Gaisberg, William Brother of HMV record producer Fred Gaisberg

Gamble, Kenny American record producer, worked with Leon Huff

Garbo, Greta Swedish film actress and recluse (1905–1990)

Garland, Judy American actress and singer (1922–1969)

Garrett, Sheryl British journalist

Geffen, David American record executive and film producer

Gelb, Peter American arts administrator and record executive

Gershwin, Ira American lyricist and younger brother of George Gershwin (1896–1983)

Genghis Khan Head of Mongol hordes that swept across middle Asia to Europe (1162–1227)

Gilbert, Fred British music hall songwriter

Gilbert, W. S. English librettist and writer of operettas with Arthur Sullivan

Gillespie, Dizzy American jazz trumpeter (1917–1993)

Gilman, Lawrence Music critic for *The Tribune* during the 1920s

Glew, Dave Head of distribution at Warner Music Group for twenty-five years

Glover, Henry American songwriter, arranger and record producer (1921–1991)

Godfrey, Arthur American radio and television broadcaster and host of TV show, *Talent Scouts* (1903–1983)

Goebbels, Joseph German's wartime Minister of Propaganda (1897–1945)

Goffin, Gerry American lyricist and co-writer with Carole King

Goldberg, Dr Isaac American writer, scholar, and musicologist (1888–1938)

Golden, Billy An American singer c.1890

Goldman, Albert American professor, author, sociologist and music critic (1928–1984)

Goldwater, Senator Barry American Senator and politician (1909–1998)

Good, Jack British TV producer

Goodman, Benny American clarinettist and bandleader (1909–1986)

Goodman, Fred American journalist and writer of biographies

Gordy, Berry American owner and head of Tamla Motown Records

Gore, Al American Senator and politician

Goring, Marius British stage and film actor (1912–1988)

Graham, Bill American rock concert promoter (1931–1991)

Graham, Roger Chicago music publisher in the early twentieth century

Granat, Mynna Irving Berlin's secretary

Grant, Peter British manager of Led Zeppelin (1935–1995)

Grasso, Francis American DJ who worked at 'the Sanctuary', a gay dance club in New York (1949–2001)

Green, Abel Editor of *Variety* magazine in 1920s and 1930s

Greenbank, Percy Writer of songs for George Edwardes' stage musicals in the early twentieth century

Greenfield, Howard Songwriting partner of Neil Sedaka

Grofé, Ferde Arranger for the Paul Whiteman Orchestra (1892–1972)

Grossman, Albert American rock manager (1926–1986)

Grubman, Allen American music lawyer who called himself 'the superpower attorney'

Gumbinsky, Aaron New York music publisher also known as Harry von Tilzer (1872–1946)

Guthrie, Arlo American folk singer and songwriter, son of Woody Guthrie

Guthrie, Woody American folk singer (1912–1967)

Haley, Bill White American singer who spread rock'n'roll around the world (1925–1981)

Hall, Owen Writer of songs for George Edwardes' stage musicals in the early twentieth century

Hallyday, Johnny French pop singer

Hammerstein, Oscar American composer of musicals and popular songs (1895–1960)

Hammond, John American record producer and writer and promoter of jazz (1910–1987)

Hampton, Lionel American jazz vibraphonist and bandleader (1908–2002)

Handel, George Frideric German-born British Baroque composer (1685–1759)

Hands, Guy British businessman and entrepreneur

Handy, W. C. American blues musician, composer, and academic, born in Alabama, known as 'The Father of the Blues' (1873–1958)

Hardin, Lil Jazz pianist from Memphis who migrated to Chicago where she met and married Louis Armstrong (1898–1971)

Harms, Tom Founder of New York publishing company T. B. Harms in the late nineteenth century

Harris, Charles K. American song writer and music publisher late 1800s

Harris, Sam Theatrical producer and partner with Irving Berlin in the Music Box theatre, New York (1872–1941)

Harrison, George British guitarist and songwriter (1943–2001)

Hart, Lorenz Lyric writing half of the songwriting duo Rodgers and Hart (1895–1943)

Harvey, Laurence Lithuanian born British film actor (1928–1973)

Hatch, Orrin American senator

Haviland, Frederick Partner in New York music publisher Howley Haviland

Hawkins, Coleman American jazz tenor sax player (1904–1969)

Heller, Jerry American hip hop record label owner and author

Henderson, Fletcher American jazz arranger, bandleader and pianist (1897–1952)

CAST OF CHARACTERS

Henderson, Ray American songwriter (1896–1970)

Hendrix, Jimi American guitarist, singer and songwriter (1942–1970)

Herbert, A. P. British humorist, playwright, novelist and lawyer (1890–1971)

Herman, Woody American clarinettist and bandleader (1913–1987)

Heston, Charlton American film and theatre actor (1923–2008)

Heymann, Klaus German entrepreneur and record executive

Hill, Lauryn American singer, once of the Fugees, latterly by herself

Hitler, Adolf Austrian-born German leader of the Nazi Party (1889–1945)

Hogan, Ernest Black songwriter and vaudeville artist in the late nineteenth century

Holiday, Billie American jazz and blues singer (1915–1959)

Holly, Buddy American country and rock 'n' roll singer (1936–1959)

Holmes à Court, Robert South African entrepreneur, businessman, asset-stripper (1937–1990)

Holmes, Sir Valentine Appointed by British government to oversee wartime committee into corruption at the BBC (1888–1956)

Holzman, Jac American record company executive

Hooker, John Lee American blues singer-songwriter and guitarist (1917–2001)

Hoover, J. Edgar First director of the Federal Bureau of Investigation of the US (1985–1972)

Hoover, President Herbert 31st President of the US (1874–1964)

Hopkin, Mary Welsh folk singer who had a hit single on Beatles' Apple label

Horne, Lena American black jazz singer (1917–2010)

Horowitz, Vladimir American classical pianist and composer (1903–1989)

Horsky, Charles American lawyer who prosecuted at Nuremberg trials

Howley, Patrick Partner in New York music publisher Howley Haviland

Howlin' Wolf American blues singer and guitarist and harmonica player (1910–1976)

Huff, Leon American record producer, worked with Kenny Gamble

Hunt, Alberta Jazz singer from Memphis who ran away to Chicago aged eleven (1895–1984)

Hunter, Meredith Member of audience at Altamont Concert who appeared to point a gun at Mick Jagger (1951–1969)

Hylton, Jack British bandleader and impresario (1892–1965)

Ibsen, Henrik Nineteenth-century Norwegian playwright

Ice Cube American hip hop artist, songwriter, record producer and actor

Ice-T American rap artist and actor

Ifield, Frank British pop singer and yodeller

Isgro, Joe American independent record producer in the 1980s

Iskowitz, Isidore Original name of Eddie Cantor

Ja Rule American rapper, singer and actor

Jackson, Michael Black American singer-songwriter, dancer and businessman, known as 'The King of Pop' (1958–2009)

Jackson, Tony New Orleans jazz pianist who migrated to Chicago (1876–1921)

Jagger, Bianca Nicaraguan wife of Mick Jagger

Jagger, Mick British rock singer

James, Clive Australian author, critic, broadcaster, poet, translator and memoirist

James, Dick British music publisher (1920–1986)

James, Harry American trumpet player and bandleader (1916–1983)

Jamieson, Bob American record executive at RCA Records who signed 'N Sync

Jay Z American rapper and music entrepreneur

Jennings, Humphrey English documentary film maker (1907–1950)

John, Elton British rock singer and songwriter

Johnson, Eldridge Engineer at Berliner Records who became first head of Victor Records (1867–1945)

Johnson, James P. American jazz pianist and composer (1894–1955)

Johnson, James Weldon American author, educator, lawyer, diplomat, songwriter, and early civil rights activist (1871–1938)

Jolson, Al American blackface singer, actor and film star (1886–1950)

Jones, Grandpa American singer, banjo and guitar player (1913–1998)

Jones, Isham American bandleader and saxophonist (1894–1956)

Jones, John Paul British bass player and songwriter with Led Zeppelin

Jones, Sidney Writer of songs for George Edwardes' stage musicals early twentieth century

Joplin, Scott Ragtime pianist and composer successful in the 1890s (c1867–1917)

Jordan, Louis American songwriter and bandleader (1908–1975)

Joy, Georgie American music co-owner of Santly-Joy music publishing company

Judge, Jack Writer of First World War hit 'It's A Long Way To Tipperary' (1872–1938)

Jules, Judge British dance DJ and broadcaster

Kahn, Gus American songwriter and lyricist, born in Germany (1886–1941)

Kalmar, Bert American lyricist (1884–1947)

Kaplan, Saul American songwriter and co-founder of Leeds Music (1912–1997)

Kapp, Jack American talent scout for Brunswick Records and founding CEO of American Decca (1901–1945)

Kaye, Sydney American attorney who conceived and founded BMI, Broadcast Musical Industries

Kelly, Chris New Orleans trumpeter and bandleader in the late nineteenth and early twentieth centuries

CAST OF CHARACTERS

Kennedy, Jackie Wife of President Kennedy, and then of Onassis, Greece's richest man (1929–1994)

Kent, Tommy German pop singer

Kern, Jerome Celebrated twentieth-century American composer of popular songs (1885–1945)

King Edward VII of Great Britain (1841–1910)

King George V of Great Britain (1865–1936)

King George VI of Great Britain (1895–1952)

King Norodom Sihanouk of Cambodia, ruled from 1941 to 1955 and from 1993 to 2004

King, B. B. American blues musician, singer, songwriter, and guitarist

King, Carole American pop singer, pianist and songwriter

King, Pee Wee American country music writer and bandleader (1914–2000)

Kirshner, Don American music entrepreneur and publisher (1934–2011)

Kitagawa, Johnny Japanese businessman and creator of boy groups known as Johnnies

Klein, Allen American businessman and music entrepreneur (1931–2009)

Klein, Carol Original name of Carole King

Knight, Gladys American soul singer

Koppelman, Charles American musician, music producer and music publisher

Korngold, Erich Wolfgang Austrian romantic music composer for films (1897–1957)

Lambert, Constant British composer and conductor (1905–1951)

Lambert, Kit British manager of The Who (1935–1981)

Lane, Frankie American pop singer (1913–2007)

Lange, Mutt Zambian-born British record producer

Lardner, Ring American sports journalist (1885–1933)

Laska, Edward American lyricist and music publisher (1894–1959)

Lauder, Harry, Sir A Scottish music hall artist and songwriter (1870–1950)

Lee, Peggy American popular singer (1920–2002)

Legrand, Emmanuel French music journalist and magazine editor

Lehar, Franz Austro-Hungarian composer of operettas (1870–1948)

Leiber, Jerry Part of songwriting team of Leiber and Stoller (1933–2011)

Leip, Hans German novelist and poet (1893–1983)

Lengsfelder, Hans American lawyer who represented music publishers 1950s

Lennon, John British singer, musician and songwriter (1940–1980)

Lennox, Annie Scottish pop singer, one of the Eurythmics

Levy, Alain French record executive

Levy, Lou American music publisher, founder of Leeds Music (1912–1995)

Levy, Morris American music industry executive (1927–1990)

Lewis, Jerry Lee American rock 'n' roll pianist and singer

Lewis, Sir Edward Owner and founder of Decca Records (1900–1980)

Lewis, Ted Blackfaced white American bandleader and clarinettist (1890–1971)

Libbey, John Aldrich American tenor in the late 1800s

Liberace American pianist, singer and entertainer (1919–1987)

Lieberson, Goddard British head of Columbia Records, New York, in 1940s and 1950s (1911–1977)

Lil Wayne American hip hop DJ and rapper

Lippincott, Jesse H. American business man who bought rights to first gramophones and phonographs

Little Richard Early and outrageous rock 'n' roll singer

Little Tony Italian pop singer (1941–2013)

Lloyd, Marie English music hall singer and comedienne (1870–1922)

Lockwood, Joe British head of EMI Records (1904–1991)

Loesser, Frank American composer and lyric writer of musicals (1910–1969)

Lombardo, Guy American bandleader and violinist (1902–1977)

Lopez, Jennifer American singer, dancer, and TV personality

Lunceford, Jimmy American bandleader (1902–1947)

Lunsford, Orville American rhythm & blues singer (1926–2010)

Lymon, Frankie American rock 'n' roll singer (1942–1968)

McCarthy, Joseph American Senator besotted with rooting out communists in US society (1908–1957)

McCartney, Linda American daughter of Lee Eastman and wife of Paul McCartney (1941–1998)

McCartney, Paul British singer, musician and songwriter

McCormack, John Irish operatic tenor (1884–1945)

McCoy, Van American musician, record producer, and songwriter (1940–1979)

McHugh, Jimmy American composer of popular songs (1894–1969)

Mack, Cecil American composer, lyricist and music publisher (1874–1944)

McKenzie, Scott American pop/rock singer and songwriter (1939–2012)

MacLaine, Shirley American theatre and film actress, singer and dancer

McLaren, Malcolm British entrepreneur who managed the Sex Pistols (1946–2010)

McNamara, Mary TV critic for the Los Angeles Times

McPartland, Jimmy White American jazz cornet player (1907–1991)

McRae, George American soul singer

Madonna Hugely successful American singer-songwriter, known for her ability at self-promotion and involvement in social issues

Maharishi, The Maharishi Mahesh, Yogi teacher of transcendental meditation (1918–2008)

CAST OF CHARACTERS

Mailer, Norman American novelist, journalist and playwright (1923–2007)

Maitland, Mike American head of Warner Bros-Seven Arts

Mann, William Music critic for *The Times* newspaper (1924–1989)

Manone, Wingy American jazz trumpeter, bandleader and singer (1900–1982)

Marcus, Greil American author and music journalist

Marks, Edward B. New York songwriter, music publisher and author

Marks, Herbie Son of American music publisher Edward B. Marks

Marsh, Dave American music writer and journalist

Martin, George British record producer

Martin, Ricky Puerto Rican-born American pop singer originally in the group Menudo

Martino, Al American popular crooner (1927–2009)

Marvin, Johnny American popular singer and ukulele virtuoso in the 1920s and 1930s

Marx, Jack Australian music writer and critic

Marx, Karl German philosopher and historian (1818–1883)

Maugham, Somerset British playwright and novelist (1874–1965)

Maurice, Peter British music publisher, founder of Peter Maurice Music

Maxwell, Elsa American gossip columnist, songwriter and professional hostess (1883–1963)

Maxwell, George British music publisher in New York in late nineteenth and early twentieth centuries who became the first head of the American Society of Composers and Authors

Mendl, Hugh Son of Decca's first chairman and later head of record production (1919–2008)

Mendl, Sigismund Ferdinand British lawyer and MP and first chairman of Decca Records (1866–1945)

Merrill, Bob American writer of popular songs (1921–1998)

Messier, Jean Paul French businessman and entrepreneur

Meyer, Joe American songwriter and lyricist (1894–1987)

Meyer, Max A close friend of music publisher Isidore Witmark

Midler, Bette American singer-songwriter and actress

Miles, Lizzie New Orleans blues singer who emigrated to Chicago (1895–1963)

Mills Brothers, The Four singing brothers from Ohio, US who made more than 2,000 recordings between 1930 and 1970

Mills, Claude President of Music Publishers' Protective Association

Mills, Herbert One of the four Mills brothers (1912–1989)

Minogue, Kylie Australian female pop singer

Mistinguett French cabaret artist, actress and singer, reputedly the best-paid female entertainer in the world of her time (1875–1956)

Mitchell, Guy American pop singer (1927–1999)

Mitchell, Joni Canadian singer-songwriter

Mogull, Artie American music entrepreneur and publisher (1927–2004)

Mohn, Reinhard German founder of Bertelsmann Music Group

Monckton, Lionel Writer of songs for George Edwardes' stage musicals in the early twentieth century

Monckton, Sir John Braddick Town Clerk of London in the late nineteenth century

Monk, Thelonius American jazz pianist (1917–1982)

Monro, Matt British pop singer (1930–1985)

Monroe, Marilyn Iconic American actress and singer, wife of playwright Arthur Miller (1926–1962)

Moon, Keith British drummer with The Who (1946–1978)

Mooney, Steve Personal assistant to Lou Pearlman during time he managed Backstreet Boys and 'N Sync

Moore, Gerald British concert pianist and accompanist (1899–1987)

Moore, Scotty American jazz and country guitarist

Morali, Jacques French author, songwriter and music publisher (1947–1991)

Morita, Akio Founder and original owner of Sony Coporation (1921–1999)

Moroder, Giorgio Italian record producer who did much to popularise the four-to-the-floor bass drum style of disco

Morris, Buddy Son of Warner's overseas sales executive c.1930

Morris, Doug American songwriter who became record company executive

Morrison, Van Northern Irish rock singer and songwriter

Morton, Jelly Roll American ragtime and jazz pianist (1890–1941)

Moten, Bennie American jazz pianist and bandleader (1894–1935)

Mottola, Tommy American rock manager brought into CBS Records, who then took over as president

Murray, Billy Member of the American Quartet, a four piece singing group in the early twentieth century and later a solo recording artist and performer (1877–1944)

Murray, Charles Shaar British music journalist and broadcaster

Murray, Mitch British songwriter

Nasmyth, Peter British journalist

Nathan, Syd Founder and owner of King Records (1904–1968)

Nelson, Mrs D. Head of dance music at the BBC during the Second World War

Nevins, Al American musician and songwriter and business partner of Don Kirshner (1915–1965)

Newman, Alfred Composer and head of music United Artists Studios (1901–1970)

Noel, Terry First club DJ to play music from records in a continuous dancing format, at Sybil's nightclub in New York

Norworth, Jack American vaudeville singer and songwriter (1879–1959)

Novello, Ivor British composer, songwriter, and writer of stage musicals (1893–1951)

Nyro, Laura American pianist, singer and songwriter (1947–1997)

O'Farrell, Talbot Popular British singer and actor in 1920s and 1930s (1880–1950)

Oberon, Merle Anglo-Indian actress, who moved from British films to Hollywood (1911–1979)

Oberstein, Maurice American head of British CBS in the 1970s and 1980s, and PolyGram UK in the 1990s (1928–2001)

Oblinski, Prince Serge Russian prince-cum-gigolo-cum-toyboy of the 1960s

Ocean, Billy First British black pop singer to have success in the US

Ohga, Norio Chairman of Sony Corporation (1930–2011)

Oldham, Andrew British manager of the Rolling Stones

Oliver, King New Orleans jazz cornettist and bandleader who made his home in Chicago (1881–1938)

Ono, Yoko Japanese avant-garde artist

Ostin, Mo American executive at Warner Music Group

Owen, William Started The Gramophone Company, which later became EMI

Page, Jimmy British rock guitarist and songwriter

Page, Patti American pop singer (1927–2013)

Paley, William American, principal shareholder and CEO of Columbia Broadcasting System (1901–1990)

Park, Phil Pseudonym for American writer of lyric for 'Lili Marlene', actually Mack David

Parker, Charlie American jazz alto sax player (1920–1955)

Parker, Colonel Dutch-born manager of Elvis Presley (1909–1997)

Parker, Dorothy American poet, short story writer, critic, wit and satirist (1893–1967)

Parnes, Larry British pop manager (1929–1989)

Parry, Sir Hubert British composer and teacher of music (1848–1919)

Passaro, Alan Hell's Angel member who stabbed Meredith Hunter at Altamont concert (1948–1985)

Pathé, Charles One of two French brothers who founded Pathé Records

Pathé, Émile One of two French brothers who founded Pathé Records

Paxton, Tom American folk singer

Payne, Jack British bandleader (1899–1969)

Pearlman, Lou American impresario and manager of Backstreet Boys and 'N Sync

Peer, Ralph American record company executive, talent scout, and music publisher (1892–1960)

Perkins, Carl American country and rock 'n' roll singer and songwriter (1932–1998)

Peters and Lee British folk/pop singing duo comprising Lennie Peters (1931–1992) and Dianne Lee

Peterson, Oscar Canadian jazz pianist (1925–2007)

Petrillo, James Caesar Head of the American Federation of Musicians during the Second World War (1892–1984)

Petty, Norman American record producer and musician (1927–1984)

Phillips, David J. At different times, journalist, equity analyst, contributor to *Forbes* magazine, editor at YCharts, reporter for CBS News Interactive

Phillips, Sam Memphis record producer credited with discovering Elvis Presley (1923–2003)

Piron, A.J. New Orleans jazz violinist and music publisher (1888–1943)

Plant, Robert British singer and songwriter with Led Zeppelin

Platz, David German-born British music publisher (1929–1994)

Pomus, Doc American popular songwriter (1925–1991)

Porter, Cole American popular songwriter, composer and lyricist (1891–1964)

Prado, Perez Cuban bandleader and composer (1916–1989)

Presley, Elvis American rock 'n' roll singer and actor (1935–1977)

Prince, Peter British A&R man at Pye Records in the 1960s

Provenzano, John A. New Orleans musician in the late nineteenth and early twentieth centuries

Puccini, Giacomo Italian composer of grand opera (1858–1924)

Puente, Tito Puerto Rican Latin jazz bandleader and composer (1923–2000)

Puff Daddy Alternative name for Sean Combs

Queen Mary of Teck wife of King George V of Britain (1867–1953)

Queen Victoria of Great Britain (1819–1901)

Rampling, Danny British DJ and club owner

Randle, Bill An American DJ, lawyer and university professor. In the 1950s *Time* magazine called him the top DJ in America (1923–2004)

Ray, Johnnie American pop singer (1927–1990)

Remick, Jerome H. Detroit music publisher (1867–1931)

Reynolds, Debbie American pop singer and film star

Richard, Cliff British pop singer

Richie, Lionel American pop singer

Robbins, Jack American music publisher founder of Robbins Music, in the first part of the twentieth century

Rodgers, Jimmie American country singer and yodeler (1897–1933)

Rodgers, Richard Melody writing half of the songwriting duo Rodgers and Hart (1902–1979)

Rogers, Ginger American dance and film star (1911–1995)

Romberg, Sigmund Austro-Hungarian composer resident in USA (1887–1951)

Rommel, Field Marshal German Field Marshal during Second World War (1891–1944)

Ronstadt, Linda American country rock singer and songwriter

Rose, Billy American composer of popular songs (1899–1966)

Rose, Fred American songwriter and music publisher in Nashville (1898–1954)

Ross, Adam Writer of songs for George Edwardes' stage musicals in the early twentieth century

Ross, Steve American head of Warner Music Group (1927–1992)

Roth, David Lee American rock singer and songwriter

Rotten, Johnny British lead singer with the Sex Pistols and then PiL

Roussos, Demis Greek popular singer

Rubens, Paul Writer of songs for George Edwardes' stage musicals early twentieth century

Ruby, Harry American composer of popular songs (1895–1974)

Rushing, Jimmy American blues singer with Count Basie's band (1901–1972)

Russell, Henry Robin Ian, 14th Duke of Bedford British peer and TV personality (1940–2003)

Sanders, Joseph Emile Berliner's nephew

Sarnoff, David Belorussian-born American, principal shareholder and CEO of NBC and RCA (1891–1971)

Sayer, Henry J. American music publisher in the early twentieth century

Schein, Harvey American record executive who took over the running of PolyGram America at the end of the 1970s

Schultze, Norbert German songwriter and composer of film music (1911–2002)

Schwartz, Arthur American composer and film producer (1900–1984)

Scully, Rock American manager of the Grateful Dead

Seaman, Frank Emile Berliner's head of marketing, who turned against him and tried to steal his copyright

Sedaka, Neil American pop singer and songwriter

Selvin, Ben American bandleader, arranger and record producer (1898–1980)

Sembrich, Marcella A soprano at the New York Metropolitan Opera House c.1900

Shakespeare, William British playwright (1564–1616)

Shakur, Tupac American rapper and actor (1971–1996)

Shaw, Sandie British pop singer

Shepard, Burt A British music hall artist c.1890

Shilkret, Nathaniel Composer, arranger, conductor and record producer, head of Victor Records record production division (1889–1982)

Shubert, Jacob One of the three Shubert brothers, American theatrical producers in the first half of the twentieth century (c.1879–1963)

Shubert, Lee One of the three Shubert brothers, American theatrical producers in the first half of the twentieth century (1871–1953)

Shubert, Sam One of the three Shubert brothers, American theatrical producers in the first half of the twentieth century (1878–1905)

Shuman, Mort American pianist and popular songwriter (1936–1991)

Silver, Roy American small-time agent

Silvester, Victor British bandleader famous for playing dance numbers at the strictly correct tempo (1900–1978)

Simon, Paul American singer and songwriter

Simon, Ralph South African co-founder of Zomba Records

Sinatra, Frank American singer and film actor (1915–1998)

Singleton, Zutty New Orleans jazz drummer who migrated to Chicago (1989–1975)

Smalls, Biggie American rapper also known as The Notorious B.I.G. (1972–1997)

Smith, Bessie American blues singer (1894–1937)

Smith, Charles Edward American jazz historian

Smith, Joe American executive at Warner Music Group

Smith, Mamie American dancer, blues singer and vaudeville performer (1883–1946)

Smith, Mike British record producer

Smith, Trixie American blues singer and vaudeville artist (1895–1943)

Smith, Whispering Jack Popular American baritone singer (1898–1950)

Snyder, Ted Partner in the New York publishing firm of Waterson Snyder in the early twentieth century (1881–1965)

Solomon, Phil Irish businessman and owner of Radio Caroline (1924–2011)

Sousa, John Philip Nineteenth-century American composer and leader of wind band (1854–1932)

Spanier, Muggsy American white jazz trumpeter (1901–1967)

Spears, Britney American pop singer

Spector, Phil American record producer

Spigelgass, Leonard American film producer and screenwriter (1908–1985)

Springfield, Dusty British pop singer (1939–1999)

Stafford, Jo American pop singer (1917–2008)

Stamper, Dave American songwriter (1883–1963)

Starr, Ringo British drummer

Steele, Tommy British pop singer

Stein, Seymour American record label owner and music entrepreneur

Steiner, Max Composer and head of music RKO studios (1888–1971)

Sterling, Sir Louis American who became head of Columbia Records UK in 1913, and later of EMI Records in 1931 (1878–1958)

Stern, Joseph American songwriter and music publisher in the early twentieth century

Stewart, Mike President of United Artists Music in 1965

Stewart, Rod British rock singer

Stigwood, Robert Australian music entrepreneur and manager of the Bee Gees

Stills, Stephen American rock musician and songwriter

Stokowski, Leopold British orchestral conductor and composer (1882–1977)

Strange, Steve Welsh pop singer

Stravinsky, Igor Russian-born classical composer and pianist (1882–1971)

Strayhorn, Billy Principal music arranger and composer for Duke Ellington Band (1915–1967)

Streep, Meryl American actress of theatre, television, and film

Sullivan, Arthur English composer and writer of operettas with W. S. Gilbert (1842–1900)

Summer, Donna American singer who helped launch disco music (1948–2012)

Swaggart, Jimmy American TV evangelist

Tabrar, Joseph English music hall singer and songwriter

Tainter, Charles Sumner American scientist and inventor of the wax cylinder phonograph (1854–1940)

Talbot, Howard Writer of songs for George Edwardes' stage musicals in the early twentieth century

Tanguay, Eva Canadian-born vaudeville artist of huge popularity in the US at the beginning of the twentieth century (1878–1947)

Taupin, Bernie British lyric writer, mostly with Elton John

Taylor, Deems Music critic for *The World* during the 1920s

Taylor, Elizabeth British actress who became one of Hollywood's greatest stars (1932–2011)

Taylor, James American rock singer and songwriter

Tex, Joe American rhythm & blues singer and musician (1935–1982)

Thomas, J. Parnell Wartime American congressman (1895–1970)

Thornton, Big Mama American rhythm & blues singer (1926–1984)

Tiffany American pop singer

Tilley, Vesta English male impersonator prominent in music hall, known mostly as 'Burlington Bertie' (1864–1952)

Tisch, Laurence American businessman who bought CBS (1923–2003)

Toch, Ernst Austrian composer of classical and film music (1887–1964)

Townshend, Pete British rock guitarist with The Who

Tucker, Sophie Russian émigré blues singer known as 'The Last Of The Red Hot Mammas' (1886–1966)

Turner, Big Joe American blues singer with Count Basie's band (1911–1985)

Usher American singer, songwriter and dancer

Valens, Ritchie American country and rock 'n' roll singer and songwriter (1941–1959)

Valentine, Dickie British pop singer (1929–1971)

Vallée, Rudy American megaphone crooner and bandleader (1901–1986)

Van Heusen, Jimmy American composer of popular songs (1913–1990)

Vanderbilt, Henry American railroad millionaire (1921–1887)

Vapnick, Richard The original name of Dick James

Vaughan, Frankie British pop singer (1928–1999)

Victoria, Vesta English music hall singer (1873–1951)

Vincent, Gene American rock 'n' roll singer (1935–1971)

von Siegel, Ralph Appointed by Hitler to oversee German music industry during Second World War

von Tilzer, Albert American songwriter and younger brother of music publisher Harry von Tilzner (1878–1956)

von Tilzer, Harry New York music publisher in the late nineteenth and early twentieth centuries (1872–1946)

Walker, T-Bone American rhythm & blues musician and songwriter (1910–1975)

Wallace, Mike American newsreader and journalist for CBS (1918–2012)

Waller, Fats American jazz pianist, songwriter and entertainer (1904–1943)

Walters, Ethel Black American blues, jazz and gospel vocalist, and actress (1896–1977)

Ward, Ted Australian songwriter c.1930

Warner, Harry Polish-born American co-founder of Warner Bros (1881–1958)

Warner, Lou Jack Warner's son, Harry Warner's nephew

Warren, Harry American lyricist and composer of popular songs (1893–1981)

Washington, Dinah American jazz singer and pianist (1924–1963)

Wasserman, Lew American talent agent and studio executive (1913–2002)

Waterman, Pete British DJ, record producer, songwriter and TV personality

Waters, Muddy American blues musician considered 'father of Chicago Blues' (1913–1983)

Waterson, Henry Partner in the New York publishing firm of Waterson Snyder, in the early twentieth century

Watson, Stuart British music executive who moved to Asia and specialised in promotion there for Western acts

Wayne, Artie Record producer, songwriter and blogger

Wayne, John American tough-guy film actor (1907–1979)

Weatherly, Fred British lawyer and songwriter of 'Danny Boy' (1848–1929)

Weiss, Nat American music business attorney in 1970s and 1980s

Wells, Mary American pop-soul singer (1943–1992)

West, Mae American actress, singer and playwright (1893–1980)

CAST OF CHARACTERS

Wexler, Jerry Record producer at Atlantic Records (1917–2008)

White, Barry Gravel-voiced American soul recording star and songwriter (1944–2003)

Whiteman, Paul American orchestra leader known as 'The King of Jazz' (1890–1967)

Whitfield, David British pop singer (1926–1980)

Whitman, Slim American country and western singer (1923–2013)

Wickham, Vicki Producer of *Ready Steady Go!* and manager of Dusty Springfield

Wilde, Marty British pop singer

Wilkinson, Jimmy Musician from Pee Wee King's band in the 1950s and 1960s

Williams, Bert Black American vaudeville entertainer, the biggest selling black recording artist in the US at the time (1872–1922)

Williams, Clarence American pianist, composer and music publisher, originally from New Orleans (1893–1965)

Williams, Hank American country and western singer and songwriter (1923–1953)

Williams, Robbie British solo pop singer and songwriter who started with pop group Take That

Williams, Tennessee American playwright (1911–1983)

Wilson, Jack American stockbroker who became Noël Coward's lover and manager

Wilson, Jackie American soul singer (1934–1984)

Wilson, Tom Black American record producer mainly of white folk-rock groups (1931–1978)

Winslow, Max Senior manager at the publishing company of Waterson Snyder, New York, in the early part of the twentieth century

Winters, Shelley American film, radio and television actress (1920–2006)

Winwood, Stevie British rock musician and songwriter

Witmark, Isidore Founder of Witmark & Sons a New York music publishing company in the late nineteenth century

Wodehouse, P.G. British author and songwriter (1881–1975)

Wolfe, Tom American author and journalist

Wonder, Stevie Blind American pianist, singer and songwriter

Wood, Haydn British composer and violinist (1882–1959)

Wood, L. G. Salesman at EMI in the 1930s, later CEO of company

Wood, Major-General American general during the First World War

Wooding, Sam Conductor of all black revue *Chocolate Kiddies* by Duke Ellington in the 1920s

Woolworth, Frank Founder and owner of Woolworth stores (1852–1919)

Wright, Lawrence British songwriter and music publisher (1888–1964)

Wyman, Bill British bass player and songwriter with the Rolling Stones

Yetnikoff, Walter President CBS Records International

Yoelson, Asa Original name of Al Jolson

Youmans, Vincent American popular theatre composer (1898–1946)

Young, Neil Canadian rock musician and songwriter

Zappa, Frank American musician, songwriter, record producer, and rock group leader (1940–1993)

Zavaroni, Lena Scottish pop singer and TV host (1963–1999)

Ziegfeld, Florenz American theatrical producer renown for his Ziegfeld Follies, a series of musical shows on Broadway (1867–1932)

zu Lowenstein, Prince Rupert Mallorcan-born British business manager of the Rolling Stones from 1968 to 2007

Songs in chapter titles

1 Ta-ra-ra-boom-de-ay (1850–1880)
Writers: Unknown. Originally credited to Henry Sayers who later admitted he
hadn't written it but had heard it performed in the 1880s by a black singer, Mama
Lou, in a well-known brothel in St Louis
1st publisher: Henry J. Sayers

2 Around and Around (1958)
Writer: Chuck Berry
1st publisher: Arc Music
1st recording: Chuck Berry
Record label: Chess

3 The Song is You (1932)
Writers: Jerome Kern and Oscar Hammerstein
1st publisher: T. B. Harms/Warner
Composed by Kern and Hammerstein for the show *Music in the Air* in 1932.

4 Give My Regards to Broadway (1904)
Writer: George M. Cohan
Written by George M. Cohan for his musical *Little Johnny Jones*, first performed
on Broadway in 1904.
1st published by: F. A. Mills

5 Alexander's Ragtime Band (1911)
Writer: Irving Berlin

6 Stardust (1927)
Writer: Hoagy Carmichael
1st recording: Hoagy Carmichael & his Pals, on Gennett Records

7 The Winner Takes it All (1980)
Writers: Benny Andersson and Bjorn Ulvaeus
1st recording: Abba on Polar Records, Sweden

8 Pennies from Heaven (1936)
Writers: Arthur Johnston and Johnny Burke
1st recordings: Bing Crosby, Billie Holliday

9 Pack up your Troubles (1915)
Writers: George Henry Powell and Felix Powell
The Powell brothers rescued the song from a pile of their reject songs and re-scored it to win a wartime competition for a marching song.

10 Cheek to Cheek (1935)
Writer: Irving Berlin
Written for the Fred Astaire/Ginger Rogers movie *Top Hat*.

11 Prohibition Blues (1919)
Writer: Ring Lardner, but jointly credited to Nora Bayes in return for promoting it by making the first recording.

12 I Got Rhythm (1930)
Writers: George and Ira Gershwin
Originally written as a slow song for the musical *Treasure Girl* (1928), it wasn't a success. But re-jigged at a faster tempo and sung by Ethel Merman in the Broadway musical *Treasure Girl* (1930), it became a hit.

13 On the Radio (1979)
Writers: Giorgio Moroder and Donna Summer
Written for the soundtrack of the film *Foxes*, it was released as a single by Donna Summer in 1980 and became her tenth consecutive top ten American hit.

14 Don't Trust Nobody (2013)
Writer: DJ Mustard
Recorded by DJ Mustard, featuring Killa Kam.

15 Let's Do It (1928)
Writer: Cole Porter
Written for the Broadway musical *Paris*, starring French chanteuse Irène Bordoni.

16 Brother Can You Spare A Dime? (1932)

Writers: Yip Harburg and Jay Gorney

A song from the musical *Americana*. The tune is a Jewish-Russian lullaby sung to Gorney by his mother. It was thought to be anti-capitalist and Republican politicians tried to have it banned from radio.

17 Same Old Song and Dance (1974)

Writers: Stephen Tyler and Joe Perry

1st recording: Aerosmith

The principal single from Aerosmith's album *Get Your Wings*.

18 Set 'Em Up Joe (1988)

Writers: Verne Gosdin, Buddy Cannon, Dean Dillon, Hank Cochran

Number 1 Country single from Verne Gosdin's album *Chiseled in Stone*.

19 Heard It All Before (2001)

Writers: Michael Flowers, Sunshine Anderson, Anthony Hamilton, Ricky Elliot

Number 1 Hip hop single from Sunshine Anderson's album *Your Woman*.

20 Trouble in Mind (1924)

Writers: Richard M. Jones

1st recorded: 1924 by Thelma La Vizzo with the composer as accompanist.

21 New World Coming (1970)

Writers: Barry Mann and Cynthia Weil

Written for Mama Cass as a single after she left the Mamas and the Papas.

22 She Wears Red Feathers (1952)

Writer: Bob Merrill

Recorded by US singer Guy Mitchell it reached Number 1 in the UK chart, but not in the US.

23 Brothers in Arms (1985)

Writer: Mark Knopfler

Title track and closing song from Dire Straits *Brothers In Arms* album.

24 Hound Dog (1952)

Writers: Jerry Leiber and Mike Stoller

Recorded first by Big Mama Thornton and released as a single on Peacock Records, it was Thornton's only hit single, then was later a Number 1 for Elvis Presley.

25 American Pie (1971)

Writer: Don McLean

Single from McLean's *American Pie* album. The song is about the plane crash that killed Buddy Holly.

26 Hallelujah (1984)

Writer: Leonard Cohen

Song appeared on his album *Various Positions* but took two cover versions by other people before it achieved real success – John Cale, and then Jeff Buckley. Cohen wrote over eighty verses before he arrived at the final ones.

27 Please Please Me (1963)

Writers: John Lennon and Paul McCartney

The Beatles first Number 1 single, and the title of their first album.

28 The Times They Are a-Changing (1964)

Writer: Bob Dylan

First track on Dylan's album of the same name released on Columbia Records and produced by Tom Wilson.

29 Come Together (1969)

Writers: John Lennon and Paul McCartney

The opening track of the Beatles' album *Abbey Road*.

30 Shape of Things to Come (1968)

Writers: Barry Mann and Cynthia Weil

Written for the film *Wild In The Streets* for a fictional band called Max Frost and the Troopers, which had Richard Pryor playing drums.

31 We Will Rock You (1977)

Writer: Brian May

Performed by Queen on their album *News of the World*.

32 Light My Fire (1967)

Writers: Ray Manzarek, John Densmore, Robby Krieger, Jim Morrison

From the Doors first album and later a Number 1 single for them.

33 All Around the World (1989)

Writers: Lisa Stansfield, Ian Devaney, Andy Morris

The first single to be released from Lisa Stansfield's album *Affection*.

34 Into The Groove (1985)

Writers: Madonna, Steve Bray

Single by Madonna from her *Like A Virgin* album, also featured in the film *Desperately Seeking Susan*.

35 Signed, Sealed, Delivered (1970)

Writers: Stevie Wonder, Lee Garrett, Syreeta Wright, Lula Hardaway

Steve Wonder wrote this song when he was 20, and one of the writers Lula Hardaway, is his mother.

36 Shine on You Crazy Diamond (1974)

Writers: Richard Wright, Roger Waters, David Gilmour

The song was written by Pink Floyd as a tribute to former member Syd Barrett and covers most of Side One of their album *Wish You Were Here*.

37 Money, Money, Money (1976)

Writers: Benny Andersson and Bjorn Ulvaeus

Abba's follow up single to 'Dancing Queen'.

38 Fly Me To The Moon (1954)

Writer: Bart Howard

First recorded by actress/comedienne Kaye Ballard, released on American Decca under the title 'In Other Words', which was later changed.

39 Fuck tha Police (1988)

Writers: Ice Cube, MC Ren, Easy-E

Released on Niggaz With Attitude album *Straight Out of Compton*. Although it was never a single it's listed on *Rolling Stone*'s '500 Greatest Songs of All Times'.

40 I'll Be Missing You (1997)

Writers: Sting, Faith Evans, Sauce Money, Albert E. Brumley

A mix of the Police's 'Every Breath You Take' and new writing by Puff Daddy and Faith Evans, the single was recorded Puff Daddy and the Family for their album *No Way Out*, in memory of the murdered Christopher Wallace (The Notorious B.I.G.).

41 Mad About the Boy (1932)

Writer: Noël Coward

Written for the revue Words and Music, the song was sung by various female characters and directed towards a film star – 'On the screen he melts my foolish heart in every single scene'. Coward later wrote a version to be sung by a male character in the New York production with the lines, "When I told my wife, she said, 'I've never heard such nonsense in my life'."

42 Everybody's Doing It (1911)

Writer: Irving Berlin

Written by Berlin to exploit a dance craze of the moment.

43 I've Got a Great Idea (1990)

Writer: Harry Connick

From the album *We Are in Love* by Harry Connick Jnr.

44 Where Do We Go From Here (1970)

Writer: Peter Cetera

From Chicago's album *Chicago II*.

Bibliography

BOOKS

Aldridge, John (1984) *Satisfaction: The Story of Mick Jagger,* Proteus.

Almond, Marc (1999) *Tainted Life*, Sidgwick & Jackson.

Anthony, Wayne (1999) *Spanish Highs*, Virgin.

Aston, Martin (1996) *Pulp*, Pan.

Averill, Gage (2003) *Four Parts, No Waiting: A Social History of American Barbershop Harmony*, Oxford University Press.

Badman, Keith (2007) *The Beatles Off The Record*, Omnibus.

Bangs, Lester (2003) *Mainlines, Bad Feasts and Bad Taste*, Doubleday.

Barfe, Louis (2004) *Where Have All the Good Times Gone?*, Atlantic.

Barnes, Richard (1979) *Mods!*, Eel Pie.

Bean, J.P. (n.d.) *Joe Cocker: With a Little Help from My Friends*, Omnibus.

The Beatles (2000) *Anthology*, Cassell.

The Beatles and Frank Ifield (1964) Sleeve notes, in *Jolly What! England's Greatest Recording Stars: The Beatles and Frank Ifield on Stage* [Vinyl booklet], Indiana: Vee-Jay Records.

Bennett, Robert Russell (2000) *The Broadway Sound*, University of Rochester Press.

Benson, Richard (1997) *Night Fever*, Boxtree.

Bergreen, Laurence (1990) *As Thousands Cheer*, Hodder and Stoughton.

Berry, Chuck (1987) *Chuck Berry*, Harmony.

Billboard (1943) *Music Year Book*, Billboard.

Black, David (1998) *Acid*, Vision Paperbacks/Satin Publications.

Black, Susan (1993) *Elton John: In His Own Words*, Omnibus.

Blake, John (1985) *His Satanic Majesty: Mick Jagger*, Holt.

Bockris, Victor (1995) *Lou Reed*, Vintage.

Bockris, Victor (1992) *Keith Richards*, Hutchinson.

Boosey, William (1931) *Fifty Years of Music*, Schwarz Press.

Booth, Stanley (1985) *The True Adventures of the Rolling Stones*, Heinemann.

Bordman, Gerald (1980) *Jerome Kern: His Life and Music*, Oxford.

Bowie, Angela with Patrick Carr (1992) *Backstage Passes*, Orion.

Boy George with Spencer Bright (1995) *Take It Like a Man*, Pan.

Bracewell, Michael (1997) *England is Mine: Pop Life in Albion from Wilde to Goldie*, HarperCollins.

Brant, Marley (2008) *Join Together*, Backbeat.

Braun, Michael (1964) *Love Me Do*, Jonathan Clowes.

Brewster, Bill and Frank Broughton (1999) *Last Night A DJ Saved My Life*, Headline.

Brown, Peter and Steven Gaines (1983) *The Love You Make*, Macmillan.

Burdon, Eric (1986) *I Used to Be an Animal but I'm Alright Now*, Faber & Faber.

Cacavas, John (2003) *It's More Than Do-Re-Mi*, Xlibris.

Cahn, Sammy (1975) *I Should Care*, W. H. Allen.

Carducci, Joe (1995) *Rock and the Pop Narcotic*, Redoubt Press.

Carmichael, Hoagy, Longstreet, Stephen and Hasse, John Edward (1999) *The Stardust Road & Sometimes I Wonder: The Autobiography of Hoagy Carmichael*, Da Capo.

Charone, Barbara (1979) *Keith Richards*, Futura.

Clarke, Donald (1990) *The Penguin Encyclopaedia of Popular Music*, Penguin.

Clarke, Gary (1995) *Elton, My Elton*, Smith Gryphon.

Clarkson, Wensley (1996) *Sting*, Blake.

Clayson, Alan (1997) *Hamburg*, Sanctuary.

Cohan, George M. (1924) *Twenty Years on Broadway*, New York: Harper & Brothers.

Cohen, Harvey G. (2010) *Duke Ellington's America*, University Chicago Press.

Cohn, Nick (1989) *Ball the Wall*, Picador.

Cohn, Nick (1969) *A Wopbopaloobopalopbamboom*, Weidenfeld & Nicolson.

Coleman, Ray (1994) *Rod Stewart*, Pavilion.

Coleman, Ray (1985) *Clapton*, Warner.

Collin, Matthew and John Gregory (1998) *Altered State*, Serpent's Tail.

Condon, Eddie (1947) *We Called It Music: A Generation of Jazz*, Da Capo.

Cornyn, Stan (2002) *Exploding*, Rolling Stone Press.

County, Jayne (1995) *Man Enough to Be a Woman*, Serpent's Tail.

Coward, Noël (1982) *The Noël Coward Diaries*, Graham Payn.

Cross, Craig (2005) *The Beatles: Day-by-Day, Song-by-Song, Record-by-Record*, Universe.

Cunningham, Mark (1996) *Good Vibrations*, Sanctuary.

Daley, Dan (1999) *Nashville's Unwritten Rules*, Overlook Press.

Daley, Sean and Ashley Majeski (2013) *Inside AGT: The Untold Stories of America's Got Talent*, CreateSpace Independent Publishing Platform.

Dance, Stanley (1979) *Duke Ellington in Person: An Intimate Memoir*, Da Capo.

Dannen, Frederic (2003) *Hitmen*, Helter Skelter.

Davies, Dave (1996) *Autobiography*, Boxtree.

Denselow, Robin (1989) *When the Music's Over*, Faber & Faber.

Des Barres, Pamela (1996) *Rock Bottom*, St Martin's Press.

Driver, Jim (1994) *Rock Talk*, The Do Not Press.

Dylan, Bob (2004) *Chronicles*, Simon & Schuster.

East 17 (1995) *Talkback*, Omnibus.

Eliot, Marc (2005) *To The Limit*, Da Capo.

Eliscu, Edward (2001) *With or without a Song*, Scarecrow.

Ellington, Edward Kennedy (1976) *Music Is My Mistress*, Da Capo.

Ellis, Royston (1961) *The Big Beat Scene*, New English Library.

Emerson, Ken (2005) *Always Magic in the Air*, Viking.

Epstein, Brian (1965) *A Cellarful of Noise*, Souvenir Press.

Ewing, Jon (1996) *The Rolling Stones: "Quote Unquote"*, Paragon.

Faithfull, Marianne with David Dalton (1995) *Faithfull*, Penguin.

Fox, Jon Hartley (2009) *King of The Queen City*, University Of Illinois Press.

Frame, Pete (1979) *The Complete Rock Family Tree*, Omnibus.

Freedland, Michael (1984) *The Warner Brothers*, St. Martin's Press.

Friedwald, Will (1996) *Jazz Singing*, Da Capo.

Frith, Simon (1978) *The Sociology of Rock*, Constable.

Frith, Simon and Andrew Goodwin (1990) *On Record*, Routledge.

Gaisberg, Fred (1977) *The Music Goes Round*, Arno Press.

Geldof, Bob (1986) *Is That It?*, Sidgwick & Jackson.

Gillett, Charlie (1983) *The Sound of the City*, Souvenir.

Gillman, Peter and Leni Gillman (1986) *David Bowie*, Hodder & Stoughton.

Gilmore, Mikal (1998) *Night Beat: A Shadow History of Rock & Roll*, Doubleday.

Giuliano, Geoffrey (1996) *Behind Blue Eyes: A Life of Peter Townshend*, Coronet.

Goldberg, Danny (2009) *Bumping Into Geniuses*, Gotham.

Goldberg, Isaac and George Gershwin (1930) *Tin Pan Alley: A Chronicle of the American Popular Music Racket*, John Day.

Goldman, Albert (1992) *Sound Bites*, Abacus.

Goldman, Albert (1971) *Freakshow*, Atheneum.

Goldman, Howard (1990) *Jolson: The Legend Comes to Life*, Oxford University Press.

Goodall, Nigel (1995) *George Michael: In His Own Words*, Omnibus.

Goodman, Fred (2010) *Fortune's Fool*, Simon & Schuster.

Goodman, Fred (1997) *The Mansion on the Hill*, Pimlico.

Gosling, Ray (1980) *Personal Copy*, Faber & Faber.

Grafton, David (1987) *Red, Hot & Rich*, Stein and Day.

Graham, Bill and Greenfield, Robert (2004) *My Life Inside Rock and Roll*, Da Capo.

Green, Benny (1974) *P. G. Wodehouse*, Pavilion Books.

Greenfield, Robert (2012) *The Last Sultan: The Life and Times of Ahmet Ertegun*, Simon & Schuester.

Greenfield, Robert (1974) *Stones Touring Party*, Aurum.

Hadleigh, Boze (1999) *Sing Out*, Robson.

Haldane, J.B.S. (2001) *Possible Worlds*, Transaction.

Hammond, John (1977) *On Record*, Summit Books.

Handy, W. C. (1991) *Father of the Blues*, Da Capo.

Harding, James (1997) *Ivor Novello: A Biography*, W. H. Allen.

Haslan, Gerald W. (1999) *Workin' Man Blues: Country Music in Califonia*, UCLA Press.

Heller, Jerry (2007) *Ruthless*, Gallery.

Hemphill, Paul (2006) *Lovesick Blues: The Life of Hank Williams*, Penguin.

Herman, Gary (1984) *Rock and Roll Babylon*, Plexus.

Heylin, Clinton (1992) *The Penguin Book of Rock & Roll Writing*, Penguin.

Hill, Dave (1986) *Designer Boys Material Girls: Manufacturing the 80s Pop Dream*, Blandford Press.

Hodkinson, Mark (1995) *Queen: The Early Years*, Omnibus.

Hodkinson, Mark (1991) *Marianne Faithfull*, Omnibus.

Holzman, Jac and Daws, Gavan (2000) *Follow the Music*, First Media.

Hoskyns, Barney (2005) *Hotel California*, Fourth Estate.

Hoskyns, Barney (1998) *Glam!,* Faber & Faber.

Ice-T and Heidi Sigmund (1994) *The Ice Opinion: Who Gives a Fuck?*, St. Martin's Press.

Jackson, John A. (1997) *Bandstand*, Oxford.

Jackson, Laura (1997) *Heart of Stone*, Blake.

James, Martin (1997) *The Prodigy,* Ebury Press.

Jarman, Derek (1994) *Dancing Ledge*, Quartet.

Jasen, David A. (2002) *P.G.Wodehouse*, Schirmer.

Johnson, Paul, (1964) "The Menace of Beatlism", *New Statesman*, London, February 28.

Jones, John Bush (2006) *The Songs that Fought the War*, Brandeis University Press.

Jones, Lesley-Ann (2011) *Freddie Mercury: The Definitive Biography*, Hodder & Stoughton.

Kelley, Kitty (1986) *His Way*, Bantam.

Kendall, Alan (1987) *George Gershwin*, Harrap.

Kennedy, Rick and Randy McNutt (1999) *Little Labels Big Sounds*, Indiana University Press.

King, Tom (2000) *The Operator: David Geffen Builds, Buys, and Sells the New Hollywood*, Random House.

BIBLIOGRAPHY

Knopper, Steve (2009) *Appetite for Self-Destruction*, Simon & Schuster.

Kureishi, Hanif and Jon Savage (eds) (1995) *The Faber Book of Pop*, Faber & Faber.

Lebrecht, Norman (2007) *Life and Death of Classical Music*, Anchor.

Leiber, Jerry and Mike Stoller (2010) *Hound Dog: The Leiber and Stoller Autobiography*, Simon & Schuster.

Leigh, Spencer (1996) *Halfway to Paradise: Britpop 1955–1962*, Finbarr.

LeRoy, J.T. (2005) *Da Capo Book of Best Music Writing*, Da Capo.

Lesley, Cole (1978) *The Life of Noël Coward*, Penguin.

Lines, David (2006) *The Modfather*, William Heinemann.

Locke, Alain (1968) *The New Negro: An Interpretation*, Arno Press.

McBrien, William (1998) *Cole Porter*, Vintage.

MacDonald, Ian (1995) *Revolution in the Head*, Pimlico.

MacInnes, Colin (1959) *Absolute Beginners*, Allison & Busby.

McLagan, Ian (2000) *All the Rage: My High Life with the Small Faces, the Faces, the Rolling Stones and Many More*, Pan.

Marcus, Greil (1975) *Mystery Train*, Dutton.

Marks, Edward B. (1934) *They All Sang*, Viking Press.

Martin, George (1994) *The Summer of Love*, Pan.

Matlock, Glen with Pete Silverton (1990) *I Was a Teenage Sex Pistol*, Faber & Faber.

Melly, George (1970) *Revolt into Style*, Penguin.

Michael, George and Tony Parsons (1990) *Bare*, Michael Joseph.

Miles, Barry (2005) *Zappa*, Grove Press.

Miles, Barry (1997) *Paul McCartney: Many Years From Now*, Secker & Warburg.

Miles, Barry (ed.) (1980) *David Bowie, In His Own Words*, Omnibus.

Miles, Barry (1978) *The Clash*, Omnibus.

Moore, Jerrold Northrop (1999) *Sound Revolutions*, Sanctuary.

Morley, Paul (1986) *Ask: The Chatter of Pop*, Faber & Faber.

Murray, Charles Shaar (1991) *Shots from the Hip*, Penguin.

NME (1995) *Big Mouth Strikes Again: The Book of Quotes*, New Musical Express.

Nolan, Frederick (1994) *Lorenz Hart*, Oxford.

Norman, Philip (1996) *Buddy*, Macmillan.

Norman, Philip (1991) *Elton*, Hutchinson.

Norman, Philip (1982) *The Road Goes on Forever*, Corgi.

Nott, James J. (2002) *Music for the People*, Oxford.

Obstfeld, Raymond and Patricia Fitzgerald (1997) *Jabberrock*, Canongate.

Oldham, Andrew Loog (2000) *Stoned*, Secker & Warburg.

Palmer, Tony (1976) *All You Need Is Love: The Story of Popular Music*, Weidenfeld & Nicolson.

Pandit, S.A. (1996) *From Making to Music*, Hodder & Stoughton.

Paytress, Mark (1992) *Twentieth Century Boy*, Sidgwick & Jackson.

Pearsall, Ronald (1975) *Edwardian Popular Music*, David & Charles.

Platts, Robin (2003) *Burt Bacharach & Hal David: What the World Needs Now*, CG Publishing.

Reed, John (1997) *Paul Weller: My Ever Changing Moods*, Omnibus.

Robb, John (1999) *The Nineties*, Ebury Press.

Robertson, Ian (1996) *Oasis: What's The Story?*, Blake.

Rodgers, Richard (1975) *Musical Stages*, Da Capo.

Rogan, Johnny (1998) *The Byrds: Timeless Flight Revisited*, Rogan House.

Rogan, Johnny (1988) *Starmakers and Svengalis: The History of British Pop*, Queen Anne Press.

Rogan, Johnny (1984) *Van Morrison: A Portrait of the Artist*, Elm Tree Books.

Rolling Stone Magazine (1992) *The Rolling Stone Illustrated History of Rock 'n' Roll*, Random House.

Sanjek, Russel (1988) *American Popular Music and its Business, Volume III*, Oxford.

Savage, Jon (1997) *Time Travel*, Vintage.

Savage, Jon (1991) *England's Dreaming: Sex Pistols and Punk Rock*, Faber & Faber.

Scaduto, Anthony (1971) *Bob Dylan: an Intimate Biography*, Grosset & Dunlap.

Secrest, Meryle (1998) *Stephen Sondheim: A Life*, Bloomsbury.

Segrave, Kerry (1993) *Payola in the Music Industry*, McFarland.

Shapiro, Harry (1996) *Alexis Korner: The Biography*, Bloomsbury.

Shapiro, Harry (1988) *Waiting For the Man*, Quartet.

Shapiro, Nat and Nat Hentoff (1955) *Hear Me Talkin' To Ya*, Dover.

Shaw, Arnold (1998) *Let's Dance*, Oxford University Press.

Shaw, Arnold (1987) *The Jazz Age*, Oxford.

Shaw, Arnold (1974) *The Rockin' 50s*, Da Capo.

Shaw, Sandie (1992) *The World at My Feet*, Fontana.

Shearer, Lloyd with Ger Rijff (ed.) and Jan Van Gestel (1988) *Elvis Presley, Memphis Lonesome*, Tutti Frutti Productions, Amsterdam.

Sheed, Wilfrid (2008) *The House that George Built*, Random House.

Shepherd, Don and Robert E. Slatzer (1981) *Bing Crosby: the Hollow Man*, W. H. Allen.

Shilkret, Nathaniel (2005) *Sixty Years in the Music Business*, Scarecrow Press.

Sky, Rick (1993) *The Take That Fact File*, HarperCollins.

Smith, Charles Edward (1956) *History of Classic Jazz*, Bill Grauer Productions.

Smith, Joe (1988) *Off the Record*, Warner.

Smith, Richard (1995) *Seduced and Abandoned*, Cassell.

Sounes, Howard (2001) *Down the Highway*, Doubleday.

Southall, Brian (2009) *The Rise & Fall of EMI Records*, Omnibus.

Southall, Brian with Rupert Perry (2006) *Northern Songs*, Omnibus.

Stearns, Marshall (1970) *The Story of Jazz*, Oxford University Press.

Sternfeld, Joshua (2008) *Jazz Echoes: The Cultural and Sociopolitical Reception of Jazz in Weimar and Nazi Berlin, 1925–1945*, UCLA History Department.

Stump, Paul (1997) *The Music's All That Matters*, Quartet Books.

Suisman, David (2009) *Selling Sounds*, Harvard.

Taraborrelli, J. Randy (2004) *Michael Jackson: The Magic, The Madness, The Whole Story*, Grand Central Publishing.

Taraborrelli, J. Randy (2001) *Madonna*, Sidgwick & Jackson.

Thompson, Ben (1998) *Seven Years of Plenty,* Victor Gollancz.

Timelords, The (1988) *The Manual: How to Have a Number One the Easy Way*, Curfew Press.

Tremlett, George (1996) *David Bowie: Living on the Brink*, Carroll & Graf.

Turner, Steve (1994) *Cliff Richard: The Biography*, Lion Publishing.

Tyler, Andrew (1988) *Street Drugs*, New English Library.

Victor Records (1922) *1923 Catalogue of Victor Records*, Victor Talking Machine Co., Camden, New Jersey, USA, December.

Von Eschen, Penny (2004) *Satchmo Blows Up the World*, Harvard University Press.

Vyner, Harriet (1999) *Groovy Bob*, Faber & Faber.

Wade, Dorothy and Justine Picardie (1990) *Music Man*, Norton.

Wale, Michael (1972) *Vox Pop: Profiles of the Pop Process*, Harrap.

Warren, Bruce (2007) *Wisdom of a Young Musician*, Running Press.

Waterman, Douglas (2007) *Song*, Writer's Digest.

Welch, Chris (1981) *Adam & The Ants*, Star.

Wexler, Jerry (1993) *Rhythm and Blues: A Life in American Music*, Knopf.

White, Timothy (1990) *Rock Lives*, Holt.

Wiener, Jon (1985) *Come Together: John Lennon in His Time*, Faber & Faber.

Wilk, Max (1973) *They're Playing Our Song*, Delacorte.

Witmark, Isidore (1939) *The Story of The House of Witmark: From Ragtime to Swingtime*, Lee Furman.

Wolfe, Tom (2009) *The Kandy-Kolored Tangerine-Flake Streamline Baby*, Picador.

Wood, Ron with Bill German (1987) *Ron Wood*, Harper & Row.

Yetnikoff, Walter with David Ritz (2005) *Howling at the Moon*, Abacus.

Zappa, Frank and Peter Occhiogrosso (1990) *The Real Frank Zappa Book*, Touchstone.

Zimmer, Dave (2008) *Crosby Stills & Nash*, Da Capo.

Zollo, Paul (1997) *Songwriters on Songwriting*, Da Capo.

WEBSITES

The 1709 Blog, article on royalties
   http://the1709blog.blogspot.com/2012/02/right-royalty-row-brings-out-fighting.html
ABC News, BMG statement
   http://abcnews.go.com/Entertainment/story?id=113790
American Heritage
   http://www.americanheritage.com/content/lullaby-tin-pan-alley
Artie Wayne
   http://artiewayne.wordpress.com/about-artie-wayne/
Bluegrass Messengers Website
   http://www.bluegrassmessengers.com/ralph-peer--a--r-man-for-okeh-and-victor. aspx
Blues and Soul
   http://www.bluesandsoul.com/feature/576/marshall_chess_all_the_right_moves/
Buddy Holly biography by Bruce Elder
   http://www.allmusic.com/artist/buddy-holly-mn0000538677/biography
Charleston Revisited, America Learns To Dance
   http://charlestonrevisisted.blogspot.com/2013_02_01_archive.html
Dave D, History of rap
   http://www.daveyd.com/raphist2.html
Deseret News, Mitch Miller obituary
   http://www.deseretnews.com/article/700053091/Sing-Along-With-Mitch-conductor-Miller-dies-at-age-99.html?pg=all
Digparty, translated from "The 100 Greatest Braunschweiger", Braunschweiger Zeitung Special, Issue 1, 2005
   http://www.digplanet.com/wiki/Norbert_Schultze#cite_note-1
Elvis Australia, Freddy Bienstock
   http://www.elvis.com.au/presley/freddy_bienstock.shtml#sthash.n2ng5dnp.dpbs
Elvis Australia, Sam Phillips
   http://www.elvis.com.au/presley/a_broken_heart.shtml#sthash.NaajMecW.dpbs
Encyclopaedia.com, Sam Phillips
   http://www.encyclopedia.com/topic/Sam_Phillips.aspx
Goerie.com, article on Chubby Checker
   http://www.goerie.com/article/20130912/ENTERTAINMENT0301/309129967/Chubby-Checker-brings-%27The-Twist%27-to-PI-Downs
Guardian, article on Frank Sinatra by Jon Savage
   http://www.theguardian.com/music/2011/jun/11/frank-sinatra-pop-star

Guardian, including interview with Malcolm McLaren
    http://www.theguardian.com/world/2008/jan/20/review.features7
Independent, interview with Calvin Harris
    http://www.independent.co.uk/arts-entertainment/music/features/calvin-
    harris-how-the-nondancing-foulmouthed-antisocial-scot-became-the-
    caledonian-justin-timberlake-1764506.html
Independent, Grosvenor Square riots 1968
    http://www.independent.co.uk/arts-entertainment/music/features/jagger-vs-
    lennon-londons-riots-of-1968-provided-the-backdrop-to-a-rocknroll-battle-
    royale-792450.html
Jack Hylton, biography section
    http://www.jackhylton.com
Julian Eltinge Project
    http://www.thejulianeltingeproject.com/bio.html
Kitagawa, translation of 2006 Johnny's Jimusho expose
    http://www.hellodamage.com/top/?s=kitagawa
LA Times, article on Louis Jordan and Bill Haley by Robert Palmer
    http://articles.latimes.com/1993-07-11/entertainment/ca-12191_1_
    pioneering-louis-jordan
Letters of Note, letter complaining about Elvis Presley
    http://www.lettersofnote.com/2009/10/striptease-with-clothes-on.html
Memphis Music Hall of Fame
    http://memphismusichalloffame.com/inductee/samphillips
Military Sheet Music
    http://www.militarysheetmusic.com/Popular-songs-of-America-at-war-WWI.htm
MP3fiesta
    http://www.mp3fiesta.com/ice_t_artist9813/
The National Great Blacks in Wax Museum, interview with Eubie Blake
    http://www.greatblacksinwax.org/Exhibits/Eubie_blake/Eubie_Blake2.htm
Oocities
    http://www.oocities.org/the_strath/1962.htm
PBS, on Minstrelsy
    http://www.pbs.org/jazz/exchange/exchange_minstrel.htm
Pepsi ad circa 1950
    http://johnstownhistory.blogspot.com/2011/12/7up-you-like-itit-likes-you.html
Robbie Rocks
    http://www.robbierocks.ch
Rock Turtlenec, Dylan on the Beatles
    http://rockturtleneck.blogspot.com/2012/02/really-big-show-beatles-on-ed-
    sullivan.html

Rolling Stone, article on Dylan leaving Asylum Records
http://www.rollingstone.com/music/news/bob-dylan-goes-back-to-columbia-records-19740912#ixzz2eAvpNpNC

Slate.com, article on Eva Tanguy
http://www.slate.com/articles/arts/music_box/2009/12/vanishing_act.2.html

Telegraph
http://www.telegraph.co.uk/news/uknews/1327116/30000-damages-for-composer-of-007-theme-tune.html

Telegraph, article on Ivor Novello wartime performance
http://www.telegraph.co.uk/culture/music/rockandpopfeatures/6454528/Songs-That-Won-The-War.html

Travalanche, about Ziegfeld's Follies
http://travsd.wordpress.com/2010/03/21/ziegfeld-and-vaudeville/

US government, on Irving Berlin's 'This Is The War'
http://www.archives.gov/publications/prologue/1996/summer/irving-berlin-1.html

VHSource, about Victor Herbert
http://vherbert.com/index.php?option=com_content&view=article&id=46:setting-the-stage-in-america&catid=28:herbert-biography&Itemid=57

Zoominfo, on Lou Pearlmann
http://www.zoominfo.com/p/Lou-Pearlman/1495749

Index of Quotations

14 "What will you do in the long, cold, dark, shivery evenings..." (Pearsall, 1975)

14 "the Finest Entertainer in the World" (Pearsall, 1975)

14 "two kinds of gramophone needles" (Pearsall, 1975)

14 "reproduces the voice with almost the same volume of sound as is given by the artist when singing" (Pearsall, 1975)

14 "subdues the tones and gives a very soft sweet effect as of a voice heard in the distance" (Pearsall, 1975)

15 "In the bazaars of India I have seen dozens of natives..." (Fred Gaisberg in Gaisberg, 1977)

15 "a Mohammedan, rather fat and covered with masses of gold..." (Fred Gaisberg in Moore, 1999)

15 "four musicians... a bearer for her pipe and to prepare her betel nut..." (Fred Gaisberg in Moore, 1999)

16 "for legal protection and commercial advantage" (Barfe, 2004)

Chapter 3

21 "the little fellow with tight green pants" (Edward B. Marks in Bordman, 1980)

22 "dealing with bills and invoice" (Edward B. Marks in Bordman, 1980)

22 "He said he wanted to imbibe the atmosphere of music. I decided to..." (Max Dreyfus on American Heritage Website)

Chapter 4

24 "in accordance with the very latest and most extreme modes of the moment" (*The Sketch*, 1896)

25 "shared the distinction of sitting at the bottom of the classical form" (William Boosey in Boosey, 1931)

27 "They were the big song publishers in those days.... I figured it would be useless to try" (George Cohan in Witmark, 1939)

27 "Just goes to show how smart those babes in there are..." (George Cohan in Witmark, 1939)

27 "Many a bum show has been saved by the flag" (George Cohan in Cohan, 1924)

28 "solo cellist from the Royal Orchestra of his Majesty, the King of Wurtemberg" (VHSource, vherbert.com)

29 "His motto might have been 'Easy come, easier go'" (Isidore Witmark in Witmark, 1939)

29 "He contrives to let his masculinity shine through" (Theatre critic reviewing *Mr Wix of Wickham* on the Julian Eltinge Project website, www.thejulianeltingeproject.com)

29 "towers in such an Eiffel way" that "criticism is disarmed" (Alan Dale in Bordman, 1980)

39   "as great a performer as there is today" (*Variety*)

40   "I can replace every one of you except the one you want me to fire" (Travalanche website on Ziegfeld Follies)

41   "a tingling of the spine, the raising of the hairs on the back of the neck…" (Jim Irwin in Averill, 2003)

41   "the clatter of hoofs, the whinnying of horses, and the 'yipping' of the cowboys" (*Edison Phonograph Monthly*, September 1910)

41   "teaching America to dance from the waist down" (Article by Mark Jones, 'Charleston Revisited')

42   "Fee exorbitant, absolutely forbid you to record" (Fred Gaisberg in Moore, 1999)

42   "Dressed like a dandy, twiddling a cane" (Fred Gaisberg in Moore, 1999)

42   "to get the job over quickly as he was anxious to earn that £100 and to have his lunch" (Fred Gaisberg in Moore, 1999)

Chapter 7

43   "Popular songs only required two or three pages of paper and they could be photographed or litho'ed in any old shed…" (William Boosey in Boosey, 1931)

43   "At 7 o'clock one evening, one of our agents had 38 copies seized at a street stall…" (ibid.)

45   "Imagine such a condition of copyright prevailing in the book world! An author publishes a work, say, at ten shillings…" (ibid.)

46   "Max Meyer was staging his little act at Macy's. After buying some tinware in the household department…" (Isidore Witmark in Witmark, 1939)

46   "started to walk away, keeping up a long harangue, at intervals of which he dropped pieces of tinware sounding like cannon reports" (ibid.)

Chapter 8

48   "vexatious rights of performance that never have and never will be understood here" (William Boosey in Boosey, 1931)

Chapter 9

51   "What a pity that you aren't capable of writing a wartime song as good as 'Tipperary'" (Clara Davies in Harding, 1996)

51   "Alright, dear, but one of us two is going to… and if you won't I will" (Clara Davies in Harding, 1996)

51   "I want words that conjure up images of the homes the young soldiers…" (Ivor Novello in Harding, 1996)

53   "A Nation that sings can never be beaten… Songs are to a nation's spirit what ammunition is to a nation's army" (Leo Feist on Military Sheet Music website)

Chapter 11

63 "It is true that the music is not the sole object, but neither is the food..." (Chief Justice Oliver Wendell Holmes, Supreme Court decision, 1917 *Herbert v. Shanley Co*)

65 "Nora Bayes, with her inimitable foolery and clean fun, her admirable imitations and clever and witty songs" (Victor Records, 1923)

66 "as a mark of respect" (Goldman, 1990)

66 "Fuck you" (Al Jolson in Goldman, 1990)

66 "the only Palm Court in the district where teas and light refreshments will be most daintily served" (Nott, 2002)

66 "lacquered columns, decorative fretwork and a pagoda roof with Chinese lanterns" (Nott, 2002)

67 "Orchestra, nine men in dinner jackets, start a tune. Large groups of each sex, segregated and concentrated round door..." (Nott, 2002)

Chapter 12

69 "considerably worried as to the future of our American house" (Boosey, 1931)

70 "Close Chappell's office in New York and make a deal with Max Dreyfus to run Chappell's business in America" (Ivan Caryl in Boosey, 1931)

70 "Very well, let's follow your suggestion. Will you ring up Harms on the telephone" (Boosey,1931)

70 "We were told that with prohibition people would spend more time at home around the piano... but depressed hypocritical people do not sing" (Marks, 1934)

70 "The public of the nineties asked for tunes to sing... But the public from 1910 onwards demanded tunes to dance to" (Marks, 1934)

70 "a bang of bad booze, flappers with bare legs, jangled morals and wild weekends" (Carmichael, Longstreet and Hasse, 1999)

71 "some people play so differently from others that it becomes an entirely new set of sounds" (Condon, 1947)

71 "When they gathered around a piano and harmonized, they could make anything sound good..." (Marks, 1934)

71 "They didn't want to think that Negoes read music... But all of us could read - you have to write parts out, don't you, you're a musician. But you didn't let the white people know that" (The National Great Blacks in Wax Museum interview with Eubie Blake, 1973)

72 "The world's most glamorous atmosphere" (Duke Ellington in Cohen, 2010)

72 "the recognized Negro capital... the Mecca for the sightseer, the pleasure seeker, the curious..." (James Weldon Johnson in Locke, 1968)

72 "walked out two pairs of shoes" (Perry Bradford in Suisman, 2009)

86   "The new racket" (*Variety* in Shaw, 1987)

86   "from $1,000 to $20,000 a year as salary charged against royalty" (ibid.)

86   "need to be compensated with royalty interests ... Most bandleaders consider it a poor week if they are cut in on less than fifteen new songs" (Jack Robbins in Shaw, 1987)

86   "I want you to write me the score for a musical show..." (Ellington, 1976)

86   "That night I sat down and wrote music for a whole show. I didn't know composers..." (ibid.)

86   "They started hollering 'Bis, Bis'... we thought they were saying 'beasts'..." (Sam Wooding in Sternfeld, 2008)

87   "It was so bad that we didn't even put a serial number on the records, thinking that..." (Ralph Peer in interview on Bluegrass Messengers Website)

87   "knowing where lightning is going to strike ... how in God's name you can detect that I don't know" (ibid.)

87   "If I can't get 'em in town we'll go to the woods" (ibid.)

88   "He was paid $80 a week and expenses. He took several trips and the next year asked for a raise" (Shilkret, 2005)

88   "No one on the musical staff had been offered a royalty for his arrangement or compositions, and here was a man collecting royalties with other men's compositions!" (Shilkret, 2005)

88   "I wrote this music with a view of having it appreciated by people who come to the theatre without any alcoholic stimulation" (Jerome Kern in Bordman, 1980)

88   "the jazzy types of entertainment" (ibid.)

89   "Ease, naturalness, everydayness... it is my first consideration when I start on lyrics... easy to say, easy to sing, and applicable to everyday events..." (Irving Berlin in Bergreen, 1990)

89   "His words, however clever, yet maintain contact with *hoi polloi*" (Goldberg, 1930)

89   "I sweat blood between 3 and 6 many mornings, and when the drops fall off my forehead and hit the paper they're notes" (Irving Berlin in Bergreen, 1990)

89   "My first name is Saul. My second is Oscar. My last is Bornstein. And you know what that spells!" (Saul Bornstein in Bergreen, 1990)

90   "little better than a megalomaniac looking after only himself" (Abel Green in *Variety*, 1927)

91   "We depend largely on tricks, we writers of song, our work is to connect old phrases in a new way, so that they will sound like a new tune" (Irving Berlin in Bergreen, 1990)

91   "There isn't a Belle Baker song in the score and I'm so miserable" (Belle Baker in Bergreen, 1990)

100 "Promptly at seven-thirty, Porter's private gondola pulled up outside our hotel…" (ibid.)

101 "As soon as he touched the keyboard to play 'a few of my little things' I became aware that…" (ibid.)

101 "As I breathlessly awaited the magic formula, he leaned over and confided, 'I'll write Jewish tunes'" (ibid.)

Chapter 16

102 "Who the hell wants to hear actors talk? The music, that's the big plus!" (Harry Warner in Freedland, 1984)

102 "You ain't heard nothing yet!" (Al Jolson in *The Jazz Singer*)

102 "Never before in the history of Tin Pan Alley has the average songwriter enjoyed such affluence and influence" (Abel Green writing in *Variety* July, 1929)

103 "He was just like the producers in the funny stories. He sprawled over the table and said…" (Rodgers, 1975)

104 "This morning I cleaned out that desk, I'm no longer a millionaire" (Max Dreyfus in Bennett, 2000)

104 "All hooey. Picture people don't take advice. They give orders" (Max Dreyfus on American Heritage website)

Chapter 17

107 "active, aggressive, intelligent organisation" (Louis Sterling in Barfe, 2004)

108 "You wore a hat in order to be able to take it off when you greeted the retailer, and you could also offer them a cigarette" (L. G.Wood in Southall, 2009)

108 "A company manufacturing gramophones but not records is rather like one making razors but not the consumable blades" (Edward Lewis in Barfe, 2004)

108 "Decca have carried out intensive research so as to attain the best acoustic results, and the methods adopted are based on the very latest practices" (*Phono Record* in Barfe, 2004)

108 "You don't have that sort of man as a director" (Hugh Mendl quoting his grandfather Sigismund Mendl in Barfe, 2004)

109 "Jack Hylton was there too. Flabby and pot-bellied like an English pork butcher; he was rocking grotesquely in his chair…" (Jack Hylton website, n.d.)

109 "agreements among publishers are farcical and as soon as they decide on some unanimous action, some immediately break their pledges" (Segrave, 1993)

120 "No other band of this quality had ever had such popular acceptance..." (*The Saturday Evening Post* writing about the swing era)

120 "Radio now is the thought by day and the dream by night of all song pluggers" (*Variety* in Segrave, 1994)

120 "Flattery, cases of Scotch, cigars, and floral offerings to bandsmen's wives... all with just one purpose" (Segrave,1994)

121 "See all those song-pluggers sitting there in back of the room. They're a pain in the neck. If they didn't cut me in on their songs, I'd throw them the hell out of here" (Guy Lombardo in Segrave, 1994)

121 "he doesn't feature anything he's not in on and he is supposed to be the No.1 money-getter..." (Rudy Vallee in Segrave, 1994)

121 "if payment is not made pronto" (Edward B. Marks in Segrave, 1994)

121 "People are being bribed to perform inferior music and today some of the poorest songs..." (Louis Bernstein in Segrave, 1994)

122 "curb the evil of cut-ins" (ASCAP resolution at AGM 1931 in Segrave, 1994)

122 "on a wholesale rampage of cutting-in.... one leader made no bones about telling the publishers that he is now cut-in on enough songs to carry him for two years" (Segrave, 1994)

Chapter 20

126 "working one huge squeeze play whose only virtue seems to be that it is legal" (*Variety* magazine, 1940)

127 "a program that was never before nor can ever again be duplicated this side of Kingdom Come" (W. C. Handy in Handy, 1991)

127 "Hundreds started to sing with him. Then thousands. And when he came to the end of his song, 15,000 Americans were on their feet..." (*San Francisco Chronicle*, 25 September 1940)

Chapter 21

130 "The place shook, dust showered down, the orchestra stopped, and the lights went off, then back on..." (Article on wartime performance of Ivor Novello musical, *Telegraph* website)

131 "What America needs today is a good 5 cent war song... something with plenty of zip, ginger..." (Congressman J. Parnell Thomas in Jones, 2006)

131 "Songs should avoid talking about the end of the war in terms of returning to 'peace-and ease' because it might sap the morale of the people..." (OWI's requirements as printed in *Variety* in Jones, 2006)

132 "aspect of psychological warfare" (William B. Lewis in Jones, 2006)

132 "a fresh crop of stirring songs that would intensify the war effort" (Senator Charles O. Andrews in Jones, 2006)

Chapter 22

141 "You like it – it likes you" (Pepsi ad on Vintage Johnstown, Johnstownhistory. blog.spot)

142 "To me, the art of singing a pop song has always been to sing it very quietly…" (Obituary for Mitch Miller on Deseret News website)

143 "Miller chose the worst songs and put together the worst backings imaginable…" (Friedwald, 1996)

143 "Before Mr Miller's advent on the scene I had a successful recording career which went into decline" (Frank Sinatra in Kelley, 1986)

143 "Music is your own experience, your thoughts, your wisdom —if you don't live it, it won't come out of your horn" (Charlie Parker in Shapiro and Hentoff, 1955)

143 "Take away the microphone and Sinatra and most other pop singers would be slicing salami in a delicatessen" (Kelley, 1986)

143 "musical baby food… the worship of mediocrity" (Mitch Miller in *NME*, 1958)

144 "I want to leave them happy," said Frankie Vaughan. "If you're swollen-headed they know it," said Dickie Valentine. "It gets you a bad name," agreed David Whitfield. (Muller in Kureishi and Savage, 1995)

145 "I want to congratulate you and your people, Bill. It is very good" (David Sarnoff in Lebrecht, 2007)

145 "Without ASCAP's performance revenue I couldn't survive…" (Irving Berlin in Bergreen, 1990)

145 "Where did you get these papers from?" (Saul Borstein in Bergreen, 1990)

145 "Don't you dare insult her. I've been suspicious for many, many years. I needed proof…" (Irving Berlin in Bergreen, 1990)

Chapter 23

147 "I could no longer stand to hear the term 'race records'" (Wexler, 1993)

148 "The truth is there was no state of the art in record-making at that time" (Wexler, 1993)

148 "Who the fuck okayed three thousand freebies for these guys?" (Miriam Abramson in Cornyn, 2002)

148 "I give you assholes six months" (Miriam Abramson in Cornyn, 2002)

148 "White stations would play cover version of our records but refused to play ours. They'd say it wasn't 'their' type of music. But the cover versions they were playing were exact copies" (Ahmet Ertegun, in conversation with the author, New York, 1966)

149 "You did the right thing, Copas; ain't no song in the world worth fifty bucks" (Syd Nathan in Fox, 2009)

Chapter 24

156 "Presley is a definite danger to the security of the United States" (Editor of the *La Crosse Register* in letter to J. Edgar Hoover, 1956, Letters of Note, http://www.lettersofnote.com/)

156 "reached the lowest depths of 'grunt and groin'" (*New York Daily News*)

156 "like a jug of corn liquor at a champagne party" (Review in *Newsweek* of Elvis Presley first show in Las Vegas)

156 "This rancid-smelling aphrodisiac, I deplore" (Frank Sinatra in a magazine interview referred to by Robert Hilburn in *Los Angeles Times*, 1 February 2004)

156 "I admire the man. He has a right to say what he wants to say. He is a great success and a fine actor" (Elvis Presley in a piece by Robert Hilburn in *Los Angeles Times*, 1 February 2004)

157 "all those others who have directly and indirectly injured writers by placing American music in a strait jacket manipulated through BMI" (Sanjek, 1988)

157 "breaking the power of the broadcast networks" (ibid.)

157 "the involvement of radio and television networks in music publishing and promotion" (ibid.)

157 "arbiters of the audible and viceroys of the visual ... the faucets through which music flows" (A past president of ASCAP at hearings by Senate Antitrust Subcommittee on radio and television, 1956)

157 "It's the current climate on radio and TV which makes Elvis Presley and his animal posturing possible..." (Billy Rose at hearings by Senate Antitrust Subcommittee on radio and television, 1956)

157 "gross degradation in the quality of music supplied to the public over the airwaves" (Popular author's statement at hearings by Senate Antitrust Subcommittee on radio and television, 1956)

157 "cheapest types of music" (ibid.)

157 "a gratuitous insult to thousands of our fellow Tennesseans both in and out of the field of country music" (Senator Al Gore at hearings by Senate Antitrust Subcommittee on radio and television, 1956)

158 "Never in my experience have I seen such sweeping charges made against so many people with such flimsy evidence..." (Judge summing up at court case between Arthur Schwartz and BMI, 1952)

Chapter 25

160 "You've got a million-dollar voice, son, but a ten-cent brain" (Roy Acuff in Hemphill, 2006)

161 "I have the devil in me" (Jerry Lee Lewis at 1957 recording session, http://history-of-rock.com/lewis.htm)

161 "I would ask that your precious blood would wash and cleanse every stain

169 "I don't have the talent myself... But you know... I'm the man with the golden ear" (Don Kirshner in Emerson, 2005)

171 "They were Jim Crowing the business. They controlled what could sell in a white market" (Wexler, 1993)

172 "a $10 bill attached to a new disc" (Martin Block in Segrave, 1993)

172 "$20 was our top price for getting the record played" (A record distributor in Segrave, 1993)

172 "an issue of public morality" (President Eisenhower as reported by History. com, http://www.history.com/this-day-in-history/the-payola-scandal-heats-up)

172 "This seems to be the American way of life, which is a wonderful way of life. It's primarily built on romance – I'll do for you, what will you do for me?" (DJ Stan Richard as reported by History.com, http://www.history.com/this-day-in-history/the-payola-scandal-heats-up)

172 "When hard times set in for us, I felt sure Alan would be sympathetic...." (Wexler, 1993)

172 "payola is just a symptom of the disease – the disease itself is the involvement of the entire broadcasting industry..." (Summing up of Federal Communications Commission in Segrave, 1993)

Chapter 27

174 "I'd never heard rock 'n' roll before. But when I saw those kids bopping up and down in the aisles..." (Jack Good in personal interview with the author)

175 "Certainly not" (BBC executives to Jack Good as told to the author in interview, 1998)

175 "I decided that rock 'n' roll wasn't the music itself, it was the *response* to the music – it was a riot" (Jack Good in interview with author, 1998)

175 "You can't do this!" (BBC executive to Jack Good as told to the author in interview, 1998)

175 "I'm doing it. Cut to Camera Five" (Jack Good in interview with Jack Good in 1998)

177 "One gets the impression that they think simultaneously of harmony and melody..." (William Mann in *The Times*, 27 December 1963)

178 "Those who flock around the Beatles... are the least fortunate of their generation, the dull, the idle, the failures...a fearful indictment of our education system" (Johnson, 1964)

179 "Dick wasn't unfair – it was just normal practice – like it used to be normal to send small boys up chimneys" (Mitch Murray in Southall with Perry, 2006)

179 "We were in a little mews house in Liverpool one morning and there was this lawyer, who we later found out was sort of ours..." (Paul McCartney in Southall with Perry, 2006)

191 "Motown wouldn't let the RIAA look at its books so Motown could never be awarded a platinum or gold record... even though they sold millions" (Ahmet Ertegun in conversation with the author)

Chapter 30

195 "They were doing things nobody was doing. Their chords were outrageous, just outrageous, and their harmonies made it all valid..." (Scaduto, 1971)

195 "the arrogant, faux-cerebral posturing that has been the dominant style in rock" (Australian journalist writing about Bob Dylan in *Rolling Stone*)

198 "We rolled hundreds of marbles along the floor at the mounted police. Suddenly it looked like these horses were on an ice skating rink..." (Malcolm McClaren in interview on the *Guardian* website)

198 "They never ought to have had police there... If they had no police there, there wouldn't be trouble..." (Mick Jagger in an article by Barry Miles for *International Times*, 1968 reprinted in the *Independent*, March 2008)

198 "No more revolutionary than *Mrs Dale's Diary*" (Correspondence between John Lennon and *Black Dwarf* magazine, 1968)

198 "Who do you think you are? What do you think you know? I don't remember saying Revolution was revolutionary – fuck Mrs Dale..." (ibid.)

199 "Though I walk in the shadow of the valley of evil, I have no fear, as I am the biggest bastard in the valley" (Allen Klein modified biblical quote on his desk from Wikipedia on Allen Klein)

201 "The first thing that we recorded was 'Any Way the Wind Blows,' and that was okay..." (Frank Zappa in Zappa and Occhiogrosso, 1990)

201 "assholes in action" (Frank Zappa in Zappa and Occhiogrosso, 1990)

201 "We're satirists. And we are out to satirize everything" (Frank Zappa in Miles, 2005)

Chapter 31

202 "Fifty thousand people at worship in a stadium. People aged 26 aren't equipped for that. That's like Hitler" (Tony Bennett in *NME*, 1995)

203 "Why should rock 'n' roll be meaningful?" (Alex Van Halen in Gilmore, 1998)

204 "People hear what they want to hear" (Greil Marcus writing about Bruce Springsteen quoted in Gilmore, 1998)

204 "I'm very good at the glib remark that may not mean something if you examine it closely, but it still sounds great" (Lou Reed in Gilmore, 1998)

204 "Violence and energy... *that's* really what rock and roll's all about... it's inevitable that the audience is stirred by the anger they feel..." (Mick Jagger in Gilmore, 1998)

216 "I'm with Tom and Mick and Bianca and Bette – we'll come over for a nightcap" (ibid.)

216 "We never had that problem when Sonny was here" (ibid.)

Chapter 33

218 "After we'd sold every last copy we could of it, we were told to throw more promo money at Bob Dylan's new album. It was ridiculous...' (Maurice Oberstein talking to the author in 1986)

219 "advertising its core values of non-racialism and fairness" (Von Eschen, 2004)

220 "Jazz is a cross between total discipline and total anarchy..." (Willis Conover in Von Eschen, 2004)

220 "a cattle-car for Negroes" (Duke Ellington in Von Eschen, 2004)

Chapter 34

221 "Elsa Maxwell, Countess Bernadotte, Noël Coward, Tennessee Williams, and the Duke of Bedford...' (Tom Wolfe in Wolfe, 2009)

221 "Cafe society has not gone slumming with such energy since its forays into Harlem in the Twenties" (*New York Times*, 1962)

221 "Even Greta Garbo hauled herself out of her myth-lined cocoon..." (*Time* magazine, 1962)

222 "Sweeping the South. Now for the first time in the North. Come to the Pavilion Ballroom and try it for yourself" (Oocities, http://www.oocities.org/)

222 "Stand up on the balls of your feet. Stay on the balls of your feet as you twist your body round from side to side..." (Twist instructions in BBC dance manual , http://downloads.bbc.co.uk/schoolradio/pdfs/3thetwist.pdf)

222 "It's like putting out a cigarette with both feet while wiping your bottom with an invisible towel" (Chubby Checker article on Goerie.com)

224 "Grasso invented the technique used by every DJ ever since..." (Goldman, 1992)

224 "reinvented them out of their composite parts, the top end vocals and the bottom end rhythm" (ibid.)

224 "The track was called 'Save Me' and it was released under the name Silver Convention..." (Pete Waterman in interview with author for *Black Vinyl White Powder*, 2001)

225 "We changed the song around and made it into more of a pop song..." (ibid.)

227 "There were things I did not know about running a big company and Harvey was never there to help" (David Braun in Dannen, 2003)

227 "He wanted all the candy, not the spinach" (Harvey Schein ibid.)

228 "Enough! This is not Nuremberg" (David Braun ibid.)

243 "I never met an asshole in the music industry I didn't like" (David Geffen in Cornyn, 2002)

243 "For MCA to be in the management business – it's shocking. They'll be dealing out of self-interest!" (David Geffen in an interview with *Rolling Stone*, Dannen, 2003)

244 "no fucking religion!" (Dick Asher in phone conversation with Bob Dylan in the presence of the author, 1982)

244 "I'm telling you – there'll be no fucking religion – not Christian, not Jewish, not Moslem…" (ibid.)

244 "short little Jew" (Bruce Lundvall in Barfe, 2004)

244 "But Walter, you're just a taller Jew. What sort of talk is this?" (ibid.)

244 "We're going to bury those people. We're going to have the leading market share" (ibid.)

245 Walter Yetnikoff: "You delivered! You delivered like a motherfucker!"
Michael Jackson: "Please don't use that word Walter."
Walter Yetnikoff: "You delivered like an angel. Archangel Michael."
Michael Jackson: "That's better. Now will you promote it?"
Walter Yetnikoff: "Like a motherfucker." (Walter Yetnikoff in Yetnikoff with Ritz, 2004)

245 "Go hire Allen Grubman" (Elliot Goldman quoting Walter Yetnikoff in Dannen, 2003)

245 "You're busting my balls!"
"Schmuck!"
"Cocksucker!"
"Putz!"
"Motherfucker!" (Phone conversation overheard on speakerphone by author during meeting with Walter Yetnikoff, 1986)

247 "I don't like the music and I don't like the people" (David Geffen in Cornyn, 2002)

248 "Geffen's a gentleman" (Alan Grubman in Yetnikoff with Ritz, 2008)

248 "And Hitler's in Heaven" (Yetnikoff in Yetnikoff with Ritz, 2008)

248 "You better get wise" (Alan Grubman in Yetnikoff with Ritz, 2008)

248 "If he called me a pussy lapper I wouldn't get upset… If he thinks I'm gonna stop calling him a cocksucker, he's wrong" (Walter Yetnikoff in interview with Fred Goodman, Danen, 2003)

Chapter 38

249 "My stuff is just hopped-up country" (Haslan, 1999)

250 "sniffing powdered razor blades off a toilet floor…" (Charles Shaar Murray, *NME*)

Chapter 39

Chapter 40

261 "They kept putting up people to run it who were non-music people..." (Ahmet Ertegun in Barfe, 2004)

261 "You sometimes do things you wouldn't do to a mate..." (Ed Bicknell in Barfe, 2004)

262 "The bank still owns the house after the mortgage is paid" (Senator Orrin Hatch in Hall Jr. *Smells Like Slavery: Unconscionability in Recording Industry Contracts*, Hastings Communications and Entertainment Law Journal, 2002)

263 "the most important classical label by the end of the century" (Norio Ohga in Lebrecht, 2007)

264 "I couldn't sell them at full price because these were unknown East European orchestras..." (Klaus Heymann in Lebrecht, 2007)

264 "I sat down with a catalogue and marked everything that had more than ten recordings..." (Klaus Heymann in Lebrecht, 2007)

265 "I believe in great music ... I just don't want to record it" (Peter Gelb in Lebrecht, 2007)

267 "I have a theory that when you have a circular building then you never see the angles..." (Emmanuel Legrand in Southall, 2009)

267 "low growth consumer cyclical" (ABN Amro's end of year report on EMI, 1999)

Chapter 41

268 "when God stops making little girls" (Lou Pearlman on Zoominfo website)

269 "Mr. Johnny loved to shout at someone from the bottom of his lungs..." (Kitagawa – Johnny's Jimusho expose website)

269 "I didn't intend to abuse anyone sexually..." (ibid.)

269 "The acts could not be considered child abuse because Kitagawa was neither parent nor guardian to the boys..." (ibid.)

270 "slightly off the pace, a little uncool, didn't dress quite correctly..." (Simon Draper in Knopper, 2009)

272 "You can't make money on an airline with just one airplane" (Lou Pearlman to Geoff Boucher, *Los Angeles Times*, 24 January 1999)

272 "He was arrogant and thought he was the smartest guy in the room..." (Bob Jamieson in Knopper, 2009)

272 "There was one guy in every band – one sacrifice – one guy in every band who takes it for Lou. That's just the way it was" (Steve Mooney in *Vanity Fair* 'Mad About the Boys', November 2007)

273 "It would be nice to have them as my five sons" (Lou Pearlman in Knopper, 2009)

Chapter 42

277 "Napster has pointed the way for a new direction for music distribution" (Thomas Middelhoff on behalf of BMG, ABC news website)

Index

Unbound is the world's first crowdfunding publisher, established in 2011.

We believe that wonderful things can happen when you clear a path for people who share a passion. That's why we've built a platform that brings together readers and authors to crowdfund books they believe in — and give fresh ideas that don't fit the traditional mould the chance they deserve.

This book is in your hands because readers made it possible. Everyone who pledged their support is listed below. Join them by visiting unbound.com and supporting a book today.

Armin Achtmann
Martin Adams
Matt Adey
Fran Aitch
Carmelo Alfano
Edward Allen
Mike Allen
Simon Altham
Tom Anderson
Phoebe Annett
Stephen Aristei
Paul Arnest and Tracy Miller
Eugeniearrow Arrowsmith
Sophy Ashmore
Peter Ashworth
Rob Astbury
Chiara Badiali
James Bannerman
Gilian Baracs
Louis Barfe
Michael Barnett

Anthony Baron
Brian Barton
Helen Beard
Jeff Beck
Denise Beighton
Peter Bek
Michael J. Bellis
Graham Bendel
Gerard Benedict
Suade Bergemann
Terry Bergin
Mark Blake
M. Ariel Blanchard
Tom Boardman
Andrew Bone
Martin Bowen
Boy George
Clare Bramley
Christian Brett
A.J. Brim
Emma Brining

Adam Broadway
Ed Bruce
John Bryan
Eivind Brydoy
David Buckley
Julie Burchill
Andy & Joy Candler
Xander Cansell
David Carrick
Ed Cartwright
Nathalie Cauchois
Yotin Chaijanla
Paul Chamberlin
Jill Champion Rosenlund
Cheah Wei Chun
Karen Christley
Peter Christopherson
Chris Churcher
Russell Clarke
Mary Clemente
Nic Close
Garrett Coakley
Norma Coates
Tony Cochrane
Richard Cohen
Stevyn Colgan
Dennis Collopy
Gail Colson
Simon Conway
Anthony Cooper
Keith Cooper
Miles Copeland
Richard Coppen
Charles Corn
Philip Cornwel-Smith
Sir Harry Cowell
Simon Cowell
Christopher Crader
Chris Craker

John Crawford
Melissa Cross
Cath Crow
Tracy Cunliffe
Kate Dale
Rod Dale
Raf Damiaens
John Dang
Marie D'Antonio
Hugh Davenport
Irving and Olya David
Mark Davies
Den Davis
Vlad Davydov
James Dean
Benny Declerck
Robert de Mornay Davies
Dario Dendi
Dom Denny
Julian de Takats
Björn de Water
Casper de Weerd
John Dexter
Wayne Dickson
Yolande Diver
Kate Dowman
Lawrence T Doyle
Linda Doyle
Jeremy Drew
Craig Drysdale
Yvonne Duffield
Scottie Duncan
Archie Dunlop
Adam Edwards
David Edwards
Mark Elliott
Andy Ellison
James Endeacott
Jules Evans

SUPPORTERS

Richard Evans

Richard M Evans

Warwick Evans

Rupert Everett

Alec Ewe

Mark Ewing

Madame Vivian Fabry d'Incelli-Jacobs

Charles Farthing

Michael Feasey

Peter Fenwick

Connie Filippello

James Fisher

Thomas Foley

Bruno Fortunati

Jonathan Foster-Pedley

Hon. Ronald Franklin

Rosemary Fraser

Alan Freeman

Dean Friedman

Caroline Frost

Deborah Frost

Wendy Frost

Andrew Fryer

Katharine Fuge

Mal Function

Jody Furlong

Olaf Furniss

Ray Gago

David Galbraith

Hilary Gallo

Helen Gammons

Elizabeth Garner

Timothy Gee

Amanda Gentle

John Giddings

Warren James Gilchrist PhD

Global Peoples Media

Salena Godden

Harvey Goldsmith

Apolonio Gomes

Mark Goodier

Paul Gordon

Storm Gordon

Lyle Gove

Will Gracie

Voula Grand

Adam Greenwell

Lawrence Hall

Craig Hamlin

Jenny Hammerton

Miles Hanson

Carolyn Harlow

Michael J. Harries

Greg Hart

Onno Hart

Guy Haslam

Dominic Hawken

Simon Helm

Louis Hemmings

Simon Henderson Producer

Shay Hennessy

Matt Hepburn

Michael Higgins

Peter Higginson

Jo Hilditch

Katie Hillier

Clive Hines

David Hitchcock

John Holborow

Tim Hollier

Joanne Hoppé

James Horrocks

Nicholas Horsburgh

Marie Hrynczak

Kristie Hubler

David Hughes

Penelope Hughes

Jordan A. Hulme

Majeed Jabbar
Paul Jackson
Paul A Jackson
Mick Jagger
Elton John
David Johnson
David L. Johnson
Stephen Johnson
Elspeth Johnstone
Christopher Jones
Lesley-Ann Jones
Peter Jukes
David Junk
Julius Just
Susie Kahlich
Martin, Rebecca & William Kelly
Mike Kennedy
Andrea Kerr
Rachael Kerr
Paul Kirkpatrick
Rob Kirwan
Mark Knopfler
Deborah Kohn
Juha Kolari
Aleksey Kruzin
John Kyle
Mackenzie Dylan Lambert
Ivar Lande
Jay Landers
Richard Last
Caleb Laurie
Jimmy Leach
Emmanuel Legrand
Brian Levine
Michelle Lincoln
Catherine Llewellyn
Martin Lloyd-Elliott
A.A. Loaf
Graham Logie

Mike Longley
David Lubich
Stephen Luff
The Luncheon Club Quo Vadis
Edie Lush
Paul Lyness
Dominic Lyon
Louise McCabe
Damian McCarthy
Paul McCartney
Claudine McClean
Ian Macdonald
Julian McElhatton
Neil McGovern
Beth McGowan
John Macmenemey
Wendell McMurrain
Alistair McNichol
Dave McNicholas
Alison McNicol
Andrew MacPherson
Peter McVeigh
Hedy Manders
Bobbi Marchini
Martynn Marritt
Kelly Martin
Nelson Martinez
George Michael
Tony Michaelides
Robert Miles-Kingston
Duncan Millar
Tim Millin
Andrew Mills
Barbara Minto
Justin Mitchell
Tony Mitchell
John Mitchinson
Paolo Mojo
Bonnie Molnar

SUPPORTERS

David Montague
Justin Morey
Ian Morton
Tony Moss
Wiron Mostert
Jean Nedelec
Anna Nelson
Donavon Nelson
Karina Nelson
Andrew Neve
Andrew Nicholson
Iain Nicholson
Anthoula Nolan
Phil Norris
Tristin Norwell
Dave Novik
Richard O'Brien
Andrew Loog Oldham
Dominique Olliver
Jacquie O'Sullivan
Andy Overall
David Overend
Nicky Page
Kevin Parker
Danny Parnes
Barry Parsons – 'The Groover'
Amber Pearson
PeeSIX
Anne Penberthy
Harold Pendleton
Tris Penna
Les Peppiatt
Leo Phillips
David Pierce
Justin Pollard
Alison Power
Paddy Prendergast
Gina Prince
Jason Prince

Francis Pryor
Jeanette Ramsden
Nicola Ranger
Tim Redsell
Steve Rehman
Wim Reijnen
Anthony Reynolds
Fifa Riccobono
Tim Rice
Kathryn Richards
Hamstall Ridware
Peter Robertson
Tom Robinson
Spencer Rocks
Inger Ronander
David Brent Roundsley
David Rowley
Gemma M. Rull
Allan P Russell
Benjamin Russell
Paul Rymer
Paul Sale
Paul Samwell-Smith
Anitas Sandall
James Sanger
Mat Sargent
Rod Schragger
James Scott
John Scott
Tim Scott
Kate Shaw
Reg Shaw
Sue Shaw
Micky Sheehan
Mark Sheppard
Jona Tan Sitthita
Suzi Skelton
Jonty Skrufff
Sl!m of #remarqabl

William Small
Samantha Smith
Allan Soh
Kotryna Sokolovaite
Dougie Souness
Matthew Spicer
Hugh Spring
Mark Stacey
Robin Stammers
Graham Stead
Dave Stewart
Laura Stoyanova
Chris Sullivan
Frank Sullivan
Ruth Sullivan
Jazz Summers
Andrew Sunnucks
Steve Swindells
Graham Tanker
Martin Technoarm Boettcher
Terracotta TCM
Ian Thompson-Corr
David Titlow
Rona Torrance
João Toulson
Miles Tredinnick
Michelle Tuft
Nicola Tyson
Barry Upton
Ian Usher
Stephen Vahrman
Bastiaan Van Gent

Ron van Rutten
Maryse van Vroonhoven
Mike Veale
Margaret Venables
Rupert J Voleshafter
Mike Wade
Steve Walker
Rebecca Walker-Jones
Mark Wardel
Mrs. Fee Warner
Mark Watkins
Nigel Watson
Ron Weston
Paul Whelan
Simon White
Vicki Wickham
Rénuka Wickramaratne
Anthony Wieler
Paul & Mary Wild
David Wilder
Naomi Wildey
David Williams
Orian Williams
Andrew Winder
Bob Winestain
Khun Witaya ("Tong") Kitidee
Simon Witter
Steve Woodward
John Wooler
Marc Zalcman
Peter, Kristina and Madelyn Ziolkowski